Social Security and Social Change

New Challenges to the Beveridge Model

Edited by

Sally Baldwin
Jane Falkingham

HARVESTER
WHEATSHEAF

New York   London   Toronto   Sydney   Tokyo   Singapore

First published 1994 by
Harvester Wheatsheaf
Campus 400, Maylands Avenue
Hemel Hempstead
Hertfordshire, HP2 7EZ
A division of
Simon & Schuster International Group

Printed and bound in Great Britain by
BPC Wheatons Ltd, Exeter

British Library Cataloguing in Publication Data

A catalogue record for this book is available from
the British Library

ISBN 0-7450 1524 7 (pbk)

1 2 3 4 5   98 97 96 95 94

Contents

List of Tables

List of Figures

Preface

The book had its origins in a conference on 'Social Security 50 Years After Beveridge' held at the University of York in September 1992. Most of the chapters were presented at this conference but their content has been revised and refined following discussion and developments since. The conference was jointly organised by the Social Policy Research Unit and Department of Social Policy and Social Work at the University of York, and the Welfare State Programme, Suntory–Toyota International Centre for Economics and Related Disciplines, London School of Economics. It was the annual colloquium of the European Institute of Social Security and was organised in association with the Foundation for International Studies in Social Security.

The editors are very grateful to all those involved in organising the conference, particularly Jonathan Bradshaw, Gary Craig, John Ditch, Han Emmanuel, Howard Glennerster, John Hills, Hilary Holmes, Denise Marchent, Janet Moore, Nicola Tynan and Jef Van Langendonck.

The editors would also like to acknowledge the following bodies for financial support of the conference and the work associated with it: the Economic and Social Research Council (under Programme Grant X206 32 2001), the Joseph Rowntree Foundation, the European Commission, the Department of Social Security, the Benefits Agency, the Information Technology Services Agency, the International Social Security Association, Prudential, the Council of Europe and the Social Policy Association.

Particular thanks are due to Jane Dickson who single-handedly prepared the camera-ready version of the manuscript and kept calm through all the alterations and delays.

We were deeply saddened to hear of John Blackwell's death at the final stages of production of this book. As his chapter in this book shows,

John was committed to the eradication of poverty and was a strong advocate of the social safety net. He was a true interdisciplinary scholar and his many writings are respected across the social sciences. His research on changing work patterns greatly enhanced our understanding of the important interactions between the labour market and social protection. We trust that his chapter in this volume will provide a lasting testament to his work and life.

Jane Falkingham
Sally Baldwin

Introduction

In 1942 William Beveridge published his report on Social Insurance and Allied Services which became the blueprint for the development of welfare states throughout Europe. Even at that time the report had important omissions. It failed to address the needs of the 'civilian' disabled – those whose disabilities were not the result of industrial or war injuries. It also backed away from insuring against divorce and single motherhood. In the fifty years since then the world has changed in ways which have accentuated these gaps in coverage and given rise to new, unanticipated, challenges. Changes in the patterns of family formation and dissolution; growth in the numbers of older people; increasing prevalence of lone parenthood; a steep rise in female labour force participation; the expansion of part-time work and the emergence of long-term unemployment – all call into question the appropriateness of continuing to rely on Beveridge's model of social security, with its roots in a different era.

This book examines both the gaps in the original Beveridge Report and the developments since its conception. It explores how social security should evolve and adapt and looks forward to an appropriate set of policies for the twenty-first century. The book's two key themes – gaps in the Beveridge system and adapting to change – are not mutually exclusive. For example, the failure to provide adequate benefit for lone parents can be seen as an omission in the original system as conceived by Beveridge. It can equally be argued that the social insurance model has failed to respond to the social and economic developments that have resulted in a greater number of lone parents.

The Beveridge model of social security, as first laid down in his Report (1942), aimed to provide protection from poverty by providing insurance against the interruption of earnings. Rowntree, in his first

1

classic study of the causes of poverty in 1899, had found that over half of all poverty was due to low wages, whereas only a quarter was due to the 'insurable contingencies' of old age, death of the wage earner and unemployment. By the time of Rowntree's second study in 1936 the picture was very different. Unemployment alone accounted for 44 per cent of the incidence of poverty and old age a further 18 per cent (Rowntree, 1941). Beveridge, using Rowntree's evidence as his starting point, concluded that the main cause of poverty had now altered to one which was amenable to solution through insurance benefits (Evans and Glennerster, 1993). Poverty could be eradicated in the majority of cases if workers could insure themselves and their families against the loss of income due to a range of specific contingencies such as sickness, temporary unemployment and retirement. This may have been true at the time Beveridge formulated his model of social insurance. Given the social and economic changes of the last fifty years, it is questionable whether occurrence of these key risk-events – unemployment, sickness, old age or death of the breadwinner – remains a comprehensive indicator of need today. The book begins by questioning whether, in fact, a system of poverty alleviation based on the social insurance principle remains appropriate for today's modern economies.

Steven Webb, in Chapter One, outlines some of the key social and economic changes of the last 30 years. He demonstrates how and why the link between earnings, or lack thereof, and poverty is no longer straightforward. With the growth of occupational benefits, and in particular pensions, absence of earnings no longer necessarily implies poverty. Equally, receipt of earned income does not preclude the experience of poverty. Given the changing composition of the poor, Webb concludes that the contributory basis for entitlement is ill-suited to the needs of today's poor. Occurrence of a risk-event no longer leads automatically to a need situation and new needs not covered by the risk-events traditionally insured by social security have arisen. This theme is taken up again by Bea Cantillon in Chapter Three. Using the Belgian social security system as a case study she analyses the implication of changing family forms and relationships to the labour market for the development of more appropriate social security systems. Cantillon's chapter is concerned with fundamental changes in the institutions of family and paid employment – the emergence of two-earner households as the norm and the consequences for the cost, adequacy and legitimacy of the current arrangements. Her critical appraisal of future policy possibilities, though based on the Belgian situation, is highly relevant to the UK situation. Her analysis points to the need for a new conception of social security based on a broader understanding of work, a different response to the risk of unpaid work, a more realistic and flexible response to family circumstances and an awareness of the need to avoid perverse incentives.

The continuing relevance of the contribution principle inherent in a system based on social insurance is the central theme running throughout the remainder of the book. The social insurance principle of the Beveridge Report rested upon three basic assumptions: full (male) employment; the one-earner family with a gendered division of labour between male wage-earner and female home-maker; and stability of the family, with the unit being broken only by death. The relevance of these assumptions was questioned at the time. As they have become increasingly unrealistic, has the contribution principle also become less relevant?

Related to the contribution principle is the gendered notion of citizenship that underlies the Beveridge Report. Beveridge was caught between the desire to provide a universal system of benefits for all, based on citizenship, and one based on an insurance principle where benefits would depend on contributions (Evans and Glennerster, 1993). He reconciled these competing principles by assuming that men would qualify as citizens through contributions made in the workplace; women's rights to citizenship would rest largely on their reproductive role within the home. Women would not qualify through their reproductive role *per se*, but would depend on the contribution record of their spouse. Thus, citizenship acquired through reproductive and other home-making duties was valid only if it operated via the family. In reality, therefore, the Beveridge Model was far from universal and excluded many individuals from full citizenship. As Ruth Lister shows in Chapter Two, this has had important consequences for the continuing economic and social dependency of women.

In addition to the assumption of a gendered division of labour within the family, Beveridge also assumed that the family would be stable, only exceptionally being broken in circumstances other than death. Separation and divorce were anomalies and, as such, were not considered, except in limited circumstances. Only marriage breakdowns where the woman was not 'at fault' were thought fit by Beveridge to be considered as an insurable contingency; insurance is for events which happen by chance and not those which happen by choice. Jane Millar addresses this question in Chapter Four, asking whether the failure to ensure financial security for lone parents is a consequence of a gap in the Beveridge national insurance scheme that can simply be plugged by a new benefit, or presents a challenge to the social insurance model requiring a fundamentally different solution.

At the heart of the Beveridge model is the 'standard employment relationship'. This is essentially a standard of the full-time male employee and, as is clearly demonstrated by the contributors in Part II, one increasingly at variance with actual employment patterns. Since the Beveridge Report was published the labour market has undergone a dramatic restructuring, not only in Britain but throughout Europe. The last 30 years have seen an increase in the relative importance of new forms of paid work; self-employment, part-time work, temporary work, contract work. These are not the exclusive preserve of males. Even the 'typical' full-time employee is now half as likely to be female as male. Rising female employment has meant that the family with a single male breadwinner is no longer the norm. Equally, in many instances, one income from the labour market no longer provides sufficient income for support of the family. Beveridge saw the labour market as the primary cure for poverty and social insurance as a means to protect those who were disengaged from it. These structural changes over the last fifty years send a challenge to the very roots of his model.

While not all of the new 'atypical' forms of work involve economic disadvantage, the majority do. The earnings of temporary and part-time workers tend to be relatively low and subject to interruption over time. More importantly for the context of this book, the rights these workers have for contributory benefits under social security tend to be less favourable than for other workers and in some instances those in 'new' forms of work can end up with no entitlements at all. Benefit entitlement in a social insurance system is often dependent not upon the fact of contribution alone but also upon amassing a required level of contribution over a certain minimum period. Low earnings can thus effectively exclude many workers from benefiting from social insurance protection, particularly unemployment insurance. Equally, they are often excluded from of the occupational benefits that are seen in many countries as complementing social security, particularly with regard to income support in later life. Many atypical workers are thus forced to rely on means-tested benefits, in direct conflict with Beveridge's original aims. The structure of the social security system can serve to reinforce the marginalisation of part-time and temporary workers, particularly if employers are excused from paying contributions for workers of certain types or those working below a certain number of hours. This makes the cost of labour cheaper, and so influences the nature of work on offer. The contribution threshold can act to benefit the employer while ensuring that the worker is excluded from full social rights. Perhaps we are in danger to returning to the world as surveyed by Rowntree, where low earnings rather than lack of employment *per se* are a key cause of poverty.

In the opening chapter of Part II John Blackwell examines changes in employment patterns across different forms of working for the OECD countries, and explores the implications of these labour market trends for social protection in the member states. Subsequent chapters focus more directly on three main trends in the post-war labour market: the growth in part-time working, the rapid increase in self-employment during the 1980s and the rise in early retirement from the labour force.

Perhaps the most notable feature of the post-war labour market has been the increase in female labour force participation. In 1947 only 1 in

5 married women were economically active compared to 7 in 10 in 1992. The majority of the increase in female work has been in part-time employment. In Chapter Six, Hilary Land traces the gendered growth of part-time employment in post-war Britain. To a certain extent this has been due to a change in the structure of demand for labour. Land details the restructuring of the civil service and the growth of the welfare service sector which has provided much of the stimulus to the increase in part-time employment. However, as she points out, demand does not operate in isolation from supply and here the interaction with the family and the social security system is of paramount influence. As we have already stated, women's wages are important to the economic survival of many families. At the same time many social policies have made it harder, rather than easier, to combine full-time paid employment with family responsibilities. Britain lags behind its European neighbours in the provision of child care facilities. Services to enable carers of older and disabled relatives – mainly women – to stay in or re-enter paid employment are even less developed.

Although the concept of the male breadwinner may be an anachronism in practice, parts of the social protection system still operate as though it is the norm. Land cites the example of the exclusion of married women from entitlement to Invalid Care Allowance until challenged in the European Court as just one illustration of the lack of importance given to their earnings. The relationship between the social security system, the structure of the labour market and the family clearly needs urgent re-examination, a view shared by other contributors such as Cantillon, Lister and Millar.

One atypical form of working that was included in Beveridge's conception of social insurance was self-employment. He recognised that self-employed people, such as shopkeepers and fishermen, could be poorer than wage-earners and as such should be included within the same contributory national insurance scheme as employees. However, as Tony Eardley and Anne Corden report in Chapter Seven, the position of the self-employed within the social security system in Britain has remained ambiguous. Successive governments have continued to regard them primarily as responsible for their own financial security, with the state as guarantor in the last resort. This view finds support in the numerous fiscal incentives and concessions that have been given to self-employed individuals when taking out private insurance arrangements, particularly pensions.

The current structure of national insurance provides for different contributions and corresponding entitlements for employees and the self-employed. The self-employed are not entitled to unemployment benefit or statutory sick pay. They are also excluded from additions under the State Earnings-Related Pension Scheme (SERPS), despite the fact that SERPS was introduced to provide an alternative to occupational pension schemes, to which self-employed people do not have access. Eardley and Corden argue that many self-employed people will enter old age with nothing more than their basic state pension, currently payable at a level below means-tested benefits. Dependence by the self-employed on means-tested benefits is not, however, limited to old age. It is also likely during any period of unemployment, and there is evidence that growing numbers are claiming in work means-tested benefits like family credit. Thus, means-tested benefits are assuming increasing importance rather than being a residual social safety net of the last resort limited to very few, as envisaged by Beveridge.

Structural changes within the labour market have particular implications for social policy in relation to older women and men. The assumption of continuous (male) employment as a basis for securing financial provision in old age has been undermined by the emergence of atypical work patterns. For women this premise has never held true. Furthermore, the period of time spent in the labour market has been shrinking from both ends; with the raising of the school leaving age and increased participation in post-school education at the lower end and early retirement at the upper. Chris Phillipson argues in Chapter Eight that the social security system has failed to adapt to this changing pattern of the life course. The increasing trend to early exit from the labour market and reduced participation rates at ages beyond statutory pensionable age, particularly for men, have meant that the period spent in retirement is lengthening. Many older workers are not choosing early retirement as such. Instead, they 'retire' through the alternative, and financially insecure, pathways of unemployment, long-term sickness, disability and redundancy. Those who do so are at a much higher risk of experiencing privation in old age. Phillipson argues that any attempt at reducing poverty amongst those already in and reaching old age in the next century must address the problems experienced prior to retirement in middle and late working age itself.

Part III examines the relationship between disability, labour force participation, formal and informal support in more detail. Lone parents were not the only group specifically excluded from the Beveridge Model of social insurance; disabled civilians were left to rely either on short-term sickness benefit or social assistance. This remained the case until 1971 when Invalidity Benefit (IVB) was introduced as an income replacement benefit for workers unable to continue in paid employment on account of ill-health. The years have seen the proliferation of benefits covering extra costs and other aspects of disability. Income replacement on account of disability remained an 'all-or-nothing' system in Britain until the introduction of the Disability Working Allowance in 1992.

Virtually all OECD countries have experienced a rise in the number of people receiving disability-related benefits. This trend does not reflect an increase in the incidence of disability, but rather administrative changes in eligibility criteria, and other economic and demographic factors such as rising unemployment and the changing age structure of the population. Susan Lonsdale and Jennifer Seddon, in Chapter Nine, examine changes in the receipt of disability benefits across a number of OECD countries with diverse disability benefit programmes. They argue that some of the observed increases may be due to labour market pressures and the potential of disability benefits to provide an alternative route out of the labour market. Indeed, in several countries the function of disability benefits has been extended to cover unemployed older workers whose health problems have made it more difficult to return to employment. However, as Lonsdale and Seddon suggest, we are now entering a period of retrenchment as countries try to curb public expenditure. Their chapter evaluates the various measures that have been adopted in an attempt to reverse dramatic increases in the cost of disability benefits.

The need for care on account of disability, or frailty in later life, was not regarded by Beveridge as a social security responsibility. Rather it was a responsibility for families and the voluntary sector, backed up by statutory health and welfare services. Likewise the consequences of providing care to a relative were not considered. Beveridge's conception of the division of labour within families clearly viewed care-giving as the married woman's responsibility. Compensation for earnings forgone was unnecessary since 'she would have been at home in any case' performing her other household responsibilities. Demographic and social changes – the growth in the numbers of frail older people, improvements in their material circumstances and the increased labour force participation of married women – pose questions about the relevance of Beveridge's prescription for care. Sally Baldwin's chapter traces the subsequent development of policy in relation to care needs in the UK. This is characterised by a growing acceptance of care-giving as a contingency to be covered by social insurance, unlike the need for care in later life. Public policy continues to regard the provision of care primarily as the obligation of families, backed up, as necessary, by discretionary services in kind. Baldwin's chapter discusses different options for financing, and increasing a sense of entitlement to, long-term care for older people, drawing on policy in a number of countries. In the short term, the most realistic option is to increase notions of entitlement and procedural rights for both older person and carer within the reformed arrangements for community care currently being implemented. In the longer term, better and more creative solutions are needed.

The community care reforms implemented in April 1993 place an increased emphasis on the market to provide the care older people need. They also embody a commitment to increasing the role of charging, and thus means-testing, for community services. The implications of both developments are unclear as yet. The feasibility of developing 'quasi-market' systems and their ability to allocate care services efficiently and equitably is much discussed (Le Grand, 1991; Le Grand and Bartlett, 1993). Less thought has been given to the consequences of means-testing for care, though evidence is beginning to emerge that it can deter the utilisation of services such as home help. Given the emphasis on the need to reduce public expenditure and the role of the market in achieving this, British policy makers increasingly look to the American model of social protection for inspiration. Any model, however, has its short-comings. In Chapter Ten Emily Abel examines the inadequacies of the US long-term care system, particularly for the disabled elderly and their carers. By relying on the market to provide long-term care services, the US helps to contain public spending, but at a cost to older and disabled people and their families.

Beveridge himself identified the problem of adequate support in old age as 'the most important, and in some ways the most difficult, of all the problems of social security' (Beveridge, 1942, p. 90). In the 50 years since the Report, the age structure of the population has changed considerably. In 1939 there were 4.4 million retired persons representing 9.4 per cent of the total population. By 1991 this group had more than doubled to 10.5 million, comprising 18 per cent of the UK population. Part IV is devoted to exploring issues concerning income support in later life in greater depth.

The contributory nature of the current British basic state pension and the State Earnings-Related Pension raises particular issues for women. The Beveridge model, of husbands providing the main source of insurance for married women, is clearly out of date. However although an increasing number of women are employed, they do not, in the main, follow the traditional male pattern of work. A disproportionate number of the new atypical workers identified by Blackwell in Chapter Five, particularly part-time workers, are women. Such workers often fail to accumulate adequate contribution records and are in marginal forms of employment. Women have the added burden of shouldering the majority of reproductive and caring responsibilities.

The difference in employment histories between the sexes is reflected in the sources of income available to women in later life and their greater experience of poverty. Only 37 per cent of older women in 1990 had entitlement to a full state basic pension in their own right (DSS, 1992b). Perhaps this is not surprising as the Beveridge Model assumed that married women would draw their entitlement from their spouses' contribution. The option of a reduced rate married women's contribution was only withdrawn in April 1977. Given the increase in female labour force participation one might expect that women retiring in the future would have access to an independent income in old age. However, as Jay Ginn and Sara Arber demonstrate in Chapter Thirteen even full basic pension entitlement remains far from providing women an adequate income. The basic state pension is now payable at a level below means-tested benefits. Implicit in this is the assumption that older people will have accrued rights to additional pension income, either from the state earnings-related supplement or private occupational pensions. Receipt of occupational and private pensions has assumed an increased importance in determining the financial well-being of older people. Increased reliance on earnings-related pensions only serves to perpetuate the inequalities of the labour market into later life. Titmuss' two nations in old age are well and truly here.

Ginn and Arber explore how the current mix of pension provision in Britain acts to discriminate against women. It is not only the state system which marginalises women; the operation of the occupational pension sector also acts to exclude women. Women are less likely to work for employers who have an occupational pension scheme and, where they do, are less likely to belong to the scheme. Given many women's non standard employment histories, with interruptions for childcare and care of older relatives, they are also more likely to have lost any entitlements they were fortunate enough to acquire. A greater understanding of the way in which the non-state sector interacts with the labour market experience of women is particularly important at a time when current government policy emphasises personal rather than collective provision. Both the private and public sectors have failed to acknowledge the growth of different types of paid employment and the greater diversity in the organisation of working life.

Sandra Hutton and Peter Whiteford compare the extent to which different social security systems promote equal treatment, and outcome, for men and women in retirement. The mix of benefits between flat rate and earnings-related, means-tested and universal benefits, and the share of public and private provision all act to discriminate between the sexes. Their analysis serves to demonstrate the range of different options available to policy makers and their different outcomes. It is important to bear in mind that different systems not only serve to treat the sexes differently but also vary widely in their generosity. Nevertheless useful lessons for Britain can learnt from the experience of other countries.

Given the well-documented failure of the Beveridge state pension in ensuring a poverty-free old age (Johnson and Falkingham, 1992) the final two chapters assess some alternatives. Both employ simulation modelling to evaluate different policy options for reform of the current system of pension provisioning. Heather Joshi and Hugh Davies consider how pension policy could be adapted to recognise the importance of both the paid and unpaid aspects of women's work. Improving Home Responsibility Protection, providing better childcare facilities (and so reducing interruptions to women's earning histories) and raising the level of the basic fate rate pension are all examined. Paul Johnson and

Jane Falkingham take a more radical approach, proposing that we abandon the current system entirely in favour of a Unified Funded Pension Scheme. Whether or not such a fundamental reform is feasible, they outline a number of attributes they think desirable in *any* reform of the British pension system. We leave the results from these two simulation exercises to speak for themselves.

No one consensual view on the future of social security emerges from this book; however, it is clear from each of the chapters that the Beveridge model is in need of fundamental reform. Our contributors are not alone in this view. At the time of writing, the UK Government is conducting a major review of social security. Simultaneously, the Labour Party's Commission for Social Justice is reconsidering the Left's position on social protection. Both parties are apparently united in a desire to contain public expenditure on social security. The possibility of extending means-testing and targeting is being explored. At the heart of this lies an assault on contributions as a basis for entitlement to benefit and hence on the philosophy of Beveridge himself. Once the link between contributions and accrual of rights disappears, so too does the notion of social insurance.

Although many of the chapters in this volume point to the weakness of the present contributory system, especially for women and people engaged in non-market activities, this need not imply that we are, or should be, ready to jettison social insurance. An alternative is to look for ways of altering its present formulation to better reflect contemporary needs and mores (Atkinson, 1993). Many of the chapters in this book point to ways of reforming the current social insurance system to overcome these defects. Increased provision of child care, more active education and labour market policies to maximise access to (better) paid work, a comprehensive policy for carers and reform of the divorce law particularly with regard to sharing of accrued entitlements would all go a long way to including Beveridge's 'excluded citizens'.

Social insurance is more than the sum of its parts. It is not just a system of poverty alleviation but provides a social vision; one incorporating notions such as solidarity and citizenship. Before accepting a route which abandons social insurance, such as the Australians have taken, we (the editors) would look for assurances that levels of relative benefits would be vigorously defended. The coercive institutionalisation of deserving and undeserving poor that pre-dated Beveridge must not be allowed to re-emerge. This is particularly important in a country such as the UK where there is no constitutional right to a minimum income and no subjective rights to claim it. We are at a crossroads in British social security policy. Whatever new blueprint is adopted it is important that the worst elements of social assistance do not become the standard of a residual state social security in the future.

Chapter 1

Social Insurance and Poverty Alleviation: An empirical analysis

Steven Webb[1]

1.1   Social Insurance in Theory and in Practice

A social insurance scheme would be expected to work in a society where two conditions are met:

- employed earners are numerous and relatively prosperous;
- poverty arises primarily from an interruption to earnings, mainly of a short-term nature.

In such a society, a system where employed earners make contributions to an insurance fund and non-earners receive payments from the fund will be effective at relieving poverty. It will also provide income security for members of the current earning population should they in turn face a period of interrupted earnings.

Whether British society ever fitted this description is open to debate, but it seems clear that it no longer does. Three examples illustrate where this simple model provides an inadequate account of the social and economic conditions in Britain today. Firstly, absence of earnings need no longer necessarily imply poverty. The growth in employer-provided benefits such as occupational pensions is probably the single most important reason for this development. Secondly, those who are poor are now far less likely to be so simply because of short-term interruption to paid employment. The long-term unemployed, young unemployed

---

1   The author would like to thank colleagues at the Institute for Fiscal Studies and conference participants for helpful comments on earlier drafts of this paper. The Central Statistical Office supplied anonymised Family Expenditure Survey data, but is not responsible for subsequent interpretation.

and lone parents exemplify this trend and these groups have grown significantly in size in recent decades. Finally, those who do have earned income are now less likely to be in well-paid, secure employment than was the case fifty years ago. The growth of both self-employment and part-time employment has contributed much to this trend. Similarly, there has been a growing recognition that even some full-time workers may have difficulty in making ends meet when the costs of children are taken into account.

This chapter documents the social and economic changes which have called into question the appropriateness of a social insurance system for the United Kingdom (and by extension, for many modern economies). Many of these changes are dealt with separately and in more depth in the subsequent chapters of this volume. Here we focus on the question of whether a social insurance system is any longer an effective means of alleviating poverty.

The first part of the chapter describes the way in which some of those covered by the UK National Insurance system would no longer be regarded as poor, whilst at the same time many of those who are poor are not covered by the system. Administrative and survey data is then used to assess the importance of these trends. In the light of this evidence, the prospects for social insurance in the UK are assessed.

1.2   The Trends Described

1.2.1   The growth of occupational/private provision

National Insurance (NI) benefits could be regarded as well targeted (and hence effective at poverty alleviation) if they go to those with little or no other income. Initially, this was a fair assumption for the unemployed, the sick, the widowed and the elderly. However, the steady growth in provision of occupational benefits and other private income has altered this pattern, particularly for the short-term sick and for the recently retired.

Occupational sick pay
Figure 1.1 is based on alternate years of Family Expenditure Survey (FES) data from 1970–90 and shows the proportion of employees coded as 'temporarily away ill' for less than six months who were in receipt of either full or partial sick pay from their employer. The proportion of employees receiving some pay from their employer during a short spell of sickness rose from around five in ten in 1970 to more than eight in ten by the end of the 1980s. There also appears to be a general trend towards more comprehensive forms of occupational sick pay, although it still

remains the case that many of those temporarily sick suffer some loss of employer-provided income.

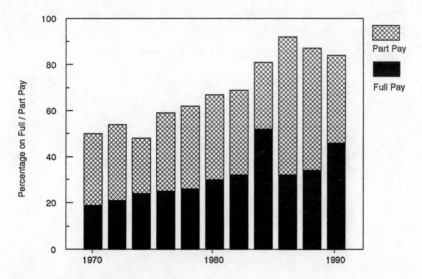

Sample: Employees temporarily away ill.
Note: The figures for 1984 may be affected by respondent confusion following the introduction of Statutory Sick Pay in 1983.
Source: Author's calculations based on Family Expenditure Survey Microdata.

Figure 1.1 Occupational Sick Pay Coverage, 1970–1990

One consequence of the growth in occupational coverage was that increasing numbers of temporarily sick employees were receiving sick pay from their employer in addition to NI Sickness Benefit. In some cases this left them better off when sick than when working! In response to this trend, the Government introduced a system of Statutory Sick Pay in 1983 which was ultimately to replace NI Sickness Benefit for all employees. Under this scheme most employees are entitled to receive a set level of Sick Pay from their employer during the first 28 weeks of sickness, and the majority of this is refunded to the employer by the Government. The employer is however free to supplement this with additional Sick Pay and, as Figure 1.1 shows, large numbers of employers are continuing to do so.

Occupational pensions
A second trend has been towards greater receipt of occupational benefits by the elderly and by widows. Although the number of members of such schemes has been remarkably steady since the early 1960s at around 11

million or approximately 50 per cent of all employees (Government Actuary's Department, 1990a), only in recent years have large numbers of the retired population received significant income from such pensions. Figure 1.2 shows the growth in the proportion of those over state retirement age and of widows with some income from occupational pensions.

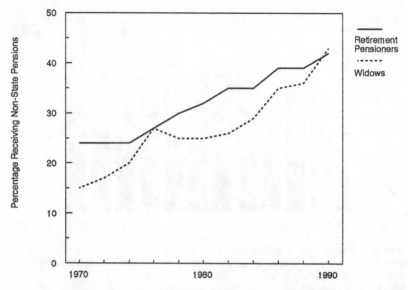

Source: Author's calculations based on Family Expenditure Survey Microdata.

Figure 1.2 Receipt of Non-State Benefits, 1970–1990

Private incomes
In addition to occupational benefits, income from investments is providing a steadily increasing contribution to pensioner incomes. Published FES reports indicate that for households headed by over-65s, the contribution of investment income rose between 1971 and 1990 from 11 per cent to 16 per cent of total income. The combined category of 'annuities/non-state pensions' rose more sharply still, from 12 per cent in 1971 to almost 20 per cent of household income in 1990.

For all of these reasons, there is an increasing minority of those in insurable categories who would not necessarily be regarded as poor. Given the contemporary emphasis on 'targeting' this has led some to question whether uniform benefits to all who satisfy a particular contingency are the most effective use of social security spending. We return to this issue in our concluding section.

1.2.2   Gaps in coverage I: the causes

Whilst some members of insurable groups have prospered, receiving occupation-related and other private income to supplement their NI benefits, others have fared less well. In particular, there is a growing number of groups who are in the non-earning population but who do not satisfy the conditions for receipt of NI benefit. In this section we outline the factors behind the rise of the excluded groups.

Long-term unemployment
In most countries operating an insurance-type benefit system, benefits for the unemployed are of fixed duration. In the UK entitlement to NI Unemployment Benefit ceases after twelve months and those who are still unemployed move on to exclusive dependence on the main social assistance benefit (Income Support) if their incomes are inadequate. Where unemployment is a temporary phenomenon, this restriction will be of little practical importance, and the social assistance scheme will bear little burden. However, as Table 1.1 indicates, for many unemployment has been far from temporary.

Table 1.1 Long-term Unemployment in the UK, 1970–1992

Year	Long-term Unemployed	Total Unemployed
1970 (GB)	97,000	609,000
1975 (GB)	143,000	1,042,000
1980	364,000	1,897,000
1985	1,327,000	3,235,000
1990	514,000	1,624,000
1992	747,000	2,674,000

Note: All figures for July, except 1992 which is for January. Long term unemployment defined as 52 weeks or more.
Source: Department of Employment, *Employment Gazettes*, various years.

The number of UK individuals out of work for a year or more and registered unemployed rose more than threefold between 1970 and 1980, and a further threefold between 1980 and 1985. Since then the numbers have fallen back, but there are still three-quarters of a million people who have been out of work for a year or more. The implications of such changes for the NI system are profound. An insurance-type benefit where entitlement is restricted to the first twelve months of unemployment is likely to exclude large numbers of unemployed people. This is in direct conflict with Beveridge's original view that: 'To reduce the income of an unemployed or disabled person ... because the unemployment or disability has lasted for a certain period, is wrong in principle' (Beveridge, 1942, p. 57).

Youth unemployment
Entitlement to a contributory benefit implies a previous record of
contributions. Although contributions are 'credited' in some cases (e.g.
during full-time education) it is also necessary for some contributions to
have been actually paid by the claimant. In the case of the young
unemployed it may be impossible to satisfy this requirement. Table 1.2
indicates the growing scale of youth unemployment in the UK.

In early 1992 more than three-quarters of a million under-25s were
unemployed and very few of these have had the opportunity to acquire
a record of NI contributions. Again this bodes ill for a social security
system for the unemployed partially based on contributions during
previous employment.

Table 1.2 Youth Unemployment in the UK, 1970–1992

Year	Age 18–19	Age 20–24	Total Unemployed
1970 (GB)	41,000	65,000	609,000
1975 (GB)	128,000	158,000	1,042,000
1980	188,000	327,000	1,897,000
1985	335,000	720,000	3,235,000
1990	131,000	357,000	1,624,000
1992	219,000	517,000	2,674,000

Note: All figures for July, except 1992 which is for January. Subtotals for 18–19
year-olds and 20–24 year-olds exclude adult students.
Source: Department of Employment, *Employment Gazettes*, various years.

Lone parenthood
Absent from a list of the contingencies covered by the UK social insurance
system is compensation for loss of earnings due to childcare
responsibilities. This is because it is implicitly assumed that childcare is
undertaken by a married woman. Although the woman may forego
earnings to care for the child, as long as the husband is earning then the
family is deemed to have an adequate standard of living.[2] Indeed
married women were until 1978 allowed to opt for a reduced rate of NI
contributions on the grounds that loss of their earnings was not a
contingency against which a family would necessarily wish to insure
itself.

Problems arise however when the person with childcare
responsibilities is also the sole breadwinner, since there is a loss of
earnings with no partner to make up the shortfall. This situation has
become increasingly common, with the number of lone parents in the UK

---

2   A small number of low income one-earner couples with children are however entitled
    to additional help through Family Credit.

having more than doubled from under 0.6 million in 1971 to stand at around 1.3 million in 1992 (Haskey, 1989a; DSS, 1992a, p. 42).

Furthermore, not only has the number of lone parents increased dramatically, but so has the proportion who are out of employment and dependent on benefits. In 1971 around one-third of lone parents were receiving Supplementary Benefit whilst in 1992 that proportion had risen to two-thirds (Bradshaw and Huby, 1989; DSS, 1992a). In part this reflects the growing proportion of lone parents with young children, as well as the diminishing role of maintenance in the incomes of such families.

A further feature of this group is that they are likely to be dependent on benefits for a considerable length of time. As Table 1.3 shows, among non-pensioners, lone parents are highly likely to be in receipt of benefits for several years. As a result a system where entitlement is dependent on recent contact with the labour market is likely to be ill-suited to the needs of this group. These issues are discussed more fully in Jane Millar's contribution to this collection.

Table 1.3 Duration of Income Support Receipt Among Lone Parents, 1990

Duration	Lone Parents	All IS Recipients Under 60	Lone Parents as Percentage of all IS Recipients
< 12 months	216,000	995,000	21.7
12–23 months	124,000	368,000	33.7
24–35 months	72,000	170,000	39.2
> 35 months	381,000	972,000	39.2
All Durations	793,000	2,505,000	31.7

Source: DSS, *Annual Statistical Enquiry of Income Support Recipients*, 1990.

Disablement

A small but growing group of non-employees who are excluded from NI benefits is those long-term sick or disabled people whose disability struck before they had acquired an adequate contributions record. The three main groups affected are married women who had opted to pay a reduced rate of NI contributions and who are not now entitled to NI Invalidity Benefit, those who were young when they became disabled, and others with patchy employment histories. The role of the first factor is likely to diminish, given that the option of a reduced rate ceased in 1978, but the numbers of young disabled and of others with poor contributions record have seen a modest increase during the 1980s.

The total numbers receiving the non-contributory Severe Disablement Allowance (SDA) (and its predecessor benefits) have increased from 175,000 in 1980 to 285,000 in 1990. Given that those who start to receive SDA will typically continue to do so for many years, this suggests that the uninsured disabled are likely to form an increasingly important group in coming years. The reasons for this growth in claimant numbers, which has occurred in a number of European countries, are discussed in the chapter by Susan Lonsdale and Jennifer Seddon in this volume.

Former part-time/contract/seasonal workers
One of the preconditions for entitlement to Unemployment Benefit is that a claimant must have actually paid a minimum level of NI contributions in at least one of the preceding two tax years. For most employees in regular employment for six months or more in a given tax year then this condition is easily satisfied. There will however be a number of groups who, though they have worked recently, will fall at this hurdle and be disqualified from NI benefit.

The first is those who earn less than the 'Lower Earnings Limit' (LEL). This threshold (£56 per week in 1993–94) is the point below which no NI contributions are due. Although this is a relatively small sum, the 1990 FES suggests that there were more than two million employees earning less than the relevant lower earnings limit for that year and who would thus be unlikely to receive NI benefit should they lose their job. Indeed there is evidence that because of the requirement for both employees and employers to pay contributions on earnings above this level, some employers may have deliberately kept part-time pay below the prevailing LEL (Dilnot and Webb, 1988). Although recent reforms to the structure of employee contributions may have reduced this incentive (Dilnot and Webb, 1989), the imposition of any earnings limit will inevitably exclude some claimants from benefit.

This issue is one which has become increasingly important because of the continued rise in part-time working. As Table 1.4 indicates, the number of part-time employees has almost doubled over the last two decades.

Table 1.4 Part-time Employment in Great Britain, 1971–1990

Year	Males	Females	Total
1971	600,000	2,800,000	3,400,000
1981	700,000	3,800,000	4,500,000
1986	1,100,000	4,500,000	5,600,000
1990	1,500,000	5,200,000	6,700,000

Source: HMSO, *Social Trends*, 1987, Table 4.10; 1992, Table 4.18.

A second group of recent employees which may fall foul of the contributions rules for Unemployment Benefit are those whose previous employment was on a short-term contract or was of a seasonal or casual nature. The contribution requirement would be satisfied by anyone earning over the LEL for 25 weeks or more, but this may not be possible where that employment was of a short-term or flexible nature.

It should also be noted that it is only since October 1988 that this contribution requirement has been quite so stringent. Until then, adequate contributions had only to have been made during any previous tax year, rather than necessarily in one of the previous two. This change is estimated to have saved the NI Fund £350 million in 1990–91, and represents a further restriction of coverage of NI benefits among those very groups for whom such benefits were originally designed.[3]

Many of the problems facing those in insecure or low-paid employment with regard to Unemployment Benefit will also affect their entitlement to Statutory Sick Pay. Those earning below the LEL are disqualified from SSP, as are those on contracts of less than three months. Evidence on the implications of these and similar restrictions for benefit receipt in the UK is given in section 1.2.3 below. A discussion of trends across the OECD in so-called 'atypical' work of this sort is presented by John Blackwell in this volume.

Former self-employed
The National Insurance Contributions paid by the self-employed give entitlement to NI benefits for sickness, widowhood, maternity or old age but not unemployment. In part this arises from the practical difficulty of defining when a person ceases to be self-employed and becomes unemployed. In return for this exclusion, the self-employed typically pay a lower level of contributions than employees on similar earnings. Nonetheless, the phenomenal growth in self-employment during the 1980s from 2,060,000 in 1981 to 3,220,000 in 1991 (Central Statistical Office, 1992, Table 4.11) has enlarged substantially a group for whom the move into unemployment does not bring entitlement to NI benefits. Tony Eardley and Anne Corden, in their chapter in this volume, discuss more fully the reasons for the growth in self-employment and also assess the problems facing self-employed people who miss out on NI benefits.

Divorcees
In the Beveridge Model it was assumed that the breadwinner in a household would typically be male and that the role of a married woman would primarily be that of housewife. The implications of these assumptions are discussed more fully by Ruth Lister in her chapter in this volume. However, leaving aside the question of the appropriateness of this assumption for married couples, it is clear that in a society where

---

3   See Atkinson and Micklewright (1989) for a comprehensive discussion of this and other restrictions to entitlement to Unemployment Benefit.

many marriages end in divorce a new approach will be required to ensure that once-married women have adequate incomes.

To some extent, the modern National Insurance system has begun to come to terms with this problem. In particular, divorced women do have rights to benefit in respect of those NI contributions of their ex-husband made during the period of the marriage. There are however two main reasons why this level of cover may be inadequate.

In the first place, many men will have 'contracted out' of the State Earnings-Related Pension Scheme into an occupational or personal pension. In this case, a divorced woman who reaches retirement age would only be entitled to (some fraction of) the basic state pension in respect of her ex-husband's contributions. She could, of course, seek some share in her husband's occupational/personal pension through the divorce courts, but the law in this area is still highly unsatisfactory. These issues are discussed more fully in Joshi and Davies (1991a, b).

A second problem relates to the period after the divorce. In principle, and subject to childcare responsibilities, a divorced woman could acquire her own record of NI contributions in the remaining years before she retires. However, if she has taken years out of the labour market to look after children, her earnings potential on re-entering the labour market may be substantially diminished. In consequence, her subsequent state earnings-related pension will be lower, and she may end up substantially worse off than had she remained married.

At present this type of situation applies to only a small number of retired women. According to Joshi, in 1985 only around 3 per cent of women over 60 were divorced. This number is however forecast to rise to around 13 per cent by 2025. Though the divorce rate has been steady for many years at round 160,000 per year, the numbers of divorced women who have not remarried has increased sharply over recent decades as Table 1.5 indicates. As these women reach retirement age there is likely to be a sharp increase in the numbers of elderly women with relatively small entitlements to NI pensions who may well become dependent on income-related benefits.

Table 1.5 Estimated Number of Divorced Women who had not Remarried, 1961–1987

Year	Divorced Women Not Remarried
1961	184,000
1971	317,000
1981	890,000
1987	1,327,000

Source: HMSO, *Social Trends*, 1992, Table 2.16.

1.2.3 Gaps in coverage II: the evidence

In Section 1.2.2 we set out a number of reasons why non-earners may none the less not be entitled to NI benefits. In this section we examine DSS administrative data and FES data to see the impact of these trends on the pattern of receipt of NI benefits. We consider five groups: the unemployed, the short-term sick, the long-term sick/disabled, the elderly and lone parents.

Benefit receipt among the unemployed
Claimants of unemployment-related benefits may receive NI Unemployment Benefit, income-related Income Support, both benefits or neither. Table 1.6 shows how the distribution of unemployed claimants between these four categories has changed over the last thirty years. Perhaps the most striking trend is that the percentage of unemployed people receiving NI Unemployment Benefit (with or without income-related benefit) has plummeted from more than half in 1961 to fewer than one-quarter in 1990.[4] All of this decline has occurred during the last two decades and can largely be accounted for by four of the factors outlined in Section 1.2.2 – youth unemployment, long-term unemployment, the growth of self-employment and the tightening of the contributions requirements.

In 1990 of the 1.5 million unemployed people, 0.5 million had been unemployed for more than twelve months (and were thus disqualified from UB), whilst of the 135,000 under-20s, only 3,000 were entitled to UB.

Table 1.6 Benefit Receipt Among the Unemployed, 1961–1990

Benefits Received	Numbers Receiving (thousands)				Percentages (%)			
	1961	1971	1982	1990	1961	1971	1982	1990
UB Only	173	352	714	288	45	41	25	18
UB + Income Support*	30	108	262	60	8	13	9	4
Income Support* Only	74	223	1428	969	19	26	50	62
Neither	107	177	466	246	28	20	16	16
TOTAL	384	860	2870	1563	100	100	100	100

Note: * National Assistance, 1961; Supplementary Benefit, 1971, 1982.
Source: DSS, *Social Security Statistics*, various years.

---

4   Since 1990 the proportion receiving UB has climbed back to around one third, mainly because of the rise in short term unemployment. This higher coverage is however unlikely to be sustained.

There is less evidence on how many of the unemployed had previously been self-employed (and hence disqualified from UB), but given the dramatic growth in the sector documented earlier, this is likely to have added a further downward impetus to UB coverage among the unemployed.

The pattern of benefit receipt revealed in Table 1.6 has implications for the administrative costs of benefits for the unemployed, since each claimant for unemployment benefits is first assessed for NI Unemployment Benefit. According to Table 1.6, in 1.2 million cases the verdict will have been that no UB is payable and then an assessment for Income Support will be made. The administrative costs of this process are enormous. The 1992 Annual Report of the DSS reveals that the average administrative cost per successful claimant of UB is £8.20 per week. This compares with a figure of £2.75 per week even for a relatively complex benefit such as Family Credit. Given the circumscription of entitlement to UB detailed above it seems rather inefficient to continue to test all unemployed claimants for UB entitlement in the knowledge that the vast majority will fail the test.

Benefit receipt among the short-term sick
Prior to the introduction of Statutory Sick Pay, the conditions for entitlement to NI Sickness Benefit were similar to those for Unemployment Benefit with the principal exception that the contributions of the self-employed could count towards entitlement. Under SSP the eligibility rules are different and the absence of a record of NI contributions is not itself an obstacle to receipt.

None the less, during the financial year 1990–91 more than 50,000 claims for SSP were rejected either on the grounds that the claimant was earning below the lower earnings limit or was only on a short-term contract. Furthermore it is likely that these figures understate the effects of such exclusions since many employers would not even register a claim in respect of an employee whom they knew would not be entitled to SSP.

Benefit receipt among the long-term sick/disabled
Those who have been sick for more than 28 weeks and who satisfy the necessary requirements on NI contributions are entitled to receive Invalidity Benefit (IVB). Those with inadequate contributions generally receive the (lower) non-contributory Severe Disablement Allowance. Table 1.7 indicates the trend in claimant numbers for these two benefits since the mid-1970s.

Table 1.7 Numbers Receiving Invalidity Benefit/Severe Disablement
Allowance, 1975/76 - 1991/92

	1975/76	1980/81	1985/6	1991/92
Invalidity Benefit	460,000	620,000	870,000	1,325,000
Severe Disablement Allowance*	130,000	175,000	230,000	300,000

Note: * Prior to 1985/86, Non-contributory Invalidity Pension / Housewives Non-Contributory Invalidity Pension.
Source: HMSO, *The Government's Public Expenditure Plans*, various years.

The dramatic growth in claimant numbers for these benefits has been widely discussed (see for example Disney and Webb, 1991). What is surprising in view of the foregoing discussion is that the split between contributory and non-contributory benefit receipt has, if anything, moved in the direction of the contributory benefit. The main reason why the general trend of more limited NI coverage has not applied in this case is that the population affected is predominantly older men. In 1990, out of 1,200,000 IVB recipients, more than 700,000 were men over the age of 50. For this group many of the factors listed in section 1.2 will be largely or wholly irrelevant (youth, lone parenthood, previous insecure employment, previous self-employment, divorce) whilst length of time on benefit will not be a barrier since there is no limit on duration of IVB receipt.

However, whilst claimant numbers on the contributory benefit have risen faster than those for the non-contributory benefit, average amounts paid have risen more rapidly for SDA. In part this is due to an upgrading of benefits under SDA (with the introduction of age-related additions in December 1990), but there have also been a number of cuts in the amount of IVB to which a claimant is entitled. The most important of these have been the restrictions to earnings-related supplements to IVB which are now available only to those over pension age. This would seem to be an area where the Government has decided that those who miss out on contributory benefits are receiving an inadequate income and has in effect funded increases for that group by cuts in the benefits of the insured population.

Benefit receipt among the elderly
The vast majority of those over state pension age receive some amount of NI pension, either in respect of their own or their partner's contributions. The residual Non-Contributory Retirement Pension has declined in significance and is now received by only around 35,000 people, compared with 130,000 in 1971. The NI Retirement Pension is however now the only NI benefit where the amount of benefit paid may be reduced for those who only partially satisfy the contribution

requirements. Table 1.8 shows, for the period 1975–1990, the numbers affected by such a scaling down.

Table 1.8 Retirement Pensioners Receiving Less than the Full Basic Pension

	1975	1980	1985	1990
Pensioners receiving less than 100% of basic pension	543,000	513,000	775,000	848,000
All pensioners		8,141,000	8,675,000	9,163,000	9,371,000

Note: Excludes pensioners resident overseas.
Source: DSS, *Social Security Statistics*, various years.

Perhaps surprisingly, the proportion of recipients of retirement pensions who are receiving reduced amounts of pension has increased in recent years. A significant majority of those not receiving full benefit are women claiming pensions on the basis of their own contributions. In more than one in four of these cases the woman concerned is receiving less than one-third of the full pension. Such an outcome, which awaits many divorced women now approaching pension age, may undermine the contribution of NI benefits to the incomes of a growing minority of pensioners.

Those pensioners with insufficient income from the state pension alone are generally entitled to a top-up through the Income Support system. The numbers affected have been relatively stable over the past two decades. From 1970 to the end of the Supplementary Benefit system in 1988, there were always between 1.5 and 1.8 million pensioners receiving SB. Since then, the number receiving Income Support has been slightly lower at around 1.4 million. With the present policy of continued price-indexation of the basic pension, and with periodic above-inflation increases for older pensioners, it seems likely that Income Support will continue to play an important part in the incomes of a large number of elderly people.

Benefit receipt among lone parents
As was indicated in Section 1.2.2, lone parenthood is typically a lengthy state and is seldom compatible with a recent record of National Insurance Contributions. Confirmation of this hypothesis is difficult from DSS administrative statistics alone, since they do not separately identify which lone parents are also receiving NI benefit. However, analysis of FES data indicates that NI benefits are largely irrelevant to lone parents. In 1970 such benefits accounted for only around 2 per cent of the household income of such families, and even where NI benefit was present it was usually being received by another household member. By 1990 the proportion was just 1 per cent. Over the same period the share

of non-contributory benefits in the income of lone parent households had risen from 21 per cent to 37 per cent.

1.2.4 National Insurance benefits and targeting: the evidence

Before considering the implications of our analysis for the future development of social insurance, we consider finally some direct evidence on the link between NI benefits and low incomes. This evidence draws together the various trends which we have documented and shows their combined effect.

Figure 1.3 is based on Family Expenditure Survey data for 1970, 1980 and 1990 and shows the contribution of NI benefits to the total income of households at various points of the income distribution in each of these years. The definition of income is gross household equivalent income (i.e. adjusted to allow valid comparison to be made between households of differing sizes) but taking no account either of housing costs or housing benefits. To avoid a discontinuity, Statutory Sick Pay has been treated as a National Insurance benefit. The most striking feature of Figure 1.3 is the way that between 1980 and 1990 the incidence of NI benefit receipt has moved from being concentrated amongst the poorest decile, to being most heavily concentrated among the second poorest tenth of the population. This result is likely to have arisen for two main reasons.

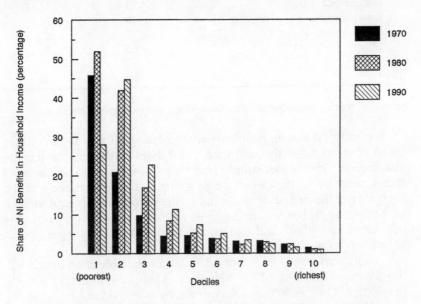

Source: Author's calculations based on Family Expenditure Survey Microdata.

Figure 1.3 Contribution of NI Benefits to Household Income, 1970–1990

Firstly, as we have seen, non-NI groups have either increased in number or seen their incomes grow by less than their NI counterparts. The uninsured unemployed have grown greatly in number since 1970. Lone parents are also more numerous and are far less likely to have paid employment than in 1970. This account is confirmed by the detailed breakdown of the composition of the bottom decile group given in Table 1.9.

Table 1.9 Composition of the Bottom Decile, 1970–1990

(percentages)	1970	1980	1990
NI Benefit Recipients	59	57	30
Of which:			
Retirement pensioners	47	39	22
Long-term sick	3	4	3
Short-term sick	1	1	1
Widows	3	2	1
Unemployed	5	11	3
Non-Recipients	41	43	70
Of which:			
Long-term sick	0	1	1
Unemployed	3	13	17
Lone parents	11	16	23
Full-time workers	22	7	13
Other	5	5	15
Total	100	100	100

Source: Author's calculations based on Family Expenditure Survey Microdata.

Secondly, NI benefit recipients are increasingly likely to have other forms of income and this will tend to lift them further up the income distribution. This is particularly true for pensioners, who, as Table 1.9 shows, were by far the largest single group in the bottom decile at the beginning of the period. This decline in the proportion of pensioners in the bottom decile has occurred despite a growth in their numbers in the population as a whole, and also despite a rising tendency for pensioners to be living in smaller households.

The pattern shown in Figure 1.3 is also attributable to an increase in the average amount of NI benefit payable, particularly among pensioners. On this account the reason why more NI benefits are going to slightly better off households is that NI benefits are now at such a level that they lift people out of poverty. However, whilst the growth in SERPS entitlements has boosted pensioner incomes, cuts in the level of

Unemployment Benefit and Invalidity Benefit will have partly offset this trend for other groups of NI benefit recipients.

Taken together, these trends suggest that recipients of NI benefits are no longer necessarily among the poorest households and similarly that poor households will not necessarily be in receipt of NI benefits. In our final section we consider how the social insurance system should respond to such a situation.

1.3 Prospects for Social Insurance

In assessing the future prospects for social insurance benefits in the light of our analysis it is helpful to consider the defining characteristics of this group of benefits. Broadly speaking social insurance benefits are those where entitlement is:

- related to previous contributions;
- based on contingency (e.g. unemployment, old age etc.) rather than income; and
- largely unaffected by the income of other household members (apart from the rules on additions for dependent adults).

Of these three features it is the first which seems least appropriate in a modern economy. It is clear from our analysis that today's poor are increasingly unlikely to have a record of contributions which would bring entitlement to insurance-based benefits. Though it is possible to contrive variations on the present contribution rules where some of the excluded groups would be brought back in to benefit, it is hard to believe that anything but the most convoluted set of contributions rules could cater for the diversity of excluded groups which we have identified.

Indeed it is far from clear that even a rejuvenated contributory principle is any longer worth retaining. Probably the sole reason for retaining a link between previous contributions and current benefits is that unlike income-related benefits, contributory benefits are seen to have been 'earned' and so there is no stigma to taking them up. In large part this perception is however a myth.

Those who receive income-related benefits will by and large have 'earned' them through the taxes they have paid. Though some may not have paid much income tax all will have paid VAT, excise duties and, through their contributions to company profits, corporation tax. It could be argued that it is only the preservation of a two-tier benefit system which preserves the view that some benefits are 'earned' whilst others are no more than charity. If the 'National Insurance' label were to be dropped from benefits, and the separate system of National Insurance contributions similarly ended, then it would be clear that taxes pay for benefits and that there is no stigma attached to taking up benefits when entitlement arises.

We must be careful however not to do away with all of the properties which make NI benefits relatively popular among recipients. Clearly targeting by contingency rather than income produces administrative savings and helps take-up. For as long as particular groups are still highly likely to be poor then a contingent approach is to be welcomed. Perhaps today however it is lone parents and the very elderly who fall into that category rather than some of the NI groups such as the short-term sick or newly retired.

A further attraction of targeting by contingency but without complex insurance rules is that of flexibility. We have observed that even in the last twenty years the pattern of poverty has changed considerably and only the most optimistic could expect to know what the causes of poverty will be two decades into the next century. The National Insurance system has been slow to adapt, not least because its main role is to pay benefits to groups identified half a century ago as likely to be poor. A system not linked to previous contributions can respond more rapidly to the current needs of the poor and does not need long periods of phasing out while entitlements in respect of previous contributions are honoured.

Similarly attractive is the third feature of NI benefits, namely the use of the individual as the unit of assessment. Individually assessed benefits overcome the problems associated with uneven distribution of resources within the household, and also reduce labour market disincentives for the partners of recipients.[5] However, they do so by continuing to pay benefit to those even in relatively well off couples, and inevitably the cost implications of this are considerable. Consequently, even those most wedded to the idea of individual assessment (see, for example, Parker, 1990) recognise that such benefits could only be a modest part of the overall system for the foreseeable future.

Insurance-based benefits have had a crucial role in the founding of the modern British welfare state. All our evidence suggests however that that role has now been completed and that a contributory basis for benefit entitlement is ill-suited to the needs of today's poor.

---

5   For UK evidence on the incentives issue, see Kell and Wright (1990). For evidence from other European countries see Micklewright and Giannelli (1991).

Part I

Adapting to Change: Gender roles and the family

Chapter 2

'She has other duties'- Women, citizenship and social security

Ruth Lister

2.1   Introduction

The focus of this chapter is the implications for women of the gendered notion of citizenship that underlies the Beveridge Report. It discusses why the question of women's economic (in)dependence – central to feminist critiques of the Beveridge model – is key in the evaluation of social security systems from women's perspective.

This perspective raises both specific questions about possible future developments in social security and more general questions about the contribution of social security to women's rights of social citizenship and the nature of these rights and associated obligations.

2.2   Beveridge: Partnership or dependency for women?

Carol Pateman's (1989) observation that 'paid employment has become the key to citizenship' (p. 184) is exemplified by the Beveridge Plan. This key was held out to men who were deemed responsible for their families' maintenance. Married women were mothers and housewives.

Nevertheless, Beveridge (1942) was at pains to stress that his plan treated housewives 'not as dependants of their husbands, but as partners sharing benefit and pension when there are no earnings to share' (para. 117). This partnership was based on their 'other duties'(para. 114); their 'vital unpaid service' (para. 108), 'in ensuring the adequate continuance of the British race and of British ideals in the world'(para. 117). The racial connotations of Beveridge's citizen-mother (underlined by Fiona Williams (1989)) can also be found in earlier developments in welfare policy in the United States (Mink, 1990).

On marriage, a woman was to become 'a new person' trading any rights to insurance benefits already accrued in her own right for derived rights through her husband. These new rights were codified in a 'Housewife's Policy' not all of which was actually implemented.

Many women, including some women MPs, welcomed Beveridge's recognition of the value of married women's unpaid work (Pateman, 1989; Brown, 1990a). Seventy per cent of women represented on the Mass Observation panel gave the report unqualified support (Jacobs, 1992). The welcome was not, however, universal. In a pamphlet entitled *The Woman Citizen and Social Security*, Elizabeth Abbott and Katherine Bompas (1943) of the Women's Freedom League brushed aside Beveridge's attempts to clothe women's continued dependent status in the trappings of partnership, arguing that 'the failure to treat women as full and independent fellow citizens with men' (p. 18) was a basic flaw in the Plan.

Thus, the rhetoric of Beveridge and his support for the introduction of family allowances notwithstanding, the Beveridge welfare state privileged 'citizen the worker' over 'citizen the mother' (Hernes, 1988, p. 200). This points to a central question posed by this chapter: who is a citizen and which activities constitute citizenship obligations from which independent social rights derive?

2.3   50 Years On: Equal treatment or equal outcome?

Fifty years on from Beveridge, his family/employment model, despite modifications, still shapes women's position in the social security system. The achievement of equal treatment, defined as the removal of explicit sex discrimination, has not guaranteed equal outcome (Land, 1988).

This is largely because the 'standard employment relationship' (Muckenberger, 1991), which stands at the heart of the Beveridge model, is essentially a male standard. It is at increasing variance with actual employment patterns, to the detriment of so-called 'atypical' workers in general and women in particular, an increasing number of whom (at least in the case of white women) are employed in part-time work, the average number of hours of which are diminishing (see Hilary Land's chapter in this volume.)

The contributory principle, which was central to the Beveridge plan, accommodates caring work in only limited ways, mainly through a degree of protection of contribution records (even more limited following the reforms of SERPS enacted under the Social Security Act 1986). It excludes completely about 2.25 million women earning below the lower earnings limit (House of Commons, 1991a) and an estimated further 1.5 million women doing occasional or irregular work (including homeworkers, many of whom are Asian women) (Hakim, 1989a).

Those working less than full-time, especially if on an irregular basis, are handicapped in building up the required earnings factor to meet the contribution conditions attached to the main contributory benefits. They are also more likely to pay 'wasted contributions' for which no benefits are received (Luckhaus and Dickens, 1991). The abolition of reduced rate benefits and the introduction of more restrictive eligibility rules for some contributory benefits have aggravated the bias against women in the national insurance scheme (Lister, 1992).

It is in the inferior, non-contributory parts of the social security system that the main recognition of unpaid caring work is to be found, albeit not always explicitly and rarely adequately.

The invalid care allowance (ICA) is an example of a non-contributory, non-means-tested benefit, introduced to fill a gap in the contributory system. The adult rates are, however, deliberately kept below those of the contributory benefits and therefore at a level insufficient to provide genuine economic independence. The ICA does, though, represent the most explicit recognition of the impact of caring on the standard employment relationship although only in so far as it ruptures it virtually completely. From an international perspective, it is unusual in providing 'citizen the carer' of disabled people with an earmarked income in her own right. Nevertheless, two recent research studies have underlined the fact that 'social security provision for carers is still far from adequate' in the UK (Glendinning, 1992a, p. 106; see also McLaughlin, 1991b).

The costs of reproduction are recognised through the child benefit scheme, the daughter of the family allowance which was described as a share of the national income 'assigned to those individual citizens who are undertaking the rearing of the citizens of the future' (Beveridge, 1949).

However, even though it provides some mothers with the only independent income they receive in their own right, child benefit is essentially a citizen's income for children rather than for women (which is not to underestimate its importance for women who still take the main responsibility for their children's welfare). It is a benefit which is supposed to contribute towards the *direct* costs of raising children and not the *indirect* costs associated with caring for them. It is in relation to the latter that the UK scores particularly badly in comparisons with the rest of Europe (see, e.g., Moss, 1988/9).

Reproductive work is also recognised, implicitly, in parts of the means-tested benefit system. For example, the UK is fairly unusual in providing lone parents with entitlement to social assistance without the requirement to register for work until the youngest child has reached school-leaving age. Carers of a claimant of attendance allowance enjoy a similar right.

The UK is also unusual in the provision of a means-tested benefit specifically for families with children where at least one parent is in full-time work (now defined for social security purposes as 16 hours a week). As the income limits exclude the great majority of two-earner families, in two-parent families family credit (which is paid to the mother against the original intentions of the Government) has, in effect, become a payment to women who stay at home to care for children. As such it can be seen as a subsidy to low-paid work which redistributes income from low-paid male wage-earners to non-employed mothers, thereby creating a potential disincentive for the latter to enter the labour market themselves. The other side of this coin is that it is the woman who stands to lose from any 'poverty trap' effect of a pay rise gained by the male worker (Brannen and Wilson, 1987; Corden and Craig, 1991). This points to one of the disadvantages of means-tested schemes which inevitably base entitlement on the couple as the unit.

The differential recognition of reproductive work in the different parts of the social security system is reflected in the pattern of receipt of benefits as between men and women below pension age. The general picture is one in which men represent the majority of recipients of contributory benefits and women the majority of recipients of the non-contributory categorical and means-tested benefits.

Women also form the overwhelming majority of indirect recipients of social security through their partners. It has been estimated that a social security benefit of some kind is paid to 3.7 million married men on behalf of their wives (Esam and Berthoud, 1991). In total, nearly two-thirds of all adults reliant on income support are women. This benefit still bears the imprint of the Beveridge family model, although, since 1988, couples have had a genuinely free choice as to who should be the claimant. Only one in twenty couples has opted for the woman to claim which at least is an advance on the one in 2041 in 1983 when a more restricted choice was first introduced (House of Commons, 1991b).

In a less extreme form, the gendered pattern of benefit receipt mirrors the 'two-channel' welfare state analysed by American feminist scholars (see, e.g., Nelson, 1984, 1990; Acker, 1988), in which masculine and feminine sub-systems 'are not only separate but also unequal' (Fraser, 1987, p. 110). Fraser argues that '"masculine" social insurance schemes position recipients primarily as rights-bearers ... They therefore qualify as social citizens in virtually the fullest sense that term can acquire within the framework of a male-dominated capitalist society' (p. 111). She contrasts their status with that of female recipients of assistance who are 'essentially clients'; and to be a client in such circumstances 'is to be an abject dependant'. They are 'effectively denied the trappings of social citizenship as the latter are defined within male-dominated capitalist societies' (p. 112).

It has also been suggested that the greater invasion of personal life involved in the receipt of assistance may be 'important in shaping the gendered meaning of receiving state benefits' (Acker, 1988, p. 493). As in the UK, welfare 'dependence' is deplored whilst women's dependence on men is taken as given and encouraged (Gordon, 1990).

Pateman (1989) suggests that this gendered pattern is perhaps even sharper in Australia, like the US, a 'liberal' welfare-state regime in Esping-Anderson's (1990) typology.

Despite her criticisms of 'the patriarchal welfare state', Pateman (1989) has nevertheless stressed that it has 'helped provide a basis for women's autonomous citizenship' (p. 195). Similar arguments have been advanced in the US by, for example, Fox Piven (1990) and Acker (1988). For all its inadequacies, the welfare system does, at least, enable poor women to live independently of men.

2.4   Freedom, Economic Independence and Citizenship

Implicit in this argument is the view (to which not all feminists would subscribe) that economic dependency on even a woman-unfriendly state is more conducive to women's autonomy than economic dependency on a man.   However inadequate and oppressive the nature of state provision, it potentially offers women more rights and control than 'chancy dependence' (McIntosh, 1981, p. 34) on male 'benevolence' (Pateman, 1989, p. 200).

The case for women's economic independence, through their ability 'to earn their own subsistence, independent of men' as 'enlightened citizens', was made 200 years ago by Mary Wollstonecraft (1792/1985, p. 283) in *Vindication of the Rights of Woman*. Two centuries later many women are still unable to achieve genuine economic independence through paid work (Lister, 1992).   The question of economic (in)dependence has thus continued to be influential in feminist analysis and has been seen as central to a gendered understanding of social citizenship (Cass, 1990; Pascall, 1986; Lister, 1990).

Dependency, has not, however, been an unproblematic concept. White feminists' preoccupation with it has been criticised by black feminists who point out that women's economic dependency is much less common among Afro-Caribbean households (cf. Carby 1982; hooks, 1982). (Nevertheless, it is only the most privileged women who are completely immune to the impact of the ideology of dependency which governs the general position of women in the labour market.)

There is also a potential contradiction between demands for women's economic independence on the one hand and a rejection of the false dichotomy between dependence and independence in favour of notions of interdependence on the other (Land, 1989; Wilson, 1983). However, the unequal power relationships that underpin women's economic dependency mean that the interdependence of which it is a part is skewed in favour of men. The latter's dependence on women for care and servicing, which facilitates their own independence as workers and citizens (Pateman, 1989), is conveniently obscured.   This has led Cass

(1990) to argue that 'it is not women's "dependency" therefore which is the problem for public policy, but men's "independence", with the negation of welfare which this implies and which is its consequence' (p. 15).

The problematisation of men's independence in this way is important in rethinking the meaning of dependency and of men and women's claims to citizenship (to which I will return later). However, it does not mean that women's economic dependence thereby ceases to be a problem for public policy and for their position as citizens.

There are a number of perspectives on the problem of economic dependency which can be summarised with reference to philosophy, poverty and power. In his recent defence of state welfare, Taylor-Gooby (1991) argues that basic human needs constitute rights against the state, as components of citizenship. He identifies human freedom or autonomy as 'a basic principle' in 'the field of needs as goals for social welfare policy' and 'as an essential component in any account of human welfare' (p. 172). A gendered interpretation of human needs, which lifts women's needs out of the 'private' domestic sphere into that of public policy, underlines the relationship between freedom and economic independence.[1] The case is elaborated in a Norwegian treatise on feminist jurisprudence by Tove Stang Dahl (1987).

Within a framework of the central values underlying 'women's law' – those of justice, freedom and dignity – she argues that 'a minimum amount of money for oneself is a necessary prerequisite for personal freedom, self-determination and self-realisation' (p. 91). Conversely, economic dependency is portrayed as the negation of freedom. From a human rights perspective 'women's dependency on men' is she contends, 'a moral problem, both on an individual and a societal level' (p. 97).

Dahl thus argues that

> access to one's own money should be considered a minimum welfare requirement in a monetary economy ... An independent income of one's own is a prerequisite for participation in and enjoyment of life, privately as well as publicly. Lack of money, on the other hand, gives a person little freedom of movement and a feeling of powerlessness. (p. 111)

She quotes research showing that women experience economic dependency as a threat to their dignity. The importance to many women of an independent source of income has similarly been highlighted by a number of pieces of British research (cf. Callender, 1992; Cragg and Dawson, 1984; McLaughlin, 1991b). Dahl's account points us also to the

---

1   Nancy Fraser (1987 and 1990) argues the case for a feminist intervention in 'the politics of needs interpretation' so that women interpret their own needs and secure their political status.

relationship between economic dependency and a gendered understanding of poverty.

As Atkinson (1991a) observes, if poverty is conceptualised in relation to a 'right to a minimum level of resources', 'we may question whether the dependency of one partner, typically the woman, on the other is acceptable' (pp. 9 and 10). Stephen Jenkins (1991) develops this to suggest that a feminist concept of poverty concerns 'the individual right to a minimum degree of potential economic independence' (p. 464).

Both the actuality and the ideology of women's economic dependency serve to make them more vulnerable than men to poverty (Glendinning and Millar, 1992; Lister, 1992). The longstanding failure to recognise the family as 'an important sphere of distribution' (Moller Okin, 1989, p. 31), reflected in the typical measurement of poverty at the level of the family or household, means that the poverty of some women, fully or partially economically dependent on men, remains invisible.

The distribution of resources (including work and time as well as money) within the family is partly a function of power relationships which, in turn, reflect the relative economic resources that each partner commands independently (Fuchs, 1988; Moller Okin, 1989; Pahl, 1989). The unequal power relationship typical of full or partial economic dependency is experienced by many women as a lack of control over resources; a lack of rights and a sense of obligation and deference (Pahl, 1989).

If it is accepted that the question of economic (in)dependence is critical to women's welfare and economic position, it needs to be incorporated into cross-national analysis of welfare states and regimes (Hobson, 1991). Langan and Ostner (1991, p. 130) point out that, as it stands, 'the question of gender is not systematically built into' the increasingly influential framework developed by Esping-Anderson (1990). In particular, they argue that his use of the concept of 'decommodification' – 'the degree to which individuals, or families, can uphold a socially acceptable standard of living independently of market participation' (Esping-Andersen, 1990, p. 37) (note the elision of individuals and families here) – takes no account of gender differences. Lewis has taken the argument further, analysing welfare regimes according to the strength of the male breadwinner family model (Lewis, 1992).

Arguably, the dimension of decommodification needs also to be complemented by that of what we might call 'defamilialisation', if it is to provide a rounded measure of economic independence. Welfare regimes might then also be characterised according to the degree to which individual adults can uphold a socially acceptable standard of living, independently of family relationships, either through paid work or through the social security system.

2.5   Individual Benefits

This brings us to the question of women's access to social security benefits in their own right as individuals. The importance of this to the achievement of genuine equal treatment has been underlined by the International Labour Office (Brocas et al., 1990). It has also been argued that individual benefits can provide greater protection in the face of trends in family break-up and cohabitation.

Strong support for individual benefit rights has come from the Council of Europe (1989). However, a proposal for a further EC social security directive (Com[87]494), which promotes the individualisation of benefits as a means of completing the implementation of equal treatment, has been deferred indefinitely by the Council of Ministers, although it does have the support of the European Parliament. Discussion of the directive has tended to focus on the implications for derived rights, dependants' allowances and survivors' benefits. In this context, a House of Lords Select Committee report has warned that any process of individualisation would need to be very gradual so as not to deprive women of the protective rights that many still need. This raises more generally the need for caution about reforms introduced in the name of an economic independence which for many women is still, at best, limited (Joshi, 1989a).

The growing support for a basic or citizens' income scheme, internationally, is also relevant here given that, in its pure form at least, such a scheme is predicated on the individual as the benefit unit.

However, the actual trend in the UK and more widely, is in the opposite direction – towards greater emphasis on means-testing. In couples, even where means-tested benefits are paid directly to the woman, they inevitably take the couple as the unit of assessment. The wider the gap between assumptions about equitable intra-family income-sharing implicit in means-testing and the reality, the lower the accuracy of means-tested benefits in targeting help on *individuals* in need. Moreover, two problems endemic to means-tested benefits – low take-up and work disincentives – have gendered dimensions which are rarely appreciated.

The intermittently fashionable notion of some kind of negative income tax, which effectively takes means-testing to its logical conclusion, largely addresses the problem of take-up but aggravates the others. In particular, it would institutionalise the couple as the benefit unit and would represent a major reverse for women's access to an independent benefit income, unless the principle of aggregation were abandoned. This is unlikely, given the expense and the problems that it would create.

Progress towards individual benefits appears to be greatest in social democratic welfare regimes where there is less reliance on means-testing and the links between employment and social security status are weaker. For instance, all the Nordic countries and the Netherlands (and also, perhaps more surprisingly in the framework of Esping-Anderson's typology, New Zealand)[2] provide a basic pension without either contribution or means test. Women tend to rely disproportionately on this basic pension only.

Within the context of the current UK benefits structure, a strategy to enhance women's independent benefit status could either aim to reduce/remove the barriers to women's access to the contributory scheme and/or improve and extend the non-contributory (Lister, 1992). Ultimately, the contributory principle itself comes into question.

Both the contributory and non-contributory schemes are linked to specific contingencies. Reforming them in order to provide women with an independent benefit income inevitably raises questions about gaps in the contingencies covered. The most obvious gap concerns the care of children. This in turn raises more fundamental questions about women's claims as citizens.

2.6   Citizen-Mother vs Citizen-Worker

The question 'who is a citizen?' is central – either explicitly or implicitly – to twentieth-century debates about women's relationship to the welfare state. The model handed down from the classic theorists of the British welfare state, including Beveridge, was, Pederson (1990) observes, one in which the citizen

> not only participates in the political life of the community and holds political rights but also contributes to its social and economic well-being, drawing from it social and economic entitlements ... By imagining a polity in which social rights stem from social functions, they begged the question of which forms of activity would properly be considered citizenship functions. If soldiering and working are to bring with them citizenship entitlements, will housekeeping or mothering do so as well? (Pederson, 1990, p. 983)

There was a strong strand in early twentieth-century feminism which argued that they should, typified in the campaign for the endowment of motherhood. This appealed to a 'rhetoric of motherhood as national

---

2   Esping-Anderson (1990) does not include the existence or relative value of universal non-contributory pensions as a variable in his de-commodification of pensions index. Yet arguably, this is a more telling indicator of de-commodification than those he does include.

service' (Pederson, 1990, p. 1006), the ethical equivalent of military service, as a basis for social citizenship and economic independence.

Others, such as Ada Nield Chew (1912), argued that participation in waged work was the key to women's economic independence. Eleanor Rathbone attempted to synthesise the two positions by arguing that the endowment of motherhood would encourage equal pay by undermining the case for the family wage (Pederson, 1989).

Nevertheless, the long-standing tension between these different approaches to women's economic independence and citizenship has not been dissolved. Pateman (1989) has conceptualised it as 'Wollstonecraft's Dilemma'. On the one hand, she writes, women

> have demanded that the ideal of citizenship be extended to them, and the liberal-feminist agenda for a 'gender-neutral' social world is the logical conclusion of one form of this demand. On the other hand, women have also insisted, often simultaneously, as did Mary Wollstonecraft, that *as women*, they have specific capacities, talents, needs and concerns, so that the expression of their citizenship will be differentiated from that of men. Their unpaid work providing welfare could be seen, as Wollstonecraft saw women's tasks as mothers, as women's work as *citizens* , just as their husbands' paid work is central to men's citizenship. (Pateman, 1989, p. 197)

The dilemma epitomises the long-standing tension between 'equality and difference'. Carol Bacchi (1990 and 1991), among others, has criticised the dichotomy as conceptually inadequate to address women's needs. The male standard, predicated on 'men as abstract individuals without family commitments' (1991, p. 83) goes unchallenged by it, she argues. A false choice between equal and different treatment diverts attention from the more fundamental issues of 'social responsibility for basic human needs such as child-bearing and child nurture' (pp. 83–4).

As Leira (1989) has observed, from a Norwegian perspective, 'what is lacking is a concept of citizenship which recognises the importance of care to society' (p. 208). The problem is how to provide this recognition without locking women further into a caring role which excludes them from power and influence.

Pateman (1989) suggests a way through Wollstonecraft's Dilemma by posing the question: 'what form must democratic citizenship take if a primary task of all citizens is to ensure that the welfare of each living generation of citizens is secured?' (p. 203). Part of her answer is that 'the opposition between men's independence and women's dependence has to be broken down, and a new understanding and practice of citizenship developed' (p. 204).

These approaches to equality and difference usefully shift the focus of attention away from women to men as well as to wider societal responsibilities for children and others in need of care.

Cass (1990) and Taylor-Gooby (1991) have developed the point, the latter using the concept of 'moral hazard' in relation to men's evasion of caring work, which is encouraged by government policies. Cass turns the argument on its head with a claim that men should not be 'accorded full citizenship if they do not fulfil their caring obligations in private life' (p. 15).

While it is difficult to see how the State could enforce such a notion of citizenship, there are certainly many ways in which it could encourage it. This has been attempted in the Scandinavian countries, by means of parental leave provisions and campaigns to encourage men to take the leave and to care for sick children. These have had some impact. There has been a gradual increase in the number of men taking parental leave and a relatively high proportion of men claim the temporary parents' allowance, paid when a child or the regular carer of a child is ill (Nasman, 1990). Nevertheless, it is still women who take the main responsibility for caring work.

Whilst the Scandinavian countries have been unsuccessful in shifting the division of caring labour between women and men in any significant way, there has been a clear shift in the balance of responsibility for reproduction between individual families and the state, most markedly in Denmark and Sweden. Lewis (1990) suggests that the experience of the latter may offer some lessons with regard to how a synthesis of equality and difference can strengthen women's claims as citizens. She notes that

> since the early 1970s, Swedish women have first had to become workers in order to qualify for the parental leave scheme at a favourable level of benefit, but, paradoxically, having taken a job they could then exert a claim to be mothers and to stay at home for what has proved to be a steadily lengthening period. (Lewis, 1990, p. 19)

Thus, she argues, in grafting a right to benefit on 'the basis of difference onto a policy based on equal treatment', the Swedish system has 'moved beyond the severely formal equality on men's terms offered in Britain and the USA to encompass women's needs as mothers' (pp. 19 and 15).

Sweden now provides 450 days of parental leave, some of which may be taken until the child is aged eight. Norway provides a year and Denmark 24 weeks. Sweden and Norway also make provision for time off to care for sick children. The contingency of caring for very young children is thus recognised through parental leave rather than through social security as such.

The ILO notes that no country has introduced what might be called a 'maternal wage' other than in 'a rudimentary form in the shape of income-tested family allowances' (Brocas et al., 1990, p. 89). However, young child allowances, paid for a period of 18 months to three years, where a parent (in France the mother only) stays at home to care for a new-born child, are now available in France, Germany and Luxembourg. In each case there is an element of means-testing, although only in

Luxembourg is a means test applied from the outset (Brown, 1992a). Finland has introduced a home care allowance, payable after the end of maternity/parental leave at nine months until the child is aged three. Alternatively, under-three-year-olds are entitled to a place in a communal day centre. A partial home care allowance also exists where a parent chooses to work shorter hours. The introduction of the home care allowance has been interpreted as a shift in ideology to encouraging mothers to stay at home for longer. Fears have been expressed that it will increase divisions between working and middle class women as it is the former who are more likely to take up the allowance (Simonen, 1991).

The Scandinavian experience suggests that if a benefit is made available to parents to stay at home and care for their children, mothers will be the main claimants.

While such a benefit paid beyond an initial parental leave period would provide full-time mothers with a citizenship income and therefore a modicum of economic independence, its longer-term implications for women's more substantial economic independence through the labour market would almost certainly be negative (cf. Joshi's (1991) work on the lifetime costs of mothers' absence from the labour market). Mothers' work as citizens in the 'private' sphere would receive greater recognition, but at the expense of locking them out of the 'public' sphere, economically and politically. This would reduce further women's power to influence social and economic policy. The dangers of this are underlined by Scandinavian feminists' warning from their own experience that, if women are to achieve full citizen status in modern welfare states, they must 'participate in the determination of what their social needs and political interests actually are' (Borchorst and Siim, 1987, p. 154).

In fact, the trend in welfare policy in recent years has been in the other direction, in particular in relation to lone mothers, the main focus of workfare-oriented policies in the US.[3] This policy shift has been articulated by people like Lawrence Mead in the language of citizenship obligation (Mead, 1986).

A similar shift in policy emphasis has been noted in some European countries (Room, 1991). In the Netherlands, all those who reached the age of 18 in 1990 or thereafter are expected to try to provide for their own livelihood. Thus, with the exception of a parent caring for an under-12-year-old child, every able-bodied individual (including in couples) must be available for work as a condition of entitlement to social assistance. This latter concession has been criticised for prioritising home child care

---

3 Brown (1989), commenting on the lessons to be learned from American workfare policies, has argued for a policy which encourages and facilitates lone mothers' labour market participation rather than one based on compulsion. The evidence suggests that most lone mothers want to return to paid work when they feel it is in their children's interests. She also argues for the need for a period of adjustment following marital breakdown or bereavement.

by one parent over improved child care facilities and encouraging shared care between parents (Bussemaker, 1991). Nevertheless, it does at least recognise the constraints on mothers' participation as full economic citizens on male terms.

So long as mothers continue to do the bulk of caring work, without fathers and the wider community sharing the responsibility, a social security policy which treats them as unfettered individuals in the labour market will simply increase the burdens on them.

This has implications for the conclusion reached by the ILO report on women and social security: that women will only achieve adequate personal rights when they 'are fully integrated into the world of work' (Brocas et al., 1990, p. 95). If this integration is to be on women's terms, it will, on the one hand, require changes in the world of (paid) work and on the other hand, the better integration of men into the world of (unpaid) care work. Adequate facilities for the care of children and to support those caring for older or disabled people must also be part of the equation.

From an income maintenance perspective, it underlines the importance of generous schemes of parental leave and leave for family reasons designed to encourage male participation in them. A starting point would be the lifting of the British veto on the draft European Directive in this area. It would be possible to recognise the value of child-rearing after the parental leave period, without undermining the incentive for mothers to take paid employment, if a benefit were paid for all those raising children, including those in paid work (see Esam and Berthoud (1991) who have modelled such a benefit). This would recognise that raising children incurs costs, including 'time-costs', regardless of the parents' employment status. Consideration of a benefit of this kind would need to be in the context of a comprehensive child care policy.

However, at a time when a growing number of commentators are questioning even a universal child benefit (ironically just as the Conservatives finally committed themselves to its index-linking), such an extension of universal benefits for families with children is not very likely in this country.

2.7 Conclusion

Policy debates around social security tend to be conducted on an implicit assumption that social security is a gender-neutral issue. Attempts to inject a woman's perspective thus come to be seen as raising 'other' questions which are somehow tangential. Yet women represent the majority of those reliant, either directly or indirectly, on most social security benefits.

This chapter has argued that, from the perspective of women's claims as citizens, a central question for the social security system is how it can best facilitate women's autonomy by contributing to their economic independence.

Broadly, a two-pronged approach has been suggested. On the one side, those elements of the present social security system which enhance women's economic independence (in particular, the non-contributory contingency benefits) need to be strengthened and the barriers to the core contributory benefit scheme need to be removed or, at least, reduced. In the long run, such an approach could be seen as consistent with a basic income scheme. However, it is out of tune with current developments which are placing growing emphasis on means-tested benefits which take the couple rather than the individual as the unit of assessment.

On the other side, a generous system of parental leave and leave for family reasons, designed in such a way as to encourage male participation, would provide some recognition of the value placed by society on child-rearing without reinforcing women's responsibility for it.

A sub-theme of the chapter has been that the contribution of the social security system to women's economic independence cannot be considered in isolation from other factors which undermine that independence. Of central importance is the division of responsibility for the care of children and of older and disabled people between women and men and between individual families and the State. This raises the question of men's responsibilities and the use of their time (Marsh, 1991) as well as of the adequacy of community support for parents and carers.

Underlying this approach is a conception of citizenship very different from that which informed the Beveridge Plan. Like Beveridge it recognises the value for citizenship of reproduction as well as production. But it sees the 'duties' associated with reproduction as falling on men as well as women and on the wider community, through child care and related provisions.

It also pays attention to the political dimension of citizenship. The history of women's attempts to create a welfare state in their own image underlines the importance of women being the subjects and not just the objects of welfare policy-making. Abbott and Bompas (1943) wrote of the Beveridge Plan that it is 'mainly a man's plan for man'. The final words of their critique of the Beveridge Plan are as relevant half a century later:

> One thing is certain. To continue to give women what seems to others to be good for them; to give them indeed anything with an ulterior motive – be it the preservation of marriage and the family, or a rise in the birth rate – is doomed to failure. To respect women as individuals, to give them what is their right as citizens and workers, may, on the other hand, have great and beneficial effect far beyond any immediate object. For both security and progress are rooted in justice. (Abbott and Bompas, 1943, p. 20)

Chapter 3

Family, Work and Social Security

Bea Cantillon

The increasing participation of women in the labour market and the destabilisation of the family have profoundly affected the adequacy of social security. On the one hand, fragmented family lives increase the risk of slipping through the family-centred social security net. On the other hand, the growing number of two-earner families has meant that in many cases the wages of one income families – and also the social security income derived from those wages – have become insufficient to cover minimum family needs. At the same time, changes in values are eroding the legitimacy of the family-adjusted system, not least through the emergence of new forms of discrimination between insured men and women and between paid and unpaid work.

Thus, social and demographic changes and their consequences for the structure of needs, as well as for the cost, effectiveness and legitimacy of social security, give rise to a complex problem. This problem is how to optimise social protection in response to the increased social burden resulting from ageing or plural populations and to the problems of poverty and inequality arising from social and demographic developments. The problem is compounded by the need to take into account the fundamental principles of non-discrimination, prevention, strengthening self-sufficiency and avoiding perverse impacts on the social and demographic behaviour of individuals and families. This chapter asks whether and how individualisation of social security can solve these problems. The first part documents the consequences of socio-demographic developments for the cost, adequacy and legitimacy of social security. The second part investigates the main objectives of future policy. The third part contains some practical recommendations for policy.

45

The analysis is based on the Belgian social security system, which is characterised by moderate earnings relations in contributions and benefits. However, the diagnosis of the relationship between social security and the basic institutions of the family and work probably applies to most social security systems in rich industrialized countries.

3.1   The Diagnosis: Social security and the basic institutions of family and work

The socio-demographic context in which social security was conceived was marked by one-earner families – if not as a rule then still as the ideal to be striven for – and by stable family structures that were threatened only by the death of one of the members. Socio-demographic developments have now thoroughly changed this situation, and herein lies an important cause of the inadequacy and legitimacy crisis of social security.

3.1.1   Inadequacy

In the socio-economic and demographic context in which the foundations of social security were laid down, the occurrence of one of the risk-events covered by social security almost automatically gave rise to a situation of need. Because unemployment, sickness, old age, or death of the breadwinner often led to the loss of the only family labour income, these risk-events were good indicators of need. Conversely, need situations arose primarily from the loss of income from the full-time job of the breadwinner by unemployment, sickness, old age, or death. Thus a universal protection system was structured in which risk was the basis for benefits and stigmatising means tests could be avoided. This system offered, in the given socio-demographic context, the advantage of the virtual coincidence of 'contributional equity' and 'distributional equity'.

Socio-demographic developments have now changed this situation fundamentally. The occurrence of a social risk-event no longer leads automatically to a need situation, and new needs not covered by the risk-events traditionally insured by social security have arisen.

A new relationship between needs, risk, and risk coverage
The increase in two-earner households, solo men and women, and single-parent families has created two polarised categories, one for whom the occurrence of a social-risk event leads to a severe – and generally too severe – drop in income, and another which can partially absorb the loss of income because of the presence of another income in the household. Replacement incomes are very inadequate for households that have to live exclusively from them, but for two-income families, the

social protection system is more adequate. After social transfers, 14 per cent of two-income married couples have an income below the poverty line, compared to about 58 per cent of one-income families (see Table 3.1).

Table 3.1 Adequacy of Income Replacement Benefits of Social Security by Type of Household (Belgium, 1985)

	Person living alone	Couple with one income	Couple with two incomes	One parent families
Percentage of households above subsistence level* before benefits	8.7	6.5	42.3	26.3
Percentage of households above subsistence with benefits	44.7	35.5	44.0	31.6
Percentage of households below subsistence in spite of benefits	46.6	58.0	13.7	42.1
Number of respondents	103	169	345	90

Note: * The subsistence level is here measured with the subjective poverty standard developed by the Centre for Social Policy. For this method, see Deleeck and Van den Bosch, 1990.
Source: Centre for Social Policy survey, 1985.

The occurrence of a social-risk event has divergent consequences in terms of needs for different groups of beneficiaries. This leads to tensions within the social security system between the principle of solidarity and the principle of insurance. Because a risk-event is no longer a good indicator of need, it has become very difficult to satisfy in one universal system both 'guaranteed minimum income as a function of needs' and 'income maintenance as a function of risks and contribution payment'. The question now arises whether and how distributional equity can be reconciled with contributional equity.

New social risks
Socio-demographic changes gave rise to new needs that are not, or only partially, covered by social security. Here it is important to note that only 40 per cent of households below the poverty line are beneficiaries whose replacement incomes are too low. Sixty per cent of households with incomes below the poverty line have inadequate incomes from labour (mainly one-income households and single parents).

This indicates that the inadequacy of social security is associated not only with social security benefits that are too low, but also with insufficient protection of unpaid work, too little compensation for the costs of children, and the almost complete absence of any protection in the event of divorce. Within social security, the necessity of double incomes, the indirect costs of children (and, more generally, of unpaid work), and marital instability thus create problems for the link between social protection, work and the family.

The risk of unpaid work
'Very few men's wages are insufficient to cover at least two adults and one child' (Beveridge, 1942). What was the case in 1942 is no longer so today. This problem is generally not taken into account, either in studying the factors determining the 'new' poverty, or in studies of the adequacy of social security.

The risk of unpaid work has changed in nature. Previously, this occurred only when the income of the main breadwinner ceased because of death, and it was satisfactorily taken care of by the system of survival pensions.[1] The high degree of insecurity of subsistence among one-income families and one-parent families (even when working) shows that the risk of unpaid work also occurs now even if there is an employed breadwinner in the family, covered by social security.

This insecurity is caused by the necessity for double incomes and the enduring incompatibility of two full-time jobs with the care of children. Because of changed consumption patterns (particularly the shift from consumption of self produced goods to the consumption of market goods which can only be acquired by cash incomes) and the increasing prevalence of women in paid work, the double income has increasingly become the reference income. Today, with one modal labour income, let alone one replacement income, the poverty level can hardly be attained (see Table 3.2). Belgian data indicate that the average wage level of unskilled workers is 14 per cent less than the minimum for a household with one child and 20 per cent less than the minimum for families with two children. Consequently, the income of almost a quarter of one-earner families with the head of household in paid work is not enough to meet needs.

This situation has led to a problem of security of subsistence for single-income households, especially where there are dependent children. For more than 30 per cent of these households, a single income is not enough to make ends meet. Considering only those households that live on social security, the proportion is more than 58 per cent. If the women's income were to disappear, the number of double income households not attaining the poverty level would, other things being equal, rise from five to 47 per cent.

---

1   In Belgium the spouse of a deceased, insured employee or self-employed person is entitled to widow(er)'s pension of 80 per cent of the retirement pension of the deceased insured person, subject to the condition that the widow(er) is over 45 years of age or has a dependent child, or is incapable of work.

Table 3.2 The Necessity of Two Incomes: Percentage of Households below the Poverty Line among One-earner Families and Two-earner Families measured with the CSP-standard (Belgium, 1985)

	Percentage of households below CSP-standard*
One-earner family	30.8
One-earner family with paid work	24.1
One-earner family with social security income	58.0
Two-earner family	5.5
Two-earner family minus the income of the wife	47.1

Note: * See Table 3.1.
Source: Centre for Social Policy survey, 1985.

The indirect cost of children

In the two-earner era, the idea that child benefits will provide the working population with the means necessary to bring their family income up to the poverty level has been superseded. Child benefits cannot compensate for the inadequacy of one income and no longer guarantee a minimum income to many single-income families with children. Indeed, the persisting incompatibility of two jobs and caring for two, three or more children, particularly in lower social strata,[2] makes the well-being of families with children no longer solely a function of the direct costs of children but also and primarily of their indirect costs. These costs, which have arisen as a consequence of the increasing prevalence of two-income families, are not adequately corrected by the child-benefit system. This system is now inadequate to assure child-poor and child-rich families the same level of well-being and an equal degree of security of subsistence. Young families with three or more children have on average a lower living standard than small families in the same age group. In spite of the relative generosity of current family policy in Belgium, and positive correlation between fathers' incomes and number of children, the standard of living of large young families is on average ten per cent lower than that of small families in the same age group (see Table 3.3).

---

2   Among mothers of three or more children it is almost exclusively those with a high educational level who are in paid work. Among low-skilled women, the participation rate drops from 61 per cent when they have only one young child to 13 per cent when they have three or more. Among women with higher education, the participation rate remains much higher: 88 per cent when they have only one young child and 79 per cent when they have three or more.

Table 3.3 Indicators of the Standard of Living of Couples whose Youngest
Child is less than 6 Years Old, by Number of Dependent Children
(Belgium, 1985)

	One child	Two children	Three children
Average equivalent income* (BF/month)	49,963	45,370	44,816
Percentage of couples in:			
Quintile 1	10.6	13.9	15.0
Quintile 2	13.9	22.2	31.4
Quintile 3	22.6	23.7	23.6
Quintile 4	33.6	27.4	15.0
Quintile 5	19.3	12.4	15.0
Total	100.0	100.0	100.0
Number of respondents	208	274	140

Note: * Using the OECD scale (1976), which is fairly close to the geometric mean derived from a number of equivalence scales in international research (see Whiteford, 1985, p. 109). The scale is as follows: single person: 0.666; two-person household: 1.00; three-person household: 1.25; four-person household: 1.45; five-person household: 1.60; + 0.15 for every extra person. Dividing the disposable income of each household by the appropriate equivalence factor gives household equivalent income.
Source: Centre for Social Policy survey, 1985.

Divorce

The inadequacy of social protection upon divorce is, in quantitative terms, relatively unimportant. Only four per cent of households below the poverty line in Belgium are one-parent families. Qualitatively, however, the problem is highly significant because the adaptation of the social security system to the risk of divorce implies a thoroughgoing rethinking of the structure of social protection.

In Belgium, as in other industrialised countries, there is a much higher poverty risk among divorced one-parent families than in other types of household, including those of elderly persons. Moreover, one-parent families are likely to stay longer in poverty than the average poor household. The high poverty risk faced by single divorced mothers is the result of several factors, including the need to 'make ends meet' with only one income, socio-economic disadvantage related to the fact of being a woman (educational level, amount of time spent in paid work and low wages), and the inadequacy of private and social protection mechanisms (low social security benefits and maintenance payments).

The limited coverage of the dual risk of 'unpaid work – divorce' is a consequence of economic and family linkages in the social protection system. Because of the economic link (both the right to benefits and their amount depend on contributions to the scheme), people who have not completed a full working career or have been working part-time can only claim reduced entitlements and benefits. Those who have not been in the labour market have no direct social security entitlements at all. In both cases, those affected are mainly women.

The family linkage of benefits is even more important. This basic principle of social security finds its concrete expression in the system of derived entitlements (old-age pensions, family allowances and health care). As the effectiveness of such a system depends on the stability of family bonds, fragmented family patterns increase the risk that people will slip between the meshes of the net that protects them. Here one should mention the (mainly administrative) difficulties faced by single-parent families in obtaining their entitlements to family allowances.

3.1.2   Unemployment and improper use of unemployment benefits

The flow of women into the labour market resulted in the growth and the feminisation of the labour force, sharply increased unemployment rates, and the *de facto* change of the concept of 'full employment' (previously one worker per household, now two workers per household). In spite of decreased fertility rates, which have already led to a drop in the number of persons of working age, the expected increase in women's participation rate will in the near future be responsible for further growth in the labour force, assuming that men's participation rate does not change.   Consequently, unemployment will remain high and the feminisation of the labour force will increase.

For social security, this raises both a cost problem and a problem of adapting to the needs of the new type of worker who, more than her predecessor, 'the breadwinner', has to combine paid work with unpaid work (care of children, sick or elderly parents).   At present, neither the labour market nor social security is sufficiently adapted to deal with this new type of worker. Full social security protection presumes a complete career and full-time work.   This creates problems of insecurity of subsistence for families who decide to have several children.   The interruption to the wife's working life leads to the problem of making ends meet on a single income. This also leads to abusive, but necessary, utilisation of unemployment benefits.

According to data from the Centre for Social Policy, there is a positive correlation between unemployment for married women[3] and the number of children, even after controlling for age, level of education, occupation and sector of activity. These data show that two-income households are more often subject to unemployment, and for longer periods. This is

---

3   In Belgium unemployment benefits are not time-limited.

because they are less available for work. But these data also show that unemployment benefits received by married women with children are a necessary complement to the household income for a large number. For more than 16 per cent of these households, the single labour income plus unemployment benefit is not enough to make ends meet. If women's unemployment benefit were to disappear, the number of double-income households with an unemployed wife not attaining the poverty level would, other things being equal, rise to over 52 per cent.

The abusive but necessary utilisation of unemployment benefits in Belgium therefore reflects the negative effect of the failure to adjust working conditions and social security to the specific problems of combining two full-time jobs with child care requirements, especially for women with a low level of education and in the lower social groups.

3.1.3 Discrimination

As a consequence of socio-demographic developments and related changes in values, social security has created new forms of discrimination, while older forms of discrimination are becoming more visible. This evolution is so important that social security policy is increasingly dominated by discussion of the extent to which and how such direct and indirect discrimination should be combated. The most important type of discrimination is that between men and women covered by social security on the one hand and that between paid and unpaid work on the other.

With the exception of the difference in retirement ages and in the maximum amounts of pensions for employees with a complete career, almost all the forms of direct discrimination against women have been removed from Belgian law. Problems now primarily concern the application interpretation of the principle of indirect discrimination (see Article 4 of Directive no. 79 (7) EEC of the Council of 19 December 1978). In general terms, indirect discrimination arises because an apparently neutral procedure turns out in practice to predominantly affect one sex. In Belgium, discussion of this legal principle concentrates primarily on the question of whether the 'family adjustments' to earning related benefits should be removed from the unemployment, sickness, disability, and retirement schemes because statistically women are predominantly disadvantaged.

There are two lines of argument regarding the unequal treatment of paid and unpaid work. Some contend that working married women pay contributions 'for nothing' because derived entitlements cannot or can be combined only partially with individual rights. Therefore, derived entitlements emerge as a discriminatory and anti-emancipatory system, 'coming from those households that contribute twice to those who contribute only once' (*Université des Femmes*, 1987). The problem arises particularly with family allowances, where women's work has entirely changed the relationship between benefits and contributions and has highlighted the distortions in the nature of the two sides of the balance sheet – benefits and contributions. 'One thus sees a redistribution from working to non-working women, irrespective of the incomes of their spouses and the size of the family ... By their contributions, women contribute to financing family policy, without receiving any counterpart' (Ekert, 1985; see also Coutière, 1983; Hatchuel, 1985).

The alternative argument is that in the wage labour centred social security system, unpaid work is rarely covered by specific benefits and individual social security rights. This is seen as discrimination against socially and economically important unpaid labour.

3.1.4 Calculating behaviour

Because choices regarding marriage, cohabitation, divorce, and remarriage are no longer ruled by the values of the past, it is generally accepted that some (potential) beneficiaries may use the opportunities offered by complex social security provisions, sometimes even adjusting their demographic behaviour to the institutional environment. Social security is not neutral towards the family. Nor can it be, even if based on the strategy of basic income. This leads to a self-reinforcing mechanism whereby social protection itself could act as a factor affecting socio-demographic behaviour (Murray, 1984; Sullerot, 1984).

The empirical data are unsurprisingly equivocal when it comes to the existence, scope, and nature of behavioural effects. Decisions about the organisation of family life are influenced by a multiplicity of social, cultural, and psychological factors. Financial incentives (including social protection) are only one influence. An empirical separation of the direct influence of social security on behaviour is difficult to achieve. Nevertheless, the question of the influence of social security benefits on marriage, divorce or remarriage is of great political significance. Indeed, regulations that discriminate against marriage and for divorce impair the legitimacy of the system and thus must be avoided as far as possible.

3.2 The Objectives of Future Policy

Three policy problems emerge from this diagnosis. First, within the universal context of the social security system, how and in what degree can selectivity be built in so that need and risk coverage can converge (the tension between solidarity and insurance)? Second, how can protection be adapted to the new family context (relationship between social security, individual, and the family)? Third, how must the new risk-event of unpaid work be defined and with what resources can it be covered by social security (principle and interpretation of the requirement of willingness to work)?

These questions are difficult to answer. As noted by Titmuss, 'not all good things are compatible, still less all the ideas of mankind, in the realm of social security as in other areas of human life' (1970). Nevertheless, in what follows we attempt to link concrete policy recommendations to our empirical analysis. We start from the following principles.

3.2.1   The relationship between insurance and solidarity

The objective of social security is twofold: guaranteeing a minimum income by virtue of the principle of solidarity (protection against poverty) and income maintenance by insurance (graduated benefits related to previous working income). Both objectives are necessarily complementary. The unavoidably low level of minimum protection requires supplementing with higher, wage-related benefits. Conversely, insurance is also a necessary basis for solidarity. Because of the insurance principle, social security can raise the total resources necessary to offer acceptable minimum security to high risk and/or low income groups, that is, those with little capacity to contribute. In this sense, minimum protection is consonant with insurance. Income maintenance is a necessary condition for achieving an acceptable level of minimum protection. Moreover, the inequalities of compulsory income-related schemes are nevertheless motivated by egalitarian considerations. Through state insurance systems the possibility of income maintenance is made available to all workers (and not only to white collar workers and 'good risks' as in the private market).

Nevertheless, future social security policy will have to be inspired more by solidarity than by insurance. For example, consideration will have to be given to higher minimum benefits, particularly for one-income families; more solidarity among pensioners and within the self-employed scheme; more solidarity between individual saving and private pensions, on the one hand, and the state pensions, on the other. This is necessary because of the immense welfare expenditure (which will automatically increase in the future because of ageing and other institutional and socio-demographic factors) and because of current inadequate protection against want with large numbers still living 'in poverty'.

3.2.2   The relationship between work and social security

Sixty per cent of households with an income below the poverty line are living on the labour income of one earner. This indicates that poverty (and the inadequacy of social security) is related both to benefits that are too low in the event of unemployment, sickness, and old age, and to the inadequacy of the sole labour income for many one-income families.

Despite the fact that annual social security expenditure in Belgium corresponds to one-fifth of gross national product, and 78 per cent of all households are in receipt of a cash benefit of some kind at any one time, the inadequacy of the single wage is one of the main reasons why these vast social security outlays seem insufficient.

There are two possible responses to this. One maintains that the problem of one-income families relates to the labour market and therefore can be resolved by an active employment policy (generating more two-income families by more labour and better adaptation of the labour market to family life). Or one argues that the high degree of insecurity of subsistence of one-income families with children arises because social security no longer adequately covers the social risks linked to unpaid work, the care of children, and divorce. Derived rights to benefits (e.g. for survivor pensions, child benefits, and health care) no longer provide adequate protection and should be supplemented by direct, individual coverage of the risks associated with the performance of unpaid work (care).

Because of the complexity of these problems, the diversification of preferences and values, the inter-relatedness of distinct state and private welfare provisions, and the necessity for cost containment in social security, neither of these remedies is sufficient by itself. Integrated action in several sectors of social policy is necessary.

In the context of a prevention policy, not least to minimise calls on social security benefits, an active employment policy must be urged, giving particular attention to the weaker categories – the less educated, women, and immigrants. However, there are reasons to doubt the effectiveness of this option alone. First, unemployment rates have remained consistently high, and will in all probability stay high at least until the year 2000. Second, the increasing labour market participation of women has thoroughly changed the content of the notion of 'full employment' and therefore the post-war consensus according to which social security and full employment were complementary.

Because of this change and the importance of more than one income for security of subsistence, the link between paid work, unpaid work and social security is up for revision. The question of the concept of work and the requirement of willingness to work cannot be avoided.

A radical strategy would be to strive for some kind of basic income. It is not possible to discuss here the many arguments that have been advanced against basic income (work incentives, level of benefits, costs, injustices linked to over-simplification of social protection, given the complexity of social problems). What is central is that basic income – a version of post-modern tolerance – rejects the possibility of influencing the use of time spent, or not spent, in paid employment for socially useful purposes. In our view the question of how 'socially useful work' is defined cannot be avoided and must be publicly discussed. What constitutes a legitimate reason to receive social benefits – only care for children under three years of age; care for sick, disabled or elderly persons; employment interruptions for training purposes?

In the past, by widening the concept of work, social security has substantially supported the policy of 'redistribution of the scarce available work'. Today, we have to evaluate, quantitatively and qualitatively, the results of these policies and consider adjustments. Most important is the dramatic change of the distribution of work between age categories since 1960. Falling labour participation among the young and older workers, together with the increasing prevalence of two-earnership, have made the active life span very short and concentrated in the family formation phase (see Figure 3.1).

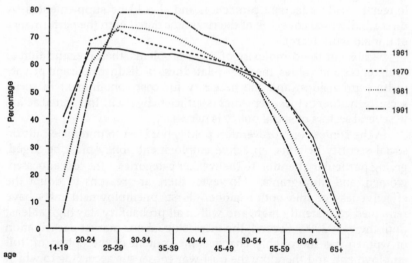

Source: Nationaal Instituut voor Statistiek, Census, 1961, 1970, 1981; Labour Force Survey, 1991.

Figure 3.1 Net Activity Rates (working men and women/population) by Age (Belgium, 1961–1991)

3.2.3 The relationship between individual, family, and social security

Despite social trends towards individualisation, the security of subsistence of individuals remains determined largely by the structure and composition of their household – by the incomes of others within it, the costs of income-dependent members, the advantages of common housekeeping, the benefits of domestic production. If the social security system is intended to offer a minimum income guarantee as well as income maintenance to individuals and households, these factors have to be taken into account.

A micro-simulation exercise helps to draw out the cost and efficiency effects of individualisation of social security benefits in Belgium. In a scenario of fully individualised benefits (same benefit for all beneficiaries at the – fairly low – EC poverty level)[4] social security costs would rise by 9 per cent, while the efficiency ratio would drop from 59.2 per cent to 56.1 per cent. In general terms this exercise shows that, given the high number of social security recipients and the costs involved, it is very difficult to achieve greater adequacy with universal policies. We must therefore try to target within universalism. One of the possibilities is family adjustment of benefits.

The social security system has to monitor the striving for an equal distribution of income and welfare between men and women. However, emancipation is, for the social security system, not a primary objective. If the principle of minimum income guarantee imposes this, and in so far as no direct discrimination is built into the system, family adjustments of benefits are thus possible. Moreover, given persistent gender-related socio-economic inequalities and the division of paid and unpaid work, it should be considered that a complete individualisation of social security benefits can only work to the disadvantage of women.

3.3   Some Practical Recommendations for Future Policy

Complex problems cannot be solved by social security alone. In particular, in relation to covering the cost of care for children, disabled and elderly people, the development of a policy for community services and facilities, assistance at home and family adapted working conditions is essential. Such a policy would make it possible to assist families to reconcile the requirements of paid work and family responsibilities, thereby guaranteeing income from work. The challenge is to find a just balance between various social measures for family members who provide care, mainly women. In any event, co-ordination between social security measures, tax reliefs and the system of community facilities and services must improve.

Considering social security in a strict sense, arguments that these discrepancies can be completely eliminated if the system were fully individualised overlooks the factors discussed above. The first of these is the inadequacy of social benefits for families that have to live exclusively from them, particularly if there are dependent children.

---

4   As defined by O'Higgins and Jenkins (1990), using an elaboration of the poverty line used in the first EC-programme against poverty. This is 50 per cent of average equivalent household income for single-person households.

Second, high levels of unemployment imply that it is illusory to think that the problem of one-earner families will be resolved in the short or even the medium term only through the implementation of an employment policy. Third, because of enduring inequalities between men and women, complete individualisation can only work to the disadvantage of women.

These considerations mean that only qualified responses can be given to questions of the need for individualisation or family adjustments to social benefits. The following principles can serve as guidelines.

3.3.1 Family adjusted benefits

As noted, there has been a polarisation between households for whom social risks involve a substantial loss of income, and households who can partly compensate for the loss of one income since they have another income available. This leads us to ask how to increase selectivity within the universal framework of social security so as to achieve more convergence between the concepts of need and risk coverage.

Given the inadequacy of replacement incomes for families who have to live exclusively from them, there must be positive discrimination for one-income families, not only to guarantee a minimum income for these families but also to assure them income maintenance at a sufficiently high level. After the introduction of separate taxation, family adjustments remain the only possible way – while maintaining the universal nature of social security – for taking account of the fact that for different groups of beneficiaries the occurrence of a social risk-event has widely divergent effects on needs.

However, the possibility of achieving a more adequate distribution of resources by means of family adjustments is limited for three reasons. First, positive and negative discrimination assumes that target groups are homogeneous. The expanding, and thus ever more heterogeneous, group of two-income families appears incapable of fulfilling this condition. This makes it difficult to reduce benefits by simple reference to the presence or not of other family incomes, without taking account of actual income levels.

Second, the third EC Directive forbids all forms of direct and indirect discrimination against women. The European Court of Justice in May 1991 rejected the complaint submitted by the 'Comité de Liaisons des Femmes' against the Belgian State regarding family adjustments in unemployment, sickness, and disability insurance. The grounds were that indirect discrimination is permitted in so far as this is necessary to assure a minimum income. Although the insight has thus rightly emerged that 'equal treatment' can hardly have first priority on the list of social security objectives, this important judgement means, *a contrario*, that benefits for dependents and for loss of the sole income are only possible in the minimum part of the protection system, not in the supra-minimum (see the previous Teulings judgement).[5]

Third, even strong positive discrimination towards one-income families cannot fundamentally resolve the problems of the high degree of insecurity of subsistence and the pronounced inadequacy of benefits for these groups. Indeed, the essential core of the problem is outside the social security system – the necessity for two incomes. Even a substantial increase in replacement incomes for one-income families can do nothing in the face of this structural problem. Such an increase can only be small (because of the relationship to minimum wages), while the inadequacy of low wages remains, inevitably, unresolved. Therefore, solutions have to be sought outside the framework of the risks traditionally covered by social security. The risk of unpaid work (care) should be secured not only by derived rights but also by direct benefits.

Given these restrictions, necessary adjustments to social protection to reflect family circumstances can be achieved by granting individual benefits for unpaid caring work, and maximum coverage of the costs of children. While equal benefits may apply to a very large group of beneficiaries under these forms of assistance, some adjustment of amounts remains necessary. This is because of the scale advantages from joint housekeeping and because not all one-income situations can be covered by special benefits, given available resources.

To keep the level of replacement incomes from being either higher than necessary for couples with two incomes or too low for one-income families and especially people living alone, the level of benefits must be differentiated according to the presence or absence of dependants and/or of other family income. For example, the following adjustment scheme could be used:

- couple, two incomes   100
- couple, one income   200
- single person   140
- one-parent family   180*

(* insofar as child benefits should appear not to cover costs completely).

---

5   In this judgement, the European Court of Justice ruled that 'objective reasons' constituted acceptable grounds of excuse for an existing form of discrimination. Teuling had received a Dutch sickness benefit that was not increased because her husband's income was too high. On this, the Court ruled that Article 4 of Directive No.79(7) EEC of the Council of 19 December 1978 has to be interpreted in such a way that a system of entitlements for labour disability where the level of the benefit is partially determined by marital status and the income from or in connection with the labour of the spouse, is in harmony with this regulation, when this system has the objective of guaranteeing an adequate subsistence level by means of an increase in social security benefits to beneficiaries with a spouse or dependent children by offering compensation for the higher expenses relative to those of people who live alone (for a further discussion, see Sjerps, 1988).

In the application of this adjustment scheme, account has to be taken of the actual criterion of dependency and of joint housekeeping. Because one proceeds from a basic rate for couples with two incomes to which supplements can be granted under certain conditions, the problem of proof is no longer insurmountable. Whoever claims supplementary allowances has to supply the proof.

3.3.2   Individualisation of social security entitlements

Marital instability and the participation of women in the labour force raise problems for the adequacy and legitimacy of derived rights to benefits through the contributions of others. As discussed, fragmented family careers increase the chance of slipping through the social security net, while working women pay contributions 'for nothing' because derived entitlements cannot or can be only partially cumulated with individual entitlements. In the light of these problems, the possibility of individualisation and universalisation of cost-covering benefits (child benefits and health care) must be investigated as a priority. In Belgium the problems of such reform are more political and institutional than substantive.

The idea of individualisation of derived entitlements to replacement incomes should be considered with more caution. If one wants to provide universal income maintenance, the only solution is to maintain the system of derived entitlements. Indeed, individuals' living standards are not only a function of individual incomes from labour, but also of the family unit of which they are or were a part. It should be remembered that, because of the enduring wage differentials between men and women (partially because women take more family responsibilities), complete individualisation of pension entitlements can only work to disadvantage women (and, more generally, both women and men who during a particular period of their life are more concerned with unpaid work than with paid work).

Social protection should be responsive to the problems linked to family breakdown, and those arising from the increasing number of two-earner families (i.e. double contributions and living standards determined by the incomes of both men and women), as well as with the desire of many women to have an independent income. The form of derived entitlements should however be adjusted in the sense of individual derived entitlements, for example, by the system of 'credit splitting'. As with old age pensions for divorced women, individual entitlements could be assigned according to shares determined by the entitlements that were built up jointly by the partners during the period of marriage/cohabitation.

3.3.3   A broader concept of work

The adaptation of social protection to social and demographic changes should be guided, first, by the idea that the increasing number of two-income households has given rise to a new type of worker who, more than his or her predecessors, is faced with problems resulting from the combination of paid and unpaid work. Second, the striving for 'full employment' in the sense that each individual will have a complete career during the entire active working age is neither feasible nor desirable. The prevalence of two-earner families thus supposes an employment policy oriented to better tuning of work and family circumstances, and redistribution of available work over the active life span of individuals, with due regard for the possibilities and needs proper to each family and life phase.

Social security should support this policy by taking account of family circumstances to a higher degree. What is central here is that the risk of unpaid work has changed substantially. Formerly this occurred only when the income of the breadwinner disappeared on death. The high level of insecurity of subsistence of single income households shows that the risk relating to unpaid work now arises also where there is a 'breadwinner' wage or replacement income. The logical consequence of these observations is that the new risk of unpaid work must be financially covered within the social security system. Not only should periods during which individuals decide to reduce or temporarily cease their work on account of family or parental responsibilities be taken into account in calculating benefit entitlements, but social security should also provide direct benefits enabling persons to interrupt their work temporarily. This coverage should be conceived as a horizontal redistribution between those at a stage in their family life during which they can combine two full-time jobs and those for whom the double income is necessary but difficult to reconcile with unpaid work. Provided that such coverage is combined with public arrangements in the field of child care and improved re-employment possibilities, compensation of the risk relating to unpaid work would make it possible to solve the problems arising from the inadequacy of social security for both single and two-parent families who have only one income. This could be achieved without violating the principles of action programmes for equal opportunities for women.

Chapter 4

Lone Parents and Social Security Policy in the UK

Jane Millar

Beveridge's plan for social insurance rested on the three key assumptions about work and the family (Beveridge, 1942). One of these – full employment – was explicitly set out as a pre-condition for the success of the plan. The other two were implicit rather than explicit. One was the assumption of a gendered division of labour in the family, with the man supporting his family financially by earning a 'family wage' and the woman providing domestic work in the home. The other was an assumption that families would be stable, broken by death but not, except rarely, by separation and divorce. Thus marriage would provide income security for women, and it would be enough for the state to guarantee men's incomes for women also to be financially secure.

All three assumptions are now out of date: unemployment and underemployment are widespread; two out of three married couples have two earners; one in two marriages ends in divorce and one in five families has only one parent living in the household. There are now about one and a quarter million lone-parent families in the UK and these are some of the poorest families in the country. In 1991 the average disposable income of lone-parent families was just £145 per week compared with an overall average of £299 (Central Statistical Office, 1992). Fifty per cent of lone-parent families have incomes of less than half the average compared with 22 per cent of all households (DSS, 1992c). Six in ten lone parents have no income from employment and even among those who are employed two-thirds are low paid (Bradshaw and Millar, 1991). In 1992 there were about 871,000 lone parents receiving income support and about 136,000 receiving family credit (DSS, 1992d).

Is this failure to ensure financial security for lone parents the consequence of a gap in the Beveridge scheme of national insurance that could be plugged by a new benefit or combination of benefits? Or does it represent a challenge to the social insurance model that requires a different sort of solution? The aim of this chapter is to consider these questions through an analysis of social security policy for lone parents in the UK since Beveridge: how has the 'problem' of lone parenthood been defined and what 'solutions' have been offered?

4.1   Lone Parents and the Beveridge Report

Beveridge made housewives a separate insurance class whose social security entitlement was derived from their husbands (Wilson, 1977; Pascall, 1986; Lister 1992 and this volume). The logical corollary of this status for women is that they should be insured against the loss of this financial support, just as men would be insured against loss of employment. Beveridge accepted this and proposed a number of benefits for women at the ending of marriage. In this he included widows (whose claim as dependants of their husbands was clear) and some, but not all, separated women. The claim of formerly married women was not so clear as that of widows, he argued, because of the insurance model unpinning entitlement to state benefits. Insurance is for events and circumstances which happen by chance and not those which happen by choice. If a man chooses to leave his job voluntarily then he should not be entitled to unemployment benefit; if a woman chooses to leave her husband voluntarily then she should not be entitled to benefit either. Therefore only women who were not 'at fault' in the marriage breakdown could be eligible for benefit. Unmarried mothers would also excluded since the insurance would be for loss of economic support not for the failure ever to obtain that support.[1]

Beveridge's plan was accepted only in part. The proposals to make married women a separate insurance class were adopted in the 1946 National Insurance Act but none of his proposals about the ending of marriage were included. There were a variety of reasons for this including concern about the exclusion of childless widows; difficulties about establishing fault in marital breakdown; lack of clarity about the relationship between the legal requirements for maintenance and the proposed social security benefits (which Beveridge discussed but without making any proposals); and continuing ambivalence about whether separated and divorced women were really deserving of state support (see Finer, 1974; and Brown, 1988 for further discussion). Widows were granted a pension for an indefinite period whether they

---

1   There is an obvious parallel here with young people who become unemployed without ever having been in paid work. These people were also excluded from the national insurance system and also later became a significant group dependent on social assistance.

had children or not; other lone parents got nothing except a claim to national assistance.

Beveridge's proposals for the ending of marriage would probably have been very difficult to implement[2] and, even if implemented, would still have left many lone parents (unmarried mothers, lone fathers, and separated women 'at fault') outside the national insurance net. Nevertheless the outcome of the Beveridge report was fairly disastrous for lone mothers in future years. On the one hand, the special insurance status of married women gave further legitimacy to the construction of women as secondary earners. Women were defined as working for 'extras' and so not in need of a living wage, with no claims on the state for compensation if wages were lost, and with no help with employment-related services such as child care. On the other hand, women were expected to rely on their husbands as their main source of income but were not insured against the risk that this source of income might prove insecure, as it increasingly did. The result was a steady increase in the number and proportion of lone parents receiving social assistance payments. In 1942 public assistance payments were being made to about 14,000 separated women with about 17,000 children (Brown, 1988, p. 28). In 1955 just over 50,000 lone mothers (including unmarried mothers) were receiving national assistance, by 1965 this had risen to about 110,000, and by the early 1970s the figure was up to almost 240,000 (Finer, 1974, para. 5.7).

4.2   The Finer Report

By the late 1960s the two assumptions about the family that Beveridge had taken for granted were both under pressure. Rising rates of female employment meant that the male breadwinner/female homemaker family was giving way to a more varied set of family work arrangements, and rising divorce rates meant marriage was not always stable and long-lasting. Both of these are recognised, and commented on, by the Finer Committee in the introductory section of the report. After locating the problems of lone parents in the context of the rediscovery of poverty in the 1960s, the report starts by discussing changes in employment:

> Until the eve of the second world war, all but a small proportion of women stopped work when they got married. Today most married women bear their children within the early years of marriage and then

2   Although this benefit never came into being in the UK, in the 1970s Ireland introduced a 'deserted wives' benefit. This national insurance benefit is paid to women who have been 'deserted' by their husbands and where they are not at fault. Many of the claims to the benefit are disallowed, often because of the difficulties in meeting these criteria (Millar, Leeper and Davies, 1992).

go back or out to work until they retire ... Fatherless families on supplementary benefit have to depend on a single wage at a time when men have largely ceased to be the sole breadwinners for their families save for a short period early in the family building cycle. (Finer, 1974, para. 2.5)

They go on to comment on rising divorce rates, putting these in a very positive light:

When Victorian parents told their daughters about to be married that they were making their beds and would have to lie on them, they spoke the precise truth. Wives were then held in marriage by legal, economic and theological bonds: the bonds of matrimony were bonds indeed. These have now dissolved into ties of choice, and modern marriages are sustained by affection or by loyalty or by use and wont. The discipline of marriage has become the consent of the partners and derives no longer from external compulsion. The family has evolved into a democratic institution. (Finer, 1974, para. 2.6)

The Committee were rather overstating both cases: in 1971 about 39 per cent of married mothers with children were economically active, including about 20 per cent of those with children aged under four (Finer, 1974, Table 7.2). So in the majority of families men were still the sole breadwinners and, for the vast majority, male wages still remained the main source of income. Whether or not marriage has become a 'democratic institution' still remains open to dispute (Moller Okin, 1989; Pahl, 1989) but certainly the concept of marriage as something that individuals should be able to choose to enter and to choose to leave was accepted at that time, as illustrated by the 1969 Divorce Reform Act, which made the sole grounds for divorce the 'irretrievable breakdown' of the marriage.

At the time of the Finer Committee the number of lone parents was starting to rise more rapidly, following the implementation of the 1969 Act. According to the estimates in the Report, in 1971 there were about 620,000 lone-parent families, of which about 520,000 were headed by women.[3] This represented about 8 per cent of all families with dependent children. Of the lone mothers about 17 per cent were single, about 23 per cent were widowed and the remaining 60 per cent were formerly married (37 per cent separated and 23 per cent divorced). Thus it was ex-married women who were the most numerous group. About 45 per cent of lone

---

3 The figures given here are those used in the Finer report, i.e. they represent the estimates at that time. Subsequent analysis suggests slightly different population figures for 1971. Haskey (1989a) gives the following 1971 estimates: single women 90,000; separated women 170,000; divorced women 120,000; widowed women 120,000 and lone fathers 70,000. This gives an overall figure of 570,000 rather than 620,000, the difference being mainly because Finer estimates rather more lone fathers (+30,000) and rather more separated women (+20,000). The Finer figures are used here to reflect how the situation was perceived at the time.

mothers were estimated to be employed, higher than the proportion of employed married mothers (about 39 per cent). However the employment rates of lone fathers were estimated to be twice as high as those of lone mothers (90 per cent). About 40 per cent of lone mothers were receiving supplementary benefit compared with about 10 per cent of lone fathers. Single and separated women were especially likely to be on benefit.

Having examined the financial circumstances of lone parents in comparison with the circumstances of two-parent families, the Finer Committee was quite clear in the conclusion to be drawn:

> The statistical material and the research studies we have examined overwhelmingly confirmed the general impression of financial hardship amongst one-parent families ... It has been consistently shown that, with only a few individual exceptions, fatherless families are considerably worse off financially than two-parent families. (Finer, 1974, para. 5.36)

The Committee directed attention to three particular areas where they argued reform was especially needed. The first was the 'lack of any worthwhile financial gain by combining part-time work with supplementary benefit' (para. 5.49). Being able to combine part-time work with supplementary benefit receipt would, they argued, improve the morale of lone parents, enable them to improve their incomes and make the transition to full-time work easier when children are no longer dependent. The second issue was 'the low level of income among working lone parents compared with two-parent families' (para. 5.49). Here they noted the problem of low pay among women and the large gap between male and female earnings and also the restrictions on employment that follow from having the sole care of children – less access to overtime, what to do during school holidays and when children are sick (although the more general problem of childcare is not mentioned at this point). Thirdly there was 'the inadequacy and uncertainty of maintenance payments' (para. 5.49) and especially the way in which this uncertainty might prevent some who might otherwise work and combine wages with maintenance from doing so.

Thus the central problem was defined as a problem of poverty, arising because of the low level of resources (benefits, earnings and maintenance) available to lone parents and because of the impossibility of creating an adequate level of income by combining income from these different sources. The Committee went on to discuss whether these problems could be solved by reforms to existing provisions but concluded that they could not, and thus what was required was a new social security benefit designed to meet the needs of lone parents: the 'guaranteed maintenance allowance'.

4.2.1   The guaranteed maintenance allowance

The proposed GMA consisted of two parts, each with a rather different structure. The adult component would be means-tested, after an initial disregard and after deducting work expenses, at a rate of 50p in the pound and would extinguish altogether at the level of average male earnings. The child component would be non-means tested and so payable regardless of other income or earnings. This would represent 'a contribution by the state to all lone parents, irrespective of means, to help with the extra costs of caring for a child where one of the parents is not available' (Finer, 1974, para. 5.129). The level of the GMA would be sufficient to take lone parents off supplementary benefit rates, but not so far above as make lone parents significantly better off than other families claiming benefits.

The GMA was to be available to all lone parents, regardless of marital status or 'fault', and every lone parent would receive at least some payment, in the form of the child component. In relation to the other sources of income potentially available to lone parents the GMA was intended to combine with earnings but to replace maintenance. The means test, with the earnings disregard and the long taper, was designed to encourage part-time employment in combination with benefit receipt. Since the benefit would be payable to all lone parents who earned less than average male earnings then the vast majority of working lone parents would be eligible. Thus low wages would be supplemented for those lone parents who chose paid employment.

As regards maintenance the Committee argued that there were three main problems in relying on this as a source of income. First enforcing such obligations is very difficult, especially if the absent parent has a new partner and/or second family. Secondly, the amounts of money that could realistically be expected from maintenance would not provide an adequate income for lone parents. Finally, if maintenance obligations were substantially increased then the absent parent, and his second family, might themselves be pushed into poverty. These problems meant that, from the point of view of the lone parent, maintenance could provide only a 'inadequate and uncertain' income. Hence the need for the GMA to replace maintenance, so that the incomes of lone parents could be guaranteed and not be dependent on the willingness or ability of the absent parent to pay. However this did not mean that the absent parent had no financial obligations but rather that this obligation should be discharged by a payment to the state, to offset the cost of the GMA, and not by payments made directly to the lone parent. The Committee also proposed that the amount to be paid by the absent parent should be determined by a standard formula. The incomes of lone parents would therefore be determined by their entitlement to the GMA plus any earnings they had, and whether or not maintenance was paid would be irrelevant to their actual income level.[4] Both the collection of maintenance and the payment of the GMA would be the responsibility of a new administrative body.

According to Marsden (1974) the government response to the Report was 'guarded' but it was made clear that the GMA would not be accepted. The timing of publication was probably unhelpful. The government were preoccupied with the introduction of child benefit (which replaced family allowances and child tax allowances in 1975). More generally, also, the recommendation for a new benefit seemed more in tune with the welfare expansion of the 1960s than the emerging welfare 'crisis' of the mid to late 1970s. By 1974 unemployment was on the increase and government attention was starting to focus on how to contain social security expenditure rather than how to improve and extend it. Thus the only immediate outcomes of the Finer Report were the introduction in 1975 of 'child-benefit increase' (later renamed 'one-parent benefit') as a small weekly addition to child benefit; and an increase in the earnings disregard for lone parents on supplementary benefit. However two principles were established in the Finer Report which were to have some influence on policy for lone parents over the next two decades.

The first of these concerned 'extra needs'. The Committee went to some length to demonstrate that, not only did lone parents have comparable costs to two-parent families in relation to items such as housing and fuel, but also that they incurred extra costs for child-minding and for services which a second parent might be expected to do in two-parent families (the examples given include lone mothers paying for household maintenance work and lone fathers paying for domestic equipment). The exact extent of these extra costs is difficult to establish empirically (see Whiteford and Hicks, 1992) but the principle has been adopted across various benefits which are available to both lone-parent and two-parent families. Thus one-parent benefit is an addition to child benefit, lone parents on income support receive a 'lone-parent premium', and the means tests for family credit and housing benefit treat the needs of lone parents as comparable to the needs of couples.

The acceptance of the existence of extra needs has therefore made some difference to the incomes of lone parents. However the second principle accepted since Finer – that lone parents should have a choice whether or not to work – has arguably been much more important in rhetoric than practice. Lone parents are not required to register for employment nor to look for work as long as they have dependent children and are thus free to choose whether or not to take paid employment. In practice, however, many commentators have argued that the choice to work has been constrained by both the structure of the

---

4   Although the proposal did include some extra maintenance to be paid to lone parents
     if the absent parent had a very high income.

benefit system and the lack of the type of services – in particular child care provisions – which would make such a choice possible (Brown, 1989; Joshi, 1990a; National Audit Office, 1990; NCOPF, 1990).

The Finer proposals for a single administrative body calculating maintenance obligations according to a standard formula made almost no impact at the time. But something similar has re-emerged in recent policy although, as we shall see, with some key differences in both form and objectives. The next section therefore moves on another fifteen or so years to the late 1980s and to the next attempt to reform financial support for lone parents.

4.3   Into the 1990s

By 1989 there were estimated to be about 1.15 million lone-parent families, about twice as many as in 1971 (Haskey, 1991). This meant that about 17 per cent of all families with children were headed by a lone parent, a figure which Roll (1992) estimates to be the highest in the EC – followed by Denmark at 15 per cent; France and Germany at 11 to 13 per cent; Belgium, the Netherlands, Ireland, Luxembourg and Portugal at 9 to 11 per cent; and Greece, Spain and Italy at 5 to 6 per cent. Almost all these EC countries had, like the UK, seen an increase in the number and proportion of lone-parent families in the 1970s and 1980s, as indeed had most industrialised countries. Using Luxembourg Income Study data, Mitchell and Bradshaw (1992) estimate that lone parents headed 12 per cent of all families with children in Australia (1985), 11 per cent in Canada (1987), 16 per cent in Sweden (1987) and 21 per cent in the USA (1986).[5] In all countries lone mothers form the vast majority of all lone parents and marital breakdown is the most common route into lone parenthood (Ermisch, 1990).

During the 1970s and 1980s employment rates for both lone mothers and lone fathers fell. For lone fathers the decline appears to have been very steep, from an estimated 90 per cent in 1971 to about 61 per cent in 1990. However the earlier estimate should probably be treated with some caution given the small sample sizes on which it was based. For lone mothers the estimated employment rates were 45 per cent in 1971 and 41 per cent in 1990. These two snapshots actually hide a steeper fall in employment rates to the mid-1980s, when only about 39 per cent were estimated to be employed, and some increase since then. Among the

---

5   These trends have meant that many other countries have also been faced with the question of whether, and how, policy should be adapted to deal with this emerging family type. There have been a number of studies comparing different approaches (see, for example, Deven and Cliquet, 1985; Kamerman and Kahn, 1988; OECD, 1990b; Millar *et al.*, 1992; Roll, 1992).

different types of lone mothers it was the single mothers whose employment rates fell most sharply (from 39 per cent in 1971 to 25 per cent in 1990). Furthermore, while the employment rates of lone mothers have been falling, those of married mothers have been rising. In 1990 61 per cent of married mothers were employed compared with 41 per cent of lone mothers (Bartholomew *et al.*, 1992).

Receipt of social assistance rose among all types of lone-parent family. In 1971 about 40 per cent of all lone parents were estimated to be receiving supplementary benefit and by 1989 this had risen to about 67 per cent. Among lone fathers only 10 per cent had been on benefit in 1971 but this was up to 26 per cent in 1990. Among lone mothers the increase was from 41 to 72 per cent. Thus, as employment fell, receipt of benefits increased rapidly and, not surprisingly, poverty increased. In 1979 about 19 per cent of lone parents had incomes of less than half the average, by 1989 this had risen to 50 per cent (DSS, 1992c) .

4.3.1   Children come first?

Whereas the Finer Report was the report of an independent committee set up by the Secretary of State for Social Services, *Children Come First* is a White Paper and therefore a statement of intended policy. Thus it starts, not from any strategic discussion of policy options and objectives, but from an analysis of the specific problems with maintenance. Maintenance is seen from the start as the solution to the 'problem'. But what is the problem as it is perceived here? The Foreword provides the clearest statement:

> Government cannot ensure that families stay together. But we can and must ensure that proper financial provision for children is made by their parents whenever it can be reasonably expected.

> While many absent parents make regular payments, 70 per cent regrettably do not. The inevitable result is that more and more caring parents and their children have become dependent on income support. This makes it difficult for them to achieve greater independence through working. And, at the same time, it places the responsibility for maintaining the children on other taxpayers, many of whom are raising children of their own.

> It is indeed in everyone's interests that the system should be reformed. It is in the interests of children that they should be maintained by their parents. Maintenance provides them with a reliable source of income and they learn about the responsibility which family members owe to each other.

> It is in the interests of their caring parent if they have maintenance for their children. Maintenance provides an invaluable bridge from reliance on Income Support into the world of work. (DSS, 1990a, *Foreword*)

There are a number of points worth noting about this set of statements. First the starting point is that parents are always financially responsible for their natural children. As is made clear throughout the White Paper this responsibility is defined as unconditional – it lasts for as long as children are children and exists regardless of the relationship between the two parents and regardless of the relationship between the parents and the children.[6] Secondly there is an emphasis on the burden imposed on the rest of the community, and especially the taxpayers, by the failure of the maintenance system. Thirdly there is a strongly didactic element to the policy – by enforcing maintenance obligations the government will help both parents and children to learn about 'the responsibilities which family members owe to each other'. Later this perspective appears again in relation to the reasons why lone parents should be encouraged to take paid work: 'if the period on Income Support is reduced, then the children themselves are likely to gain a more positive attitude to work and independence' (DSS, 1990a, para. 6.1). Finally, maintenance from the absent parent and employment of the lone parent are seen as closely linked with maintenance providing a way of facilitating employment.

Three main proposals are put forward in the White Paper. First a standard formula will be introduced to assess how much child maintenance should be paid (the issue of maintenance between spouses is excluded from these provisions). Second, in order to assess, collect and enforce these child maintenance payments, a Child Support Agency is to be established as part of the Department of Social Security. Lone parents receiving means-tested benefits will be required to cooperate with the Agency in tracing the absent parent and will suffer a benefit penalty if they refuse to do so. Third, there will be encouragement to caring parents to go out to work through changes in the rules for social security benefits. This encouragement takes two main forms: family credit becomes payable at 16 hours of work per week instead of 24 hours (and correspondingly income support will only be available to those working less than 16 hours); and £15 of child maintenance will be disregarded against family credit although none will be disregarded against income support. Thus lone parents who stay on income support will receive no financial gain from maintenance but those who go out to work for at least 16 hours will be both eligible for family credit and maintenance will add to their incomes. These measures have been introduced in the 1991 Child Support Act and should be fully operational in 1993.

The move to reform the maintenance system has been to some extent welcomed but there have been a number of criticisms of the structure of

---

6   The financial obligation even extends to children born as a result of sperm donation, where this was done as a private arrangement, according to the Child Support Agency guidelines (Brindle, 1993).

these changes (Eekelaar, 1991; Family Policy Studies Centre, 1991; Hayes, 1991; Millar, 1992 and 1993; NCOPF, 1991; Social Security Committee, 1991). There are three issues in particular that have caused concern. First lone parents receiving income support will not gain financially from any child support collected, as benefit will be reduced pound for pound against maintenance. Since the majority of lone parents are on income support few will benefit – unless they can find employment which also, of course, means finding and paying for child care. This means that these measures will do little to reduce poverty among lone parents. Secondly lone parents receiving benefit are required to pursue child support through the Agency and will lose benefit if they refuse to do so. Thus some lone parents will actually be worse off as a consequence of this legislation. In addition, the requirement to cooperate in tracing the absent parent might, it has been suggested, put some lone parents at risk of retaliation, including violence, from former partners. Thirdly, concern has been raised abut the impact on second families, whose incomes may be substantially reduced by the much higher levels of maintenance required (although they will be 'protected' so that their incomes cannot fall below a level set just above income support levels). Thus the net result is likely to be that many lone parents will not benefit at all from this legislation, while many second families suffer a fall in income.

The Child Support legislation also raises fundamental issues about the role of the state in providing financial support for families, and about the obligations of family members to each other. The final section examines these issues, first by means of a comparison of the objectives of the Finer Report with those of the *Children Come First* proposals.

4.4   The Family and the State

In a number of respects these two policy documents concerned with lone-parent families seem to share a similar approach: both seek to make it easier for lone parents to combine income from different sources, especially a combination of benefits and part-time work, and both propose standard maintenance payments determined administratively rather than through the courts. However, as discussed above, each defines the 'problem' of lone parenthood in a different way and this leads to some significant differences in the proposed 'solutions'. For the Finer Committee poverty was the central problem and the proposed GMA was based on an acceptance that such families, because of their high risk of poverty, have a claim on the state for financial support. Although the benefit was to be partly means-tested, the approach can be described as almost universalist in that all lone-parent families would have received at least the child component of the benefit, and many would also have received at least some of the adult component: what might be called a 'selective universal' benefit. The GMA was to replace private with public support, and thus give lone parents rights to benefits derived not from their situation as dependents within the family but from their situation as families with additional needs.

By contrast, in *Children Come First*, the central problem is defined as a failure of individuals to meet their responsibilities to themselves and to their families: lone parents are dependent on state benefits mainly because they are not supported by their former partners but also because they do not seek to support themselves through employment. Thus the role of private maintenance is to be strengthened, with the state taking responsibility for enforcing, rather than replacing, maintenance, and employment encouraged. In this respect the White Paper is part of a wider perspective which defines the problem of welfare as a problem of private dependency on public benefits. This view derives much from the US 'underclass' and 'rights versus obligations' debates (Roche, 1992, provides a summary). It also has close links with the way unemployment in the UK has been defined as a 'problem' of the attitudes of unemployed people (McLaughlin, 1992a); and with increasingly privatised family policy in general (Brown, 1992a). The 1991 Child Support Act is aimed at shifting the balance between the family and the state: at making families more 'responsible' for themselves.

However, in order for this policy to succeed, it is essential that the measures proposed carry some legitimacy. Absent parents must accept that they have an ongoing financial obligation to their children and to their former partners and be willing to pay child support at average levels of about £48 per week (Brindle, 1993). Lone parents must accept that they must always take action to pursue maintenance claims. The public in general must agree that these obligations should be enforced, regardless of the particular circumstances of different families. Whether this legitimacy exists in practice, however, remains to be seen. At the moment only 29 per cent of lone-parent families are in receipt of regular maintenance (Bradshaw and Millar, 1991), which suggests either widespread unwillingness or widespread inability to contribute regular support. Inability to pay maintenance certainly plays some part, for example the study of maintenance awards carried out as background to the White Paper found that absent fathers had higher rates of unemployment and lower than average earnings (DSS, 1990a, vol. 2). Similarly in Australia unemployment has been the largest single factor in the non-payment of maintenance under their child support scheme (Millar and Whiteford, 1993). However there is also some evidence that absent parents do not themselves always accept such responsibilities as unconditional, but instead relate them to issues such as fault, access to children and contact with children (Bradshaw and Millar, 1991; Davis and Murch, 1988). Bradshaw and Millar also found that 20 per cent of lone parents not receiving maintenance said they preferred not to receive any, and 24 per cent said they had not or would not give details of former partners to the DSS. The benefit penalty for those who do not cooperate suggests that the government are not confident that lone parents will accept this policy.

In terms of general opinion the 1990 *British Social Attitudes Survey* asked respondents whether they thought a father should make maintenance payments for his children after divorce (Kiernan, 1992). Almost all said that he should (90 per cent of men and 95 per cent of women) and most agreed that this should apply to cohabiting as much as married fathers. But there was less agreement about what should happen if the woman remarried. Here 51 per cent said maintenance payments should continue, 13 per cent said they should stop, and 33 per cent that it would depend on the new husband's income. The unconditional obligation that underpins the White Paper does not seem to command widespread support. Moreover, as Finch and Mason (1992) demonstrate from their empirical study of family responsibilities, there may be some considerable distance between publicly expressed norms about obligations within families and what actually happens in practice. Finch and Mason do not examine the issue of financial obligations from absent parents to children but their analysis of the way family responsibilities are negotiated over time suggests that separation and divorce would be likely to have a profound impact on how these responsibilities are viewed. Bradshaw and Millar (1991) found that only just over half of children in lone-parent families are in contact with their absent parent and this would seem to mitigate against feelings of ongoing obligation among the parents, although which is the cause and which the consequence is not clear. Arguably policy about financial obligations after couples separate, or where parents have never lived together, has been – and continues to be – developed with little information about how these obligations are actually perceived in practice.

The Child Support legislation is presented as being a policy that will produce greater responsibility and reduce dependency. The meaning of 'dependency' is by no means clear but it could be argued that these measures will actually increase dependency among lone parents, in the sense that control over their own incomes will be reduced. Lone parents will become more financially dependent on their former partners because their incomes will directly depend on the absent parent's actions and circumstances, and will be affected by any changes in his employment, family status or housing. Since the majority of lone parents are women and the majority of absent parents are men this means the financial dependency of women on men is extended and reinforced. In addition the central role given to means-tested benefits, especially family credit, sets a ceiling to the level of income that can be achieved (except for those few who can earn enough to get outside the range of the benefit). The complex means test, involving both earnings and maintenance, will lead to both uncertainty and insecurity since many lone parents will find it difficult to predict what their incomes will be. Thus more, and not less, dependency is likely to be the result.

As the Finer Committee recognised, none of the three sources of income potentially available to lone parents can alone make an adequate family income, and in particular few lone parents can support themselves through employment without some form of supplementation of wages. But increasingly this is not a problem unique to lone parents. Trends in the labour market have lead to many countries experiencing high levels of long-term unemployment, a growth in part-time employment and in seasonal and other forms of less than full-time working (Hakim, 1987; Room, 1990). Much of this type of employment is associated with insecurity and low pay. For many families it is thus increasingly the case that employment, especially of a sole earner, cannot secure an adequate income. In essence the key assumption in the Beveridge Plan – that wages are the main source of subsistence – appears to be false for an increasing number of people, including the vast majority of lone parents. Replacing wages during short-term interruptions of earnings is therefore no longer enough to maintain adequate standards of living and benefits like family credit, which act as wage supplements, may reflect the future of income support policy more generally. There are, however, other possible approaches. For example, Finch (1992) argues that the state should take a much larger role in the financial support of children, so that individual wages do not have to cover these costs. Advocates of basic income schemes go even further in arguing that the state has to take responsibility in securing income for all individuals and not just for children (e.g. Jordan, 1987; Parker, 1991; Standing, 1992). Land (1992) argues women in particular would benefit from a greater emphasis on the 'social wage' – the services that have a direct impact on living standards – rather than on individual economic wages. Seen in this context the 'problem' of lone parents is not simply a gap in the Beveridge scheme but follows from a more fundamental challenge to the assumption that the labour market can provide the means of subsistence for the majority of people.

Part II

Adapting to Change: New work patterns

Chapter 5

Changing Work Patterns and their Implications for Social Protection[1]

John Blackwell

5.1 Introduction

The focus of this chapter is the increase in the relative importance over the past fifteen years in OECD member countries of so-called 'atypical' or new forms of work – part-time work, temporary work, contract work. The first part of the chapter outlines the changes that have occurred in these forms of work. The second part is concerned with the implications of these labour market trends for social protection. Some of the policy issues which arise are outlined.

5.2 'New Forms' of Working

Three 'atypical' forms of work – which are also called non-standard, peripheral, non-regular, flexible (Hakim, 1987) – are considered here: part-time work, temporary (including casual) work, and self-employment which can overlap with work done on a contract basis. There is an overlap between the various new forms of working: for instance, some part-time workers are temporary. Where possible, an allowance is made for this.

---

1 The views expressed are those of the author and do not necessarily reflect those of the OECD. Helpful comments on a draft were received from John M. Evans and David Grubb. The usual disclaimer applies.

5.2.1   Part-time work: trends and features

The trend over time in part-time work for both men and women as a proportion of total employment is shown in Table 5.1. There are two major features. First, in most of the countries, there has been a growth in the proportion of total employment which is part time. Second, the proportion of employment which is part time is far higher among women than among men. The majority of part-time workers are women. Part-time work among males tends to occur at the two ends of the age spectrum – among those aged under 25 and among those aged 60 and over. For young workers, part-time work can be a way of entering the labour market and can also provide them with an opportunity to combine work with study. By contrast, female part-time employment tends to be more evenly spread across the age groups.

The extent of part-time working can be affected by social security arrangements. For instance, Sweden has the highest proportion of part-time to all employment for males aged 60–64. This is influenced by the availability of a part-time pension in Sweden through the social security system for those aged 60–64: an eligible employee must agree to reduce his or her working week by an average of at least 5 hours and subsequently to work part-time for a minimum of 17 hours a week. For some workers, this part-time pension has eased the transition from 'full' work to retirement. In Sweden, the numbers in this pension peaked at 68,000 in 1980 and were 39,000 in 1989 (National Social Insurance Board, 1990). Similar schemes have been available in Denmark and in Finland from 1987.

Stability of part-time employment
The stylised picture of the bottom end of the labour market is that marginalised workers are prone to instability in terms of their job tenure, have a relatively high turnover through jobs and can suffer spells of unemployment between jobs. Table 5.2 provides some support for this proposition. The average job tenure of part-time workers is less than that of full-time workers, though this difference is more pronounced among men than among women. For the UK, Bosworth (1991) finds that part-time working is closely linked with shorter tenure of employment in the case of older women, but that the opposite is the case with younger people. He also finds a strong relationship between part-time work and temporary/casual work.

The information on job turnover among the part-time workforce complements these data. In the mid-1980s, in Canada, Great Britain and the United States there was a greater job turnover among the part-time workforce than among full-time workers (OECD, 1986, p. 19). A higher proportion of part-time workers than of full-time workers had been employed in the current job for less than a year. However, there is one

Table 5.1 Share of Part-time Workers in Total Employment, Selected Years, 1982–1991

Country		1982	1985	1988	1989	1990	1991
Australia	M	6.0	6.2	7.0	7.8	8.0	9.2
	W	36.2	37.3	39.5	40.1	40.1	40.1
Austria	M	1.5	1.2	1.0	1.6	1.6	
	W	18.6	15.4	17.2	20.0	20.2	
Belgium	M	2.0[a]	1.8	2.0	1.7	2.0	
	W	19.7[a]	21.1	23.4	25.0	25.8	
Canada	M	6.9	7.6	7.7	7.7	8.1	8.8
	W	25.1	26.1	25.2	24.5	24.4	25.5
Denmark	M	6.6[a]	8.4	9.0	9.4	10.4	
	W	44.7[a]	43.9	41.5	40.1	39.1	
Finland	M	4.1	4.6	4.4	4.6	4.4	5.1
	W	11.6	12.1	10.4	10.4	10.2	10.2
France	M	2.5	3.2	3.4	3.5	3.3	3.4
	W	18.9	21.8	23.8	23.7	23.6	23.5
Germany	M	1.7[a]	2.0	2.1	2.3	2.6	
	W	30.0[a]	29.6	30.6	30.7	33.8	
Greece	M	3.7[a]	2.8	2.9	2.4	2.2	
	W	12.1[a]	10.0	10.3	8.0	7.6	
Ireland	M	2.7[a]	2.4	3.8	3.1	3.4	
	W	15.5[a]	15.5	17.1	16.6	17.6	
Italy	M	2.4[a]	3.0	3.2	3.1	2.4	
	W	9.4[a]	10.1	10.4	10.9	9.6	
Luxembourg	M	7.3	7.5	7.6	8.0	9.5	10.1
	W	29.1	30.1	30.9	31.9	33.4	34.3
Netherlands	M	7.2[a]	8.2	15.5	15.6	15.8	16.7
	W	50.1[a]	53.1	60.8	61.5	61.7	62.2
New Zealand	M	8.0	9.2	9.8	11.0	8.5	9.8
	W	33.9	35.5	36.0	36.6	35.2	35.8
Norway	M	5.7	5.4	6.2	8.3	8.8	9.1
	W	48.1	46.2	43.1	48.9	48.2	47.6
Portugal	M	n.a.	3.4[b]	3.6	3.1	3.6	4.0
	W	n.a.	10.0[b]	10.5	10.0	10.1	10.5
Sweden	M	6.4	6.1	6.9	7.2	7.3	7.5
	W	46.5	44.0	43.3	41.7	40.5	40.5
United Kingdom	M	3.3[a]	4.4	5.5	5.0	5.3	
	W	42.4[a]	44.8	44.2	43.6	43.2	
United States	M	10.6	10.1	10.2	10.0	10.0	10.5
	W	28.1	26.6	25.7	25.5	25.2	25.6

Notes: a. 1983; b. 1986. In each case, part-time employment of men is expressed as a proportion of all employment by men; correspondingly for women. Definitions are given in OECD, 1989, Annexe 1.B.
Source: OECD, 1989.

caution: in Australia and North America, young people tend to have a higher share in part-time employment, by comparison with Europe. Hence, some of this instability in part-time employment, can be related to the job turnover which one finds among young people.

Table 5.2 Average Current Job Tenure for Full-time and Part-time Workers in Four OECD Countries (first half of 1980s)

	All persons		Males		Females	
	f-t	p-t	f-t	p-t	f-t	p-t
Australia (1981)	6.4	4.7	7.1	4.7	4.5	4.6
Canada (1985)	8.8	4.6	n.a.	n.a.	n.a.	n..a
United Kingdom (1985)	9.0	6.0	9.9	6.0	6.8	6.1
United States (1981)	7.2	4.2	8.2	4.2	5.6	4.2

Source: OECD, 1986, Table 5.

Other evidence comes from the Federal Republic of Germany (Büchtemann and Schupp, 1988) concerning 'marginal or irregular' part-time employment, a distinction which in most cases corresponds to the categories of 'marginal' (part-time) employment by contrast with (part-time) employment which is subject to compulsory social insurance. The group of female 'marginal' part-time employees shows a significantly higher than average degree of employment instability, judged by the proportion who have worked with their current employer for less than five years or for less than one year.

'Voluntary' part-time working
One can define involuntary part-time employment as occurring where workers would have preferred full-time jobs if they could have found them. The question of whether part-time working is 'voluntary' or 'involuntary' is of interest for a number of reasons, aside from the implications for economic well-being (below). First, when aggregate demand falls, the proportion of involuntary part-time working can be expected to rise. If one is interested in the long-run trends in part-time work, there is a need to remove this type of cyclical influence. Second, the degree to which part-time working is voluntary can be influenced by social security arrangements. An example, referred to above, is the availability of part-time pensions in some of the Nordic countries.

Those who work part-time voluntarily comprise essentially three groups: young workers who use part-time work as a means of combining work and study; older workers who wish to move down to part-time work from full-time employment as a way of easing into retirement; and those who wish to combine market work with child-rearing and with household work. The latter, who consist almost entirely of women, may wish to work part-time for only a part of their working lives, to be followed by full-time work.

Table 5.3 gives some evidence on the degree to which part-time work is involuntary. The relative amount of involuntary part-time working among women tends to be lower than among men. For women, the proportion of part-time work which is involuntary is less among those aged 25–54 than among those aged under 25. These differences between men and women undoubtedly reflect the need for women to combine paid employment with household work and child rearing. This begs the question of what one means by 'voluntary', given the unequal division of labour between women and men within the home. Any increase in involuntary part-time jobs cannot be assumed to be merely a short-run response to downturns in economic activity. For instance, evidence for Canada (Economic Council of Canada, 1990) is that nearly half of all the additional part-time jobs since 1981 have been classified as 'involuntary' part-time.

Table 5.3 Incidence of Involuntary Part-time Employment by Age and Sex, 1986–1987

			Involuntary part-time as a proportion of all part-time employment		
	Men	All		Women	
			Aged 25–34	Aged 35–44	Aged 45–54
Australia	28.6	16.2	15.9	15.2	11.2
Canada	27.7	26.2		28.5	
Italy	41.5	33.7		31.2	
Sweden	15.2	12.1	8.9	11.0	10.5
United Kingdom	21.8	8.0			
United States	23.6	16.7	19.0	16.0	17.3

Source: OECD, 1988, Table 1.5.

Reasons for the growth in part-time working
Among the reasons for the growth over time of part-time working are the following influences from the demand side of the labour market.

• A shift in the composition of employment towards the services sector, which contains a relatively high proportion of the part-time work force.

• The shift to an individual basis of taxation in a number of countries has generally reduced the tax rate on part-time earnings (though not necessarily full-time earnings) of married women (OECD, 1990a, Chapter 6).

- The influence of non-wage labour costs: that is, employers' contributions to social insurance and to private pension and insurance schemes, together with recruitment and training expenditure, and expenditure associated with redundancies.

First, in some countries, once the employee work week falls below a certain threshold, the rate of social insurance contribution of employers can fall, or social security contributions are paid subject to a wage floor. Second, in a number of countries, certain non-wage labour costs such as maternity pay and leave do not arise in the case of part-time workers. Third, in some countries, coverage for unemployment compensation is not mandatory for part-time workers. Finally, the coverage of part-time workers under occupational welfare, such as company sick pay and pensions, is often less than in the case of full-time workers. Employers can save on the costs of occupational welfare by hiring part-time workers. There has been a rise over time in non-wage labour costs as a proportion of total labour costs (OECD, 1986). In this light, there has been some incentive to shift towards the hiring of part-time employees.

5.2.2   Temporary work

Temporary work includes seasonal, casual, or intermittent work and interim contracts through a temporary employment agency. There is a degree of overlap with part-time work. Table 5.4 shows that temporary employment has generally risen as a proportion of total wage and salary employment since 1983. Table 5.5 shows the share of temporary workers, other than the self-employed, in employment across certain EC countries: shares range from around 4 to 10 per cent for men and 10 per cent for women.

Temporary work is more common among young people than across the population as a whole. Bosworth (1991) for the United Kingdom finds that temporary or casual contracts are important among new entrants and re-entrants into employment. Some of the increase over time in temporary employment in certain countries reflects the growth of government employment schemes aimed at young people and schemes which have been aimed at the long-term unemployed.

Based on evidence from a number of OECD countries, people who were previously unemployed or out of the labour force account for much of the movement into temporary work (OECD, 1987, pp. 37–39). Some 20–30 per cent of temporary workers over the period 1983–85 had typically not been in the labour force a year earlier and 10–20 per cent had been unemployed a year earlier. Data for the Netherlands for the mid-1980s suggest that a significant minority of temporary workers remain in that state over time, rather than move into permanent employment (OECD, 1987, p. 38). In Spain, only 15 per cent of those in temporary employment move to permanent employment (Alba-Ramírez, 1991).

Table 5.4 Temporary Employment as a Proportion of Total Wage and Salary Employment in Selected Countries, 1983, 1989 (percentages)

	1983	1989
Belgium	5.4	5.1
Denmark	12.3	9.9
France	3.3	8.5
Germany	10.0	11.0
Greece	16.3	17.2
Ireland	6.2	8.6
Italy	6.6	6.3
Luxembourg	3.3	3.4
Netherlands	5.7	8.5
Portugal	17.0	18.7
Spain	15.6	26.6
United Kingdom	5.5	5.4

Source: OECD, 1991a, Table 2.11.

Table 5.5 Share of Temporary Workers (other than self-employed) in Total Employment, 1985 and 1986 (percentages)

	Men	Women
Belgium	4.6	10.2
Denmark	10.2	10.7
France	4.8	4.9
Germany	8.9	9.6
Netherlands	5.4	9.7
United Kingdom	4.3	6.4

Source: OECD, 1989, Table 5.6.

To what extent does the coming to an end of a temporary job lead to a major flow into unemployment? Work for Britain (Casey, 1988) shows that between 6 and 16 per cent of those who finished a temporary job entered unemployment (depending on the survey); redundancy and dismissals were more important reasons for entry to unemployment. There was, however, evidence of a relationship between temporary employment and recurrent unemployment. Those whose first job on leaving unemployment was a temporary one were more likely to suffer multiple spells of unemployment over the 20 months following their initial registration than those whose first job was a permanent one. Longitudinal data for Germany show that a large proportion of the temporary workers (especially the unskilled) fluctuate between those jobs and unemployment (H.-G. Brose, W. Meyer and M. Schulze-Böing, 1989, cited in Hinrichs, 1991, p. 118).

Fixed-term employment contracts
Little systematic information is available on the extent of employment on fixed-term employment contracts. In the 1980s, for countries where information is available, there was an increase in the number of registered agencies handling temporary work contracts (European Industrial Relations Review, 1989). The rise over time in the number of workers on temporary work contracts in Belgium, Canada and the Netherlands is documented in OECD (1991a, Chapter 2), as are the sharp increases in the importance of fixed-term contracts that occurred in France, Portugal and Spain. By 1986 in Germany, a significant proportion of workers were on fixed-term, part-time contracts (European Industrial Relations Review, 1988). Taking all fixed-term contracts, there has been a rise over time in contract employment in Germany since the 1960s (Dombois and Osterland, 1987). The percentage of employees on fixed-term contracts in the private sector in Germany increased from 4 per cent in 1984 to 5.6 per cent in 1988 (Hinrichs, 1991, p. 117). A survey of eight sectors in the Netherlands showed that between 1982 and 1985 the incidence of part-time contracts increased by 14 per cent and of on-call contracts increased by 17 per cent (European Industrial Relations Review, 1987). In Portugal and in Spain, the 1980s saw a sharp increase in the number of temporary contracts and in their proportion of total employment (Ferreira *et al.*, 1989; Guillen, 1989).

5.2.3   Self-employment

Self-employment – and in particular, those instances where no employees are employed – is the third 'non-standard' form of work. Table 5.6 shows that self-employment varies from 6 per cent of employment in Norway to 27 per cent in Greece. In the 1980s, self-employment outside agriculture grew rapidly in many OECD countries, both in absolute terms and as a proportion of total employment (OECD, 1992, Chapter 4). There has been a rise over time in the proportion of women in employment who are self-employed (OECD, 1988a, Chapter 5). In Canada over the past decade, 10 per cent of overall job growth has been in self-employment without employees (Economic Council of Canada, 1990).

There is an overlap between fixed-term contract work and self-employment without employees. There has been a tendency for employers to opt to employ workers on a contract basis for specific periods rather than on a permanent pensionable basis (evidence for Great Britain is presented in Creigh *et al.*, 1986).

Table 5.6 Share of Self-employment in Total Employment, Selected
Countries, 1979, 1990 (percentages)

	1979	1990
Austria	8.9	6.4
Belgium	11.2	12.9
Denmark	9.2	7.2
Finland	6.1	8.8
France	10.6	10.3
Germany	8.2	7.7
Greece	32.0	27.2[a]
Ireland	10.4	13.3
Italy	18.9	22.3
Netherlands	8.8	7.8
Norway	6.6	6.1
Portugal	12.1	18.5
Spain	15.7	17.2
Sweden	4.5	7.0
United Kingdom	6.6	11.6

Note: a. 1989.
Source: OECD, 1992, Table 4.1.

5.2.4 Overview and the future for new forms of working

Among the three 'new' forms of work considered, part-time work (other
than self-employed and temporary) comprises the biggest share, 43 per
cent of the total, with self-employment 34 per cent, and temporary work
(other than self-employment) 23 per cent. The degree of overlap between
the categories is particularly marked in the case of women, with
self-employed women appearing to be highly 'marginal' (British data:
Casey and Creigh, 1989). In Canada between 1981 and 1986, four forms
of non-standard employment (part-time work, short-term work or jobs
of less than six months in duration, own-account self-employment and
temporary-help agency work) accounted for about half of all new jobs
and currently represent nearly 30 per cent of total employment
(Economic Council of Canada, 1990, p. 12).

It is not clear to what extent the growth in new forms of working has
been a long-run or structural feature of the economies of member states,
and to what extent it has reflected cyclical down-turns in economic
activity across the OECD area. This is a desire on the part of employers,
in sectors with periodic fluctuation in activity, to reduce the amount of
slack time and to concentrate their use of labour on peak periods, thus
reducing risks in the face of uncertainty about demand. However, there
does not seem to have been a notable increase in 'new' temporary work
on grounds of handling uncertainty in Germany and Great Britain (Casey
et al., 1989). Nevertheless, the data are consistent with an increased

propensity on the part of firms to make use of atypical forms of work. It seems likely that the incidence of new forms of working is likely to persist. With the exception of women in self-employment, all the non-standard work forms are more in evidence in growing sectors (in terms of employment) than in declining sectors (Table 5.7). Among service workers, there is a high proportion of part-time employees. Thus, a continuance of the growth in service occupations should bring with it a further growth in part-time work.

Table 5.7 Non-standard Forms of Working across EC Countries, Categorised by Nature of Employment Change (percentages)

		All sectors	Growing	Middle	Declining
Share of self-employment in total employment	Men	12.1	14.4	11.8	10.2
	Women	8.7	7.0	8.8	10.8
Share of temporary workers (other than self-employed) in total employment	Men	6.3	7.5	6.2	4.9
	Women	8.6	9.9	8.4	6.6
Share of part-time workers (other than self-employed and temporary) in total employment	Men	4.1	5.2	4.0	2.4
	Women	26.8	30.0	26.5	22.4

Note: Data are simple averages of 1985 and 1986 for the following EC countries: Belgium, Denmark, France, Germany, Netherlands, United Kingdom.
Source: OECD, 1989, Table 5.6.

5.3   Implications of these New Forms of Working for Economic Well-being of Individuals

Undoubtedly, not all of the atypical forms of work involve workers who are in a disadvantaged position. There can be marked differences in levels of well-being across individual workers who are classed as 'atypical'. For instance, while temporary employees have less access to training and promotion, high turnover through jobs can give opportunities for work experience and for finding a job which better matches the person's abilities. Nevertheless, these workers as a group can be regarded as being on the 'fringe' of the labour market. In many instances, their earnings are relatively low or are subject to interruption over time. Often, they are not entitled to the same occupational benefits (e.g., holidays, pensions) as are permanent full-time employees, they can have less access to training, limited opportunities for promotion, and are typically not on incremental scales. They may not be covered under employment protection legislation which can assure minimum conditions about notice to quit and redundancy payments.

While there is a paucity of information about the earnings of part-time workers compared with full-time workers, evidence suggests (e.g., OECD, 1983, p. 51 for manual workers; Belous, 1989, for the United States; Blackwell and Nolan, 1990 for Ireland) that part-time workers earn less than full-time workers on an hourly basis. Some of this differential is likely to be related to the 'gender effect': the persistently lower hourly earnings of women than of men. Ideally, there is need to allow for skill levels when making these comparisons. Blank (1990) finds that in the United States, most part-time workers appear to earn lower wages than equally skilled full-time workers in the same industry or region, that part-time workers are unambiguously less likely to receive fringe benefits, and that those who are involuntarily in part-time work receive lower wages and are even less likely to receive fringe benefits than equivalent voluntary part-time workers.

Relatively little systematic information is available on the earnings of workers on fixed-term contracts. However, in Germany, workers on fixed-term contracts have lower incomes than those on permanent employment contracts (Büchtemann and Quack, 1989). These lower relative earnings are not fully accounted for by the lower average skill level of their jobs or their relatively lower average age. Some at least of the remaining wage differential can be explained by relatively low length of service. Those with a succession of fixed-term contracts, with intermittent spells of unemployment in between, never achieved enough seniority to qualify for wage increases and fringe benefits. In Spain, temporary workers other than seasonal workers (the majority of them with a fixed-term contract) earn 12 per cent less than permanent workers; temporary workers get lower additional earnings from experience and education than do permanent workers (Alba-Ramírez, 1991).

5.4   Implications of New Forms of Employment for Social Protection

For a number of reasons, the 'new' forms of work have implications for social security. First, each of these forms has a particular aspect which means, even for people who are in employment, there can be a need for social protection. In self-employment, earnings are erratic over time; part-time work tends to be low paid, not just in weekly terms but in hourly terms; and temporary work is insecure. The low pay of many atypical workers has implications not just for their current income but also for their ability to acquire resources over their working lives.

Second, while the treatment of 'atypical' workers under social security varies across the OECD member states, in general, the rights which these workers have for contributory benefits are less favourable than for other workers. In some instances, those in 'new' forms of work can have no entitlement to social security. (For reviews, see Calcoen *et al.*, 1988; Euzéby, 1988; Maier, 1991; see also International Labour Office, 1989.) Benefits are often calculated on the basis of contributions which are built up over a certain period, or only if their remuneration reaches a certain minimum level during the reference year. In some countries (e.g., in Germany, for pension and sickness insurance coverage) a minimum number of hours per week and minimum monthly earnings are specified. In Ireland most social insurance benefits are not available to those who work under an hours threshold (18 per week) and whose part-time earnings amount to only a secondary income. Across countries, access to social benefits and to social security is generally best for part-time workers who work more than 20 hours a week and worst for those working less than 17–18 hours a week.

Many countries require that part-time workers receive proportionate sick pay. However, minimum hours thresholds exist in a number of countries: for instance, one-fifth of normal working hours in Austria, a minimum of 40 hours during the last four weeks in Denmark, 200 hours of work in the preceding three months in France. Some of the thresholds result in the exclusion from coverage of those workers with working hours which are not distributed evenly over the week or the month, and of those with irregular working patterns who have no earning in some weeks. This is unless the hours worked are averaged over a relatively long period. For example, the averaging is done over only a month in Denmark.

Temporary workers can have no entitlement to social security. In general, the self-employed are not eligible for unemployment benefits and can be covered less favourably than employees for pension benefits; when benefit cover does exist, the benefit levels can be lower than for those on wages and salaries. Self-employed workers are either not covered for social security or have access to fewer benefits than have employees.

In some countries, full public pensions are paid only to those who have worked full-time over their whole working life – examples are Austria, Belgium, Germany. In these countries, part-time workers who fall below hours or income thresholds are not entitled to public pensions. Eligibility for public pensions can be based on minimum income (Austria) or on both income and hours minima (15 hours a week and minimum income in Germany). When pension benefits are calculated on the basis of the most recent earnings, as in Greece where they are based on the last two years, a move from full-time to part-time work in the later part of the life-cycle can lead to a reduction in the pension. In other countries, part-time work for a limited number of years does not reduce the pension which is based on a number of 'best' years: in France, Germany, Norway and Sweden.

5.4.1 Coverage of social security, occupational welfare and personal pensions

Over time, there has been an increase in the absolute number of part-time workers who usually work 20 hours a week or less (OECD, 1991a, p. 53). This could be expected to have led to a decline in the proportion of these workers who are covered for social security.

It is estimated that one in four female part-time employees in the Federal Republic of Germany lack entitlement to social security (Büchtemann and Schupp, 1988). It is estimated for Britain that 26 per cent of part-time workers have earnings below the NI threshold, and there are indications that there has been a gradual increase, both absolute and relative, in the workforce outside the social insurance net in the second half of the 1980s (Hakim, 1989a). Luckhaus and Dickens (1991) estimate that in 1988 over two million part-time employees in Britain (generally working under 16 hours and earning under £40 a week) had insufficient earnings to participate in the contributory scheme.

There is also the question of coverage for occupational welfare and personal pensions, which are increasingly seen as complementing social security. For a number of countries in recent years, incentives have been given for private pensions, either through tax incentives for occupational pensions or by incentives to take out personal pensions. Part-time workers tend to be excluded from occupational schemes. A survey carried out in Great Britain at the end of 1988 showed that, for women, those who had always been in part-time work and those who, although they had experience of full-time work, had most recently only worked part time, were much less likely to have joined an occupational pension scheme than women whose jobs had always been full time (Bone et al., 1992, Table 6.13; see also Chapter 13 in this volume by Ginn and Arber). In the specific case of the UK, 'personal' pensions have been encouraged since 1986, but these require regular contributions over a long period and hence can cause difficulties for women.

Another form of occupational welfare is the provision of occupational sick pay. While existing occupational sick pay schemes improved their provisions in Britain in the 1980s, many employees are not covered, either because they work part time or because they have not been working long enough (Dean and Taylor-Gooby, 1990).

5.4.2   Structure of social security

The implications of the 'new forms' of work for policy on social security are now considered. At the outset, some broad points about the systems of social security are made. To a considerable extent, social security systems have been designed for an economy where the characteristic job was a full-time one with some degree of stability. The very idea of 'social insurance' reflects this, with its spreading of risks across a large group of workers, for each of whom the probability of a contingency such as unemployment is assumed to be small. Thus, social insurance is designed to replace income lost in the short term for reasons such as sickness and unemployment; or for longer periods such as occurs with retirement pensions and long-term invalidity payments; it has not been designed for those in intermittent unemployment or in part-time jobs.

The response on the part of social security systems to the growth of 'atypical' forms of work has had some resemblance to the attitude adopted by governments to the existence and presumed growth of employment in the informal economy. In the latter case there has been an inherent tension in the concerns of governments. On the one hand, they have wished to maintain social cohesion and to respond to the grievances of workers in the 'formal' economy who pay direct taxes and whose tax rates are presumably higher, the larger the extent of the informal economy. On the other hand, governments may not want to inhibit entirely 'those who may be too enthusiastically enjoying the enterprise culture' (Pahl, 1988) on the grounds that economic activity is being generated.

A similar tension is discernible in the area of social security. Governments may feel that on equity and efficiency grounds, there is a case for bringing atypical workers more fully into the social security system. But at the same time, there may be a temptation to continue to give, effectively, exemptions from social security coverage in order to encourage the employment of the more marginal workers and improve the competitiveness of firms.

There is an implicit assumption in social security systems that the very fact of full-time, stable employment means that there will be little or no need for social protection. Admittedly, efforts have been made in some countries to direct social transfers to those families which depend on income from low pay: for instance, Australia, Ireland and the UK have attempted by family income supplements to augment the income of those families. In each of these cases, the take-up of the benefit has been disappointingly low.

Incentives

Many of those who have been in atypical work have a tenuous contact with the labour marker, in the sense that they have moved in and out of employment, possibly in between spells of unemployment. There are features of social security which penalise the acceptance of paid work by these individuals.

First, the structure of social security facing lone parents can act as a disincentive to the acceptance of paid work. The 'poverty trap' which faces lone parents in France and the UK, where net income may rise by a negligible amount in response to increases in gross earnings from work, is outlined in Ray (1990) and Joshi (1990a) respectively. Second, there can be a withdrawal of benefit from those older workers who combine work with acceptance of a pension. In a number of countries – Belgium, Canada, France, Japan, the United States – an earnings rule applies, under which there is a reduction in public pension benefits once earnings reach a certain level. This amounts to an implicit marginal tax on work income for pension recipients, which can be as high as 100 per cent.

Third, it can be impossible for unemployed workers to continue to receive benefit while engaged in part-time work, due to a sharp withdrawal or termination of social security benefits. Even though part-time work could suit some workers, the benefit rules mean that there can be a disincentive for people to move from unemployment to part-time employment. Fourth, in certain instances in member countries, workers can lose entitlement to benefit as a result of a number of moves between employment and unemployment. Administrative delays involved in restarting unemployment benefit payments by themselves are a major disincentive to taking a short-term job. This is likely to arise for those who are most marginalised, who suffer the highest incidence of unemployment and multiple spells of unemployment.

Finally, when people have lost a full-time job and have an offer of a part-time job, the net earnings from the part-time job may not be greatly different from the unemployment compensation. In a number of countries, rules about the granting of unemployment benefit have been relaxed for those who find a part-time job, partly in order to encourage a re-entry of the unemployed into employment. For instance, in Belgium, an unemployed person who takes a part-time job obtains partial unemployment compensation. In Denmark and in Spain, those receiving unemployment benefit who accept part-time work can continue to receive a benefit, reduced proportionately to the difference between the hours worked and normal hours. In France in 1985, an allowance was introduced equal to the difference between net monthly unemployment benefit and net monthly pay from a part-time job. This allowance does not really give an incentive to unemployed people to take on part-time work, since there is in effect a marginal tax rate of 100 per cent.

Safety nets and means testing
The reliance by increasing numbers of unemployed people on means-tested social assistance has a number of implications. The 'safety

nets' which exist in different countries can in principle provide a minimal amount of protection to those people who are not covered for social insurance, including those who have been in atypical employment. However, across the different countries there are a number of reasons why this 'second tier' of social assistance may fail to ensure an adequate minimum income for all, or there can be particular problems associated with its operation. This is aside from the adequacy of the social assistance levels, given that those on social assistance receive lower levels of income support by comparison with those on unemployment insurance. They can be encapsulated as follows.

First, some sections of the population are not covered for social assistance. One such group consists of low-paid workers. Second, means testing is also associated with problems of low take-up of benefit by those who are eligible for benefit. This can be due to the stigma which can be attached to their receipt, the lack of information among potential recipients about their eligibility, an erroneous perception that they are ineligible for benefit, or the costs of time spent claiming and obtaining benefit in those cases where the benefit entitlements are relatively small.

Third, means testing on the basis of household income results in many women who are 'secondary earners' being denied benefit. Means testing is done on the assumption that income sharing occurs within the household. If income sharing does not occur, women can be disadvantaged. Fourth, there can be implications for incentives to work. Means testing can add to the problems of the poverty trap, with high effective marginal tax rates on those low-income households who wish to increase their earnings from work. One instance is where the earnings of one partner are set off against the benefit of the other, leading to a ceiling on the income of the household. Women may be allowed to earn only a small amount before there is a reduction in social security benefits due to the level of family income. One result is that in two-parent families where the male partner is unemployed, the labour force participation rate of the woman partner is significantly lower than in cases where the man is employed. Where women work part-time, the incomes of the families may be insufficient for them to be lifted off social assistance. Admittedly, other influences are also at work here. Cooke (1987) points out the possible influence of elements, such as health, attitudes, and the roles of male and female partners in the family. Women may be reluctant to seek work if their partner is unemployed, since this could undermine his role as the main breadwinner.

5.4.4   Financing of social security

Social expenditure is financed partly from tax revenue and partly from social security contributions. The latter have many of the characteristics of a tax and are not insurance contributions in the pure sense: benefits are not always covered by revenue and there is little risk rating. However, there is an argument made that workers are more prepared to pay social insurance contributions or earmarked taxes, than they are prepared to pay taxes on the basis that they are building up entitlement to benefit. There is little evidence on this. One could argue that in the sphere of pensions there has been a 'social contract' whereby workers of one generation are prepared to pay 'contributions'/taxes on the basis that when they in turn become eligible for pensions, they will receive them, funded from a new generation of workers.

There are a number of implications of changes in new forms of work for social security funds. First, the changes in the economic structure and in the labour market may weaken the solidarity which up to now has been a feature of social security. Workers may have been prepared to contribute to funds on the basis that people with a risk of being (for instance) unemployed will currently benefit. That preparedness to fund contributions may weaken as a divide in the labour market opens out between workers with different forms of security. Second, for any given structure of contributions and for any given set of contribution rates, the changes in the labour market may lower the income of social security funds.

5.5   Conclusions and Policy Implications

5.5.1   Broad implications

This chapter has focused on three atypical forms of work: part-time work, temporary work and self employment including work done on the basis of fixed-term contracts. Over time, there has been a rise in the incidence of these forms of work, expressed as a proportion of total employment. This has partly reflected a relative increase in employment in those sectors where atypical forms are prominent, and has been related to an increased search for more flexible forms of work by firms. There are reasons to believe that further increases in the incidence of atypical work are likely.

At first sight, the implications for social protection are that many atypical workers are either not covered for social security or are covered less fully than are employees in full-time and year-long employment. The coverage can depend on the number of hours worked per week and on earnings. Workers who fall below a threshold of hours per week, or who are in or out of work over their lifetime (hence with a lower than average stream of contributions for social security) will tend to have lower than average entitlements to social security. Women are especially affected by the less favourable coverage for those in part-time work.

These general conclusions need to be amplified in a number of respects. First, in some countries, people have been encouraged, by means such as tax incentives, to provide their own social protection, especially through personal pensions. For those in atypical employment, this is likely to be more difficult. Their coverage for occupational welfare is also likely to be lower than average.

Second, there is a two-way interaction between work patterns and the structure of social security. The nature of social security can influence work patterns. One example noted above is the Swedish part-time pension, which has encouraged older workers to move down from full-time to part-time work. Another example is that women are likely to receive lower public pension benefits, reflecting intermittent work patterns, among other things. Many of them are not likely to become vested in an occupational pension. Hence, one reason why some women may defer their departure from the labour force is in order to build up future pension entitlements.

Third, the focus should be extended to examine the interaction between atypical employment and those work patterns which can adversely affect people's well-being. Of particular importance is the degree of the correlation between new forms of employment and (a) low earnings, (b) multiple spells of unemployment, (c) shorter than average duration of spells of employment, (d) intermittent patterns of work involving exit from and re-entry to the labour force over the life cycle, especially in the case of women. While evidence on these correlations is less than adequate, there is some evidence for a link between temporary work and multiple spells of unemployment, and between part-time work by women and interrupted work spells over the life cycle. It can be easier for those in atypical employment to move in and out of the labour force over time, but a price paid can be reduced entitlement to social security benefits. There are other life-cycle aspects: the limited access of women, especially those ever-married, to occupational pension provision, reflects their lifetime labour market status (Groves, 1987a).

Fourth, the impacts of any increases in the insecurity of male employment can have been offset for some households by increases in female participation in the labour force. However, in most circumstances, the coverage for social protection of a family with two intermittent workers is likely to be inferior to that of a family with one non-intermittent worker at the same number of annual hours.

5.5.2   Policy alternatives: building on social insurance

Some of the main policy alternatives which arise in relation to the reform of social security are now considered, designed to cope with the growth in atypical forms of work and to improve equity of treatment under social security. Reform could build on the existing structure of social insurance.

An instance is unemployment insurance. An advantage of retaining the structure of unemployment insurance is that contribution conditions give people an incentive to enter or re-enter the labour force or to seek stable, regular employment in order to build up future entitlements. One option would be to extend the coverage of benefits such as unemployment insurance, extending a greater degree of coverage to those in new forms of work. The problems which arise in the case of broken contribution records by women could be handled (as suggested by Atkinson and Micklewright, 1988) by the crediting of contributions. The alternative option of a second-tier insurance programme with lower benefits for those in the lower tier would hardly be desirable on grounds either of horizontal equity or the pooling of risks.

There are a number of different ways in which social insurance could be extended to part-time workers. One would be through lowering the thresholds which currently can be set in terms of minimum earnings or minimum hours of work. In order to minimise hardship for low-paid workers, this could be combined with a lower rate of contribution set on earnings below a certain level. With regard to the payment of benefits, one option would be to pay a proportion of the full benefit levels to those who work under a certain threshold of hours per week or under a certain threshold of earnings per week. Alternatively, the benefits paid could be related to the earnings level.

Even if the current broad thresholds were maintained, the thresholds could be made more flexible. For instance, the period over which the average number of working hours is calculated, for the purpose of establishing entitlement to benefit, could be extended. If a greater proportion of workers were brought within the scope of social insurance, they would have lower disposable income in the short-term but enhanced protection in the long term. There is little evidence on the extent of any adverse impacts on the demand for labour by employers, but some might be expected in labour-intensive sectors subject to a good deal of competition.

If the social insurance coverage of atypical workers was improved, would there be adverse implications for the financial structure of social insurance? This is not necessarily the case. The outcome would depend on the benefit/contribution ratio which varies across the age groups and also depends on the mixture of tax financing and social security contributions that are used to fund benefits.

Supplementing income from work
Given that many of those in atypical work are in receipt of low and irregular pay, one possibility would be the supplementation of low income from employment through social transfers. This would be likely to be a limited solution, partly because atypical workers are in need of income maintenance in other circumstances, such as unemployment and

sickness. Moreover, countries which have attempted to supplement low pay through family income supplements have found a low rate of take-up of the supplement.

Means testing
Quite a different option would aim to direct a given amount of resources towards those whose resources fall below their needs. This can be done through increased use of means testing. In the limit, this would mean that, for the poor, exactly 100 per cent of the difference between needs and resources would be made up. There would be a number of drawbacks with this approach, some of which are evident from the discussion of means testing. This approach would mean that high effective marginal tax rates would be imposed on households. The dilemma is that if marginal tax rates of less than 100 per cent are to be achieved, either not all of the deprivation would be made up, leaving people in poverty, or some households would be given more than is necessary to eliminate poverty. For any given level of public expenditure, lower marginal tax rates on those of low incomes could be achieved only by either increasing marginal tax rates further up the income scale or by lowering the minimum income guarantee. The alternative is to increase public expenditure on income transfers. The objectives of providing a minimum income guarantee, providing incentives to work by putting a limit on marginal tax rates, and containing public expenditure, are in conflict with one another.

Unemployment benefit rules
With the increase in non-standard forms of employment, it has become more difficult for those in public employment services to apply in a consistent and equitable way the rules with regard to the award of unemployment benefit. One particular group for which there could be a loosening in conditions are those who quit a part-time job and seek to enter more stable employment via a spell of unemployment. Greater flexibility in dealing with new forms of working would also be achieved by allowing people in certain cases to receive income from work, including from temporary work, without disqualifying them from receipt of social security including unemployment insurance. Related to this is the desirability of loosening up the application of 'availability for work' criteria in the case of part-time workers, who currently may be denied benefit even if the work offered is not suitable for the person.

5.5.3   Coverage for occupational pensions

In the sphere of pensions, many atypical workers are not covered for occupational pensions. Others may be covered but can be disadvantaged if pension calculations are done on the basis of final salary. Any encouragement to move away from the final salary basis, towards a number of the 'best' years, could improve the pension entitlements of atypical workers. Furthermore, regulation could ensure that a higher proportion of atypical workers were covered under occupational pension schemes. For instance, in the Netherlands, recently under consideration has been a proposal which would forbid the exclusion of part-time workers (most of whom are women) from participation in occupational pension schemes.

5.5.4 Policy alternatives: grand designs

The most radical alternative would be to replace the current structure of social insurance/social assistance with a guaranteed minimum income through some form of basic income or negative income tax. A uniform benefit would be payable to all, regardless of work history or current labour force status, replacing means-tested benefits with a tax-free basic income, above which income would be taxable. This could take the form of tax credits which could be paid in cash or else used to reduce tax liability. Contribution record or past and current participation in the labour market would not be a condition for benefit entitlement. Nor would benefits depend on how income was distributed within the year. Those in low-paid and irregular work would in effect receive income supplementation. There would be similar treatment of those with the same income but with different labour force status, including the unemployed and those who return to the labour force after an absence. This would be in contrast with current forms of income supplementation, which can treat claimants differently according to whether they are insured or in receipt of social assistance, and which can confine supplementation for the low paid to those with children.

Less radical but halfway towards comprehensive reform would be a breaking of the connection between elements such as contribution record and the entitlement to unemployment compensation. Distinctions based on elements such as contribution record and the length and continuity of the contribution period lead to systems which are administratively complex. As a result, resources are used up to administer them and inequities occur between the treatment of different people. As long as the claimant meets the criterion of being available for work, there is a case for moving to finance unemployment benefit out of general taxation or out of a merger of the schedules of social security contributions and income taxation. This could result in greater equity between different claimant groups.

Chapter 6

The Demise of the Male Breadwinner – In Practice but not in Theory: A challenge for social security systems

Hilary Land

> You can't abolish Want unless you make sure that everybody willing to work, everybody subject to occasional accidents and misfortunes that interrupt his earnings, has at all times, for all his responsibilities, the income necessary to meet those responsibilities. (Beveridge, 1943, p. 82)

Want was the giant that Beveridge's plan for social security was to overcome. The other giants were Disease, Ignorance, Squalor and Idleness. These were to be tackled by other social and economic policies. In particular, 'the destruction of Idleness means ensuring for every citizen a reasonable opportunity of productive service and earning according to his service' (Beveridge, 1943, p. 43). His use of the male pronoun was deliberate: breadwinners were male. Women and children were to be shielded from Want by guaranteeing men paid work, replacing their husband's earnings when they were interrupted and by introducing a system of children's allowances.

6.1   The Beveridge Model of the Family

Beveridge's social security systeM was based on a model of the family in which men were in full-time paid employment and women were primarily wives and mothers. In his proposed national insurance scheme men were categorised according to their employment status and women according to their marital status. In other words a man's membership of the scheme and entitlement to benefit depended primarily on his relationship to the labour market and a woman's on her relationship to a man. Although the scheme accommodated those in temporary or casual jobs and the self-employed, part-time workers were not even discussed.

100

This is not surprising. When the Beveridge Committee were sitting, part-time employment involved a small proportion of the female workforce and a tiny proportion of the total workforce. In June 1942 out of a total civilian workforce of 17. 8 million, there were 6.6 million women of whom only 380,000 were employed part-time. Six months later the demand for labour was such that compulsory registration was extended to include all single women up to the age of 50 years. Employers were encouraged to offer part-time employment, provide canteens and give time off (unpaid) for shopping. The school meals service was expanded (by ten-fold between 1940 and 1945, reaching one in three school children by the end of the war).

By mid-1943 it was estimated that 80 per cent of single women aged between 14 and 59 years, 41 per cent of wives and widows without children and 13 per cent of mothers were either in the Forces, in industry or in civil defence (Ferguson and Fitzgerald, 1954, p. 6). The numbers in part-time employment had doubled. A year later there were 900,000 part-time workers (Ministry of Labour (MoL), 1947a). These part-time workers were almost entirely married women or women with domestic responsibilities.

Beveridge was clear that such changes were temporary. Once the war was over married women would and indeed should return to being full-time housewives and mothers. Although not discussed in the Report, Beveridge recognised the importance of services for wives and mothers and wanted to increase these too. He was interested in developing their opportunities for leisure rather than for paid work. He wrote that better housing and equipment were needed along with communal services so that

> some of what has now to be done separately in every home – washing all clothes, cooking every meal, being in charge of every child for every moment when it is not in school, can be done outside the home. (Beveridge, 1944a, p. 264)

Against a background of concern about a birth rate below replacement level, it was considered important that women be encouraged to take motherhood seriously.

In contrast married women's paid work was treated lightly. First, it was not regarded as important to the economic viability of the family.

> Unless there are children, the housewife's earnings in general are a means, not of subsistence but of a standard of living above subsistence, like the higher earnings of a skilled man compared with a labourer: the children's allowance proposed ... will make this true in most cases in future, even where there are children. (Beveridge, 1942, para. 108)

Although there was a need to replace a housewife's services when she was ill there was no need to replace a housewife's earnings when she was sick or unemployed. After all social insurance should aim at guaranteeing the minimum income needed for subsistence. (Beveridge, 1942, para. 27)

Only the husband's income needed replacing when he was ill or unemployed because he was the breadwinner.

Second, those involved in developing the British social insurance system from the outset believed married women themselves did not take their paid work seriously. When the national health insurance scheme was introduced in 1912, including in it 800,000 married women, the government was surprised at the high rate of sickness among married women. A committee of inquiry to investigate these 'excessive claims' was established within months. Ignoring the evidence that many married women were in a poor state of health the majority of the committee concluded that at best women did not understand the social insurance system and at worst they were claiming benefit when they were not really ill.

Nearly thirty years later Beveridge and several members of his committee held rather similar views. At an early meeting of the committee, Beveridge said 'notoriously, married women have not got the same urge to keep continuously at work' (Public Records Office (PRO), Social Insurance Committee (SIC), 11 March 1942, Q.1610). He proposed paying a lower rate of sickness and unemployment benefit to those married women who chose to continue as contributors to the national insurance scheme in their own right rather than to rely upon their husbands. They would however receive maternity benefit at a higher rate. As he explained to the National Council of Women, who in their evidence to the Committee argued for men and women to receive equal benefits,

> Assume you equalise benefits and still have the woman's wage, as I am afraid you are likely to have ... you are getting your benefit very much nearer your wage for women than it is for men ... it would be bad obviously to weaken the already weaker incentive for women to get employment. (PRO, SIC, 11 March 1942, Q.1387)

He ignored the National Council's suggestion that equal pay would reduce this problem.

The Government Actuary was even more reluctant to take married women's needs for sickness benefit seriously. When preparing the legislation necessary to implement the committee's proposals in a memorandum entitled *Rough Notes on married women's benefits* he wrote:

> The finance of married women's sickness insurance has throughout the history of the National Health Insurance, been a source of difficulty and trouble owing to very heavy claims as compared with unmarried women. This is due only in part to genuine extra risk and more to
> (i)   dependency on husband;
> (ii) lack of incentive to women to return to work;

(iii) casual and part-time nature of occupations. (PRO, ACT/1702, 21, 1944).

With these attitudes firmly embedded in the minds of the social policy makers in the mid-1940s, the neglect of part-time workers in the proposed social security system is understandable. Nevertheless it is important to note that the national insurance scheme was still being used as a means of extending the boundaries of the formal labour market. This had been one of the aims in 1911, and although married women's needs were not fully acknowledged (the unemployment benefit scheme initially covered only male trades so all women were excluded), the government did insist that the employers of casual and outworkers paid contributions to the national health insurance scheme, even if the workers did not do so because they were 'not wholly or mainly dependent on earnings for livelihood' (i.e. mainly married women). If employers had been excused from contributing on behalf of these workers then they would have been cheaper to employ than single women or men.

That would have run counter to the prevailing view that a married woman's place was in the home. It did not of course accord with the views of those who relied on outworkers. They warned they would have to replace their outworkers with full-time workers, which was of course the intended outcome. In Beveridge's scheme, although married women had the option of not contributing to the national insurance scheme, their employers did not. Paradoxically the phasing out, starting in 1978, of the married woman's option not to contribute may well have made part-time workers *more* marginal rather than less, as will be discussed below.

6.2 The Labour Market in the early Post-War Years

As Beveridge expected, once the war was over, married women did return to the home, albeit many very reluctantly. Nevertheless by 1947, only 18 per cent of married women were economically active. However the government was faced with a labour shortage and the attitudes of those concerned with economic and labour market policies were rather more ambivalent about married women's proper place. The Ministry of Labour's Economic Survey for 1947 reported that it would be necessary to increase the total labour force in civil employment and 'women now form the only large reserve of labour left, and to them the government are accordingly making a special appeal' (Ministry of Labour, 1947b, p. 183). However, it was stressed first that women would not be asked to do men's jobs and second, that the labour shortage was only temporary.

Those services associated with the expansion of the welfare state particularly looked to women. Marriage bars in teaching had been removed in 1944 and from the Civil Service in 1946. The practice of firing nurses when they married was abandoned. The Ministry of Labour collaborated with the Ministry of Health to organise recruitment drives for part-time workers. Shortages of hospital and other institutional cleaners were so great that the British government launched recruitment campaigns in the British West Indies and in Europe.

The shortage of labour was far from temporary and by the early 1950s the picture was changing again. The demand for women's labour in health, education and welfare services ranging from professional to manual workers continued to grow as the welfare state became established. The raising of the school leaving age to 15 years in 1947 had increased the demand for teachers. In 1951 there were 1.2 million more children under the age of 15 years than there had been in 1941. The British involvement in the Korean War, rearmament policies and the introduction of national service for all young men made women's labour rather less dispensable than Beveridge had envisaged. The Ministry of Labour forecast that the number of men and women in the Armed Forces would increase from 713,000 in 1950 to 860,000 in 1952. It was recommended therefore:

> that something can be done to encourage more people to go to work, by the adjustment of working hours to allow more women with domestic duties to work in industry and by special arrangement to retain the services of the elderly and disabled. (Ministry of Labour, 1951, p. 142)

By 1951, one in four of married women (3.2 million) were economically active, double the proportion Beveridge had assumed in his Report (see para. 108). According to the 1951 census there were nearly 7 million women in the working population, including 779,000 part-time workers (defined as working less than normal hours in their particular occupation) (see Table 6.1). Eighty per cent of the women part-time workers were married. Viola Klein and other social researchers argued that this was almost certainly an underestimate, for she had found part-time and full-time workers in equal numbers in her survey (see Klein, 1960).

During the 1950s women continued to be drawn into the labour market and by 1961 there were 4.4 million married women in paid work, including 1.5 million employed part-time. First, there were financial pressures on them to do so. Family allowances which Beveridge had thought would reduce the financial pressure on mothers to take up paid employment had only been increased twice during the 1950s: once in 1952 and once in 1956 (and then only for the third and subsequent children). On both occasions these coincided with the withdrawal of food subsidies.

Second, there was still a labour shortage. The number of people of working age remained nearly static during the 1950s, and concern about shortages in nursing and teaching in particular continued despite the fact that in 1951 one and a quarter million people were employed in the education, health and welfare services – about double the numbers in 1931 (Rosenbaum, 1971, p. 6). Britain continued to look to its colonies and ex-colonies for health workers and the government exempted the NHS from the restrictions of the Immigration Acts of 1962 and 1965. Although local authority day nursery provision had declined in the 1950s, both the Ministry of Health and the Department of Education and Science sanctioned the establishment of day nurseries and nursery schools to help mothers return to nursing or teaching while the children were still young.

Table 6.1 Historical Trends in the Numbers in Part-time and Full-time Employment (Great Britain)

Year	Full-time (000s)		Part-time* (000s)		Ratio of f-time to p-time
	Total	of which female	Total	of which female	
1951	19,239	6,041	832	779	23:1
1961	19,794	5,698	1,999	1,851	10:1
1971	18,308	5,413	3,341	2,757	6:1
1981	16,407	5,481	4,442	3,789	5:1
1988	16,549	5,890	5,194	4,284	4:1

Note: * except for 1951, part-time work defined as working less than 30 hours per week.
Source: House of Lords Select Committee on the European Communities, 1982, p. ix; House of Commons Employment Committee, 1990, p. 157.

Table 6.2 Proportions of Women with Dependent Children Working Full-time and Part-time at Different Dates by Age of Youngest Child

Age of youngest child	Work status	Date (end December)				
		1949	1959	1969	1979	1990
0–4	Full-time	9	8	8	7	13
	Part-time	5	7	14	19	28
	All	14	15	22	26	41
5–10	Full-time	-	20	23	18	19
	Part-time	-	24	33	45	47
	All	-	44	56	63	66
11–15	Full-time	-	36	31	31	32
	Part-time	-	30	29	47	46
	All	-	66	60	78	78

Source: Equal Opportunities Commission, 1986, p. 87.

Official policy, however, was not to encourage or facilitate the employment of mothers with young children and the proportion of mothers working full-time declined slightly. Mothers were increasingly likely to take up part-time paid employment (see Table 6.2): a trend which has continued. Indeed the proportion of mothers in full-time paid work declined steadily from 1951 to the end of the 1980s; it was not until 1989 that there were as many women in full-time employment as there had been in 1951.

6.3   The Growth in Part-time Employment

In order to understand why the supply of, and the demand for, part-time employment increased it is necessary to analyse the changes in the labour market and family structures and processes together, as well as the part social policies, including social security systems, play in facilitating or modifying these changes.

6.3.1   Changes in the demand for labour

The structure of the labour market changed substantially over the next three decades, these changes accelerating in the 1980s. The manufacturing sector fell from nearly two-fifths (8.7 million) of jobs in 1971 to a little over one-fifth (4.7 million) in 1991. Most of the 4 million jobs lost were full-time. In contrast jobs in the service sector increased by more than 4 million to over 15 million. In 1991, over a third of these jobs were part-time. These changes affected men and women differently. Both lost full-time work in the manufacturing sector (in which a third of all female employees were found in 1961 compared with only one in eight in 1991), but it was predominantly women with family responsibilities who became part-time workers in the service sector.

Welfare services continued to provide an important source of employment for women. By 1988 there were 3.1 million people employed in this sector, 1.5 million of them employed part-time. Of the latter 1.3 million were women. In other words about one in three of all women working part-time are now found in the welfare service sector. During the 1970s there was an increased emphasis on part-time employment. In the health service this was partly because of a shift in policy away from employing full-time immigrant labour. During the 1960s pressure for tighter control over immigrant workers increased and the 1971 Immigration Act ended the automatic right of entry of prospective nurses. A report by the Prices and Incomes Board published at the end of the 1960s, when one in seven pupil nurses and midwives were being recruited overseas (Rosenbaum, 1971, p. 6), advocated the greater use of part-time labour in hospitals. They commended the practices of local education authorities in attracting back trained staff with family commitments:

> there are still many thousands of trained nurses to be attracted back into nursing ... it has to be accepted that hospitals will in future become increasingly dependent on this type of labour and many of them will

have to adopt a more flexible and accommodating attitude to it than they do at present. (National Prices and Incomes Board, 1968, p. 21)

By 1983 entry of overseas nurses had come to a standstill as work permits were withdrawn. Fewer than 9 per cent of nurses employed by the NHS in 1983 were born in developing countries (Commission for Racial Equality, 1983). The NHS is the largest employer of black people in the UK, relying heavily on them for domestic, catering and other manual work, but the service no longer looks for so many overseas.

The use of part-time staff in the welfare services is partly then a reflection of the supply of labour available to work full-time and this has varied between services since the Second World War. It may also be determined by the nature of the service itself. As Olive Robinson and John Wallace explained to the House of Lords Select Committee on the European Communities in 1982:

> Expansion of school meals provision, for which the majority of employees are required for no more than 2 hours daily, is an obvious instance of a service creating a demand for part-time labour. In health and social services part-time labour is an advantage ... in staffing centres with limited opening hours. (House of Lords Select Committee on the European Communities, 1982, p. 91)

If part-time employees have fewer rights than full-time employees they are cheaper and can be used more flexibly than full-time employees. These advantages to health, education and welfare budget holders became important with the onset of public expenditure cuts after 1976. As budgets remain very tight, or as more services are transferred to the private sector, managers concerned about maximising profits will prefer part-time workers. In the 1980s compulsory contracting out of services such as school meals and cleaning, previously provided directly by local government or health authorities together with the abolition of Fair Wages clauses, has meant hours and wage rates have been cut.

Part-time employees became more desirable in other sectors too. Just as Beveridge did not think through the consequences of an expanded welfare state for the demand for women's labour, he did not consider who was going to provide the services which would enable housewives to have the increased leisure he thought they deserved. In 1988 catering and hotels, which are highly labour intensive and the services provided require varying staffing levels to meet fluctuations in customer demand, employed 1.2 million people, double the number in 1961. Altogether 51 per cent of these employees were part-time and they accounted for one in eight of all part-time workers. The wages for both full-time and part-time employees in this sector are amongst the lowest of any industrial or services sector. In such labour intensive sectors high profits can only come from keeping wages low. This sector is expected to expand because as a junior Minister at the Department of Trade and Industry forecast:

Tourism will be the principal growth industry in the service sector for the rest of the century. (Waldegrave, quoted in *Municipal Journal*, April 1987)

This sector also depends on workers from minority ethnic groups.

The retail distribution sector had also come to rely heavily on part-time labour. In 1988 there were nearly one million part-time employees, 45 per cent of the total workforce in this sector, and accounting for nearly one in five of all part-time workers. Full-time jobs for women have been replaced by part-time jobs, as the trading day and week has lengthened and sophisticated technology allows very close monitoring of fluctuations in customer demand.

The other sector in which part-time employees have increased significantly is the banking, insurance, finance and business services sector. In 1988, out of 2.5 million employees just over 400,000 people were employed part-time, including 332,000 women. This accounts for one in twelve of all part-time employees. The growth of part-time employment has enabled banks and other financial establishments to meet uneven and changing levels of customer demand which, like the retail trade, has been affected by changes in the availability and use of technology. It has also been used to overcome shortages of full-time labour with specialist skills.

These changes in varying degrees are shared by our EC partners, as John Blackwell shows in Chapter Five. It is important to emphasise, however, that the meaning of part-time employment varies markedly between countries. Part-time can mean 'shorter working hours than statutory, collectively agreed or usual hours'. In the UK since 1961 it is defined as working fewer than 30 hours a week, in Sweden fewer than 35 hours, in France two-fifths of normal hours, but two-thirds of normal hours in Spain. It is therefore more illuminating to look at the distribution of hours of work between one country and another.

As Table 6.3 shows, while on average only 5 per cent of all employees in the EC worked fewer than 15 hours a week in 1988, in the UK and Denmark the proportion was double this, and in the Netherlands it was 15 per cent. The trend in the UK has been towards part-time work, meaning ever shorter hours. In 1979 among part-time workers, 30 per cent of manual workers and 23 per cent of non-manual workers worked fewer than 16 hours, by 1988 this had increased to 41 per cent and 32 per cent respectively. Those working less than 8 hours increased from 1 per cent to 12 per cent for manual workers and 6 per cent to 8 per cent for non-manual workers. During the same period their hourly earnings as a proportion of average full-time female hourly earnings fell from 80 per cent to 74 per cent. This deterioration is explained in part by the most rapid increase in part-time jobs occurring in the distribution, hotel, catering and retail sector. Significantly together with agriculture, this sector has the lowest hourly earning rates for both full and part-time workers. As the service sector grows and agricultural and manufacturing sectors decline, if left to market forces alone this trend towards shorter hours will grow in other EC countries.

Table 6.3 Distribution of Total Actual Hours Worked by Employees in Reference Week[a] in Main Job (per cent) 1988[b]

	1–15 Hours	16–29 Hours	30–45 Hours	46 Hours and over	Legal Provision on hours[c]
Belgium	3	12	81	4	40
Denmark	10	14	69	7	-
France	3	10	74	12	39
Federal Germany	3	9	79	9	48
Greece	2	8	76	14	48
Ireland	3	8	75	13	48
Italy	1	8	82	8	48
Luxembourg	2	6	87	4	40
Netherlands	15	16	57	12	48
Portugal	2	7	81	10	48
Spain	2	10	81	7	40
UK	11	15	55	19	-
Eur 12	5	11	73	12	-

Notes: a. Includes paid and unpaid overtime but excludes meal breaks and travel time; b. Includes people who did not answer and those who worked no hours in the reference week; c. Maximum statutory normal hours (although there are exceptions). Source: Eurostat, 1988.

6.3.2   Changes in the supply of labour

Part-time employment is sought for very different reasons as Table 6.4 shows. The reasons given for seeking part-time employment gives some indication of the factors affecting the availability of women, and men, for paid work.

Among those of working age the proportions of part-time workers who either could not find a full-time job and therefore had no alternative but to work part-time or did not wish to work full-time varied within the EC. The proportion in the UK stating that they did not wish to work full-time (64 per cent) is one of the highest in the EC and nearly all of these workers are mothers of dependent children or women with caring responsibilities. At first sight this confirms the view held by Beveridge fifty years ago that women's, particularly married women's, attachment to the labour force is weaker than men's and their earnings are merely an optional extra.

Certainly the DHSS (as it was at the time) and the DE, as illustrated for example in their evidence to the various Select Committees studying part-time employment, are still influenced by this view. For example, the DE said to the House of Lords Select Committee in 1981 when asked to comment on the DHSS figures showing that three times as many two parent families with a working father would have been in poverty if the mother had not been in paid work:

> Although the statement is true, it misrepresents the situation in that the absolute number involved was small: about 80,000 couples actually below supplementary benefit level rising to 220,000 if the wives had not worked. Furthermore no account was taken of the means-tested benefits to which couples may have been entitled if the wife had not worked. (House of Lords Select Committee on the European Communities, 1982, p. 133)

Table 6.4 Reasons for Working Part-time (per cent), Employees in 1988

	Student still at school	Ill or disabled	Could not find a f-time job	Did not want a f-time job	Some other reason	All[a] p-time employees (000s)
Belgium	2	2	37	13	46	314
Denmark	29	1	11	59	0	594
France[b]	-	-	-	-	-	2,158
FRG	8	2	7	68	16	3,039
Greece	5	2	50	18	25	74
Ireland	9	1	41	47	2	67
Italy	3	4	51	29	13	747
Luxembourg	24	1	8	52	16	9
Netherlands	18	3	30	36	12	1,529
Portugal	3	6	47	31	12	138
Spain	3	1	41	8	47	388
UK	10	1	9	64	15	5,084
Eur 12	10	2	17	56	16	14,140

Notes: a. Includes people who did not state a reason for working part-time. The definition is based on respondents' own assessment, not on the number of hours usually worked; b. Data on reasons for working part-time are not collected in France.

Even on these figures mothers' employment was keeping at least three-quarters of a million adults and children out of poverty. Is this 'small'? Women's wages are important to the economic survival of many families and are growing in importance as more married couples depend on two earners. Marriage rarely ends women's paid employment as it did for middle-class women earlier this century and the interruption due to children is shortening. In the early 1980s women on average spent less than 7 years out of the labour market because of their responsibilities for children. This is less than half the time spent out of paid employment by their mothers. The proportion of couples dependent entirely on the husband's earnings fell from a third in 1979 to a quarter in 1988. In the 1988 Family Expenditure Survey, nearly 40 per cent of women working part-time and 55 per cent of those working full-time said their earnings were used to pay for basic essentials. Unfortunately, the period when a family has only one earner coincides with the time when there are children, especially young children.

At the same time changes in a number of social policies have made it harder rather than easier to combine full-time paid employment with family responsibilities. Day nursery provision was not extensive in the post-war years, as discussed above. In 1965, among children whose mother were employed full-time, just over 10 per cent aged under 3 years and 7 per cent aged 3–4 years were cared for in a nursery (Hunt, 1968, p. 165). In 1980, 15 per cent of pre-school children of mothers in full-time employment were cared for in a nursery. However, by 1990 this proportion had fallen to 4 per cent. Childcare provided by relatives (other than husbands) declined in the 1980s (Macrae, 1991) and heavier reliance placed on paid care, either in the carer's or the mother's home. Childcare workers are another group of poorly paid women workers. Nannies and *au pairs* often come from abroad and are most open to exploitation.

For lone parents the changes have been even more dramatic for in addition to cuts in local authority nursery provision, where until the late 1970s they had priority for places, changes in their household circumstances have reduced the availability of childcare from relatives. A study in the 1950s found that a third of the pre-school children of lone parents were in day nurseries while their mothers worked. In this study three times as many lone mothers were working full-time than part-time. There was also heavy reliance on grandmothers to provide childcare in school holidays and after-school.

> This great reliance on the grandmother suggests that a large proportion of the sole supporters were living in their parents' home, as was found to be the case in the Douglas and Blomfield survey. (Yudkin and Holme, 1963, p. 78)

At this time far fewer lone parents lived in separate households. Ten years later the Finer Committee found that 45 per cent of lone parents were living in multi-unit households. The report states:

> from the very high proportions of working mothers with a child under 5 in multi-unit households (90 per cent) it can be inferred that the presence of others in the household is a key factor in determining whether the mother worked at all. (Finer Report, 1974, p. 255)

In 1990, 88 per cent of lone parents were living in households on their own, and grandmothers were more likely to be in paid employment themselves.

Lone mothers in the UK have the lowest economic activity rates in the EC and in the 1980s the numbers and proportions in full-time employment fell (see Table 6.5). Bradshaw and Millar's study found that many lone mothers on income support would take paid work if childcare was available (Bradshaw and Millar, 1991). In France, for example, where childcare provision is extensive both for pre-school and school-age children, the number of children, in particular the presence of a third child, is a much better predictor of women's economic activity than age of child and marital status. Nevertheless French mothers' availability for paid work is affected by the school week and childcare provision. With no school on Wednesdays, mothers who wish to work part-time do not work a shorter day as in the UK, but do not work on Wednesdays. French employers therefore pattern part-time work differently from UK employers (see, for example, O'Reilly, 1992).

Table 6.5 Lone Mothers in Paid Employment

Year	% in full-time employment	% in part-time employment	Total
1971	25	20	45
1977–79	22	24	46
1981–83	19	23	41
1986–88	17	22	39
1990	16	21	38

Source: Finer Report, 1974, p. 409; Office of Population Censuses and Surveys, 1990, p. 157; DE, 1992a, p. 570.

The Equal Opportunities Commission has pointed out that a number of research studies have demonstrated a significant number of all mothers in the UK would work longer hours if childcare provision was improved. Carers of dependent adults make up one in twelve of all full-time and one in six of all part-time workers. The exclusion of married women from entitlement to the invalid care allowance in 1975 until challenged in the European Court in 1986 is an example of the lack of importance given to their earnings. A national survey of carers published in 1991 found half of all carers not in employment would take paid work if there were adequate facilities available to provide the necessary support (Department of Health, 1991, p. 10). Men are much more likely to combine caring with full-time employment than women (45 per cent compared with 16 per cent of those providing at least 20 hours of care a week) (Office of Population Censuses and Surveys, 1990a). They are, after all, more likely to be able to afford to pay for substitute care and both they and their employers expect continuation in full-time employment.

6.4   Implications for the Social Security System

The cost as well as the availability of childcare has become a much more vital issue to all mothers of young children, but particularly to lone mothers. It is in this context of changing levels of state provision, and changing family and household structures that the social security rules have to be judged. These include eligibility criteria and level of benefits, how much can be earned without losing benefit, and how much work expenses can be offset against earnings. The latter became more generous in the mid-1970s following the Finer Report's recommendations (see Chapter Four by Jane Millar, this volume) but became less generous in 1988 when the level of earnings disregarded was based on gross earnings rather than earnings net of childcare costs. All these factors, together with higher levels of unemployment make it unsurprising that the proportion of lone parents dependent on state benefits (Income Support) increased from half to two-thirds during the 1980s.

On closer examination it is therefore difficult to sustain the argument that women 'choose' how much paid work, if any, to take up. The economic and social context in which families have to survive has changed, particularly in the last ten years. Beveridge envisaged a system in which men's wages would at least be sufficient to support a wife and one child. Minimum wage legislation together with a social security system which relied heavily on the contributory principle thus discouraging casual and irregular employment would help to ensure this. Adequate family allowances for second and subsequent children would adjust family income to family size without putting pressure on mothers to take up paid work.

Since 1979 the UK has had a government committed to reducing wage costs. The UK still has no minimum wage legislation and Wages Councils, which protected some of the lowest paid, have been abolished. The social security system is no longer being used to extend the boundaries of the formal labour market. On the contrary, it is one of the factors pushing workers – male and female – to the periphery. It has become harder for men as well as for women to be sole breadwinners. Earnings rules have been tightened for unemployed and part-time workers so that it is harder to combine anything but very marginal paid employment with receipt of benefit. Family allowances, or child benefits as they became in 1978, are still nowhere near providing for the cost of the child (although the first child has been included since 1978) and for much of the 1980s were frozen.

It remains to be seen whether the reduction of the threshold to 16 hours to qualify for family credit and conversely the ceiling of 16 hours to retain eligibility for income support will make it harder or easier for claimants with children to make the transition from dependence on benefits to dependence on earnings from employment. Hours and earnings ceilings can have the effect of trapping claimants in very low paid work (and note 16 hours is the limit for most employment protection as discussed above) and some employers exploit this.

While some EC countries have been putting full-time and part-time employees on a similar footing during the 1980s, as illustrated in John Blackwell's chapter, there is evidence in the UK that, in contrast, more part-time workers have been excluded from the social insurance system altogether. In 1991, 2.25 million women part-time workers earned insufficient to contribute to the national insurance scheme (Lister, 1992, p. 27). In 1981, when there were 3.8 million women working part-time, 40 per cent or 1.5 million were earning below the national insurance threshold (House of Lords Select Committee on the European Communities, 1982, p. 131). The comparable figure in 1971 was 20 per cent or 0.5 million women. While the withdrawal in 1978 of the married women's option not to pay full contributions to the national insurance scheme did not change the employer's position – any worker earning above the threshold had to have a contribution paid on his or her behalf – it did make married women aware there was a threshold of pay above which it was not worth increasing their earnings unless they could be increased substantially. This is the result of levying the contributions on the whole of earnings once the threshold is reached rather than only on those earnings above the threshold. Nigel Lawson when Chancellor of the Exchequer modified this effect by introducing in 1989 reduced contribution rates for those whose earnings were just above the threshold. Nevertheless the fact that income tax thresholds are now very close to the national insurance threshold makes it significant to employees. Prior to 1978 three-quarters of married women chose not to pay full contributions so the threshold was a matter of indifference to them.

A significant proportion of part-time workers therefore are cheaper than full-time workers in the UK because the threshold above which employers and employees have to contribute to the social insurance scheme is higher than in many EC countries' schemes. In addition, protective legislation giving workers rights concerning redundancy, unfair dismissal, maternity leave, statutory holidays, etc., only applies when workers are employed at least 16 hours a week which is also higher than in many other EC countries. (The Social Charter proposes a threshold of 8 hours for both social security membership and for protective legislation.)

6.5   Conclusion

The way in which employers use their employees and the willingness of workers to take up certain jobs are not only affected by the changes in the nature of the jobs on offer but also by the structure of the social security system. The extent to which part-time employees are cheaper to employers depends to some extent on whether or not they are included in any state or occupational social security scheme. This varies over time within one country and varies between countries within the EC. A social security system can work either to increase or to decrease the marginalisation of certain groups of workers. The EC draft directives on part-time or atypical work proposed that such workers should be entitled to the same state and occupational benefits as full-time workers on a pro-rata basis. The Social Charter contains similar proposals. The effect would be to decrease the marginalisation of those working less than 'full-time' however defined. However, the UK is opposed to these proposals on the grounds that it would be too costly to employers and would make UK production uncompetitive. There are echoes here of the complaints of the employers of outworkers in 1912, mentioned above. This time the UK government is listening to them and as long as it does so, the social security system will fail to meet the needs of many individuals and families.

There is no doubt that the relationship between the social security system and the structure of the labour market and of families needs a thorough re-examination. In doing so, it is important to remember that these structures are interdependent in a complex way. As Freiderike Maier concluded in an international comparison of part-time work and social security provision:

> instead of being taken for granted as a norm, full-time work needs to be treated as problematic; a more general process of overall working time reductions would provide a mechanism for breaking down the distinction between full-time and part-time work which is so overlaid with gender and the domestic division of labour. Working time, social and employment policies that do not consider the gender specific labour market situation will otherwise be in danger of keeping women in a position described as 'living on half rations'. (Maier, 1991, p. 10)

'Living on half-rations' is in part a result of clinging to the outdated concept of the male breadwinner and means for too many women and children, living with the giant Want whom, fifty years ago, Beveridge hoped to vanquish.

Chapter 7

Dependency or Enterprise? Social security and self-employment[1]

Tony Eardley and Anne Corden

Many independent workers – small shopkeepers, crofters, fishermen, hawkers, outworkers – are poorer than many of those employed under contract of service and are as much dependent on good health for their earnings. (Beveridge, 1942, para. 118)

7.1   Introduction

One striking feature of change in the British labour market during the 1980s was the rise in self-employment. The rate of increase – some 75 per cent between 1979 and 1990 – was surprising given that self-employment had previously been in decline as a form of economic activity. How are these new self-employed different from traditional groups of independent workers and are many still relatively poor?

The above observation from the Beveridge Report, that self-employed people could be poorer than wage-earners, was used to justify including self-employed people within compulsory social insurance. Beveridge did not see the lack of an employment contract as a reason to exclude people from collective, contributory protection, particularly where without such protection they and their families might face Want. Yet the self-employed have historically had an ambiguous relationship with the social security system in Britain. Since the 1940s they have been in the mainstream of state social security arrangements –

1   The paper draws on research carried out at the Social Policy Research Unit as part of a programme of work commissioned by the Department of Social Security. Any views expressed are those of the authors and not necessarily those of the Department.

116

in contrast to many other European countries where the independent status of the self-employed has often been reflected in the development of parallel, occupationally-based insurance systems. On the other hand, successive governments have continued to regard the self-employed as primarily responsible for their own financial security. They are given various fiscal incentives to make private financial provision, but are excluded from some of the more important areas of social insurance.

There is evidence that many recent entrants to self-employment are by no means affluent and cannot always guarantee financial security for themselves and their dependants purely through their own enterprise. Consequently, more are coming to rely on means-tested state benefits.

This chapter examines the recent growth of self-employment and considers whether the picture is primarily one of continuity or change. We then review briefly the limited evidence on incomes of self-employed people and look at the development of policy for their social protection, in the realm of both social insurance and means-tested benefits. One aspect of particular interest is the measurement of self-employed earnings for means-tested benefits, and this is explored in some detail.

7.2   The Resurgence of Self-employment in Britain

The dimensions of growth in self-employment in the 1980s are now fairly familiar. One and a half million more people were self-employed in Great Britain by 1990 than when the Conservatives took office in 1979, bringing the total to 3.44 million or 13 per cent of the work force (DE, 1991a). This increase was unmatched by any other European or OECD country: between 1979 and 1989 non-agricultural self-employment in the UK grew by more than three times the average rate for the EC as a whole (OECD, 1991c). Moreover, the sharp rise in the 1980s followed a long period of stagnation: between 1949 and 1979 the numbers of self-employed fluctuated between 1.8 and 2.0 million (Institute for Employment Research, 1987).

It is not yet clear how the new self-employment will survive the economic climate of the 1990s. Curran (1990) argued that the 1990s would be less favourable to small business, a prediction which has so far been accurate. In 1990/1991 self-employment dropped for the first year since 1979 and has continued falling since then. By Spring 1992 it had dropped by 310,000, or nine per cent from its 1990 peak (DE, 1992b).

It is also unclear what the resurgence of self-employment represents. Research has identified important distinctions to be made in patterns of self-employment, including by gender and ethnicity, between those entering self-employment by different routes, and in the divergent conditions of work experienced in different sectors. There is some consensus that self-employment as a form of employment status is becoming more heterogeneous. Substantial increases have taken place in homeworking, sub-contracting, franchising and other forms of what has been called 'quasi self-employment' (Casey and Creigh, 1988) or 'disguised employment' (Rainbird, 1991). Here people's legal status may be that of self-employment, but actual work situations, levels of autonomy and control, and methods of remuneration may differ little from those of employees (Dale, 1986; Hakim, 1987) and may bring inferior legal protection (Hepple, 1986; Leighton, 1983, 1986).

It should not necessarily be assumed, however, that all such work is marginal or enforced. Opportunities offered by technological change have led to considerable growth in sub-contracting and self-employment of a skilled and professional nature, such as 'teleworking'. Nevertheless, the overall picture is one of instability: fluctuating flows of people coming into self-employment each year are offset by a large and steady stream of people giving up, with around a third returning to unemployment (Daly, 1991). Most self-employed people work on their own or with help only from family members. Much of the growth has been concentrated among providers of small-scale services or retail outlets in sectors characterised by high rates of business failure and low levels of earnings. These new self-employed seem often to be motivated in part by aspirations towards independence and self-reliance traditionally found among the small business-owning *petite bourgeoisie* (Lee, 1985; Hakim, 1989b; Leece, 1990; MacDonald and Coffield, 1990). Nevertheless, for many in the 1980s the alternative was unemployment.

The link between unemployment and self-employment is one of a number of unresolved questions in the debate over the growth of self-employment. There is no single explanation for the resurgence of this kind of work: self-employment rates in different countries appear to depend on the interacting combinations of different factors on both the demand and supply sides. It has been suggested, for example, that periods of economic recession can encourage the growth of self-employment as unemployed people seek alternative strategies for work (Steinmetz and Wright, 1989; Bogenhold and Staber, 1991), though attempts to derive macro-economic models of the relationship have not been particularly successful (Meager, 1992). There is also an argument that opportunities for self-employment are greater (and risks are smaller) in periods of expansion (Campbell and Daly, 1992). Overall it appears that both these economic cycles can foster certain kinds of self-employment if other conditions are favourable. The 1980s in Britain saw periods of both high unemployment and economic boom, and a restructuring of industry from manufacturing towards a burgeoning services sector (Pollert, 1988). This favours the growth of self-employment since the service sector offers the greatest opportunities for individuals to try working on their own. There is also some evidence that employers have specifically encouraged the substitution of employee jobs with 'flexible' work arrangements through subcontracting, franchising and other forms of self-employment (Atkinson, 1985; Hakim, 1985, 1987; Fevre, 1987, 1991; Wood and Smith, 1989), though Pollert (1991) and others have disputed whether such practices represent a significantly new development.

A further factor has been the promotion by government of an 'enterprise culture'. Curran (1990), among others, has queried the validity of this concept, arguing that its suggestion of bold entrepreneurialism misrepresents the nature of much small scale self-employment, which he characterises as cautious and conservative. Nevertheless, the notion of 'enterprise' has been persuasive ideologically in the construction of a favourable political discourse around job creation during a period of high unemployment and business failure. In practical terms it has led to the creation of financial incentives to take up self-employment, such as the enterprise allowance scheme, and other grants and concessions for small businesses.

One notable feature of the upsurge in self-employment was the involvement of women: according to labour force statistics their numbers grew proportionately by 125 per cent between 1979 and 1990, more than double the rate for men. However, this rate of growth was measured from a very small base and much of the recorded increase can be accounted for by greater participation by women in the labour force as a whole. As a share of all employment self-employment did not increase for women nearly as much as it did for men. Nevertheless self-employment for women may be seen as significantly different from that of men, because women are much more likely to be working part-time. Between 1981 and 1984, when self-employment grew most rapidly for women, four-fifths of the increase was among women working 16 hours or less per week (Casey and Creigh, 1988).

It may be misleading to rely too heavily on official statistics of women's self-employment. Women are often informally involved in small enterprises with husbands and partners, though their contributions may not always be acknowledged. Also, as Arber and Gilbert (1992) point out, certain forms of self-employment, including child-minding, outworking and home production, lie on a continuum of economic activity between waged work and unpaid domestic labour, which can blur women's relationship with the formal labour market. The invisibility of this work is one reason why the involvement of women in self-employment may tend to be underestimated (Allen and Truman, 1992).

As more has become known about the new self-employment of the 1980s, policy and research interest has begun to focus on the interaction between self-employment and social security (Lynes, 1988, 1989; Eardley, 1991; Luckhaus and Dickens, 1991; Brown, 1992b). Qualitative studies have suggested that activity carried out within the framework of 'self-employment' is often closely associated with other forms of so-called 'atypical' work and with activity labelled as part of the informal or 'hidden' economy (Pahl and Wallace, 1985; Jordan et al., 1992). The gender dimension has already been mentioned, but more broadly the fluidity of the concept of self-employed work tends to cut across the boundaries commonly used to define economic activity. This is one reason why data on self-employed incomes is often regarded as misleading.

7.3   The Incomes of Self-employed People

The economic position of self-employed people remains poorly understood. Household surveys and Inland Revenue data suggest a bimodal distribution of incomes, with clusters at both ends of the scale. A substantial proportion of incomes falls below the threshold for national insurance contributions (Hakim, 1989a). These data, however, are often disregarded because it is widely assumed that self-employed people under-report their income, both for tax and household surveys. Estimates of the informal economy also frequently highlight self-employed people as the main participants (Smith, 1986; Pissarides and Weber, 1989), though the empirical evidence to support these assumptions is inconclusive. Such studies are mainly based on apparent shortfalls in the national accounts (for example, MacAffee, 1980; Smith, 1981), or on discrepancies in household survey microdata between reported incomes and expenditure (Dilnot and Morris, 1981; Pissarides and Weber, 1989). Their estimates of informal economic activity vary enormously and the methodologies of both strands have been subject to criticisms (Brown, 1988; Thomas, 1988; Hakim, 1989a; Harding and Jenkins, 1989). The technical problems of self-employed earnings data in household surveys were one of the issues discussed in the DSS's recent review of its Households Below Average Income (HBAI) data (DSS, 1991).

Our own interviews with self-employed people detected scope for inaccurate reporting of income, partly because earnings and expenses are often haphazardly recorded. Inaccuracies can also arise from the way surveys ask income questions and from problems in gathering up-to-date estimates. There is some evidence suggesting that where marginal self-employed activity takes place alongside receipt of income support or unemployment benefit, concealment of earnings may be widespread (Jordan et al., 1992). Nevertheless, empirical research has failed as yet to provide much useful information about the level of under-reporting and what kinds of activity are most commonly involved, beyond conventional reference to subcontracting and the 'lump'.

In the absence of such information we are forced to rely on existing data, albeit with some qualifications. In fact the various sources are reasonably consistent. According to the 1989 Family Expenditure Survey (Central Statistical Office, 1990b), households with a self-employed head had incomes 52 per cent higher than the average for all households. However, self-employed incomes are also distributed across a wide range: nearly two-fifths had gross weekly household incomes of less than £275, compared with only a quarter of employees. Seven per cent of self-employed households had weekly incomes of under £100, as against less than half of one per cent of employees. At the other end of the scale, nearly 11 per cent of self-employed households had weekly incomes of £750 or more, compared to 6 per cent of employees. The 1988 General Household Survey gives a broadly similar picture, with the self-employed as a whole having higher mean incomes than employees, but those without employees, particularly women, falling below the employee mean (Office of Population Censuses and Surveys, 1990a).

Inland Revenue data, drawn from a census of taxable incomes rather than sample surveys, are less vulnerable to problems of small samples or variations in response rates (though not necessarily to concealment of income). They are based on individual not household incomes, but they support the picture of a bimodal earnings distribution. More than two-fifths of individual gross incomes from self-employment assessed for taxation in 1988/89 (nearly 1.5 million people) were less than £5,000 and three-fifths were below £7,500 (Board of Inland Revenue, 1991). Some people with self-employed earnings also had other sources of income, but total incomes for all those with self-employed earnings below £5,000 still averaged less than £6,000.

The official Households Below Average Income statistics, based on the FES, have also highlighted the low incomes of the self-employed. In 1988/89 they comprised 27 per cent of the bottom 5 per cent of incomes, mainly because of an increase in reporting of zero or negative earnings (DSS, 1992c). The accompanying DSS press release points out that household expenditure of those reporting nil incomes was above the average for the population as a whole, suggesting that: 'Their low reported incomes do not imply low living standards' (DSS, 1992e). This may be the case, but it does not entirely dispel the picture of an employment sector where earnings are fragile and vulnerable to market forces.

Other evidence of low earnings among people entering self-employment comes from evaluations of the enterprise allowance. Between 1982/83 and 1990/91 some 566,000 people started small enterprises with help from the scheme (DE, 1991b). In 1985 the median gross weekly profit figure for all the businesses surviving one year after the ending of enterprise allowance payments was £100 (Allen and Hunn, 1985). Participants were all previously unemployed so might expect to make relatively low profits, at least in the early years. Nevertheless these findings support the broad picture of a substantial low income sector within self-employment.

7.4   Social Security for the Self-employed

We have suggested that many people entering self-employment in the 1980s were not high-earning entrepreneurs. Some may differ little from employees in their conditions of work but lack the protections which come from the full-time waged relationship. What does this mean for social security? Luckhaus and Dickens (1991) and Brown (1992b) have described how independent workers were largely excluded from the nascent social insurance systems which developed in the early years of the twentieth century. These social insurance schemes were founded on the tripartite system of contributions from employers, the state and the employee. Without an employer as the other party to a contract of service, the self-employed could not easily be incorporated into these schemes. More fundamentally, they were also regarded as affluent and capable of private provision (Forde, 1979).

The Beveridge proposals, however, while continuing to adhere to the tripartite principle of insurance funding, ended the exclusion of those in paid work but not under a contract of service. Beveridge's advisers were clearly familiar with the situations of low income self-employed people: the Report begins by stating categorically that 'Many persons working on their own account are poorer and more in need of state insurance than employees' (Beveridge, 1942, para. 4). This recognition brought independent workers into the mainstream of social security protection in the UK for the first time.

Since Beveridge, self-employed people have remained within the same contributory national insurance scheme as employees, but the structure now provides for different contributions and different entitlements. Self-employed people pay flat-rate Class II contributions, and Class IV profit-related contributions on a band of income above and below specified thresholds. They are not entitled to unemployment benefit (apart from share fishermen), or to earnings-related additions to the basic state pension under the State Earnings-Related Pension Scheme (SERPS), both of which require Class I contributions.

Another area identified by Brown (1992b) where the self-employed are relatively disadvantaged is that of sickness and occupational injury. Self-employed people are not entitled to the industrial disablement benefit or to the earnings-related addition to invalidity benefit, although agriculture and construction – two sectors where industrial injuries are relatively common – have high concentrations of self-employed people, often working alongside employees under similar safety conditions

(Industrial Injuries Advisory Council, 1991). Since self-employed people have no employers they cannot receive statutory sick pay, which is paid through employers and based on previous wages or salaries. Instead they are entitled to the lower-rated sickness benefit. Our interviews with self-employed people suggest that the difficulties of replacing lost earnings and of finding people to take over businesses during periods of ill-health mean that they often continue working when sick.

SERPS is one of the major innovations in social insurance since Beveridge and it has been argued that the self-employed have been particularly disadvantaged by not having access to it. Many employees have the possibility of an occupational pension as an alternative, but by definition self-employed people have no access to employer-based schemes (unless they have acquired entitlement through earlier periods of employment). The Government's position has been that national insurance contributions paid by the self-employed tend to be proportionately lower than those of employees. The primary responsibility thus lies with self-employed people themselves to make personal provision for retirement or sickness through private insurance (DHSS, 1980). To this end tax concessions have been granted which recognise and assist self-employed people's personal financial responsibilities.

Private pensions may have a number of disadvantages compared with SERPS and occupational pensions, including higher premia and administrative costs, and returns dependent on the fluctuations of investment markets rather than final or best earnings (Brown, 1990b). To what extent self-employed people actually subscribe to private pensions and insurance is not at all clear. Few had private pensions in the early 1980s (House of Commons Social Services Committee, 1982; Legal and General, 1984) and by 1988 only 36 per cent of self-employed people were claiming tax relief for retirement annuities (Inland Revenue, 1992). The Government introduced enhanced tax incentives for private schemes in 1988 and by 1992 an estimated 4.6 million employees had contracted out into approved private plans (DSS, 1992a). Published data do not indicate how far coverage has spread among the self-employed, however, and the Inland Revenue has been unable to supply any detailed information.

Many lower income self-employed families are clearly not protected for retirement in this way. Secondary analysis of administrative statistics on family credit recipients found that only 17 per cent of families with self-employed earners were making any pension contributions in April 1991 (Eardley and Hutton, 1992). In 1988 the DSS estimated that around a third of all self-employed people were also not paying National Insurance contributions, either because of low earnings or through default or late payments (Brown, 1992b). Even taking into account entitlements to state or occupational pensions accrued through periods of paid employment, and the possibility for some of selling businesses with capital assets, it seems likely that many self-employed people and their spouses may reach retirement without pension incomes sufficient to keep them above the level of means-tested benefits.

But it is not only in retirement that self-employed people have to resort to means-tested benefits. In the event of unemployment income support may be the only help available since they cannot claim unemployment benefit. Growing numbers, mainly those with children, are claiming in-work means-tested benefits like family credit.

7.5   Means-tested Benefits

Contrary to Beveridge's vision, a combination of policy and demographic change has led to a rise in the relative importance of means-tested benefits within the UK social security system (see Webb's chapter in this volume). Treasury figures analysed by Barr and Coulter (1990) show that expenditure on means-tested benefits rose by 171 per cent in real terms between 1979 and 1989, compared with a 14 per cent rise for contributory and other non-contributory benefits combined.

Consequently, while much of the development in social security since Beveridge has passed self-employed people by, one of the few areas where there has been expansion in provision has been in the field of means-tested benefits. The Beveridge scheme included self-employed people within national assistance and they have continued to be entitled to subsequent schemes – supplementary benefit and income support. They were also covered by the major innovations in means-testing of the 1970–74 Conservative government, including rent and rate rebates, and family income supplement. Since then self-employed people have continued to be eligible for the in-work benefits – family credit, housing benefit and community charge benefit – which replaced their predecessors following the 1988 social security reforms. The most recent extension to the range of in-work means-tested benefits was the disability working allowance, introduced in April 1992, in which self-employment was anticipated by the Government as a likely growth area.

Whatever view is taken on the extension of means-testing in general, it might be expected that these benefits could be particularly helpful to low income self-employed people. As well as being low, incomes often fluctuate widely with the seasons, the agricultural cycle, or the vicissitudes of market forces – changes in demand, prices, competition and production cycles. Whereas some self-employed people may need preliminary financial security while struggling to start up a business, others need support through business decline. Means-tested benefits would seem to fill a useful role in maintaining minimum income levels and standards of living for people prepared to face the risks of enterprise, as well as an increasing number whose self-employed status is determined by employers and contractors. Possibilities of combining paid work with caring responsibilities might be increased by availability of financial support for 'flexible' or 'home' working, usually self-employment. Employment possibilities for people with disabilities or health problems might be expected to increase in a similar way. The disability working allowance is of special interest not just because it is the first benefit specifically for disabled people to be means-tested, but also because of the Government's assumption that it might prove particularly attractive to disabled people wanting to work in self-employment.

Moreover, the majority of self-employed people are middle-aged married men so we might expect the means-tested benefits, with the children's premia, to help target resources on families with children. At the same time, recent growth in women's self-employment, in combination with availability of in-work means-tested benefits, could indicate an avenue of opportunity helping some lone parents towards financial independence. This was one of the explicit motives underlying the recent reduction of qualifying weekly hours of work for family credit from 24 to 16 (DSS, 1990a). Finally, in recent years when social security policy has been increasingly concerned with management of unemployment and incentives to work, we might expect the in-work means-tested benefit schemes for self-employed people to work in tandem with promotion of job creation through the enterprise allowance, to provide opportunities to move out of unemployment.

This chapter continues by looking for evidence as to whether these expectations are being fulfilled. We consider the extent to which self-employed people claim means-tested benefits, and how well the benefits appear to be working. There are interesting conceptual issues about the measurement of earnings in adjudication of benefit applications which are shown to affect administration and delivery.

7.6   The Self-employed and Take-up of Benefits

The lack of general research on self-employed people until recently means that we know little about their use of social security. Brown (1992b) has demonstrated the deficiency in knowledge at all levels and our own review of research on self-employment (Eardley, 1991) also points more towards gaps in knowledge than towards major areas of research activity. The self-employed have been almost invisible – either included in research studies without identification as a special group, or, more often, excluded from surveys and samples altogether on the grounds that they are difficult to contact, respond poorly and provide unreliable income data (Hancock, 1988; Fry and Stark, 1993).

Access to and use of means-tested benefits by self-employed people has attracted little attention. Indeed, it has sometimes been assumed to be unproblematic. Luckhaus, for example, in discussing disadvantages faced by self-employed people in the social security system, suggested that they have 'ready access to all the means-tested benefits' (1991, p. 3). The little research which has been carried out suggests, however, that applying means tests to self-employed incomes and delivering benefits to this group is hardly unproblematic.

It is difficult to get an overall picture of the take-up of means-tested benefits by people who are (or have recently been) self-employed. One reason is that available data are not sufficiently disaggregated. Income support is available both to people who have recently ceased being self-employed and to those who work less than 16 hours a week with very low incomes. The DSS has not routinely collected data about the number of people applying for income support after leaving self-employment. It is possible to identify self-employed people among those who supplement low earnings with income support. In May 1989 some 162,000 income support claimants also had some earnings (DSS, 1990b), but very few of these had income from self-employment – only 1,200 according to Brown (1992b). This suggests that most self-employed people either work more than 16 hours weekly or have earnings and other sources of income which bring them above income support level. It is also possible that some may be unaware of their entitlement, may not wish to claim, or may have had difficulty establishing their incomes.

While more self-employed people supplement low earnings with in-work benefits than with income support, numbers in receipt are still quite small. Some 15,200 people with self-employed earnings were receiving housing benefit payments for rent in May 1990, three-fifths of whom were local authority tenants (DSS, 1992b). This does not include any who might also have been receiving income support. Such apparently low numbers are hardly surprising since the vast majority of self-employed people are owner occupiers. Most self-employed people receiving housing benefit payments for rent are likely to be families with children: a 1990 survey carried out for the National Audit Office (National Opinion Polls, 1990) found that nearly a third of self-employed family credit recipients also received housing benefit (around 15,000 in May 1990). Community charge rebates were available also to home owners and the number of individuals or couples with self-employed income receiving them in May 1990 was 36,900. While we know how many self-employed people receive means-tested benefits towards housing costs we do not know what percentage take-up this represents, since estimates of take-up for housing and community charge benefit again generally either exclude the self-employed or do not disaggregate them.

The main focus of our research on low income self-employed families has been family credit. The number of self-employed families claiming family income supplement and its replacement family credit grew more than five-fold in the 1980s and doubled as a proportion of all recipients. In April 1991 53,000 families received family credit on the basis of self-employed earnings, representing 16 per cent of all recipients (DSS, 1992b). Of special policy interest is the relatively high proportion who receive maximum levels of payment. In March 1991, 44 per cent of all self-employed families received 90 per cent or more of their maximum family credit award, compared with only 11 per cent of employed families (Eardley and Hutton, 1992). While a small element of this difference could be attributed to factors such as family composition and other sources of income, the difference lay primarily in the substantially lower earnings of the self-employed compared to employees. Does this reflect genuinely lower earnings among self-employed families, or does it result from more favourable treatment in the earnings assessment procedure, or under-reporting of income? How do apparently very low earnings among the self-employed families match their living standards? These are some of the issues addressed by the research programme.

Despite the recent increase in numbers of self-employed recipients of family credit and the relatively high value of their benefit awards, it has been suggested that take-up may be lower than among employed families (Lynes, 1988, 1989). This is difficult to test since take-up is generally calculated from FES data which deliberately excludes the self-employed because of small sample sizes and doubts about the accuracy of reported earnings (DHSS, 1989).

7.6.1 Recognition and demonstration of entitlement

Previous research on family credit and its predecessor family income supplement (FIS) suggests a number of reasons why take-up of in work benefits might be low among self-employed people. Failure to recognise eligibility may be a particular problem for self-employed people, who are used to being ineligible for many benefits (Corden and Craig, 1991). A study of unsuccessful applicants for FIS showed that self-employed people often experienced considerable difficulties in presenting accounts or other financial data for assessment (Corden, 1987). Administrative problems in dealing with some self-employed applicants have led to considerable delays. These are partly caused by the time it takes some self-employed applicants to produce the required information for assessment, but this in itself may compound their difficulties. The National Audit Office (1991) found that 10 per cent of claims in 1989/90 took longer than 35 days to clear and a quarter of these were from self-employed people.

Some of these qualitative findings are supported by other recent research on family credit take-up using housing benefit records (Noble et al., 1992). This was carried out in only two local authorities, neither of which followed the practice operated in some areas of routinely informing claimants of their possible eligibility for family credit. Nevertheless, one of the main reasons cited for non-take-up among those potentially eligible was previous experience of unsuccessful claims or difficulties with the application process. In practice most difficulties arise in the assessment of self-employed earnings.

Delays in the application process can present special problems for people making the transition from income support. Previous research suggests that low income families may be reluctant to take risks with their incomes, especially when there is an expectation of delay in delivering a benefit (McLaughlin, 1991a; Jenkins and Millar, 1989). The 'risk' for a person contemplating moving from income support to self-employment may seem even greater, since they cannot rely on wages while waiting for an adjudication.

Self-employment has not had a high profile as a problem area in housing benefit, possibly because of the relatively few claimants. Because of individual rent levels, it is also difficult to compare the value of awards made to self-employed people and those made to employees – one of the points considered in our family credit study. Nevertheless, research by Walker et al. (1987), prior to the 1988 changes in the scheme, showed that self-employed incomes presented problems for local authorities, even though the number of cases was relatively small. Housing benefit officers had devised a range of ad hoc procedures in order to penetrate the information provided. In a recent research workshop with housing benefit officers it was clear that local authorities had developed approaches on a number of key issues that differed substantially both from those of the Family Credit Unit and from each other, despite the requirement to operate the same basic system as for family credit. Our interviews with self-employed family credit recipients found that some had experienced applying for housing benefit as much easier and quicker than family credit, as suggested by Noble et al. (1992). Others, however, had found the process so problematic that they had given up. These differences are perhaps not surprising given the known variations between administrative practices of different local authorities.

While income support may not be used extensively to supplement part-time earnings from self-employment, it can be important for those whose self-employment is intermittent, whose business fails, or who leave self-employment for some other reason. People who are or have been self-employed have to meet the same conditions of entitlement as any other claimant. Cases taken to citizens' advice bureaux (Brown, 1992b) and interviews conducted by the authors suggest that they may sometimes find it more difficult to demonstrate their entitlement: they may have problems, for example, proving that all trading has ceased or providing figures for 'final earnings'. Residual capital from a previous enterprise can also take people over the capital threshold even though they have no current earnings. Business assets must be realised, although time is allowed for sale. It is not known how many people ceasing to be self-employed apply for income support; at the time of writing, the National Audit Office was conducting research on this subject.

7.6.2 Measuring self-employed income

Underlying the practicalities of administering means-tested benefits for self-employed people are a number of interesting conceptual issues concerning the assessment of earnings to determine entitlement to social security benefits. The same issues arise in all the different benefit schemes (and, of course, have parallels within taxation policy). How they are resolved (or not) affects the various administrative approaches and techniques, and the responses of the potentially eligible population. One of the most important is equity.

The measurement of income should be such that there is equity between self-employed people in different occupations and at various stages of business development, and between self-employed people and wage earners. This raises complex questions of accountancy about different ways of measuring income (Corden, Eardley and Smellie, 1993). The measurement of employees' income is based on weekly available cash. It is possible to arrive at some similar measure of self-employed earnings, by using estimates based on cash flow (receipts less expenses) but decisions have to be made about the relevant basis period for this measurement. Many self-employed people have no receipts over long periods. Lengthening the basis period for assessment may produce a more realistic figure, but creates new problems: for example, historical business data may give an inaccurate picture of current needs and circumstances. In any case, historical business information is traditionally dealt with by accruals-based accounting practices, which measure different aspects of business activity from those measured by cash flow figures. Whatever measure is used for people established in self-employment, a scheme must also aim to provide equitable treatment for recent entrants who can provide no retrospective financial data.

Another key issue is the cost to the applicant. A means-tested scheme must give applicants opportunity to apply at minimal cost to themselves in terms of financial expense (accountants' fees, photocopying, etc.), time (earnings forgone), difficulty, and procedures experienced as intrusive. All these costs may act towards depressing take-up and reducing the effectiveness of the benefit in raising the incomes of low earning families.

While the concept of equity can be pursued at a theoretical level, by considering different types of accountancy procedures and techniques for measurement, how far it can actually be achieved will depend on administrative and operational effects. The centrally-operated postal scheme for family credit, for example, constrains interaction with applicants whose work situations and methods of record keeping vary substantially. Achieving consistency in adjudication requires well developed regulations and guidance about treatment of income, as well as sufficient discretion in the system for dealing with the wide variety of circumstances presented.

A further key requirement is speedy delivery of benefit. If family credit and housing benefit are to maintain their roles in providing incentives to start or stay in employment, they must be available immediately families become eligible. Thus the income assessment scheme has to work within quite different parameters from those, for example, of Inland Revenue, who can afford to wait for end of year statements.

On the one hand there appear to be a number of potential barriers, in claimants' expectations and in the design and delivery of benefits, limiting their usefulness for the growing ranks of lower earning self-employed. On the other hand there is a suggestion that current methods of assessing self-employed earnings may produce an unrealistic picture of money available for household expenditure and that self-employed families receiving benefits may have higher living standards than those of employed recipients, one of the issues addressed in the authors' current research programme.

7.7   Discussion

In this chapter we have discussed the resurgence of self-employment and looked at what is known about the financial position of people working as self-employed in the 1980s. Although historically self-employment is associated with entrepreneurialism, people working for themselves may be relatively disadvantaged in the British social security system, especially in relation to social insurance benefits. Moreover the heterogeneity of self-employed work makes the position for means-tested benefits particularly complex.

What we are describing is not entirely a new phenomenon. All those occupations identified by Beveridge as poorly remunerated still exist in some form and many people working in them are still amongst the lowest earners. However the picture is not just one of continuity. Changes in the labour market and the promotion of enterprise have brought whole new swathes of people into forms of insecure self-employed work where some may lose more from restricted access to social protection than they can gain from fiscal concessions available. Working independently does not necessarily free people from dependence on financial support through means-tested benefits, but the more self-employed people claim them the clearer it becomes that assessing their incomes for benefits is fraught with difficulty.

Until recently these issues have received little attention in either research or policy despite the extension of means-testing since Beveridge and the more recent growth of self-employment. According to Brown (1992b), governments have resisted such demands as there have been for change for reasons including ambivalent attitudes towards the self-employed and administrative difficulties such as perceived problems of benefit control. On the whole the self-employed themselves have rarely drawn attention to their position in social security, which may not be recognised as a high priority by people concentrating on building up a business. There may be temptation to sacrifice poorly understood future entitlements in favour of short-term cash flow by delaying or avoiding paying national insurance contributions. The self-employed have also traditionally worked long hours, often in relative isolation from others similarly occupied. For many there are no professional associations that represent their particular occupational interests and no tradition of collective representation. Even though since Beveridge's time some of the self-employed trades and professions have become more politically organised, they have rarely been united in making common demands on social security. The attitudes and values of self-employed people generally emphasise the importance of independence and autonomy. It appears that many do not expect to be entitled to benefits and are unused to the ideas and processes of claiming, or may hope to be free of the benefit system altogether. These factors may help to explain why the use and experience of benefits by self-employed people have not been prominent in the policy arena.

Experience of recession and the restructuring of the labour market seem likely to bring new occupation groups and people with different backgrounds and expectations into eligibility for means-tested benefits. For example, people who until recently were running successful and profitable businesses will be comparing social security adjudication with other processes with which they are familiar, such as the Inland Revenue, Customs and Excise, and negotiations for bank loans and mortgages. It may be these kinds of changes that will attract greater attention to the position of self-employed people in the social security system, both in terms of national insurance protection and in access to means-tested benefits.

Chapter 8

The Modernisation of the Life Course: Implications for social security and older people

Chris Phillipson

8.1 Introduction

Social policy in the 1980s and 1990s has faced a number of significant challenges in terms of divisions and inequalities operating through the life course. These developments have been variously related to the restructuring of the welfare state (Johnson, 1991); to the social implications of an ageing population (Jefferys, 1989); to the problems facing women as paid and unpaid workers (Williams, 1989; Land, 1989); and to the increasing importance of ethnicity in the production of disadvantage within society (Patel, 1990). These developments have been reinforced through the changing political economy of the labour market over the past twenty years, with the vulnerability of certain groups to prolonged unemployment, early exit from work, or consignment to low-paid employment (Offe, 1985; Kohli *et al.*, 1991).

It is these structural changes within the labour market that are addressed in this chapter, together with their implications for social policy towards older women and older men. The chapter briefly outlines, from an historical perspective, two contrasting aims within social policy. It then describes labour market changes which, it is suggested, are undermining the basis for financial arrangements for older people. These developments are then interpreted in respect of the changing shape of the life course, especially in terms of the opportunities for full-time paid employment. Finally, the chapter concludes with a review of policy alternatives, with particular attention to social and financial issues.

8.2   Social Policy and Full Employment

Post-Beveridge social policy has operated within a framework with two potentially conflicting sets of aims and assumptions. One has concerned the role of social insurance in relieving groups such as the old, the sick and the unemployed, from the pressure of having to compete for paid employment (Korpi, 1989). Social insurance, from this vantage point, has been seen as essential in ensuring that people maintain their dignity and status as citizens despite the loss of the various rewards associated with paid employment. Accompanying this perspective, however, has been a view that activities outside paid employment are of a secondary nature, resulting in an increase in social as well as economic dependency, both for the individual and for the community at large. There has been a sense of hostility to those outside the labour market, or at the very least, a view that it is only through paid employment that people can gain a full measure of self-esteem and purpose (Beveridge, 1944b).

The importance of work in the marketplace was discussed by T. H. Marshall (1963) in his essay 'Citizenship and Social Class', where he reviewed the changing balance of rights and duties attached to each citizen. One of his concerns was how, given full employment, society revives the personal obligation to work. For Marshall, the commitment to work (and by this it is clear he means work as paid employment) is an essential part of being a 'good citizen'. But the issue is not simply one of having a job, something which is relatively easy to secure, according to Marshall, in a situation of full employment. The real test is seen to be the willingness of the individual to: '... put [their] heart into [their] job and [to] work hard' (Marshall, 1963, p. 124). Marshall went on to argue that in terms of reviving a clear concept of the duties of citizenship, society might turn to the more limited loyalties towards the local community and especially the working group. He suggested that: 'In this latter form, industrial citizenship, devolving its obligations down to the basic units of production, might supply some of the vigour that citizenship in general appears to lack' (Marshall, 1963, p. 124).

The benefits to individual welfare arising from participation in productive employment had already been identified in the Beveridge Report (1942). In his report, Beveridge gave particular emphasis to the value of work in respect of personal fulfilment:

> ... income security which is all that can be given by social insurance is so inadequate a provision for human happiness that to put it forward by itself as a sole or principal measure of reconstruction hardly seems worth doing. It should be accompanied by an announced determination to use the powers of the State to whatever extent may prove necessary to ensure for all, not indeed absolute continuity of work, but a reasonable chance of productive employment. (Beveridge, 1942, p. 163)

Beveridge's view has to be set against the wider policy objective of preventing mass unemployment as set out in the 1944 *Employment Policy* White Paper. In theory, this committed future governments, through the exercise of Keynsian economic policies, to maintain full employment. The practice however was somewhat different. According to Rodney Lowe:

> [The White Paper] did, admittedly, commit future governments to an aggregate view of, and more positive intervention, in the economy. Apart from that, however, it was both vague and contradictory. At a late stage in drafting, the phrase 'high and stable level of employment' was substituted for 'full employment' and deliberately left unquantified. It was also deliberately elusive on what many have seen to be the key Keynsian remedy for unemployment: deficit finance. Moreover, very few practical policies were proposed other than the varying of insurance contributions to regulate aggregate demand – and that policy ironically was never implemented. (Lowe, 1992)

But the symbolism of the commitment – to prevent mass unemployment – was to exert an important influence in debates on social policy. Thus, even if the possibility of full employment broke down – especially from the late 1960s onwards – the idea that it was a desirable goal seemed difficult to dispute (Sinfield, 1981; Showler and Sinfield, 1981). The arguments for and against the policy are not in contention in this paper. What is of concern is the persistence of the view that work in the market place is both a defining characteristic of citizenship and the major (or indeed the only) source of independence.

8.2.1   Paid employment and the welfare state

The significance of paid employment has been emphasised in a wide range of perspectives on the welfare state (Land, 1989). For example, the importance of the independence arising from waged work, in contrast with what is seen as the dependence created by the welfare state, has been a persistent theme of new right perspectives (Glennerster and Midgley, 1991). However, as Hilary Land points out: 'Those on the left make similar assumptions about the locus of productive work and hence the source of an individual's independence' (Land, 1989, p. 142).   One example which she cites is the theory of the 'structured dependency' of older people developed by Peter Townsend (1981) and Alan Walker (1980). An assumption in this approach is that older people, by having to retire from gainful work, are pushed into a position of heightened dependency. This is seen to arise partly because of the severe loss of income for many workers, but also because of the social and psychological deficits presumed to arise from separation from work in the market place. This argument, however, as a number of commentators have pointed out, is somewhat contentious. Paul Johnson, for example, has argued: 'There is no theoretical reason to suppose that a transition from labour market income to state benefit income induces the onset of dependency: indeed logically the reverse should happen, as individuals shift from being dependent on finding employment in the labour market, to being in receipt of an independent income guaranteed by the taxable capacity of the state' (Johnson, 1989, p. 67; see, also, Kohli, 1988).

A second argument is that there is no strong evidence that paid employment necessarily provides the kind of social benefits with which it is associated. Indeed, as Land suggests, dependence on a guaranteed pension, even if modest, may well be preferable to dependence on the vagaries of the labour market and an exploitative employer. Galbraith's analysis is especially relevant here:

> There is no greater modern illusion, even fraud, than the use of the single term *work* to cover what for some is ... dreary, painful, socially demeaning and what for others is enjoyable, socially reputable and economically rewarding. Those who spend pleasant, well-compensated days say with emphasis that they have been 'hard at work', thereby suppressing the notion that they are a favoured class. They are, of course, allowed to say that they enjoy their work, but it is presumed that such enjoyment is shared by any *good* worker. In a brief moment of truth, we speak, when sentencing criminals, of years of 'hard labour'. Otherwise we place a common gloss over what is agreeable and what, to a greater or lesser extent, is endured or suffered. (Galbraith, 1992, p. 14)

But whichever view is adopted about the nature of work, the reality of the late twentieth century (and for the foreseeable future) is a continuing decline in the relevance of paid employment for defined groups in society. Kohli and Rein (1991) summarise these changes in the following way:

> The period spent in gainful work is shrinking, with an early exit at the upper end and the extension of schooling at the lower end of the work life contributing to this outcome from both directions. The period spent in retirement is also expanding in both directions as a result of early exit at the lower end and increasing life expectancy at the upper end. Thus, what has been the 'normal life course' is being massively reorganised, and the relations between age groups and generations are being redefined. (Kohli and Rein, 1991, p. 1)

At the same time, it is clear that the social policy implications of labour market changes have received limited acknowledgment in terms of arrangements for pensions and social security. Before discussing some of the implications arising from these developments, the main trends in respect of labour force participation will be reviewed, particularly as applied to older men and women workers.

8.3   The Decline of Labour Force Participation

Although economic activity rates of older workers have been falling throughout this century, this was not viewed as either a permanent or indeed desirable trend when the Beveridge Report was being discussed. The Second World War had itself led to an increase in employment for older workers: by the end of the war, 750 000 pensioners were in work and nearly 300 000 had returned to the labour force after having retired (Brown, 1990b). Beveridge himself was influenced by concerns about the likely pressures arising from demographic change, and the consequent need, as he saw it, to encourage people to stay on at work after retirement age, as a means of saving on pension costs. He made it clear that 'early retirement of men on pension is not wanted or useful as a cure for unemployment' (cited in Brown, 1990b, p. 143). While it was not considered feasible to raise the pension age – because the individual capacity to work was seen to vary so much – incentives could be offered for those over pension age to stay in the labour force as long as work was available to them. The retirement pension itself would be paid only to those who had retired from work. Those who worked on could pay National Insurance contributions and could as a result earn a higher pension.

In the immediate post-war period the approach taken by Beveridge was echoed in reports such those from the Royal Commission on Population (1949) and the Phillips Report (1954), both of these stressing the financial costs associated with an ageing population and, in the case of the Phillips Report, recommending the raising of the retirement age to 67.

The assumption that economic activity would continue at a high rate amongst older workers underpinned policy debates in the post-war period. Indeed, even up to the mid-1960s, the then Ministry of Labour was projecting that, based on trends up to 1965, economic activity rates for older men and women would remain stable over the period 1966 to 1981. The expectation was that economic activity rates for men would continue exactly as they were, at 98 per cent for men aged 50–54, 96 per cent for 55–59, and 90 per cent for 60–64 year olds. A slight dip, from 38 per cent in 1966 to 30.5 per cent in 1981, was envisaged for those 65 and over. For women the rates were seen as holding steady for those not married, at 62 per cent for 55–59 year-olds and 29 per cent for 60–64 year olds, and increasing for married women, from 39 per cent to 52 per cent and 21 per cent to 26 per cent for the respective age groups (cited in Schuller, 1989).

These projections were, of course, well wide of the mark – especially in respect of the male workforce. Table 8.1 examines the changes in the position of older men during the 1970s and 1980s. This confirms the steep fall in economic activity for men aged 60–64, especially in the 10 years from 1976–1986 (a drop of 27 percentage points). The change for men aged 55–59 was also highly significant, showing a decline of 11 percentage points. By the end of the 1980s, only around 50 per cent of men aged 60–64 would be counted as economically active.

Table 8.1 Percentage of Each Age Group Economically Active (men; estimates)

	45–54	55–59	60–64	65–69	70+
1971	97.6	95.3	86.6	30.6	11.0
1972	95.8	93.0	82.7	29.3	10.3
1973	96.0	93.0	82.6	28.2	9.6
1974	96.1	93.0	82.4	27.0	9.0
1975	96.2	93.0	82.3	25.9	8.3
1976	96.1	92.4	80.4	23.9	8.0
1977	96.0	91.8	75.8	19.4	6.8
1978	95.7	91.3	75.8	19.4	6.8
1979	95.4	90.8	73.0	16.8	6.1
1980	95.1	90.1	71.2	16.6	6.3
1981	94.8	89.4	69.3	16.3	6.5
1982	94.0	86.8	64.3	14.8	5.9
1983	93.1	84.1	59.4	13.3	5.3
1984	92.6	82.1	56.7	13.6	5.5
1985	92.4	82.2	55.4	14.4	5.2
1986	91.8	81.1	53.8	13.2	4.7
1987	91.0	79.4	55.2	13.3	4.6
1988	91.3	80.3	54.9	12.2	5.4
1989	91.7	79.8	54.6	14.6	5.5
1990	91.5	81.0	54.4	14.4	5.2

Source: Department of Employment, *Employment Gazette*, May 1987; April 1992.

The trends amongst older women are more complex to assess because of inadequacies in manpower statistics: in particular, the failure of many women to register as unemployed or the omission of part-time workers (the majority of whom are women) from some labour statistics (Dex and Phillipson, 1986). The official statistics (see Table 8.2) for the 1970s and 1980s indicate a marked decline in the percentage of women aged 60 and over who are defined as economically active. In contrast, the rates for women aged 55–59 fluctuated between 51 per cent and 56 per cent throughout this period and for women aged 45–54 there was a gradual rise in economic activity. Although the employment situation for mature women workers appears more stable than is the case for men, this is mainly because the decline in older women's activity rates has been masked by the tendency for each succeeding generation of women to have a higher activity rate than its predecessor. Trinder, Hulme and

McCarthy (1992) note that this effect is brought out in a comparison of the number in employment of 55–59 year-old women in 1984 with that for the same cohorts who were 50–54 in 1979. This shows a drop in employment of 23 per cent.

Table 8.2 Percentage of Each Age Group Economically Active (women; estimates)

	45–54	55–59	60–64	65+
1971	60.6	51.1	28.2	6.4
1972	63.2	51.1	28.8	6.0
1973	64.8	51.4	28.7	5.6
1974	66.0	51.9	28.7	5.3
1975	66.3	52.4	28.6	4.9
1976	66.5	54.3	26.9	4.7
1977	66.7	56.1	25.2	4.4
1978	66.9	55.0	23.3	3.9
1979	67.0	53.8	21.5	3.4
1980	67.6	53.6	22.4	3.6
1981	68.0	53.4	23.3	3,7
1982	68.1	52.0	21.9	3.5
1983	68.1	50.6	20.5	3.2
1984	69.2	51.1	21.3	3.0
1985	69.5	52.1	18.9	3.0
1986	70.5	51.8	19.1	2.7
1987	70.8	53.0	19.2	2.7
1988	70.5	52.7	19.9	2.8
1989	72.2	54.3	22.9	22.7
1990	72.8	54.9	22.7	3.3

Source: Department of Employment, *Employment Gazette*, May 1987; April 1992.

Taking both men and women, the evidence suggests that the marginalisation of older employees gathered pace from the 1970s onwards. This arose through, first, their concentration, in many cases, in contracting industries; secondly, the operation of particular schemes to promote worker redeployment (e.g., the Redundancy Payments Act) or replacement (the Job Release Scheme); thirdly, the pressure of mass unemployment; fourthly, changing attitudes amongst government, business, trades unions and older people themselves, in respect of the older workers' right to employment in relation to other, younger age groups (Bytheway, 1986).

There is some evidence that in the move out of recession around the mid-1980s, there were increased opportunities for individuals either to delay their retirement or to find employment after they had left their main work career (Bone *et al.*, 1992). However, the rise of unemployment (and especially long-term unemployment) in the early 1990s, is likely to have produced further restrictions on the job opportunities available to older workers.

At the same time, for those who remain in work there has been the emergence of greater flexibility in patterns of employment (Brown, 1990; McGregor and Sproull, 1992). In part, this reflects a marked change over the past 10 years in the nature of the labour market for older workers, with the increasing importance of the self-employed, part-time workers and mature women workers (see Blackwell, Chapter Five in this volume). Across the British labour market as a whole there has been an increase in the proportion of people in 'non-standard' forms of employment, with a significant increase in self-employment both in the total workforce and amongst workers 60 and over (Casey and Laczko, 1991; Hewitt 1993). A higher proportion of the labour force in self-employment implies that more people approaching retirement age will not face retirement at a fixed age. Traditionally, the self-employed are more likely to work beyond state pensionable age: first, because they can adjust their hours of work more easily; secondly, for financial reasons (they are unlikely to have index-linked pensions). A higher proportion of older workers in part-time work also suggests more flexibility, with more people likely to combine elements of work and retirement.

8.3.1 The transition to retirement

Trends in labour force participation have produced significant changes to the institution of retirement. Retirement (defined in terms of entry into a public old-age pension scheme) and withdrawal or 'exit' from the workforce, no longer coincide for increasing numbers of workers (Kohli and Rein, 1991). Thus it is misleading to view the fall in male participation rates simply as part of a trend toward earlier retirement. Retirement, as it is traditionally defined, is seen to come at a predictable point, accompanied (for most men at least) by a pension provided by the state (Laczko and Phillipson, 1991a). In contrast, the retirement which emerged – in many industrialised countries – from the 1970s, did not come at the traditional stage in the life course. Moreover, many people who are generally considered to be retired do not receive a public pension and may not even consider themselves retired.

These developments reflect the emergence of a new phase in the history of retirement. In general terms we can distinguish between, first, the gradual consolidation of retirement from 1950 through to the mid-1960s; second, the acceleration of early exit and completion cessation of work after 60/65 in the period after 1970. The contrast between these periods is important to establish: in 1951 to 1960 the annualised labour force participation rate for 65–69 year old men was 50 per cent; for men aged 70 plus the figure was 20 per cent. The equivalent figures for the period between 1971 to 1980 were 24 and 8 per cent, and for 1981 to 1990 were 14 and 5 per cent.

The first period can best be described in terms of a steady consolidation of retirement as a social and economic institution (Phillipson, 1978; Harper and Thane, 1989), with the growth of occupational pension entitlements (Brown, 1990b; Hannah, 1986), and the gradual acceptance of retirement as an accepted stage of life (Phillipson, 1993). Sociologically, this period can be identified as one in which retirement is viewed as a largely male phenomenon (and problem), a phase which is still subordinate in length and status to that of paid employment.

The second phase of retirement, from the mid-1960s onwards, is marked by a number of critical changes, these arising from the development of more flexible patterns of work and the emergence of high levels of unemployment. These produced what may be termed the reconstruction of middle and old age, with the identification of a 'third age' in between the period of work (the second age) and the period of physical and mental decline (the fourth age).

A characteristic feature of this new period of life is the ambiguity and flexibility of the boundaries between work at the lower end, and the period of late old age at the upper end of the life course. Both now have complex periods of transition, with the ambiguity of 'work-ending' (Schuller, 1989) in the first period, and the blurring of dependence and independence in the second (Bernard and Meade, 1993).

In the case of the retirement transition, the template of previous generations – long work, short retirement – is being dissolved (Schuller, 1989). For many (mostly male) workers, the predictability of continuous employment is being replaced by insecurity in middle and late working life – an experience shared with the majority of women workers (Itzin and Phillipson, 1993). Older workers increasingly find themselves on the margins of the labour market but with a number of years ahead of them before they reach the comparative safety of retirement. The retirement transition itself has become a period of increasing length and complexity. From the 1970s onwards there was an increase in the range of pre-retirement categories and statuses as well as an increase in the number of people entering these positions (Laczko and Phillipson, 1991a). The transition has come to be organised on a much more flexible basis with a number of different pathways (e.g. unemployment, long-term sick, redundancy) which people follow before they either describe themselves or are defined within the social security system as 'wholly retired' (Kohli et al., 1991). The result of this has been increasing uncertainty as regards the position of older workers, both in their attitudes towards leaving work and in terms of their position within society (Estes 1991).

8.3.2   Retirement and the life course

At least two interpretations may be placed upon the changes described above. One view is that they represent a fundamental break from the tripartition of the life course around one of preparation, one of 'active' work and one of retirement. In terms of the last of these, Guillemard describes the changes in the following terms:

> The retirement system has lost its central function of regulating labour force withdrawal. The other subsystems (principally unemployment compensation and disability insurance) that now do this introduce their own logic for regulating the transition from work to non-work. As a result of this replacement of retirement, the chronological milestones that used to mark the life course are no longer visible; and functional criteria have assumed importance in organising the later years of life ... The time for definitive withdrawal for the individual is no longer fixed ahead of time; it is not predictable. Since the chronological milestones of retirement are being torn up, the threefold model, which placed the individual in a foreseeable lifecourse of continuous, consecutive sequences of functions and statuses, is coming apart. (Guillemard, 1989, pp. 176–177)

Another view, however, would caution against exaggerating the extent to which the sequence of education, work and retirement, is breaking apart. The argument here is that whilst increasing numbers of workers experience an ambiguous status between work and retirement, there is nonetheless a clear transition between these institutions. Kohli and Rein argue as follows:

> Most people at age 55 and below still work, and most people at age 65 and beyond do not; most people below 55 gain most of their income from work, and most people beyond 65 gain most of their income from retirement pensions ... One can even argue that life-course segmentation has become more important in relation to other lines of segmentation such as gender. The work life has been shortened, but at the same time it has become more pervasive as regards women ... Thus the labour-market regime has become more exclusive and homogeneous in terms of gender, while at the same time it has become more exclusive and heterogeneous in life-course terms, with longer periods wholly outside of gainful work. (Kohli and Rein, 1991, p. 23)

Despite different points of emphasis, both the above arguments agree on certain key issues: first, that what Beveridge wanted to discourage (the growth of retirement) is now an inevitable feature of economic and social life; second, that the point of entry into this institution is one marked by increasing insecurity for many individuals.

On the first point we now have in place an institutionalised system of retirement which, although there may be significant developments in terms of future social policies, is unlikely to change shape substantially

(Schultz, Borowski and Crown, 1991). There may be adjustments in the process of transition into this institution (i.e. there may be withdrawal from work at earlier ages and/or exit via new types of pathways). However, all the evidence suggests that the institution itself will remain intact for the foreseeable future: if only because high levels of unemployment seem set to be a permanent feature of the economic landscape.

In addition, the evidence seems to be that most industrialised economies have resisted moves towards a radical redistribution of work and leisure across the life course (e.g. to cut paid working hours to say 20 hours per week and to have later retirement ages). The impact of economic recession in the 1980s led to the abandonment of policies such as 'flexible life scheduling' (Best, 1990). Priority issues become focused around economic and employment security, and savings and investment. In this environment, for those who remained in employment, working hours stayed the same or actually increased. In Britain, the historical trend towards a shorter working week was reversed in the 1980s, and men in Britain work longer hours than men in almost any other European country. Within the EC as a whole, two men in ten work an average 46 hours or more per week; in Britain, four in ten do so (Hewitt, 1993). These trends towards an intensification of work in the middle years have, of course, to be set against a major reduction in the amount of paid work both in the earlier and in the later years of life (Schultz, 1991).

The implications of these developments need to be analysed in both general and specific terms. At a general level, we are seeing the break-up of what Martin Kohli has described as 'work societies' (Kohli, 1988, p. 368). In such societies – the industrialised societies of the western world – work (as paid employment) has traditionally been viewed as forming the basis of the economy. From a sociological perspective, work has been seen to provide not only income and opportunities for consumption, but a broader structure of individual socialisation (Kohli, 1988) as well as access to citizenship (Marshall, 1963). Such a view has always been open to criticism, omitting as it does from consideration groups such as older people, unwaged women and children. However, such an approach has become, as Arber and Ginn (1991) suggest, even less sustainable as paid working life has itself shrunk, with the life course for men and women now being organised in equal measure around work (as paid employment) and non-paid activities (within and beyond the home). Following this, the key issue now is how to face the reality that 'being employed' is not really the normal state of affairs for the majority of people. Beveridge assumed – for men at least – that it always would be: that social–psychological as well as economic dislocations would result if this failed to be the case. The reality now is certainly very different. Offe and Heinze make this point in their study Beyond Employment. They argue:

The gap between the *imagined* reality of employment and a steady job and the experienced reality of unemployment, underemployment and precarious or irregular employment is widening, resulting in a growing contingent of marginalized, discouraged, powerless sections of the population, who are often called the 'new underclass'. But because it is supposedly 'normal' that entitlement to income can only be based on the performance of paid work (or that of family members, or at least on the preparedness to do paid work), the income situation suffers the same vicissitudes as the employment situation, save for a social minimum of public assistance. (Offe and Heinze, 1991, p. 2)

For older people, this economic transformation conceals divergent social trends. On the one side there is the redefinition for some social groups of the period of retirement, with what Giddens (1991) describes as the 'reflexive self' developing new projects and activities independently of work-based identities. Conversely, for other groups of elders, movement from the immediate workplace may impose new types of restrictions and dependencies. Carroll Estes (1979; 1991) views some of these as arising from the social relations between older people and welfare bureaucracies. The latter constitute, she argues, the 'ageing enterprise' which contributes to the socially constructed nature of dependency in old age. According to Estes:

> The dependent status of many older persons subjects them to a greater degree than younger persons to the social relations of subordination to public and private service agencies that act to reproduce capitalist culture and class relations. Analyses of class and age must be concerned with understanding how individual elders, given their unique biographies and historical moment, are made differentially dependent according to their preretirement class, gender, and racial/ethnic status. A 'differential process of devaluation' occurs based on class and gender. Working class elderly are more rapidly devalued in the labour market and in the society as a whole than are the aged of other classes. Similarly, women, whose labour is not generally considered productive, are more devalued than men in old age. (Estes, 1991, pp. 25–26)

These transformations and social processes suggest radical changes will be needed to social policy itself, especially as it has been applied to groups such as older people and to the development of pensions in particular. The final part of this paper will review some key areas for policy innovation, focusing in particular on older people and financial provision.

8.4   Policies for Old Age

The implication of this paper is that the assumption of continuous employment, as a basis for securing financial provision for old age, has been undermined over the last two decades (see Lister, Chapter Two in this volume). The corollary of this is that increasing inequalities will arise from taking the traditional male pattern of work as typical of workers now (and of women in particular) as a basis for organising pensions and other benefits in the future.

Inequalities have been reinforced by legislation such as the 1986 Social Security Act, elements of which (the emphasis on job-related personal pensions, the potential loss of rights for surviving partners, the penalising of those with low or interrupted earnings) will significantly affect the financial circumstances of older women (Arber and Ginn 1991; Bernard and Meade, 1993).

The problem – for some men and virtually all women – is how to secure financial coverage in the context of demographic change and the reorganisation of the life course. For many women there is a form of 'triple jeopardy' arising from these changes. First, the growth of a flexible workforce has been especially strong amongst women and has led to significant forms of discrimination in respect of wages and career development (Joshi, 1989a; Dex, 1987; Itzin and Phillipson, 1993). Second, rights to employment have been significantly affected by women's role as carers. A study of non-spouse carers by Glendinning (1992a) found that a quarter of the carers interviewed had to give up paid work altogether and most had already had to change jobs, reduce their hours of work or lose earnings for other reasons before finishing work completely. Third, low rates of pay have translated into deprivation in terms of limited access to pensions along with high levels of poverty in late old age (see Ginn and Arber, Chapter Thirteen in this volume).

Fourth, in the case of both men and women who leave employment ahead of state retirement age, the likelihood is that they will enter a financially insecure pathway in the transition from work to retirement. Kohli and Rein (1991) make the important point that pathways invariably make use of institutional arrangements that were originally constructed for purposes other than early exit – usually to cover specific risks that were thought to be the exception rather than the rule (such as employment or disability). They conclude that: 'Incorporating them into pathways of early exit means that they are now used to deal not with specific risks but with the burden of a whole age group. The old instruments came to be transformed into new tools for labour market regulation' (Kohli and Rein, 1991, p.13).

Financial insecurities in the retirement transition are especially acute in the case of Britain (Laczko and Phillipson, 1991b). Public provision for early exit from work are much less generous than in other parts of Europe. In the British case a higher proportion of older workers have been leaving work via long-term unemployment where benefits are much less generous than in many other EC countries. Laczko (1990) argues from his analysis that:

older workers who leave work early in the UK may run a greater risk of being poor in old age than older workers in other countries. The long-term unemployed are likely to have fewer savings and a poorer insurance contribution record. [Research suggests] that a record of long-term unemployment increases the likelihood of a pensioner being dependent on supplementary pension by a factor of almost five. [Other research] shows that there [is] a high level of income poverty among men aged 60–64 who left the labour force early, and that those who were long-term unemployed had the lowest incomes. (Laczko, 1990, p. 275)

In policy terms, the above trends suggest major changes are needed in the design of pensions and the support for workers when unemployed. In particular, the pension system of the future will need to be one which is detached from assumptions about continuous participation in paid work. Instead, such benefits should be attached to individual citizenship rights, reflecting the diversity of socially useful roles in which individuals engage throughout their lives (Bornat, Phillipson and Ward, 1985; Waerness, 1989; see also Joshi and Davies, Chapter Fourteen in this volume). The basis for such a system must be acknowledgement of the growth of different types of paid employment alongside greater flexibility in terms of the organisation of working life. There are a number of implications which follow from this. First, social security in the future will need to be based on a view of productive activities taking place in a range of locations, outside as well as inside the marketplace. This will entail giving equal value to both care work and waged work, ensuring that those who on a full- or part-time basis care for the old or the young do not suffer financial penalties in their own old age.

Second, social security will need to operate with a different view of the life course, one in which paid work is concentrated into a limited period of years, but where different forms of flexible working in terms of the entry and exit into work become more common. The issue for the future is how to ensure that flexibility within the occupational system does not translate into disadvantage in terms of benefits and financial provision for old age.

Third, we need to have immediate reforms to protect the position of older workers who are caught between the end of employment and receipt of a state pension (Laczko and Phillipson, 1991a). One possibility might be rights to indefinite unemployment benefit for men and women who have spent a specific number years in the labour force and/or care-work within the home (see Brown, 1990a, for one such example).

Fourth, reforms will also be needed to provide greater security in employment for older workers and mature women workers. The key to such a policy is to treat older workers as a human resource which can provide considerable benefits to an employing organisation. This means giving older workers and mature women workers full access to re-training, job re-design, staff development schemes, and related facilities (Itzin and Phillipson, 1993). At present, because of the combined effect of age discrimination at work and high levels of unemployment, older workers are treated as a marginal and disposable element within the workforce. This increases the likelihood of them experiencing forced early exit with the potential financial penalty of an impoverished old age (Laczko, 1990).

Fifth, the developments reviewed in this paper reflect changes in the meanings associated with periods in the life course, as well as transformations in economic and social relationships. The need to change the way pensions are provided is not simply because establishing eligibility through employment is becoming increasingly difficult to sustain, when the conditions for employment are either not met or only met on terms which are unacceptable. It also lies in the reconstruction of the meanings attached to retirement and old age. The Beveridge notion of retirement as a period of dependency has been replaced by an ideal (as yet fully experienced only by a minority) of retirement as a significant period of life, with a range of activity patterns open to individual choice (Kohli and Rein, 1991). Featherstone and Hepworth (1989) characterise this change in terms of the 'modernisation' of ageing, with the social reconstruction of middle age, this becoming more fluidly defined as 'mid-life', or the 'middle years'. Importantly, this period is increasingly defined and managed outside formal occupational roles: with the significance of caring responsibilities (for partners and elderly parents) for some; for others, the gradual emergence of new life styles built around changing patterns of consumption.

At present the financing of the diverse routes being taken out of work is only secured by those who combine high status positions within paid employment, with secure pathways out of the workforce. Viewed in this context, the challenge for social security lies in the way dependency and poverty in old age reflect problems experienced prior to retirement in middle and late working life itself: problems to do with ill-health, low income, unemployment, and the pressure of caregiving (Walker, 1989; Glendinning, 1992a). Resolving these issues will be crucial for tackling poverty amongst those already in and those reaching old age over the next fifty years.

Part III

Excluded Citizens: The civilian disabled and their carers

Chapter 9

The Growth of Disability Benefits: An international comparison

Susan Lonsdale and Jennifer Seddon

9.1 Introduction

Under the 'Beveridge model' of social insurance, disabled civilians in Britain had to rely on either short-term sickness benefit which under certain circumstances could be paid indefinitely, or social assistance. This model was adapted in 1971 when Invalidity Benefit (IVB) was introduced as an income replacement benefit for those unable to take up paid work on account of disability. Between then and now, there have been dramatic increases in both the numbers of people on IVB and in the cost of the disabilities programme. However, this is not a phenomenon peculiar to Britain. In recent years the size of the population in receipt of social security benefits for long term sickness or disability (henceforth referred to as disability benefits) has increased in virtually all OECD countries, five of which are considered here. They are countries as diverse as Australia which has a means-tested system of disability benefits, the Netherlands where disability benefits are almost universally available, Sweden which also has relatively liberal criteria for eligibility for disability benefits, and the United States and Great Britain where eligibility for disability benefits is controlled through insurance contributions and a recent employment history.

There is no clear evidence that these increases are accounted for by changes in the incidence of disability. But they are often associated with economic and demographic changes such as increases in unemployment and an ageing population. Explanations for the growth in these benefits include the effect of increasing levels of unemployment and the potential of disability pensions to provide a means of early exit from the labour market. In some countries, notably the Netherlands and Sweden, disability benefits have become an institutionalised way in which ageing

149

members of the workforce can effect an early withdrawal from the labour force as an alternative to unemployment (Kohli *et al.*, 1991).

From the perspective of the beneficiary, disability benefits often provide a better system of income maintenance than unemployment benefits. Reporting requirements are usually less onerous, and it is arguably easier (but not necessarily easy) to obtain medical certification than to prove that one is genuinely looking for employment. Disability benefits are usually perceived to be less stigmatising than unemployment benefits. They are often more generous, if not in the basic rate, then in the linked eligibility that they bring to other benefits, e.g. the rent allowance to which disability beneficiaries in Australia are entitled. They may also be non-taxable, for example invalidity pension for the under 65s in Australia, invalidity benefit in Great Britain and disability insurance in the USA.

Labour market pressures and the relative advantages of certain disability benefits have encouraged a growth in the numbers of recipients of disability benefits; all five countries have implemented, proposed or are considering measures to curb the growth.

9.2   Social Security for Long-term Sickness and Disability

Income replacement benefits for long-term sickness and disability vary in each of the countries under consideration here. Four have national insurance systems, although these differ in the comprehensiveness of their coverage. All adult residents in Sweden and the Netherlands are automatically covered by insurance. Britain and the USA, while also having compulsory insurance systems, usually cover only those with a recent and significant connection with the labour force. In contrast, Australia has only means-tested benefits.

The Dutch system of social security stands out from most others by its high replacement rates and the leniency in its eligibility rules. There are two main disability benefits known as WAO and AAW (Wet op de arbeidsongeschiktheidsverzekering and Algemene arbeids- ongeschiktheidswet). WAO benefits, introduced in 1967, are compulsory insurance benefits for employees only. AAW benefits were introduced in 1976 to extend insurance coverage to the self-employed and those who had become disabled before taking up employment. Married women were also included from 1980. WAO covers approximately three-quarters of all disability beneficiaries. WAO/AAW benefits are paid at a range of levels depending on the reduction of earning capacity.

Despite its comprehensiveness, the Swedish system of social security embodies the principle of aiming for employment rather than pensioning particularly in relation to disabled people. Consequently, there are both temporary and permanent disability pensions, although the majority of people on a temporary pension eventually move onto a regular or permanent pension. Temporary pensions increased significantly during the 1970s, especially among women and younger people (Wadensjo, 1984, p. 463). The disability pension comprises two components – a basic (AFP) and a supplementary (ATP) disability pension (Alman folkspension and Alman tjanste pension). The latter depends on the number of years worked and the level of earnings and increases the value of the pension. Four out of five men and three out of five women receive it.

The main income maintenance programmes in the case of disability in Britain are Invalidity Benefit (IVB) or Severe Disablement Allowance (SDA), with past employment history or severity of disability determining eligibility respectively. A residual form of provision also exists in the means-tested Income Support system which can be paid in its own right to disabled people or as a supplement to invalidity benefit when the latter falls below the means test level. Unlike the Dutch and Swedish benefits, they are paid at a flat rate. The basic rules of entitlement for these benefits are an incapacity to undertake paid employment due to physical or mental illness or disability which is expected to be long-term. Invalidity benefit can have up to three components: a basic pension, an allowance related to the age at which the recipient became disabled, and an earnings-related element based on previous earnings up to a maximum. A partial incapacity benefit known as the Disability Working Allowance is also available.

Programmes ensuring cash benefits in the case of disability in the USA include Disability Insurance (DI) and Supplemental Security Income (SSI) which is subject to an income and asset test. As with the British system of Income Support, SSI can be paid to disabled people in its own right or as a supplement to DI when a person's combined DI and other income meets the income requirement test. Whereas DI is designed to cover people with a recent and substantial connection with the labour force, the SSI programme is designed to give assistance to people who have had less or no labour force participation.

Australia stands out from all the countries discussed so far in that eligibility criteria for social security typically include a test of income and assets. Programmes include Sickness Benefit (SB) and Invalid Pensions (IP) which were replaced by Sickness Allowance (SA) and Disability Support Pension (DSP) in October 1991. The basic rule for entitlement to SB was a medical judgement certifying temporary incapacity for work, whereas for IP it was having a permanent incapacity for work. SA is generally limited to 12 months, at which point claimants will normally move on to DSP or a training/job search scheme.

9.3 Reasons for the Growth of Disability Benefits

In all five countries the number of beneficiaries of disability benefits has increased dramatically since 1970 as shown in Table 9.1. In the Netherlands, Sweden, the USA and Australia, the main increases occurred during the 1970s whereas in Britain they occurred in the 1980s. Although growth rates slowed during the 1980s, they still remained high, with all countries experiencing significant numbers of new beneficiaries.

The majority of recipients of the insurance based benefits and IP have been male. However, the number of female recipients of these benefits grew faster than male recipients over the two decades in all countries apart from Australia. In Sweden, women now outnumber men (see Table 9.2).

Some of the increase among women can be explained by changes in the rules governing eligibility, for example, the abolition in Britain of the rule allowing married women to opt out of national insurance, and the opening up of disability benefits to married women in 1980 in the Netherlands. In Australia, a change in 1977 allowed more married women to claim SB in their own right, leading to an increase in female SB recipients. The increase among women is also likely to be due to changing patterns of female employment and the increased participation of women in the labour force.

Table 9.1 Disability Benefit Recipients, 1970–1990 (thousands)

	Netherlands[1]		Sweden[2]	GB[3]	USA[4]		Australia[5]	
	WAO	AAW/ WAO	AFP/ ATP	IVB	DI	SSI	SB	IP
1970	205	n/a[a]	269	415[b]	1492	n/a[c]	9	134
1975	331	n/a	460	479	2489	1496	25	169
1980	496	657	503	633	2859	1538	32	229
1985	585	762	584	899	2657	1737	64	259
1990	636	883	676	1210	3011	2279	80	307
1991	652	903	690	1306	3253	2663	73	334
Percentage change 1970–80	142	n/a	87	53	92	3[d]	256	71
Percentage change 1980–90	28	34	34	91	5	48	150	34

Notes: a. AAW introduced 1976; b. IVB introduced 1971; c. SSI introduced 1974. Adults aged 18–64; d. Percentage change between 1975 and 1980.
Sources: 1. de Jong et al., 1990; Sociale Verzekeringsraad, 1992; 2. Social Insurance Statistics, Stockholm, 1992; 3. DSS, 1992d; 4. US Department of Health and Human Services (1992); 5. DSS (Australia), 1992.

Table 9.2 Disability Benefit Recipients by Sex, 1970–1990 (thousands)

	Netherlands[1] AAW[a]/WAO		Sweden[2] AFP/ATP		GB[3] IVB		USA[4] DI		Australia[5] IP	
	Men	Women	Men	Women	Men	Women	Men	Women	Men	Women
1970	n/a	n/a	156	113	334b	81	1069	424	75	59
1975	n/a	n/a	265	195	400	79	1710	778	103	66
1980	486	171	268	235	517	116	1928	930	158	71
1985	549	213	298	286	706	193	1785	872	189	70
1990	600	283	316	360	917	293	1965	1046	223	84
1991	601	302	320	370	976	330	2100	1154	245	89
Percentage change 1970–80	n/a	n/a	72	108	55	43	80	119	111	20
Percentage change 1980–90	23	65	18	53	77	153	2	12	41	18

Notes: a. AAW introduced in 1976; b. IVB introduced in 1971.
Sources: 1. Sociale Verzekeringsraad, 1992; 2. Social Insurance Statistics, Stockholm, 1970–1992; 3. DSS, 1992d (and previous years 1970–1991); 4. US Department of Health and Human Services (1992); 5. DSS (Australia), 1992.

The majority of beneficiaries tend to be older and, with the exception of the United States, the number of older beneficiaries has increased between 1980 and 1990 as illustrated in Table 9.3. In Britain, the increase has been especially high. IVB is a benefit which can be claimed five years into retirement (and is fiscally advantageous relative to the state retirement pension) and the number of recipients over retirement age has shown the greatest increase of all age groups.

Table 9.3 Percentage Change of Older Beneficiaries aged 55–64, 1980–1990 (percentages)

	Netherlands[1]	Sweden[2]	GB[3]	USA	Australia[4]
Men	9	-1	56	-17	29
Women	n/a	19	159	-11	13

Note: 1. 1979 and 1980; 2. 1980 and 1989; 3. 1979/80 and 1989/90; 4. 1985 and 1990.
Source: OECD Employment Outlook, Table 5.20.

In some cases, the overall increases reflect a growth in inflows or the number of people claiming disability benefits as in the United States. In other cases, they reflect an increase in durations or the length of time people remain in receipt of benefit as is largely the case in Britain.

Relative to other benefits, disability benefits have more liberal access and higher replacement rates. Increasing unemployment, the marginality of older workers in the labour force and a demand for higher qualifications among the workforce, interacting with illness or disability, may all have contributed to the increase in the number of disability beneficiaries. At the same time, there has been a debate over the relative contributions of medical and non-medical factors in causing work incapacity and the extent to which non-medical factors should be recognized in assessment for eligibility of disability benefits. Increases in the population of disability benefit recipients may, therefore, have been precipitated by labour market pressures and the potential of disability benefits to provide a pathway of early exit from the labour force, as well as relative advantages associated with disability benefits. This hypothesis is examined in more detail below.

9.3.1   Labour market pressures

The growth of disability benefits coincided with both an increase in unemployment and a decrease in the labour force participation rates of men and an increase in those of women. In the five countries under discussion, as in all OECD countries, the labour force participation of older men has fallen since 1970. In the Netherlands, Britain, and Australia, this trend has coincided with an increase in older age recipients of disability benefits.

Among certain groups such as older but pre-retirement workers, it is often difficult to make a distinction between pensioners and those who should still be regarded as part of the labour force. This is especially so in periods of high and growing long-term unemployment. Given the association that appears to exist between long-term unemployment and poor health, the function of disability benefits was extended in some countries to cover not only long term sickness or disability, but unemployed older workers who found it more difficult to return to employment, and who might well also have had a health problem.

In the Netherlands this occurred through a legal provision known as the *labour market consideration* in assessing eligibility for disability benefits. The Disability Insurance (WAO) Act made provision for the risk of unemployment as a result of partial disability to be taken into account in making an assessment of the degree of disability (de Vroom and Blomsma, 1991, p. 107). In assessing disability, adjudicators could take into account the difficulties a disabled person might face in finding employment. In other words, employer discrimination could legitimately be taken into account in assessing degree of disability. From 1973, the law began to be interpreted in such a way that poor employment opportunities were always assumed to result from employer discrimination, unless it could be proved otherwise. Although this liberal interpretation of the law was judged improper by the Court of Appeal, the practice of awarding a full WAO benefit to applicants with only a 15 per cent degree of disability became the norm (de Jong *et al.*, 1990, p. 66) The great majority (85 per cent) of WAO beneficiaries are judged to have the maximum disability and receive a full award, although theoretically there is provision for seven degrees of disability.

The labour market consideration is judged to have made a significant contribution to the increase in disability benefits. These can continue indefinitely, whereas unemployment benefits cannot and are, therefore, more advantageous to a recipient. Under this system, unemployment can be relatively easily judged as disability. From 1987, however, the impairment and unemployment components in assessing disability have had to be disentangled so that the benefit payable to a non-working partially disabled person consists of a mixture of disability and unemployment benefit. The level of benefit was also reduced. The effect of these changes has been smaller than anticipated and a range of new measures to curtail the growth is being debated, such as introducing more rigorous controls over entry to the benefit, and promoting greater employer responsibility towards disabled employees.

In Sweden, the scenario has been similar to the Netherlands despite the active and strong preference in Sweden for promoting employment. At the start of the 1970s a labour market consideration was introduced in assessing the eligibility of older workers for a disability pension, and medical considerations were no longer applied to people over the age of 63 (subsequently 60) who were long-term unemployed. A new requirement was introduced for a disability pension for the long-term unemployed – they had to have exhausted their unemployment insurance and be unable to support themselves in the same type of work.

This meant that all unemployed people over 60 years who had collected unemployment insurance benefits for the maximum period of 90 weeks (1 year 9 months) could take retirement. It became the practice for firms to lay people off at age 58 years and three months. They could then claim unemployment insurance until they reached 60 at which point they move on to a pension and out of the labour force. This practice (known as the 58.3 pension) seems to have been used to circumvent a law protecting the rights of older workers (Wadensjo, 1990b, p. 7). There is considerable informal evidence that the requirement for disability pensioning (of having a working capacity permanently reduced by at least a half) was enforced less strictly for workers threatened by unemployment (Bjorklund *et al.*, 1991). Criteria related to the labour market took precedence over health criteria.

The number of people aged 60–64 who retired for labour market reasons increased substantially from 5,000 in 1980 to 14,600 in 1988. The bulk of these were disability pensioners (Bjorklund *et al.*, 1991, p. 119). Until 1990, medical considerations were not part of the basic rules of entitlement for those over the age of 60 who were long-term unemployed. Since 1990, disability pensions are no longer granted for labour market reasons only. Older workers wishing to retire early are now encouraged to exit through early retirement schemes rather than disability pensions. However, the disability pension is often more generous than early retirement pensions (Wadensjo, 1984, p. 472).

In Australia implicit labour market considerations may have encouraged the growth of disability benefits. Sickness benefit (SB) was primarily but loosely based on medical assessment whereas Invalid Pension (IP) was assessed more broadly to include personal characteristics and employability as well as medical criteria. Although SB was originally developed to provide benefit for those with a temporary incapacity from employment, a study in 1983 found that more than half its recipients had transferred from unemployment benefit, special benefit, or had never been employed (Jordan, 1987, p. 4). SB appeared then to be serving the unemployed or marginally employable as well as the working population.

There was a steady transfer of about two-fifths of SB beneficiaries to IP during the 1980s, the great majority of whom were male (Nichol, 1988, p. 19). Over the same period the number of people transferring to IP from unemployment benefit also increased. This happened in two ways: directly as well as via SB. As might be expected a high proportion of all new SB grants came from unemployment benefit. Since about one half of all new IP grants in 1989/90 came from SB, the route to IP from unemployment is likely to have been via SB.

In addition to this, judgements regarding the degree of incapacity and the effects of non-medical factors upon an individual's work chances have always been open to considerable interpretation in determining eligibility for IP. During the 1980s, there was a juggling between the importance given to medical and labour market criteria culminating in a requirement in 1987 that at least 50 per cent of the incapacity for work should be directly caused by physical or mental impairment (Cass et al., 1988, pp. 21–2). Since October 1991, labour market criteria have been eliminated.

It is more difficult to assess the effect of labour market pressures in Britain and the USA. In Britain, a number of studies have looked at the interaction between the labour market and receipt of IVB in the 1980s. One fairly consistent finding is that higher rates of unemployment in the early part of the decade increased the likelihood of people remaining on or claiming IVB (Piachaud, 1986; Disney and Webb, 1990; 1991). Unemployment and poor labour market conditions may have induced certain people to withdraw from the labour market through a discouraged worker effect. One group whose numbers on IVB increased considerably during the 1980s were men in their pre-retirement years. The number of men aged 55–64 on IVB increased by 56 per cent between 1980 and 1990 (Table 9.3).

In the USA, the DI system has more rigorous entry conditions than either the Netherlands or Sweden which limits the numbers of older workers with declining work capacity qualifying for its benefits. The basic rules of entitlement to disability benefits have had a chequered career in recent times. Disability is determined by each state, but must conform to the federal government's definition of disability. This is the inability to engage in any substantial paid work due to a medically determined physical or mental impairment which can be expected either to result in death or last for more than one year. Impairment is tightly and medically defined as 'abnormalities which are demonstrable by medically acceptable clinical and laboratory diagnostic techniques' (Berkowitz, 1987) In determining disability, it is immaterial whether a specific job exists or even whether there are jobs available in someone's area and they would be hired if they applied for a job. Although advancing age may affect someone's capacity in competition with others, it will not be a factor taken into account in assessing ability to work. To do so would contradict the objectives of the Age Discrimination in Employment Act which prohibits discrimination on the basis of age.

Notwithstanding this, there was a steady increase in the number of older workers in receipt of DI during the 1970s. The number of DI beneficiaries aged 60–64 grew from 510,700 in 1970 to 964,100 in 1980. The growth was higher among women than men over this period i.e. 117 per cent and 77 per cent respectively. The numbers declined slightly thereafter. Even without the broadening of standards of assessment that had taken place in the Netherlands and Sweden, older and more marginal workers still moved onto the disability rolls rather than unemployment.

Part of the growth of disability benefits in these countries seems, then, to be related to high levels of unemployment, the marginality of older people in the labour force and the growing practice of using disability benefits as a means of alleviating labour market pressures. Once on a disability pension, other factors affecting work chances would come into play. Recipients are likely to lose contact with, and knowledge about, the labour market. Their skills may be superseded by others. Their confidence in getting a job may dwindle. Employers will pay more attention to their past history, such as medical records, especially if there is a surplus of labour. The older they are, the more likely it is for these effects to be felt. Elderly men generally make up the bulk of disability benefit recipients. The incentive for them to return to work is much weaker because of their lower likelihood of getting work and the relative financial attractiveness of disability benefits.

9.3.2 Advantages of disability benefits

People who have a reduced capacity for work may receive different levels of income maintenance from different parts of the social security system because of the interaction between medical conditions and the state of the labour market in affecting the ability to work – or because of the different weight placed on medical impairment and labour market conditions when determining eligibility. This creates inequities in the treatment of people in similar circumstances.

The level of disability benefit may directly impact on the number of programme claimants – the more generous the level of disability benefit the greater the incentive for unemployed people to prove permanent incapacity for work as they will get a better replacement income by doing so.

Disability benefits in the Netherlands have long been characterised by extreme generosity and leniency. The generosity stems from the emphasis placed on providing a social minimum income linked to a high minimum wage. The leniency of the labour market consideration has allowed partially disabled people to receive full disability benefits. As these benefits are earnings-related, this makes them extremely attractive.

Some of the factors affecting the increases in disability pensions in Sweden are to be found in a number of policy changes that took place during the 1970s which increased the level of the pension and liberalised eligibility for it. Disability pensions are paid out at three levels. In 1970, the lowest rate pension was raised, making the pension scheme more attractive to less severely disabled workers, or those who are more likely to be on the margins of unemployment rather than disability. The minimum requirement of waiting for six months before receiving a temporary pension was abolished. Most importantly, a labour market consideration was introduced in assessing older workers applying for a disability pension.

In Britain, IVB is of greater value than two other competing benefits. First, the basic rate of IVB plus the higher rate of age allowance is worth 50 per cent more than the basic rate of unemployment benefit. Secondly, it is not taxed unlike the state retirement pension. Between 1980/81 and 1989/90 the number of people receiving IVB grew by 91 per cent compared for example with only nine per cent on retirement pensions (DSS, 1991, pp. 109, 182). The greatest increase, however, has been amongst those who remain on IVB after pension age. In 1980/81, they accounted for eight per cent of people on IVB. By 1989/90, this had grown to 17 per cent. The tax-free status of IVB is likely to be important for the increasing number of pensioners with other incomes such as occupational pensions.

In the USA, during the 1970s, there was unprecedented growth in the disability insurance (DI) programme despite the strict test of disability. According to Berkowitz (1987) the sheer volume of the increase led to a decline in administrative control and a dramatic decrease in federal supervision leading to even further increases. The relative lack of control and supervision may have increased the attractiveness of this benefit.

9.4 Policy Responses to the Growth

Policy changes in Australia, the Netherlands, Britain and Sweden, suggest that a very different climate awaits disability beneficiaries and claimants in the 1990s. For some time the thrust in all five countries has been to curb growth and costs. The Dutch have abolished their labour market consideration, the Swedes their 58.3 pension. In Australia, a wide reaching package of reforms has reduced the range of non-medical factors taken into account when assessing disability, and introduced a number of rehabilitation and employment programmes for disabled people. In Britain, the introduction of Disability Working Allowance has recognised for the first time that a combination of part-time employment and partial disability benefits might be a means of promoting a more gradual return to work. The USA has introduced a system of regular reviews of existing recipients which has succeeded in moving large numbers of people off federal disability benefits such as DI. Their experience also shows, however, that the same people turn up on state welfare programmes. This suggests that removing people from disability benefits without dealing with their employment needs may simply mean that they find their way back onto another part of the social security system.

An important element of some of these reforms, especially those in the Netherlands, Sweden and Australia, has been a recognition that any policy to curb disability benefits will have little effect without a simultaneous policy to promote employment and re-entry to the labour force. The latter needs to focus not only on the work resumption efforts of individuals, but also on fostering employer responsibility towards disabled or older employees.

9.4.1 Netherlands

There were two main periods of change to the Dutch social security system. The first was in the late 1970s and early 1980s, when a series of incremental changes attempted to reduce social security expenditure. The second was in 1987 when more fundamental reforms were enacted to abolish the rule which enabled unemployed partially disabled people to claim a full disability pension. Whereas the leniency in awarding disability benefits only lessened with the 1987 changes, their generosity had already been reduced by the earlier changes. Both types of change can reduce the numbers on benefit. However, reducing the level of benefit seemed to have a greater effect than reducing eligibility.

The earlier changes were not very successful, by and large, in containing expenditure and a more fundamental review was carried out, leading to the subsequent reform. One aspect of this was to abolish inequities within the system, one of which was between the partially disabled and the long-term unemployed. After their unemployment benefits ran out, long-term unemployed people had to move on to National Assistance which was means- and asset-tested. By contrast, a mildly disabled person would be on a full disability pension with unlimited duration.

The main elements of the reform included abolishing the labour market consideration, introducing a more active labour market policy for disabled people, and introducing a new benefit for senior disabled unemployed people. The principle of the social minimum level of benefits was retained. Abolishing the labour market consideration meant no longer giving only mildly disabled people a full disability benefit. One objective of this was to try to contain the growth of disability benefits and their cost. Another was to decrease the component of unemployed people on disability benefit. Under the new rules, assessors have to make more accurate assessments of someone's capacity for work. To do this, they must ascertain how much of a claimant's unemployability is due to medical factors and how much to the state of the labour market. Disability insurance will now only cover the medical component. Unemployment insurance or national assistance will cover the labour market component.

More rehabilitative measures are to be introduced. These include measures aimed at the individual disabled person such as increasing their benefit if they accept a job paying less than their remaining earning capacity entitles them to, and maintaining existing job protection measures. However, measures have also been introduced which are aimed at employers. A new Act obliges employers to accommodate the functional limitations of disabled employees and makes provision for financial compensation to employers who do so. It also makes provision for wage subsidies in cases of lower productivity. An employment quota of 7 per cent is planned.

Older workers will be protected by a new benefit which acts as a more lenient form of National Assistance. When unemployment benefit runs out for workers who become unemployed after age 50, they can claim the new benefit which is only earnings, not wealth, tested in contrast to National Assistance.

9.4.2 Sweden

In 1969 a parliamentary commission known as the Disability Commission was set up to investigate the living conditions of disabled members of the community. It consists of representatives of the political parties, the disabled movement, and the national associations of county councils and municipalities. It has published four reports, the latest in May 1991.

The report stresses that disability is not just the property of the individual but refers to a relationship between the injury or disease and the person's environment. The objective of the commission is to overcome the exclusion many disabled people experience and to promote their full integration in society. Consequently, although some attention is paid to reforming and improving social insurance, it is within the context of many other measures to strengthen self-determination and influence. For example paying for the provision of a personal assistant to every person needing one is the responsibility of the municipality in the first instance, with social insurance only being called in once the need for such assistance exceeds 20 hours a week.

Integration is seen as less a matter of financial support from the central state, than of providing services locally such as housing, domestic and personal support, transport, legal aid, help with demanding social rights, and improving pathways to employment. Relying simply on the provision of centralised disability pensions may actually lead to even greater exclusion by their assumption that employment is no longer feasible – especially in relation to younger disabled people. Although labour market instruments such as wage subsidies and special induction opportunities are considered most important in promoting integration, it is recognised that this should not be at the expense of other provisions such as transport, housing and personal assistance which are often prerequisites to being able to take up employment opportunities.

In an attempt to counter the decline in labour force participation of older people, a Bill was passed by Parliament in 1990 abolishing the 58.3 pensions. Disability pensions can no longer be granted for labour market reasons only and used as a means of laying off older workers. The Bill also included measures to reintroduce the active labour market policy for disabled workers. People leaving a disability pension to return to work can automatically return to their pension if they leave work within five years of starting. A generous wage subsidy for employers hiring someone on a disability pension was introduced but is being repealed because it was severely under-subscribed (only 4 people were employed in this way during 1990).

The Swedish Working Life fund (arbeitslivsfonden) was also introduced in 1990 for an initial period of six years. It is financed by a special work environment charge on employers. The aims of the Fund are to bring back to work as many people taking long-term sick leave or drawing early pensions as possible. This will be done through programmes of rehabilitation, retraining, workplace adaptations, improved work environments and conditions that promote job satisfaction and personal development. The objectives of the Fund reinforce the approach of the Disability Commission, acknowledging the relationship between the work environment and injury and disease.

9.4.3   Great Britain

The most significant policy change in recent years relating to benefits for long-term disabled people was the introduction of the Disability Working Allowance (DWA) in April 1992. The basic qualifying condition for IVB is that a person must be incapable of work. Prior to the existence of DWA, the only way someone on IVB could take up employment without losing their benefit was through 'therapeutic work'. This enables someone to earn a small amount of money without losing their benefit, but only if the work has been medically certified as beneficial. This means that the activity must help recovery. If these earnings go above a certain amount, IVB will be withdrawn.

DWA is the first measure to reform the 'all-or-nothing' system and allow a more flexible combination of benefit and earnings. It allows some disabled people to take up employment without losing their benefit entitlement. Two groups of people are eligible: those on long-term incapacity benefits who wish to return to work; and those already in work and in receipt of disability living allowance. In the former case, DWA should have the effect of decreasing the numbers on IVB, SDA, and Income Support. In the latter case, it may have the effect of enabling some disabled people in employment to reduce their working hours.

The amount of DWA received is based on family circumstances and income. Restrictions on the benefit include a limit on income and capital and having to have an average working week of 16 hours. Two advantages of DWA relative to traditional disability benefits are its increased 'linking rule' and its form of assessment. If the recipient's attempt at work fails within two years, they will be able to return to their old benefit without having to go through a new application with the 28 week qualifying period. Secondly, there is now a new system of assessing disability which to a large extent is based on self-assessment confirmed by a professional involved in their care whom applicants are asked to nominate. Most claims will be determined without a medical examination, which represents a radical departure from traditional forms of assessment for disability benefits in Britain.

9.4.4   United States

The major growth in disability benefits in the US occurred during the 1970s. This led to the first major reform of the Social Security Disability Insurance programme in 1980 during the Carter administration. The reform was not uncontroversial as it lowered the amount that individuals would receive from DI and hence the replacement ratio. The review was concerned not only to prevent more growth in people coming on to the rolls but also to remove people already there – an altogether more difficult endeavour.

One of the 1980 reforms was to introduce a mandatory review of the situation of someone on DI once every three years – to ascertain if they were still disabled and if not, to remove them from DI (Berkowitz, 1987, p. 123). This requirement was to be phased in over three years. Prior to this, there had been very little by way of such reviews because it was felt that people would simply appeal the decision with a good chance of it being overturned. When the Reagan administration came to office in the same year, 1980, it began an immediate review and termination policy in the belief that over one-quarter of beneficiaries were incorrectly receiving benefit – or as Berkowitz (1987, p. 127) describes it, 'the Social Security Administration geared up for a major assault on the disability rolls' with a particular focus on younger people. However over two in five people whose benefit was terminated successfully appealed.

Terminations also put pressure on state welfare programmes because if someone was thrown off DI, they were denied SSI as well, because the determination of disability criteria were the same. They would then ultimately turn up on state welfare programmes, bringing a direct cost to states as well as an indirect one by no longer bringing in federal dollars to the state.

The 1984 reform really reformed the first reform. It introduced legal entitlement, swinging the pendulum back from removing people from DI to protecting their right to it. Disability benefits could only be terminated if there was significant evidence of medical improvement and an ability to work and the burden of proof lay with the social security administration.

Both reforms, therefore, were little more than incremental and political responses to various crises. They did not deal with the underlying problems inherent in determining disability and the powerful role that litigation now plays in disability insurance in the States.

9.4.5 Australia

The thrust of the Disability Reform Package introduced in August 1990 was to shift towards a more active emphasis on the labour market participation of people with disabilities. Preliminary projects established as part of the Social Security Review focused on barriers to employment and early rehabilitation as well as ways of improving placement and referral procedures. Clearly, the aim was to move to a more active labour market policy (DSS (Australia), 1990).

With effect from 1 October 1991, a Disability Support Pension (DSP) replaced Invalid Pension. A minimum impairment threshold of 20 per cent is required. The range of non-medical factors that can be taken into account when assessing disability has been reduced.

The concept of 85 per cent incapacity is replaced by an inability to work full-time at full wages in the foreseeable future due wholly or substantially to physical, intellectual or psychiatric impairment. People who are considered likely to benefit from rehabilitation and training or assistance will have their workforce participation rigorously assessed. They may then be placed in an 'active' category of DSP and will be required to undertake appropriate activities as a condition of their pension entitlement.

The amount of weekly income that can be earned before medical review is required will be increased. Rates of payment of the new DSP for claimants under the age of 21 will be in line with other levels of income support given to young people to abolish incentives to claim disability benefits.

Sickness Allowance (SA) will replace Sickness Benefit. Unlike its predecessor, it will normally be limited to a 12 month period, although this may be extended a further 12 months in special circumstances. At the end of the 12 month period, claimants will normally move over to DSP or a training/job search scheme.

These reforms to the benefit and pension system take place alongside a new Workforce Transition package aimed at assisting disabled people to re-enter the labour market. This package includes a range of incentives, increased training schemes, additional accommodation places in the community for the disabled, rehabilitation programs and other support programs.

9.5 Conclusion

Two features have characterised all these countries over the last two decades. One is the high value of disability benefits relative to other comparable benefits in the system. The other is the increasing use of labour market considerations in determining eligibility for disability benefits. Regardless of the type of social security system adopted or the underlying philosophy towards the rights of beneficiaries, all five countries displayed these two characteristics to varying degrees during the 1970s in particular. And all five countries over the following decade attempted to reverse the dramatic increase in disability benefits to which this led. Although most countries managed to slow down the growth, none was able to stop it.

The growth that occurred cannot be explained in terms of changes in the health of the population of these diverse countries. It is more likely to have been a consequence of changes in economic and social policy. Changes in the structure of the labour market and relatively high rates of unemployment in the second half of the 1970s made labour market conditions increasingly difficult for certain parts of the labour force such as older workers, partly disabled workers, less skilled workers, and those in industries which were restructuring and shedding labour.

Social security could be said to combine a humanitarian purpose of supporting those in need with an economic one of ensuring stability in the economy in times of recession by maintaining purchasing power and facilitating restructuring by employers. The latter purpose was especially evident in the Netherlands and Sweden during the 1970s when more liberal rules were introduced opening up eligibility for disability benefits. This made it easier for employers to lay off certain workers often with the consent of trade unions (Wadensjo, 1990a; de Jong *et al.*, 1990). It was less evident with regard to disability benefits in the United States although extensions to unemployment benefit served the same purpose (Reno and Price, 1985). The growth in Australia seems to have resulted less from deliberate policy changes as in Sweden and the Netherlands, but rather more from changes in practice such as looser interpretation of permanent incapacity (Cass *et al.*, 1988, p. 132).

Responses to the growth vary. According to Haveman *et al.* (1984) there are two main approaches in disability policy, the ameliorative and the corrective. The former tries to ensure that disabled people have access to a minimum level of income and is usually reflected in social security and social welfare policy. The latter tries to reduce or remove the effect of disability by altering the environmental milieu in which disabled people live, and is found in policies which open up avenues of access to employment, for instance.

Of the countries discussed, Australia and Sweden have adopted approaches which are more in the direction of corrective policies emphasising reintegration into the labour force and the promotion of employment. With its new disability working allowance, Britain may also be moving towards such an approach. The Netherlands and the United States seem to have adopted the more ameliorative approach, going for incremental reforms to lessen the attractiveness of disability benefits.

It is ironic that during the 1970s and 1980s when there were widespread attempts to assert the rights of disabled people including recognition of their productive capacity and their right to earn a living from paid employment, people were relegated to long-term dependency on disability benefits. It is equally ironic perhaps that a number of countries are looking to more active labour market approaches as an alternative to disability pensioning at a time when unemployment is again high and jobs scarce. The difficulty of disentangling the different factors affecting employment such as physical or mental impairment, low levels of skill, age, and employer prejudice against older and disabled workers remains, however, and may well turn out to frustrate rehabilitation policies as much as it did social security policy.

Chapter 10

The Limits of Social Insurance Protection for the Elderly in the United States: The two-class system of long-term care

Emily K. Abel

The system of social protection in the United States differs dramatically from that in most Western European welfare states. A nation which enshrines the virtues of individual responsibility and rejects the concept of 'social citizenship', the US lacks a national health plan, fails to grant the 'undeserving' poor the minimum necessary for a decent life, relies heavily on the private market, and allocates a relatively small proportion of the gross national product to social programmes. To some extent, the US treats elderly people very differently from members of other age groups. In contrast to the means-tested programmes directed toward the poor, the elderly have Social Security (for income maintenance) and Medicare (for health coverage). Both are federally-administered, social insurance programmes, with uniform eligibility standards and relatively generous benefits.

But the protections of social insurance programmes end when elderly people become disabled. Medicare is based on an acute-care model and thus provides minimal assistance for care of chronic diseases. Elderly people who need long-term care either pay privately (out of pocket or through private insurance) or turn to Medicaid, a federal-state means-tested welfare programme for low-income people. Although Medicaid recipients in nursing homes continue to receive Social Security cheques, they can keep only $30 for personal expenses.

At a time when social welfare schemes in the US look increasingly attractive to British policy makers, the disadvantages of these schemes demand attention. This chapter examines the inadequacies of the US long-term care system and their impact on the disabled elderly as well as the people who care for them in both paid and unpaid capacities. It focuses on the ways factors of class, race, and gender affect the distribution of services.

10.1 Nursing Homes

Nursing homes dominate long-term care in the United States, absorbing the great bulk of government funds. But public funding is available only after private resources are exhausted. Although most older people assume that Medicare covers nursing home stays (R.L. Associates, 1987, pp. 16–17), this programme pays for a negligible fraction of nursing home expenditures (Pepper Commission, 1990, p. 101).

Almost by default, Medicaid has become a primary funding source for long-term institutional care, providing 87 per cent of all public spending for nursing homes and 45 percent of total nursing home revenues (Special Committee on Aging, 1991, p. 208). Approximately one half of the nursing home residents who receive Medicaid entered the facilities as Medicaid beneficiaries; the other half became Medicaid-eligible after depleting their funds (Special Committee on Aging, 1987, p. 39). The cost of a nursing home stay is prohibitive to all but the very wealthy. The average monthly charge is approximately $2,500, a sum which exceeds the monthly income of four-fifths of elderly people (Pepper Commission, 1990, p. 100).

Not surprisingly, women and members of ethnic and racial minorities are disproportionately represented among Medicaid recipients. In 1985, 42 per cent of female nursing home residents, as opposed to 36 per cent of their male counterparts, relied on Medicaid. African Americans were almost twice as likely as whites to depend on Medicaid; 70 per cent of African American nursing home residents were Medicaid beneficiaries, compared to 38 per cent of white residents (Special Committee on Aging, 1987, p. 31).

Studies repeatedly find that nursing homes discriminate against people attempting to enter as publicly-funded patients. Because the Medicaid reimbursement rate typically is significantly lower than the amount nursing homes charge their private-pay residents, institutions look for clients who can pay their own way, at least initially (Committee on Nursing Home Regulation, 1986). Although most nursing homes receive public funds, the majority are proprietary, and an increasing proportion are controlled by major corporations. Profit-making considerations thus frequently govern admissions criteria. The heavy demand for nursing home places enables operators to give priority to applicants who have sources of support besides Medicaid. The ratio of beds to population varies dramatically throughout the US, but most nursing homes have lengthy waiting lists (Harrington and Swan, 1985).

Medicaid recipients who require intensive care are especially disadvantaged. A variety of studies report that Medicaid recipients requiring 'heavy care'[1] have difficulty finding facilities willing to accept them (Feder and Scanlon, 1980; Scanlon, 1980; Cotterill, 1983; Committee on Nursing Home Regulation, 1986; Lewin and Associates, 1987). Hospital discharge planners in California estimate that it is over four times harder to obtain a nursing home bed for a patient on Medicaid requiring light care than for a privately-funded patient needing light care and it is over seven times more difficult to place a 'heavy care' Medicaid recipient than a privately-funded patient requiring the same level of care (Lewin and Associates, 1987, pp. 31–32). Some 'heavy care' Medicaid patients are unable to find any nursing homes that will accept them (Lewin and Associates, 1987, p. 42). In short, Medicaid recipients who have the greatest need for nursing home care are least likely to receive it.

Patients who initially use their own funds to pay for nursing home care but then reduce their assets and incomes to Medicaid levels also encounter problems. Legislation in California forbids facilities from evicting patients who exhaust their resources and become Medicaid-eligible. Investigators have found, however, that some institutions circumvent the law by withdrawing from the Medicaid programme, compelling all Medicaid recipients to leave, and then applying for new Medicaid certification once their census contains what they consider an acceptable number of privately-funded patients (Blum, 1987). According to *The New York Times*, nursing homes throughout the country require entering patients to sign contracts that they will pay privately for a specified period of time and leave voluntarily if they no longer can afford to do so; some facilities also reserve a proportion of their beds for Medicaid recipients and dump patients who become Medicaid-eligible if no more Medicaid beds are available (Freudenheim, 1988).

Medicaid recipients who do gain admission to nursing homes tend to be relegated to institutions which, according to some measures, offer the poorest quality care (Rivlin and Wiener, 1988). In California, nursing homes with high concentrations of Medicaid recipients spend substantially less than others on items related to patient care. Institutions in which more than 75 per cent of their patient days are Medicaid funded spend an average of $26.68 per resident a day on nursing, dietary, and social services; institutions in which fewer than 25 per cent of their patient days are reimbursed by Medicaid spend an average of $41.85 (Lewin and Associates, 1987).

Current policies may exacerbate the access problems of Medicaid recipients. As the number of frail elderly persons soars, the high cost of nursing-home care attracts increased attention. Medicaid funding for

1   This term refers to patients who need at least $2^{1}/_{2}$ hours a day of personal and nursing care (Committee on Nursing Home Regulation, 1986, p. 9).

nursing homes jumped from $9.8 billion in 1980 to $17.3 billion in 1987 (Special Committee on Aging, 1987). The rate of increase of expenditures on nursing homes is outstripping that of the health care industry as a whole (Lave, 1985). By 1984, nursing homes consumed 44 per cent of all Medicaid spending (Burwell,1986).

A central preoccupation of policy makers thus is to keep people out of nursing homes as long as possible. Policy makers are particularly concerned with preventing or postponing the institutionalisation of Medicaid recipients and persons who are likely to become Medicaid-eligible shortly after entering nursing homes. Several states have attempted to use 'certificate of need' programmes to limit the supply of nursing home beds and instituted pre-admission screening programmes to control utilisation of those that exist. Federally-funded 'channelling' demonstration projects have sought to divert the disabled elderly from nursing homes (Kane and Kane, 1987).

Despite the various barriers to entry, poor people are disproportionately represented among nursing home residents. Public funding for non-institutional services is extremely scanty. Some low-income people who might be able to live at home if they had adequate assistance thus are compelled to enter institutions. Women also constitute a very high proportion of the nursing home population. In 1980, 26 per cent of women aged 85 and over resided in nursing homes, compared to 16 per cent of men (Rosenwaike, 1985). Because women tend to outlive their husbands, they often lack the social support that can prevent the need for institutional placement. In short, both women and the poor sometimes enter nursing homes because no other alternatives are available to them. If women and poor people are over-represented among nursing home residents, members of ethnic and racial minorities are under-represented. For example, among the population 85 and over, 14 per cent of African Americans are residents of nursing homes, as opposed to 23 per cent of whites (Special Committee on Aging, 1991). This discrepancy has been attributed variously to the concentration of minority populations in geographic areas which are under-served by nursing homes, to the greater reluctance of certain ethnic and racial groups to institutionalise family members, and especially to discriminatory admissions policies (Markson, 1980; Vladeck, 1980; Eustis et al., 1984; Wallace, 1991).

10.2 Community and Home-Based Services

Although Medicaid picks up the tab for nursing home residents who have exhausted their resources, public funding for community and home-based care is negligible. Medicare emphasises medically-oriented care, not the social services many elderly people need to remain in the community. Moreover, the home health benefit under Medicare is extremely restrictive; recipients must be confined to the home, require skilled nursing care, and need services on an intermittent, rather than continuous, basis. Home health care thus consumes just a tiny fraction of total Medicare expenditures (Special Committee on Aging, 1988, p. 4).

Medicaid regulations do not require home and community based care under this programme to cling so closely to a medical model; nevertheless, the individual states are responsible for determining eligibility and coverage, and they differ dramatically in the extent to which they fund non-institutional services (Rabin and Stockton, 1987). Section 2176 of the Omnibus Budget Reconciliation Act of 1981 allowed states to apply for waivers to include non-medically oriented home and community-based services under Medicaid. Such services can include case management, homemaker services, home health aides personal care, adult day care, and respite care. The Office of Management and Budget has discouraged the government from liberally granting such waivers. Thus, although home care advocates originally hoped that this act would significantly expand non-institutional services for the elderly and disabled, the majority of waivers have been targeted to restricted numbers of people in specific geographical areas (Feldblum, 1985; Pepper Commission, 1990, pp. 98–99).

The two major programmes that fund social services for elderly people living in the community are the Social Services Block Grant (formerly Title XX of the Social Services Act) and Title III of the Older Americans Act. The former provides coverage for homemaker and chore services, including meal preparation, house cleaning, and home repairs. The latter covers information and referral services, meals programmes, transportation, homemaker services, and adult day care. The level of resources devoted to both programmes is meagre. Moreover, the Omnibus Budget Reconciliation Act of 1981, which replaced the Title XX programme with the new Social Services Block Grant, sharply reduced federal funds and removed both state matching funds and state reporting requirements (see Bertghold, 1987).

Because government funding for non-institutional care is sparse, most disabled elderly people living at home fail to receive the assistance they need. Between one-third and one-fourth of disabled elderly people in the community use any home care services (Rivlin and Wiener, 1988; Short and Leon, 1990). Elderly people who do obtain help tend to finance it themselves. Beth Soldo and Kenneth Manton have concluded that 66 per cent of the elderly who use formal services pay at least part of the cost themselves and 41 per cent pay the entire cost (Soldo and Manton, 1985). The utilisation level of community and home-based services thus varies directly with income. Using data from the 1982 National Long-Term Care Survey, Korbin Liu and colleagues found that people with higher incomes spend far more than others on care (Liu et al., 1985).

Recent developments have accentuated the class bias of non-institutional care. Mirroring changes throughout the rest of the health care industry, home health agencies have undergone a major transformation. First, the type of ownership has changed from voluntary and government organisations to private ones. The number of Visiting Nurses Associations (VNAs) and other voluntary and government home health agencies – the entities that traditionally have been responsible for serving the poor – has remained stable. The number of private non-profit and for-profit agencies, however, has risen. In 1960, voluntary and public sector agencies constituted 92 per cent of all home health agencies; by 1983, their share of the market had declined to 43 per cent (Lindeman and Wood, 1985). The growth of the for-profit sector has been particularly striking. Legislation passed in 1980 gave a major boost to profit-making organisations by allowing them to be certified as home health agencies under Medicare. By 1986, the number of for-profit agencies had tripled (Rabin and Stockton, 1987). Second, as large corporate organisations capture an increasing share of the home health market, the number of free-standing agencies declines. Large multi-hospital systems looking for a relatively inexpensive way to expand have been particularly eager to acquire home health care (Lindeman and Wood, 1985).

As the home care environment becomes more competitive, all agencies find themselves under pressure to generate revenue by focusing on the most remunerative patients (Lindeman and Wood, 1985). Although agencies certified under Medicare are automatically eligible for Medicaid certification, non-profit as well as for-profit agencies increasingly spurn Medicaid beneficiaries (Rabin and Stockton, 1987).

Recent changes also have reinforced the tilt toward medically-oriented home care services. As noted, the Omnibus Budget Reconciliation Act of 1981 replaced Title XX of the Social Security Act with the Social Services Block Grant and reduced government funding for the new programme. Many community agencies, which relied heavily on Title XX, sought to recoup their losses by reorienting their programmes toward the medical services Medicare reimburses (Wood et al., 1986). The programmes most likely to be dropped or reduced were homemaker and chore services and personal care services, which helped to promote the self-sufficiency of elderly people living at home (Bertghold, 1987). At the same time, however, some non-profit agencies have created for profit subsidies, offering social support services to a predominantly privately-funded clientele (Lindeman and Wood, 1985).

In short, the access of low-income people to social services in the community appears to have dwindled. As the elderly population expands and hospitals discharge older patients earlier, a growing number of people require care at home. But the for-profit entities which control a growing segment of the home care industry give priority to patients who can afford to finance their own care. Researchers at the

University of California, San Francisco, have coined the term 'the no-care zone', to highlight the problems of low-income disabled elderly people searching in vain for community and home-based social services (Estes and Wood, 1985, p. 18).

Not only do low-income people have less access to home care, but programmes seeking to attract privately-funded patients tend to differ dramatically from those geared toward publicly-funded clients. Government officials frequently acknowledge that they endorse non-institutional services only in so far as they can serve as cost-effective alternatives to nursing home care. They thus want to ensure that home care substitutes for nursing home placement and that the cost of providing home care for clients is less than the cost of supporting them in institutions. Applications for Section 2176 waivers under Medicaid must contain assurances that eligibility is limited to people who otherwise would be compelled to enter nursing homes and that the cost of services is less than the cost of a nursing home stay. Many programmes funded as demonstration projects have operated under similar constraints. A key concern of researchers associated with these projects has been to perfect techniques for identifying clients at imminent risk of institutionalisation. Funding caps have limited both the range and intensity of services. The New York Nursing Homes Without Walls project did not allow expenditures on home care services to exceed 75 per cent of a year in a nursing home. The limit placed on spending on services provided under the National Long-Term Care Demonstration (Channelling) was even lower – 60 per cent of the annual cost of institutional care (Weissert, 1988, pp. 176–77). It almost goes without saying that programmes geared toward publicly financed patients rely on professional assessment (rather than consumer choice) to determine the need for social as well as medical services. A distinguishing feature of the Channelling experiment, for example, was that it employed case managers responsible for allocating whatever services were available under the programme.

Programmes serving private pay patients seek to create rather than stem demand. As a result, those that employ case managers do not expect them to serve as gatekeepers. The timing of service utilisation also tends to be different. Rather than restricting eligibility to people who are frail enough to require nursing home placement, these programmes try to reach the elderly long before they begin to consider institutionalisation. Consumers thus can obtain services which may help to prevent more serious disabilities. Finally, privately-funded patients tend to be offered a broader array of services than those relying on Medicaid or Medicare.

To be sure, the delivery of services to privately-funded patients is not without its problems. Despite the rhetoric of consumer power, programmatic decisions often are based on corporate balance sheets; some agencies may seek to stimulate demand where none exists or eliminate even essential services that do not generate profits. Moreover, many people who can afford to purchase some practical assistance at home cannot pay for a full range of services. Some also risk financial ruin if they pay for substantial levels of care over extended periods (Liu *et al.*, 1985). Nevertheless, elderly people who do have sufficient resources enjoy enormous advantages when they require care at home.

Although this chapter has concentrated on services provided through community agencies, the greatest class differences may lie in the area of services provided outside the bounds of established organisations. Equating formal services with those furnished by bureaucratic agencies, most studies ignore the vast network of helpers recruited through *ad hoc*, informal arrangements. There is some evidence, however, that elderly people rely disproportionately on this type of assistance (Brody and Schoonover, 1986; Noelker and Townsend, 1987). I recently conducted a study of 51 women caring for elderly parents. The interviewees were overwhelmingly white and middle class, and they lived in a city with a huge pool of immigrant workers. Just 15 used any service from a community agency, but 28 hired helpers who were unaffiliated with formal agencies. Moreover, they received assistance from informal helpers for many more hours. Although three women employed aides and attendants just a few hours a week, nine employed them for 40 hours each week, and 16 had helpers who stayed with their parents around the clock (Abel, 1991). The help provided by such workers rarely appears in government statistics. Nevertheless, it appears to constitute a major source of assistance to the affluent that is not available to others.

How can we account for the enormous inequities that exist in the distribution of non-institutional services to the frail elderly? One obvious explanation is that the need for community and home-based services is rising just when cost containment in health care has become a pre-eminent government concern. Many policy makers argue that we cannot afford to equalise access by expanding services for low-income people.

An equally compelling explanation may lie in the fact that, unlike acute health care, long-term care involves a combination of social and medical services. US citizens traditionally have viewed the allocation of social and medical services in very different lights. If we occasionally waver in our commitment to regarding health care as a right, surveys repeatedly demonstrate that we believe that market principles alone should not govern the allocation of medical care (Bayer, 1986–87). Publicity about the denial of critical health services provokes widespread concern. However, we never have had a strong tradition of providing social support services to dependent populations. Perhaps as a result, we find it difficult to distinguish between care for the needy and the personal services elite members of society routinely command. One Congressman explained his opposition to expanded in-home care this way: 'I'd like someone to come fix my roof or do my shopping for me too, but why should taxpayers have to provide me with that?' (cited in Vladeck, 1980, p. 217). As long as we view personal care services as a luxury to which the wealthy alone are entitled, we will continue to withhold essential care from the bulk of functionally-impaired people.

The reluctance of some policy makers to expand non-institutional services also is grounded in the fact that such services lack natural gatekeepers. Although fee-for-service reimbursement schemes encourage some physicians to over-utilise health services, these providers do help to guard the portals of the health care system. The number of case managers is growing in the US, but is still relatively small. Moreover, home care services do not have built-in limitations on consumption. As Stephen Crystal notes:

> Just as people usually subject themselves to surgery only when convinced it is needed, hardly anyone goes into a nursing home if he feels there is an acceptable alternative. There is no such disincentive for home care. In fact, help with household maintenance is a key part, in some cases all, of home care, and almost anyone, disabled or not, would appreciate having this. (1982, p. 92)

But one person's 'latent demand' is another's 'unmet need' (see Feldblum, 1985). Those who fear that the expansion of home and community-based services will open the floodgates implicitly acknowledge that the elderly are drastically under-served. Moreover, although the potential pool of clients of home care programmes is vast, an evaluation of a system of home care programmes established in Massachusetts in 1973 found that the demand for services was 'neither excessive nor uncontrollable' (Branch et al., 1981). At least some evidence suggests that the most critical issue for community agencies may be recruiting a sizeable clientele, not controlling intake (Weissert, 1985). Many elderly people share with most other Americans the belief that dependence on any social services is a sign of personal failure. Having absorbed a value system which glorifies self-sufficiency, they may be unable to rely on others even when they are desperately needy. The same ideology that retards the expansion of home care programmes thus inhibits the utilisation of those that exist. Some elderly people also may cling to housekeeping chores as a way of separating themselves from their more severely impaired counterparts. An ability to manage routine tasks may serve as a source of self-esteem, especially for those who have suffered numerous other losses. As Alan Sager comments, 'The notion of a horde of greedy old people and lazy family members anxious to soak up new public benefits appears to be more a projection by a few wealthy legislators accustomed to domestic and hotel and restaurant service than it is a realistic image of our nation's elderly citizens' (Sager, 1983, p. 15).

10.3   Private Sector Initiatives

The two-class system in long-term care may become even more apparent if private sector initiatives win increased support. Such initiatives take two forms. Some, such as home equity conversions and individual medical accounts, seek to promote private saving, which can then be used to finance long-term care. Others attempt to bring individuals together to pool the risks of paying for long-term care; these mechanisms include private long-term care insurance, continuing care retirement communities, and social/health maintenance organisations (see Rivlin and Wiener, 1988).

Advocates of such programmes argue that the growing segment of the elderly population which is sufficiently well off to be able to pay for long-term care should not rely on limited government funds (Task Force on Long-Term Health Care Policies, 1987; Ricardo-Campbell, 1988). Critics charge that the expansion of the private sector would sharpen the divide between rich and poor. Most programmes are far beyond the reach of low-income elderly people. A high-option long-term care insurance policy, for example, costs approximately $1,500 a year for persons 79 to 80 (Rivlin and Wiener, 1988, p. 60). Entry fees for continuing care retirement communities range from $50,000 to $100,000 (Leutz, 1986, p. 136). Because substantial numbers of low-income elderly people are homeowners, some potentially could take advantage of home equity conversion schemes; but many do not have enough equity in their homes to pay for adequate levels of long-term care (Leutz, 1986). Critics also note that increased private financing may well dissolve whatever popular support public programmes currently enjoy. Walter Leutz writes:

> The Medicaid budget could be cut not only because private policies keep some people from spending down, but also to encourage or stimulate the private market ... This could clearly lead to a two-class system of care, which would be rationalized by arguments that blame elderly victims for not insuring. It would not be uncommon to hear the argument that those who don't plan for the future don't deserve such a generous programme, and so on into the all-too-familiar pattern. (Leutz, 1986, p. 139)

10.4   Delivering Long-term Care

The deficiencies of the long-term care system affect providers as well as recipients of services. In the United States, as in Britain, studies consistently show that families and friends render the great bulk of services disabled elderly people receive. Between 70 to 80 per cent of long-term care is delivered by family members (Comptroller General of the US, 1977; Community Council of Greater New York, 1978; Stone,

Cafferata and Sangl, 1987). Three-quarters of unpaid carers to the non-institutionalised disabled elderly live with the care recipient, and the majority render care every day of the week, devoting an average of four hours a day to caring activities (Stone, Cafferata, and Sangl, 1987). Caring can last a long time. Approximately 44 per cent of carers have been furnishing assistance for one to five years, 20 per cent for five years or more (Stone, Cafferata, and Sangl, 1987).

Like their counterparts in Britain, researchers in the US find that care for the elderly continues to be allocated on the basis of gender. Women represent 72 per cent of all carers and 77 per cent of the children providing care (Stone, Cafferata and Sangl, 1987). Because the elderly turn first to their spouses when they become ill, we might expect spousal caregiving to be divided equally along gender lines. Partly because women tend both to marry older men and to live longer, however, a majority (64 per cent) of the spouses providing care are women (Stone, Cafferata, and Sangl, 1987). Daughters are more likely than sons to live with dependent parents (Wolf and Soldo, 1986) and to serve as the primary carers (Stone, Cafferata, and Sangl, 1987). Sons and daughters also assume responsibility for very different chores. Sons are more likely to assist parents with routine household maintenance and repairs, while daughters are far more likely to help with indoor household chores and personal care (Coward and Rathbone-McCuan, 1985; Stephens and Christianson, 1986). This gender division of labour may help to explain why caring has different consequences for sons and daughters. Sons take responsibility for tasks they can perform whenever they choose. Daughters, however, often assume responsibilities that keep them on call 24 hours a day.

A few studies suggest that husbands and wives also assume different caregiving responsibilities. For example, one qualitative, in-depth study of spousal caregivers of elderly people with dementia found that wives were more concerned about treating their spouses with dignity and more willing to respond to their changing needs (Miller, 1990).

A host of researchers has documented the costs of caring. Various studies have found that, although some family members find caregiving rewarding, many also experience a range of physical, emotional, social, and financial problems. In many cases, caring responsibilities re-ignite family conflicts, impose financial strains, and encroach on both paid employment and leisure activities (see Abel, 1991).

Low-income people face special problems in rendering care. Those who work tend to have jobs with rigid schedules, and they lack leverage to demand special consideration. They thus may suffer greater penalties if they phone disabled relatives from work or take time off to help them during the working day. Data from a government survey show that female carers employed as operatives and labourers are more likely than those employed in either professional/managerial positions or clerical/sales positions to take time off without pay; on the other hand, female carers who hold clerical/sales positions and, to a lesser extent, those in professional/managerial positions are more likely than operatives and labourers to re-arrange their schedules (Subcommittee on Human Services, 1987).

The few studies that have investigated race and ethnic differences in the provision of family care to the frail elderly are hampered by the difficulty of disentangling cultural values from socio-economic necessity. It is unclear whether variations in caring behaviour reflect ethnic differences or economic need (Rosenthal, 1986; Lubben and Becerra, 1987). Some researchers also may be cautious about pursuing this line of research because of the uses to which it can be put. They may fear that studies showing that minority communities provide extensive assistance to the elderly might encourage policy makers to conclude that such groups can take care of their own, without publicly supported services (see Hernandez, 1991).

If we still do not understand adequately how cultural variations in household structure and in the meaning of family responsibility alter the caring experience, it nonetheless is clear that racial and ethnic minorities bear a particularly large burden of care (see Worobey and Angel, 1990). I have noted that minorities are under-represented among the nursing-home population and that they therefore remain in the community with higher levels of functional impairments than do whites; in addition, members of minority groups have extremely limited access to home and community based services (Harel, McKinney and Williams, 1990; Hinrichsen and Ramirez, 1992). We can assume that a very high proportion of minority families deliver care, that the elderly people they tend are especially disabled, and that few formal services provide support or relief.

The intense involvement of many family members in caring work suggests that they are not simply responding to external pressures. Nevertheless, long-term care policies create the framework within which the experience of caring unfolds. The decisions carers make are not solely private choices. Because publicly funded services are not universally accessible, many women lack the power to determine when they will begin to care for elderly relatives, the power to control the intrusions of caring in their lives, and the power to hand over responsibilities that have become overwhelming.

We have seen that some family members lack access to nursing homes. The poor quality of institutions that are available to Medicaid recipients deters some elderly people and their carers from considering them. Although policy makers often assume that family members are overeager to exile elderly people to institutions, many relatives are reluctant even to contemplate nursing home placement (see Abel, 1991).

Access barriers to community and home-based services also affect carers. Just 10 per cent of carers receive any assistance from formal providers (Stone, Cafferata and Sangl, 1987). As we have seen, community and home-care based services tend to be distributed on the basis of financial resources, not just disability. Moreover, just as community agencies treat publicly-funded clients very differently from those who pay privately, so agencies regard the relatives of these two groups in very different lights. Agencies serving privately-funded clients increase business by relieving family members of caregiving responsibilities. They thus encourage relatives to shed the chores they find physically onerous or emotionally taxing. But the more relatives of clients dependent on Medicaid or Medicare relinquish their responsibilities, the more agencies risk exceeding their funding limits. Rather than urging family members to reduce their care, such agencies promote increased family involvement. Some agencies seek to locate relatives who have refrained from rendering care and solicit their participation. The home care programmes operated by New York City's Human Resources Administration deliver services only when family members can justify their inability to help (Caro and Blank, 1987, p. 48). Agencies also train family members to provide care to elderly people so that they can discontinue visits when eligibility for public funding ends (Lindeman and Wood, 1985, p. 40).

The shortage of resources which requires agencies to involve the families of publicly-funded patients reflects two governmental concerns. The first is a fear that, if families unload responsibilities on the state, the financial burden on the government will expand indefinitely. Many policy makers thus want to ensure that publicly funded community care does not replace services now provided 'free' by family and friends. The second is an ideological commitment to privatism. Many policy analysts contend that family care is preferable as well as cheaper. They view the family as the 'natural' locus for caring and argue that, by returning care to the home, we can reinforce traditional values and strengthen intimate ties. But the rhetoric of family love and responsibility does not extend to the very wealthy, who can afford to purchase on their own the supportive services policy makers would deny to others.

Paid as well as unpaid carers suffer from the failure to fund long-term care adequately. Nursing homes and home health agencies seek to save money by keeping wages low. A recent survey of home care workers in New York City found that 99 per cent are women, 70 per cent are African American, 26 per cent are Latina, and almost half (46 per cent) are immigrants. A very high proportion are single mothers with three or four children. They typically earn less than $5,000 a year. Eighty per cent cannot afford adequate housing, and 35 per cent often cannot buy enough food for their families (Donovan, 1989). Timothy Diamond, a sociologist who worked as a nursing assistant in a nursing home, reported that his co-workers were overwhelmingly women from third world countries. Although most took extra jobs to make ends meet, staff conversations centred 'on not having enough money for rent or transportation or children's necessities' (Diamond, 1992, p. 44–45).

I have noted that a high proportion of elderly people rely not on services from bureaucratic agencies but on aides, attendants, and companions whom they hire through *ad hoc*, informal arrangements. This work has many of the features of traditional domestic service – poor pay, few, if any, benefits, unsteady employment, and personalistic relationships. In some cases, racial prejudices may blind elderly people to the needs of the workers they hire. Although elderly people who can afford such help are disproportionately white, the overwhelming majority of the aides and attendants are African, American and Latin (Abel, 1991).

10.5 Conclusion

At a time of heightened alarm about the ability of governments in western Europe to afford social welfare programmes, policy makers increasingly look to the American system of social protection for a model. This essay demonstrates some of the dangers of doing so. By relying heavily on the market to provide long-term care services, the United States helps to contain public spending. But low-income elderly people with disabilities often cannot obtain either the institutional or non-institutional care they need; the services they do receive constitute the bottom rung of a highly stratified system.

The shortage of public resources devoted to long-term care also means that family members responsible for the disabled elderly lack the preconditions for good caring – an ability to relinquish obligations they find overwhelming and access to a broad array of supportive services. And the paucity of public funding contributes to the exploitation of some of the most marginal members of the work force. Long-term care in the United States increasingly is delivered by immigrant minority women who are denied decent pay and working conditions. The establishment of adequately-funded, universal long-term care systems must become a priority for all policy makers concerned with promoting social equity and social justice.

Chapter 11

The Need for Care in Later Life: Social protection for older people and family caregivers

Sally Baldwin

11.1   Introduction

A major gap in Beveridge's thinking concerned the care of people living outside institutions. This chapter addresses that gap – now a major concern among industrialised countries. Its central focus is on care needed in later life and the role of social security as opposed to services. The chapter focuses on the social protection, not only of older people who need care, but of relatives and friends involved in caregiving. It has as its backdrop the social and demographic changes that have happened since 1942: increasing proportions of very old people, changes in women's roles and expectations and in family forms. These changes have increasingly prompted anxieties about the costs of providing care and worries about the future supply of family carers. They also reopen long standing debates on the respective obligations of individuals, families, the wider community, and the state.

Social security could play a critical role in ensuring that appropriate care is available to older people who need it, in ways that protect their autonomy and dignity and without imposing intolerable strains on relatives. In the United Kingdom it does not. By comparison with some major successes of social security in the post-war period – notably the creation of legal entitlements to a basic minimum level of support – Britain has made little progress towards establishing basic entitlements to social care. The origins of this failure lie partly in the assumptions made by Beveridge in framing the social legislation of the 1940s.

11.2 The Break-up of the Poor Law and the Separation of Cash and Care

A dominant theme of social policy in the UK for the first half of the twentieth century was the replacement of the 1834 Poor Law. Under the Poor Law, needs arising purely from financial destitution were not distinguished from those created by frailty or disability. The 'indoor relief' offered in workhouses provided for both – though a degree of separation existed within the workhouse itself. Older people had a greater probability of receiving financial support from the Poor Law Guardians without having to enter the workhouse than the younger, able-bodied, poor.

Provision for people whose needs were primarily for medical or residential care came to be separated out from financial support for the destitute in the course of the 1920s and 1930s (Means and Smith, 1985). Following the Local Government Act of 1929, Local Authorities assumed responsibility for both. Residential care was provided in public assistance institutions; cash assistance for the destitute was dispensed by Public Assistance Committees, on much the same discretionary and judgemental basis as the Poor Law Guardians.

The subsequent chapter in the history of social security in the UK has attained the status of myth. As Bradshaw and Deacon (1983) recount, mass unemployment in the 1930s and the collapse of unemployment insurance led to the assumption by local Public Assistance Committees of responsibility for the financial support of large numbers of unemployed people and their families under what was essentially a poor law regime based on household means testing. Public resentment against the Public Assistance Committees, translated into resistance on the part of many Committees to administer the means test rigorously, led to the creation of the Unemployment Assistance Board in 1934. Renamed the Assistance Board in 1940 (under the Old Age and Widows' Pensions Act), it acquired responsibility for awarding means-tested supplementary pensions to older people. The Board was responsible at national level for fixing assistance scales, though a measure of local discretion was also employed. Thus, responsibility for social assistance in the form of cash came to be sharply distinguished from responsibility for the provision of social support and health care (see Means and Smith, 1985, for a detailed discussion of these developments).

Beveridge's plan built on, and extended, this basic separation between security in relation to income and to care. For older people, retirement pensions were to provide the main route to income security, underpinned by social assistance. Social security would play no real role in their care. Entitlement to health care would be secured by a National Health Service, free at the point of access. Social support – perceived as distinct from health care and covering both residential and domiciliary care – would be the responsibility of local agencies, statutory and voluntary.

The 1948 National Assistance Act formally completed the separation of cash and care. Part II of the Act provided for the creation of a national system of social assistance on the basis of scale rates set by Parliament. Assistance would be means-tested, though the means test would not apply beyond the immediate family of parents and dependent children.

Local authorities became responsible, under Part III of the Act, for providing residential care for 'all persons who, by reason of age, infirmity or other circumstances, are in need of care not otherwise available to them'. They also acquired responsibilities for domiciliary support. These were minimal, however, and mainly concerned with supporting voluntary organisations. Beveridge does not address the question of entitlement to domiciliary support or the need to compensate relatives heavily involved in caregiving. Nor, indeed, was there any contemporary debate about the level of support frail older people living at home – or their relatives – had a right to expect.

This largely reflects the policy priorities of the time. Two policy goals were dominant: the creation of adequate, universal, pensions; and major improvements in both the quantity and quality of residential care. The emphasis on residential – as opposed to community – care seems curious from a contemporary perspective. It is partly explained by the effects of wartime in exposing large numbers of 'respectable' elderly people to lamentably inadequate public assistance institutions following evacuation from their own homes (Means and Smith, 1985). Tremendous emphasis was given, in the post-war years, to plans for replacing these with small, purpose-built homes, on the lines of hotels rather than poor law institutions, with residents contributing to the costs of their accommodation from their pensions or payments from the National Assistance Board.

The focus on residential care also reflects the strength of contemporary assumptions about the primary role of the family in supporting older kin, and the importance of voluntary effort in supplementing that. Women were the prime movers in both spheres and assumptions about the naturalness, indeed rightness, of this permeated thinking about social support for older people. The care provided within families, and its implications for those who gave or received it, was perceived as unproblematic – part of the normal give and take of family life. Even so, to the contemporary eye the absence of any debate about the merits or costs of care in residential and community settings seems strange. This is less true of the absence of debate about entitlement to support in the form of services, which remains a feature of contemporary policy discussion. The main argument of this chapter is that the failure to develop notions of entitlement to such support was a major gap in Beveridge's conception of social protection and remains so today.

Things did not, of course, turn out precisely as Beveridge and his contemporaries expected. The next section discusses two unforeseen developments: the emergence of policies with a strong emphasis on promoting care in community settings; and of social security as an obstacle to the realisation of this policy.

11.3 Care for Older People in the Post-war Period

11.3.1 The rise of 'community' care

It is impossible to do justice to the complex history of social policy between 1945 and 1980 in a few paragraphs. At a very basic level, however, it is possible to track changes in the consensus about the best locus of care for older and disabled people, and to see the emergence of strong preferences for community, rather than residential, care.

The reasons for this change of emphasis include the dismal failure of successive post-war governments to transform public sector residential care on the lines planned by Aneurin Bevin (Means and Smith, 1983). The persistence of the bleak and squalid homes vividly described by Townsend (1962) was certainly one factor prompting a shift in policy. Throughout the 1960s institutional life came increasingly to be represented as bad for people (Goffman, 1961). This perception was reinforced by a series of scandals concerning long-stay institutions.

Probably more significant was growing awareness of the significance of demographic factors for public expenditure, as the UK economy moved from the boom years of the 1960s to the recessionary 1970s and 1980s. Consciousness of projected increases in the number of older people began to dawn just at the point when the oil crisis of the mid 1970s initiated a period of intense pressure on public expenditure. Together, these developments concentrated the minds of policy makers on the costs of residential care and the desirability of finding cheaper alternatives.

This is the background to an increasingly strong articulation of a policy of community care. In its early stages community care policy was based as much on convictions that it would deliver a better quality of life for people with long-standing care needs as on economic imperatives. Relatives and friends are acknowledged as essential elements in the (better) care provided in the community but there is clear commitment to providing reasonable levels of support in the form of statutory services (DHSS, 1978). With continuing pressure on public expenditure, the panic engendered by the 'rising tide' of frail older people and the return, in 1979, of a government ideologically opposed to state provision of welfare, a very different picture emerges. 'Community' becomes identified as a major provider – not simply the locus – of care (see Walker, 1982; Parker, 1990; and the White Paper *Growing Older*, (DHSS, 1981), as compared with the consultative document *A Happier Old Age* (DHSS, 1978) which preceded it). By 1980, then, policy had shifted significantly in two major respects. The focus was now on changing the balance from residential to community care, rather than increasing the supply and quality of residential care; and 'the community' was to provide a greater share of the support needed by people with long-term care needs – greater than before and greater than the statutory services.

It is important to recognise, against this backdrop, that the powers and duties of local authorities had increased significantly by 1970, following the Seebohm reforms (1968), as had the volume of domiciliary services they provided. Nevertheless, these services remained poor, thinly spread, inflexible and of little consequence beside the input of relatives (Sinclair *et al.*, 1990). They were also premised on ideas of kin (and especially female kin) responsibility not significantly different from those embodied in the original Poor Law legislation. Long after social security legislation had reduced the scope of extended family responsibility for the financial support of relatives (under the Determination of Requirements legislation, 1941), local authorities continued to look to extended families for the practical and financial support of 'non-dependent' parents and children. The new focus on community care was, then, less of a break with the traditions of the past than might appear. The vast majority of frail older people always have remained in the community, supported by spouses and children. The emphasis on community, rather than family, responsibility is new. As noted below, feminist analyses came to play a significant role in unpacking the consequences of this elision of 'community' and 'family' – particularly for women (Finch and Groves, 1980).

11.4   Cash for Care – The Role of Social Security

Against Beveridge's expectations, social security came to play a major role in the support of people with long-term care needs – both through income maintenance in general and benefits to help with the costs of disability. More surprisingly, it became heavily involved in financing the costs of care – both in institutions and in the community.

11.4.1 Social security, residential and nursing home care

In spite of the role envisaged for local authorities in the 1948 National Assistance Act, more than half of the people in UK residential and nursing homes in 1992 – as against 14 per cent in 1979 – were in independent sector homes and their fees were subsidised by income support. The reasons for this development have been rehearsed elsewhere (see, for example, Parker 1987; Baldwin, Parker and Walker,

1988; Bradshaw and Gibbs, 1988). The simplest reason lies in the long standing power of social assistance to meet the full costs of boarders and the definition of people living in residential homes as boarders. More complicated factors include

- the combined effects of increases in the numbers of older people, reductions in NHS long term care facilities and a slowing down after 1975 in local authority programmes to develop new residential care facilities;
- the associated growth of a large private sector industry in residential and nursing home care, encouraged by government support for a more mixed economy of welfare after 1979.

The crucial catalyst, however, was social security. Following the move to a regulated system of income support after the 1980 review of the supplementary benefits system, legal entitlements to help with residential and nursing home fees were established. Previously this was discretionary. The result was dramatic. The number of people receiving help from Supplementary Benefit (later Income Support) with residential or nursing home fees rose from 11,000 to 231,000 in twelve years, while the cost rose from just £10 million a year to around £2 billion. Clearly, this development met a need. Whether it was being expressed by the people who went into independent sector homes, their relatives, hard-pressed professionals released from managing queues for local authority beds, or local authorities who no longer had to meet the costs of care from increasingly cash-limited budgets, must be a matter for speculation.

For the last ten years, then, there has been clear entitlement to nationally established benefit limits to pay for care in residential or nursing homes, based on the financial circumstances of the individual seeking care and assessed according to clear rules about her financial resources – not those of children or other relatives apart from spouses. Adjudication and appeals mechanisms based on national regulations also existed. Alongside these procedural rights were less tangible benefits – for example, the freedom for older people or their carers to decide when it was time to enter residential care and to look for the home that best suited the individual's taste and circumstances. Within homes the relationship between resident and proprietor was, superficially at least, that of customer and contractor, not pauper and provider. Residents financed by income support mingled with those who were privately financed, instead of clustering in separate enclaves.

11.4.2 Cash for care in the community

An even more radical development was the creation of the Independent Living Fund (ILF) – an independent trust dispensing public funds to individuals to help with the costs of care for people who would otherwise have needed to move to residential settings. The ILF was created to replace the discretionary additions for 'domestic assistance' lost in the 1986 reform of supplementary benefit and the move to a simpler, non-discretionary, scheme. The significant feature of the ILF was that it paid cash directly to disabled and older people to cover the wages of helpers they decide they needed, and whom they employed. Payments were geared to individual circumstances – the average payment in 1991 was £55 a week but as much as £500 a week was paid to some people. Like benefits for residential care, the ILF has proved embarrassingly popular (Kestenbaum, 1992). The anticipated budget of £5 million a year for an anticipated 350 recipients a year grew to some £62 million for 7,724 recipients by 1991 and had to be curbed by the introduction of stricter eligibility criteria.

11.4.3   The retreat from benefits to pay for care

The escalation of social security expenditure on residential and nursing home care was a key factor in the Government's decision to remove the perverse incentives social security created to entering independent sector homes.   Under the system fully implemented in April 1993, local authorities again have power to decide whether people *need* residential or community based care and, in the latter case, how much statutory support they should have. These decisions are based on assumptions about the amount of care relatives will provide. While assessments of the need for care will, it is promised, be based on the 'clients's' perceptions, the services actually provided will – unlike social security payments – be limited by the financial resources available. They will also aim to keep people on the margins of residential care in the community as long as this is cheaper. Choice of residential homes will be limited to those with whom the local authority will deal. It also seems likely that payment arrangements will in many cases be between homes and authorities not, as currently, between residents and homes. Publicly funded residents will thus lose their status as paying customers, even if they contribute significant sums towards a home's charges.

The new arrangements signal both a significant loss of entitlement and choice and the reassertion of family responsibilities. This is most true of older people, who will no longer have access to the ILF to buy and control the community services they need. A unique period of entitlement to financial support towards one's own care in old age is disappearing.   With it goes commitment to the notion of a strong individual claim on the state for social, as well as medical, care in later life. After April 1993 the assessment of frail older people's 'resources' will encompass relatives, friends and neighbours.   Their care requirements will be determined by local authorities in the light of local budgets, on the basis of professional discretion and without rights of appeal. Nothing in the history of local authorities and their Poor Law predecessors inspires confidence that these arrangements will enhance the autonomy or dignity of the person needing care.

11.4.4 Benefits for carers

In parallel with this retreat from benefits to help older people to buy their own care we find from the mid-1970s the introduction and extension of benefits for informal carers. How did this come about? Are the two developments related?

In social security, as elsewhere in public policy, a deep anxiety exists that by supporting families with what they might do as a matter of course, the state will weaken their willingness to support relatives at all and, eventually, have to substitute for their care. In the UK social security system this fear is expressed in a range of rules preventing relatives from gaining financially by supporting close kin. It is not surprising, then, that Beveridge did not see the need for a benefit to compensate people caring for relatives. His unquestioning acceptance of the domestic division of labour and of caregiving as a central part of married women's 'duties' meant that the idea of caregiving as a contingency to be covered by social security would not have occurred to him. Unmarried carers were as invisible to him as the 'civilian' disabled and thus left to rely on National Assistance or on the goodwill of those they supported. Not until 1974 was a benefit for carers, the Invalid Care Allowance (ICA), introduced – largely in response to lobbying on behalf of single women caring for elderly parents who wanted a non means-tested benefit in their own right.

ICA was for 'those of working age who would be breadwinners but for the need to stay at home and act as unpaid attendants to people who are severely disabled and need care' (DHSS, 1974, para. 60). Married women were originally excluded because – in a phrase reminiscent of Beveridge – they 'would be at home in any case'. The exclusion of married women from ICA created widespread resentment; a central strand in feminist writing in the 1970s was the identification of caregiving within marriage as work requiring recognition and financial compensation. Nevertheless, it was not until 1986 – following a test case in the European Court of Justice on the grounds that ICA contravened a European Commission Directive on equal treatment of men and women in social security – that married women became eligible for ICA.

ICA remains a contentious, complex and unsatisfactory response to the situation of carers, in terms of its purpose, scope, criteria and level. It is not payment for caring as such but a recognition of the earnings lost by people unable to work full-time because of caring responsibilities. However it only partially replaces earnings, being set at some 60 per cent of short-term contributory benefits, regardless of how much care is needed or how long caregiving continues. At this level it falls far short of what would be required to give carers an income independent of the person they care for or of means-tested income support. McLaughlin's (1991b) evaluation of ICA confirms the benefit's weakness in replacing earnings.

Nor does ICA reach most carers. All those over pensionable age are excluded by the benefit's eligibility criteria. As a maintenance benefit it cannot be received on top of another maintenance benefit. It is lost completely by carers earning more than £50 a week. Entitlement is not determined by the carer's activity but depends on the cared-for person's receipt of attendance allowance. The number of ICA recipients is thus much smaller than the number of people heavily involved in caregiving. 'By 1988 an estimated one in ten of carers providing more than 35 hours of care a week received ICA' (McLaughlin, 1991b, p. 2).

It is difficult, then, to be clear about what ICA's purpose really is, other than to act as symbolic recognition of the work of caring and its importance for society. McLaughlin (1991b, p. 2) describes ICA as an *honorarium* – a payment which dignifies and validates the activities of those who receive it, rather than paying for caregiving. ICA gives some people an income they would not otherwise have had (mothers of disabled children whose husbands are in employment, for example). However, it does nothing for older carers and many carers of working age; does not recognise any costs incurred by carers or the situation of those who prefer to combine work and caring; and does not address the effect of long-term caregiving on living standards or on pensions.

The lack of clarity about ICA's purpose and its role in community care has been recognised in policy debate. A recent report by the House of Commons Social Services Committee called for immediate action to change some aspects of the benefit and far more radical change in the longer term (House of Commons Social Services Committee, 1990, paras. 103–111). Little change has happened, however, apart from an increase in the amount carers can earn before losing the benefit. There has been no decision to increase it to a level comparable to that of even short-term benefits. Moreover, this Committee's ideas of 'more radical' change did not extend to questioning the most appropriate way to use cash payments in providing for long-term care needs. Is an earnings replacement benefit, for example, better than direct payments for the care given? The cost of enlisting carers to community care – entitlement to benefits – is, it could be argued, more acceptable to policy-makers (because cheaper) than conferring rights to benefits for care on the people who need it. This is, of course, something of a distortion. It is unlikely that trade-offs of this kind were consciously confronted in the dealings between the separate Government Departments – Social Security and Health – involved. None the less it is probably true that the decision to take social security out of paying for care was made more palatable to the public by the commitments made at the time to increasing support for carers – in cash and in kind.

It is difficult to see this as a victory for carers. Real improvement in their support has yet to materialise. In any case, carers' situation is closely bound up with that of the people they support. Restrictions on entitlement to benefit for residential care or for purchasing domiciliary support will inevitably affect them adversely; reducing their room to manoeuvre, increasing their burdens and leaving both parties locked into the vicious circle of dependence, isolation, low income and stress that emerges from much of the current research on disability and informal care (Martin and White, 1988; Qureshi and Walker, 1989; Parker, 1990; McLaughlin, 1991b; Glendinning, 1992b). The emergence of separate, and competing, lobbies of carers and disabled people's organisations serves only to camouflage the underlying reality – that UK policy on community care does not deal well with the needs or legitimate claims of either group.

11.5   The European Debate on the Social Protection of Older People and their Carers

UK policy is, as we have seen, to separate policies for maintaining the incomes of older people, via social security, from policies to ensure that their care needs are met by services in kind. In as far as social security is involved in provision to meet older people's care needs, it is restricted to benefits for relatives and friends providing care. For this group, social security primarily takes the form of partial compensation for inability to engage in paid employment, with some additional recognition of the longer-term effects of caring provided by a carers' premium within income support. Thus, while the UK social security system acknowledges caregiving as a risk to be covered it does not similarly recognise the need for care as a risk – or at any rate a risk to be covered by social security. Other European countries face similar problems to the UK in respect of the care of growing numbers of older people. How have they have responded to questions about the supply and financing of long-term care and what role does social security play in the social protection of older people? Have they been more successful in developing clear entitlements to long term support? Does this take the form of benefits or services? What presumptions are made about the responsibilities or contributions of relatives and friends? Are they compensated in any way and, if so, what is the rationale for this?

Personal communications from colleagues with similar interests and key papers (by Morginstin, 1989, et al. 1992; Schulte, 1989; Lingsom, 1992; McLaughlin, 1992b) indicate that the majority of European countries have benefits based on care needs in their social security schemes.

However, coverage is patchy and rarely linked to the actual delivery of care. What we typically find is (see Schulte, 1989) a series of 'supplements' to long-term maintenance benefits for incapacity or, as in the case of the UK, benefits designed to help with the costs of disability but using care needs to determine eligibility. In general, entitlements to these benefits are more common and more generous when the need for care occurs before retirement or, particularly, as a result of industrial injury. Care needs arising in consequence of old age are less likely to attract a social security benefit. When they do, it is likely to be small. On the whole, then, a thoroughgoing use of the social security system to provide cash benefits for the provision of care – whether in the community or in residential settings – seems relatively rare. Exceptions, discussed further below, are Israel and the Netherlands.

State involvement in financial support for family caregivers is, on the other hand, becoming an increasingly common feature of social policy, particularly in the more industrialised European countries. Payment is not always made through the social security system. McLaughlin (1992b), in a preliminary analysis of financial support for carers in nine countries (UK, Ireland, Sweden, Norway, Denmark, Finland, Germany, France, USA), distinguishes two 'ideal types' of financial support for informal carers found in these countries:

• those based on a social security model, typically based on compensation for earnings loss and deriving from issues of equity and equality;

• those which are payments for care, and intended to act as incentives to provide care. These are typically assessed and paid through decentralised health and welfare systems.

McLaughlin spells out the advantages and, more frequently, the disadvantages associated with each. As with benefits for care it is clear that there is enormous variety in the forms, levels and criteria for carers' benefits. The conclusion drawn by Schulte from his overview of financial provision for care and carers is that the whole situation is confused and unsatisfactory.

> Currently the solutions are generally as disparate as the problem is ill defined ... No specific branch of a social security system is responsible for the risk-complex 'need for care' and even ... no particular area of social policy is solely or typically responsible. (Schulte, 1989, pp. 12,15)

Schulte is concerned with the fundamental question of how 'care security' can be guaranteed within social protection for older people and, particularly, with the role of social security in this. He argues that social security payments made to the individual have clear advantages. They convey legal rights and entitlements. Money allows choice and control. There are, however, considerable limitations on the current capacity of cash benefits to deliver real 'security' to older people needing care. Typically, benefits for care do not address questions about the supply of care, the mechanics of delivery or the quality of the care supplied. Nor can social security on its own provide a way of assessing the older person's needs in the round.

Thus, what is required is both a legal entitlement to a certain amount of care and a way of linking this to systems for ensuring the delivery of appropriate care. Such systems would include independent professional assessment, counselling, clear identification of the roles and protection of the rights of family carers, the brokerage of services with formal providers and assurance of standards.

The only countries which currently appear to have schemes approximating to this model are Israel and the Netherlands. The Israeli long-term care insurance scheme (Morginstin, 1989) is, interestingly, not driven by concern about the costs of an ageing population, but about older people's access to services and the state's obligation to share the support of older relatives with families. In response 'to a rapidly ageing population, inadequacies of existing services which were also unequally accessible, and as part of a growing recognition on the part of policy makers that the growing burden of care placed on families' (Morginstin et al., 1992) Israel's community care sector, which previously provided home care on a selective, discretionary, basis was redesigned and home care services provided under a social insurance programme (Long-Term Care Insurance).

> The primary aim of the law fully implemented in 1988 was to define the statutory obligation to provide long-term care benefits to the seriously disabled elderly, thus meeting individual needs and enhancing the role of the family as a primary caregiver. (Morginstin et al., 1992)

A benefit is provided at two levels, based on activities of daily living and providing approximately 11 and 16 care hours a week. Assessment is done by local multi-disciplinary teams which design a care plan. Services are provided on a subcontracting basis by public or private agencies. The potential contribution of relatives is ignored in making the assessment of needs, though in exceptional circumstances relatives can be paid to give support. Evaluation of the scheme indicates that the scheme works well and that, so far, relatives have not reduced their commitment to caregiving following receipt of guaranteed levels of public service. Though expensive, and not successful in postponing entry to residential care, Long-Term Care Insurance retains the support of the Israeli government (Morginstin et al., 1992). Policy for services to older and disabled people in the Netherlands demonstrates a similar commitment to linking legal entitlement to a social insurance benefit to individual assessment and designated responsibility for securing the supply of appropriate care.

Superficially, these models might seem to have much in common with the new systems of assessment and care management introduced in the UK following the implementation of the NHS and Community Care Act, 1989. The crucial difference lies in the absence of any entitlement to services for older people or any binding protection for family carers within that legislation. Systems based on social security above all protect the separate identity of the individual citizen. The discretionary system re-introduced in April 1993, while establishing some procedural rights (access to complaints procedures, for example), essentially reasserts family obligations to provide care. In so doing, it negates rather than affirms the independent existence of older citizens.

Schulte's analysis of what constitutes reasonable social protection for older citizens places the affirmation of their citizenship rights at the heart of policy. Whether 'benefits' for older people needing care are provided in the form of cash or services the key requirement is to guarantee entitlement to support. Only this can ensure that older people actually enjoy the kind of citizenship rights to which most industrialised countries pay lip service but few deliver.

Schulte confronts two important facts. First, delivering this kind of social protection requires legislative and social reform. It has to be based on the assertion of principles about the rights of older people and their claims on the community – and the separate rights of any relatives involved in their care. Secondly, it has financial implications which need to be addressed without compromising the basic principles of social protection. In a changing world, preconceptions have to be re-examined and new options addressed.

11.5.1 Implications for the development of United Kingdom policy

Beveridge did not perceive the need for care of frail older people living in the community – and the consequences for relatives of providing that care – as requiring a new policy response. That is no longer the perception of contemporary policy makers. Nevertheless, no real progress has been made in the UK towards securing older people's entitlement to care in their own right. More progress has been made in recognising the rights of relatives giving care, though social security policy for carers remains ambiguous, patchy in coverage and focused solely on carers of working age.

This chapter's starting point was a concern about older people's loss of individual social security entitlements to support with the costs of care following the implementation of the NHS and Community Care Act. The author's initial position was that older people – and their relatives – were best protected by legal rights to support, enshrined in social security legislation and delivered in the form of cash to purchase care. Reflection on policy in other European countries has slightly modified this position, particularly in relation to the shortcomings of simply providing a cash benefit for care. Mechanisms are required for ensuring that a supply of appropriate care is available, for regulating its quality and for matching the individual's needs to appropriate suppliers. All of this will often be too much to leave to the person needing care or to relatives. If, then, social protection is concerned with outcomes rather than inputs we need to link individual legal entitlements to benefits for care to systems for securing appropriate care. The Israeli and Dutch systems show that social insurance can effectively be linked to the delivery of services in kind via assessment and care management. The Norwegian experience, on the other hand, indicates that entitlement does not necessarily depend on legally enshrined rights or individual, social security based, rights. Commitment to providing high quality public services can generate strong feelings of entitlement to services. Whether this resolves problems of professional dominance is not clear.

A reading of the recent history of social policy for older people in these three countries suggests that the key issue may not be the legal underpinning of access to care services but the recognition of older people's citizenship rights and those of relatives – their separate identities and separate claims to public support. The current state of UK policy suggests that the values expressed in Dutch, Israeli and Norwegian policy are not widely held in Britain, where official policy pronouncements focus more on the problems posed by an older population than on what is owed to citizens in later life. Official pronouncements also continue to stress family rather than societal responsibilities for older people's care, although research indicates that the general public has a different, and more varied, view of family responsibility for older kin than that expressed by Government ministers (West, 1984; Finch, 1989).

Such debate as has taken place in the UK on older people's care needs is dominated by anxieties about fiscal burdens and hopes of using increases in older people's prosperity to fund their care needs. There is, for example, much discussion of funding care from occupational pensions, equity released from owner occupation and private insurance. Possibilities for pooling risks via social and health maintenance organisations are also debated (Davies, 1988). The positive aspect of these debates is the emergence of a focus on older people themselves, rather than their relatives. It is also encouraging to see the beginning of discussion about needs for care in later life as a risk that can be anticipated – whether individually or collectively.

There are clear limits to older people's ability to pay for their own care unless retirement pensions and disability benefits increase significantly. It has been demonstrated (Walker, 1988; Sinclair et al., 1990; Oldman, 1991; Craig, 1992; Groves, 1993) that at current levels of income and wealth few older people will be able to contribute significantly to the costs of their care. Moreover, unless quite fundamental changes in policy happen, some groups – women, disabled people and the long-term unemployed, for example – will always need publicly funded services in old age. The general increase in incomes that has happened since Beveridge's time clearly makes it important to focus on how individuals can contribute to the costs of any care they need in old age. However, for the foreseeable future only a small minority will be able to pay for these entirely from their own resources. Thus, while exploring possibilities for integrating private and public resources, equity release and so on, we have to confront the fact that the public resources allocated to older people's support will have to be increased if *this* generation of older people is to be confident of receiving the care it needs. This is partly because of the extent of currently unmet need and partly because needs are bound to increase (Davies, 1988).

11.5.2 A way forward?

It is unlikely that the UK Government will reverse the decision to withdraw from its brief, almost accidental, experiment in using social security to finance older people's care. A long-term social insurance benefit for care is not on the agenda – nor is any significant increase in public expenditure on services for older people. What, realistically, can be done to improve older people's confidence of receiving the care they need without exploiting relatives or damaging family relationships?

Current community care policies offer possibilities for clarifying entitlements to services and increasing choice. It should be possible to establish clear criteria for giving entitlement to a defined and costed level of service. It should also be possible to negotiate more formally with carers the inputs they can, and wish to, sustain. There is no reason why the level of expenditure authorities are willing to make in individual cases should not be made explicit. Older people and carers could then be assisted to purchase the 'care-package' they want, within that budget. Appeals mechanisms should also be possible. These developments would significantly increase security and choice – though legally based entitlements to defined levels of care would do so more effectively.

In the longer term three fundamental issues need to be addressed. The first arises from the narrow focus of the debate so far. The central problem has been defined as the cost of care and the preferred solution to target support on the very frailest. 'Care' needs are discussed in isolation from what shapes needs for social and health services in later life. However, as Sinclair *et al.* (1990) argue, the feasibility of targeting social services on the frailest – those on the margins of residential care – depends on improving support for their carers. It also depends on older people who are less frail managing without support from the statutory services. This, in turn, requires improvement in their living standards, and particularly in pensions and housing. Pensioners' living standards *are* improving, but slowly and for the foreseeable future there will be large numbers who are poor or 'not rich, not poor' alongside a much smaller number who are more prosperous. How can the living standards of this large group be improved? The second concerns the need to develop ways of financing care which build on the greater resources of some older people, provide free services for those unable to contribute at all, and sensibly address the large group falling between these two poles. This includes the difficult issue of whether, and how, to tap into assets such as housing. Cash may now be separate from care at the national level. Increasingly, however, they will have to come together at the local, and particularly individual, level. This may well require the development of semi-independent financial brokerage systems linked to care management (Davies, 1988). Finally, social security policy for carers needs a fundamental review – not least because caregiving itself contributes to the poverty of women in later life.

11.6 Conclusion

Entitlement to social care in later life remains a gap in the UK's system of social protection. As this chapter demonstrates, the issues involved are complex. There is a pressing need to establish some mechanism for serious analysis of these issues, linked to detailed and rigorous research on the costs and feasibility of alternative policy approaches. We need sound demographic projections linked to the public expenditure consequences of different programmes over the next 20 years. We need to think across programmes, making connections between pensions, housing and care services. We need to know, realistically, who will be able to contribute to their care costs and how to avoid the creation of separate, second-class, services for those who cannot. We need to know much more than we do about public attitudes to family obligation. We need to consider seriously the implications of the conflicting demands placed on women and the burdens placed on older spouses. Most of all we need these questions to be asked by government, and linked to strong and positive ideas of what social protection should look like for people who need support in old age and for people who give it. It is significant that the three other European countries whose policies are discussed here all prefaced their policy reforms with major commissions of enquiry which resulted in principled restatements of public obligations to older people and their relatives. The Labour Party's Commission on Social Justice, currently underway, may provide some answers but unilateral solutions are of limited value. A Royal Commission on Later Life?

Part IV

Excluded Citizens: Women and older persons

Chapter 12

Gender and Retirement Incomes: A comparative analysis

Sandra Hutton and Peter Whiteford

12.1 Introduction

In recent years there has been increasing concern with the equal treatment of men and women in social security systems. A major factor underlying this is the recognition of the unfavourable economic circumstances of women and the greater extent of poverty among women generally, but particularly among women in retirement (Glendinning and Millar, 1987). Using data from the 1982 Family Expenditure Survey, Walker and Hutton (1988) show, for example, that single women had the lowest equivalent household incomes and expenditures of any group in retirement, and that women – either single or widows – were significantly more likely to be dependent on supplementary benefit in retirement than either single men or couples. This is still the case – in 1989 the number of men over pension age and receiving Income Support was equivalent to around 8 per cent of the total number of men receiving retirement pensions, while the corresponding proportion for women was 18 per cent (DSS, 1990b).

According to Walker and Hutton:

> Most of the oldest pensioners and of those living alone are women. Most of those who reach pensionable age with few if any occupational pension rights are also women. The twin social phenomena of retirement and pension rights developed in response to the needs and life experiences of men. Women were left in the cold, sometimes quite literally. (Walker and Hutton, 1988, pp. 46–47)

Similarly, Lister (1992, and this volume) notes that the contributory principle is based on standard notions of employment, a male standard which increasingly differs from existing employment patterns, particularly for women. These types of conclusions have also been supported by other writers, including Walker (1987) and Groves (1987b), and has also been found to be true in other European countries (Amann, 1981; Buhmann *et al.*, 1988).

The degree of equality of treatment of men and women in retirement income systems will become increasingly prominent in evaluations of social security policy. A European Community Directive adopted in December 1978 established the principle of the progressive implementation of equal treatment of men and women in social security matters. The European Community Directive on Occupational Social Security Schemes adopted in July 1986 extended this, outlawing direct and indirect discrimination on the basis of sex, marital status or family status in all occupational schemes whether optional or compulsory which provide employees or self-employed people with benefits intended to replace statutory provided schemes (Ditch, 1992). A further directive prepared in 1987 but yet to be adopted covers retirement age, family allowances and survivors' benefits.

In this context, it is interesting to ask whether particular pension systems are more likely than others to achieve equal treatment of men and women. While there is a considerable literature comparing the outcomes of different social policies internationally, the issue of equality between men and women has not been prominent in this debate. For example, according to Esping-Andersen:

> The extension of social rights has always been regarded as the essence of social policy ... we choose to view social rights in terms of their capacity for 'de-commodification'. The outstanding criterion for social rights must be the degree to which they permit people to make their living standards independent of pure market forces. It is in this sense that social rights diminish citizens' status as 'commodities'. (Esping-Andersen, 1990, p. 3)

This definition of social rights is limited. It defines rights solely in terms of independence from the labour market, and ignores the issue of women's independent incomes, which would seem to be equally important as an issue of rights. In assessing and evaluating current systems, there is a clear parallel between the dependency of workers on the market and the dependency of women on men. The extent to which a particular system breaks both links should be evaluated.

The objective of this chapter is to assess the extent to which different social security systems promote equal treatment of men and women in retirement. The chapter compares the position of women in the retirement income systems of the UK, France, the Netherlands and Australia, using data from the Luxembourg Income Study (LIS) for the mid-1980s.

Social security systems have a range of objectives, including income replacement and poverty alleviation, as well as equality of treatment.

Systems in different countries place differing degrees of emphasis on these and other objectives, and will therefore differ in their impact on particular vulnerable or lifecycle groups. In addition, countries differ in their choice between public and private instruments for providing income security in retirement. In order to give due weight to these other objectives, the analysis compares incomes from different sources and also compares the absolute income levels of the elderly in these countries, as well as the relative incomes of the elderly in the overall income distribution. As discussed by Lister (1992), equality of treatment does not necessarily imply equality of outcome. Our analysis focuses on the impact of government social security transfers on the relative incomes of men and women, in addition to describing differences between private incomes (from earnings, occupational or private pensions, and investments). In this way, we cover issues both of equality of treatment and of outcome.

The discussion is structured as follows. Section 12.2 provides relevant details of the social security arrangements of the countries included in the analysis. Section 12.2 also reviews some of the literature dealing with differences between welfare states, types of retirement income arrangements and their outcomes. This section discusses the likely impact of differing social security arrangements, and presents the hypotheses that we test with the LIS data. Section 12.3 presents the results of the analysis of the LIS data, and the paper concludes with a discussion of the implications of these findings.

12.2 Types of Welfare States and Pension Regimes

12.2.1 The UK

The UK retirement pension scheme is based on contributory principles, and includes a flat-rate pension and an earnings-related supplement. It covers all employees, self-employed and those making voluntary contributions, but those with occupational pensions and personal pensions (post-1988) can opt out of the earnings-related element. A non-contributory pension and various allowances are paid to residents over 80. It is funded from graduated contributions from both employees and employers, depending upon earnings, employment status and whether contracted out or not. There are two main categories of retirement pension: that paid on your own contribution record; and that paid on your spouse's. Different conditions apply to married women, widows and widowers.

Apart from this discrepancy and that between widows and widowers, the contributory pension scheme treats men and women equally. The contributions and levels of pensions are the same for both.

The outcome, however, is far from equal. Fewer than a quarter of women qualify for a full pension in their own right. Elderly women are more than twice as likely as men to be receiving income-related benefits. The UK state retirement pension scheme might appear to fit within the social insurance model, and in so far as contributions are based on labour market participation, it does. However, the fact that the means-tested social assistance benefit is set at a higher level than the flat-rate retirement pension introduces a divergence from that model.

Under the means-tested 'safety net', income support, pensioners receive benefits higher than the basic retirement pension, plus their housing costs would be paid, apart from 20 per cent of their community charge.[1] Thus even those who have enough contributions for a full state pension scheme but no other income are better off claiming the means-tested benefit. Receipt of other income from occupational pensions or investment is necessary to bring pensioners above this residual level of support. Women are considerably less likely to contribute to and hence receive occupational pensions.

12.2.2 Australia

Age pensions in Australia are payable to men aged 65 years and over and women aged 60 years and over. In addition, a large proportion of the elderly population receive pensions paid by the Department of Veterans' Affairs, as a consequence of war service or related injury. Some of these pensions are more generous than the basic age pension, and are paid free of any means test to those with disabilities or their widows, where it is accepted that the disability or death was associated with war service. There is also a service pension payable to those with eligible war service, essentially on the same basis as the standard age pension, although payable to both men and women five years earlier. There are no contributions towards any of these social security cash benefits, which are flat rate and paid from general government revenue. In general, pensioners must have been resident in Australia for at least ten years. Those who do not satisfy these residence requirements may receive a special benefit, which is subject to more restrictive conditions.

The Australian system is means-tested (except the war widows and war disability pensions). The means test is applied to the combined income of husbands and wives. Entitlements and payments, however, are made individually, so that each partner in a couple receives half the assessed rate of pension in their own right. Single pensioners receive 60

---

1 The help offered under the means-tested system in the UK is mainly financial, although it does cover cost of prescriptions, dental treatment, eye-tests and spectacles, and the costs of care for those in residential and nursing homes. The National Health Service offers free treatment.

per cent of the combined married rate. Adjusted by purchasing power parities, Australian pension levels are substantially higher than either income support or the retirement pension in Britain, but there is much less assistance with housing costs. For example, public sector tenants will generally pay 20 per cent of their income in rent, while private sector tenants receive assistance with less than half of their rental costs. Roughly three-quarters of the elderly in Australia own their own home outright, however.

Since nearly all benefits are means-tested, the Australian system of social security has been characterised as a residual approach to social welfare (Esping-Andersen, 1990). This description is misleading. Because of the 50 per cent taper applying to pensions for the elderly (and those for veterans, those with disabilities, and lone parents), most persons in the eligible age groups receive some pension. In 1989, nearly 80 per cent of those eligible were receiving an age or service pension. The cut-out point for the married rate of pension exceeds average weekly earnings, and the assets test applied to pensions is structured so as to exclude those with substantial wealth, not to restrict payments to those in abject and demonstrable need. It is the special benefit that fulfils the last resort, residual function, although persons receiving this payment account for just under 1 per cent of all recipients.

12.2.3 France

In the late 1980s, the French pension scheme consisted of a main system applicable to all employees in the private sector, and a special system for public-sector employees. The main system consisted of two tiers: the *régime général* and *régimes complementaires*. The general regime is funded by the joint contributions of employees and employers but at a higher rate than the complementary scheme. The latter, however, receives some government contribution. The government covers the main part of the cost of the *minimum viellesse* system. For a full pension 37.5 years contributions are required. There are options to defer pension and for a reduced pension below the age of 65 (OECD, 1988b).

The value of the full pension in the general system is 50 per cent of average earnings in the ten highest paid years after 1947, with a minimum and maximum benefit level. The complementary system pays 20 per cent of highest ten years average earnings. This works out as a total pension of around 70 per cent of average non-executive wages.[2] For low income workers, because of the minimum pension provided in the general

---

2　The average level of earnings in France, when adjusted by purchasing power parities, is only around 75 per cent of the level of average earnings in the UK, probably as a consequence of the high level of employer social security contributions in France (see Whiteford, 1991).

system, the pension is 100 per cent of wages whereas for executives it is only around 50 to 60 per cent of earnings. There is a means-tested spouse supplement and a child supplement for those who have reared three or more children. There is also the *minimum-viellesse* means-tested pension. Depending on their earnings, some of those with full contribution records (but not all, as is the case in the UK) will qualify for full pensions lower than that offered by the means-tested system.

Since 1988, insured persons can work and draw a partial pension, provided their working hours are less than four-fifths normal working hours. A minimum contribution record is required and the insured person must be 60 years of age. The proportion of the old-age pension payable varies with the hours worked. Similar arrangements are applicable in the complementary pension schemes. The French state pension scheme is clearly insurance based and earnings-related. It is likely that the qualification period of 37.5 years for a full pension will put women, with their greater likelihood of a broken employment record, at a disadvantage. For pensioners with resources below a given level, the *Fonds Nationals de Solidarité* (FNS) provide an assistance-type payment, which is a supplementary or national 'social minimum' pension. Those over 65 qualify, but it is payable at 60 for those unable to work because of invalidity. The French social assistance scheme provides a range of other benefits including medical care and domiciliary aid (Laczko, 1990).

12.2.4 The Netherlands

In the mid-1980s, the Netherlands had a contribution-based flat-rate scheme with almost universal coverage. There was a general scheme for all residents with a special scheme for public employees, and a supplementary occupational scheme for private-sector employees. Employees contributed 11.5 per cent of gross earnings for the old age pension, but the employer made no contribution. The government paid a pension to exempted people on low incomes. The pension was paid to those over 65, and for a full pension 50 years of contributions are required, but there is no retirement condition. The pension is reduced by 2 per cent for a single person and 2 per cent for a couple for each insurance year below 50.

Equality of treatment between married and unmarried couples was introduced in 1987 under the general pensions scheme (AOW), and this applies to *de facto* couples, both homosexual and heterosexual, if there is economic dependency between the partners. From 1988 a person who has reached age 64 and is living with a partner under that age is entitled to a pension not exceeding 70 per cent of the net minimum wage. A supplement of 30 per cent of the minimum wage may be awarded to the partner, subject to income testing. When the partner reaches 65, each of the pensioners receives a single pension not exceeding 50 per cent of the minimum wage.

12.2.5 Pension regimes

According to the OECD report *Reforming Public Pensions* (1988b, p. 17):

> In many countries the historical roots of public pension schemes go back to the turn of the century, though in most OECD countries the current systems – in particular their structure and virtually universal eligibility – are the result of developments after the Second World War. The structure of the schemes can be traced back to the two polar models of public retirement provision:
> * the insurance model, which relates benefits to former earnings and contribution periods, and is mandatory for a specific occupational group (Bismarck);
> * the universal model, which provides old age income maintenance at a basic level for the whole population, financed by general taxes (Beveridge).

The OECD report goes on to argue that these distinctions have been eroded over time by moves to top-up flat-rate systems with earnings-related supplements, while the earnings-related systems have often introduced minimum standards. As a consequence, three types of pension systems are identified – the basic flat-rate system, mixed systems of basic pensions plus supplements, and the insurance systems of an earnings-related pension above some minimum standard. The OECD classifies countries with basic systems as including Australia, New Zealand, and Iceland; mixed systems include Canada, Denmark, Finland, Ireland, Norway, Sweden and the UK; while insurance systems include Austria, Belgium, France, Germany, Greece, Italy, Luxembourg, Japan, the Netherlands, Portugal, Spain, Switzerland, Turkey, and the United States. In making a comparative analysis of the position of women under different pension regimes, it is clearly important to include countries that take different approaches to the provision of income security in retirement. This was one factor leading to the choice of the UK, the Netherlands, France and Australia as the countries to be compared. On the basis of this typology, our choice of countries gives us Australia in the first group, the UK in the second, and France and the Netherlands in the third.

There are other ways of categorising pension systems. Esping-Andersen (1990) recently proposed that welfare systems can be described as belonging to three different 'worlds', in terms of the extent to which the nexus between attachment to the labour market and survival has been broken (the level of 'de-commodification' of labour). The first group comprises systems based on the principle of need, developed in the poor-law and social assistance tradition, and characterised by means-testing.[3] The European social insurance systems comprise the second group where benefits are based on the insurance principle conditional on labour-market attachment and level of contributions. The final group is founded in the principle of universal rights of citizenship, irrespective of labour market performance or level of need. As Esping-Andersen recognises, these three groups also correspond to the three systems outlined by Titmuss – the residual, the industrial-achievement and the institutional (Titmuss, 1958).

No country's welfare system is a pure example of any one of these categories, all combine differing weights of each element. Australia is usually regarded as belonging in the first group. France is an example of the social insurance group and the Netherlands fits in the universalist approach. The UK has features of all three worlds, with a universal retirement pension, an earnings-related supplement (SERPS), and a range of means-tested benefits (income support, housing benefit). Because of the importance of the means-tested system, Esping-Andersen (1990) classifies the UK as tending towards the residual approach. Thus, our four countries fall into three somewhat differing groups, depending upon the typological approach adopted.

How will these different approaches affect the relative position of women in retirement? Figure 12.1 sets out our hypotheses. It seems likely that social security systems that seek to encourage private provision for retirement will result in greater inequality between men and women than systems that emphasise public provision. The reason for this is obvious. Pension systems that rely on private provision will favour those who have been able to save for retirement, or those who have access to occupational pension schemes. Men have traditionally been more likely than women to be in full-time employment, and therefore have a higher likelihood of making private savings in the form of superannuation or investments, and to have greater access to occupational superannuation. Second, earnings-related benefits could be expected to favour men over women, since they will reproduce in retirement the inequalities that have existed in employment. While this effect could be moderated by minimum and maximum benefit levels, this equalising effect would not be as strong as that provided by flat-rate benefits. Flat-rate benefits, however, will not be as equalising as means-tested benefits. This is because flat rate benefits will not be affected by private provision. Means-tested benefits could be expected to offset the inequalities engendered by private provision.

---

3 Esping-Andersen's characterisations have been criticised by Mitchell (1991a, b) and Castles and Mitchell (1991), who argue that there are in fact four worlds of welfare capitalism, with the UK and Australia differing from the other Anglo-Saxon countries. More fundamentally, Ringen (1991) questions whether welfare states can be said to come in types at all.

While these likely effects are fairly straightforward, the overall impact of a particular country's set of arrangements is likely to be less clear. This is because all countries have a mix of arrangements. Each of the three tiers in the public system in the UK will have a different impact; their combined effect will depend on the relative size of each component, plus the scope of private and occupational arrangements. Similarly, Australia has an equalising public system of income-related benefits, but a relatively heavy reliance on private arrangements.

The Public/Private Mix
- Retirement income systems that encourage private provision will tend to favour men over women in retirement.

Public Pension Regimes
- Earnings-related public pensions will tend to favour men over women in retirement.
- Flat-rate benefits will tend to equalise men's and women's incomes in retirement.

Other Public Transfers
- Income-related benefit systems will have a stronger equalising effect on men's and women's incomes than flat-rate or earnings-related pension systems.

Figure 12.1 Working Hypotheses

12.3   Analysis and Results

12.3.1   Methods of analysis

In assessing the above working hypotheses, a number of difficult issues arise. Ideally, we would like to analyse the individual financial circumstances of women and men. Individual level income data are not, however, available for France, and individual investment income is not available for the other countries. The lack of individual level information on investment income will have a major impact on the apparent picture for Australia. A large proportion of superannuation schemes in Australia pay lump sums on retirement, rather than occupational pensions. These lump sums may be used to pay off mortgages or be invested, and will yield investment income (or capital gains) rather than pensions.

Individual incomes may not be ideal measures of individual well being, because of the possibility of sharing of resources in multi-person households. The LIS data, like other surveys of this sort, contain no information on the distribution of resources within households. By choosing the household as the unit of analysis, it is implicitly assumed that resources are shared equally by couples.

Because of the data limitations, household incomes rather than individual incomes are used, but to avoid the equal-sharing assumption, the analysis concentrates on the circumstances of single women households, and compares them with the circumstances of single elderly male households. That is, we assess equality of treatment of women by reference to single females only, and do not present results for women living in couples or in larger households. It is not possible to separate widows, divorced and separated women and women who have never married. These are significant limitations, but the results are still of interest in that single elderly women are a group particularly likely to experience low income.

Results are shown for households in three age ranges – 65 to 69 years, 70 to 74 years, and 75 years and over. These age ranges were chosen so as to exclude groups who were likely to still be working . Pensioners under 65 years are left out. The timing of the surveys differs somewhat. The data set for the UK is for 1986, for Australia it is 1985–6, France, 1984, and the Netherlands for 1987. Comparisons are made both in relative and absolute terms. All income data have been adjusted to 1985 values and subsequently converted to 1985 pounds sterling by 1985 OECD purchasing power parities. Given that the real levels of GDP per head in the four countries are very close, this seems to be an appropriate way of comparing income levels.

A number of caveats should be attached to this analysis. We have restricted our comparisons to single person households, and thus do not encompass all of the elderly. In addition, some of our specific results should be considered in a broader framework than is currently possible. In particular, income measures do not incorporate differences between countries in the provision of non-cash services. Using LIS data for around 1980, Smeeding, Saunders et al. (1992) show that estimates of poverty among the elderly drop markedly when the imputed value of health and education spending are included. Nor do the results take account of differences across countries in the housing tenure of the elderly. The imputed value of pension rights may also make a difference to comparisons between the circumstances of the retired and the non-retired. The structure of tax systems differs substantially between countries, and indirect taxes which are large in France and less significant in Australia are not taken into account. In addition, this analysis treats the current pension system in each country as being fundamentally responsible for the observed outcomes. This may not be the case, particularly in contributory systems, where the circumstances of the current elderly reflect their contributions many years previously.

12.3.2 Results

To compare the effects of the different social security arrangements in retirement for the four countries, we first examine net household incomes in each country as an outcome measure. Net household incomes are incomes after the receipt of government social security payments and the payment of direct taxes. To clarify the impact of government social security payments ('transfers') on outcomes, we consider the contribution made by original (pre-transfer) income,[4] and social security transfers, both means-tested and other. Finally, the distributional outcome for men and women in different age groups is examined.

Figure 12.2 shows mean household net incomes adjusted by purchasing power parities. The household incomes of the single elderly are much higher in France than in any other country, although they are also high for 65 to 69 year olds in the Netherlands. Incomes in the UK are well below those of the Netherlands, and those for Australia are substantially lower again. Each country shows a differing pattern of income by age. For men income tends to decline with age. For single women, household incomes are more stable, although there is an apparent slight rise with age in France.

Figure 12.3 shows the proportions of single elderly households of different ages in the lowest quintile of the net income distribution. Income has been adjusted by equivalence scales[5] to enable comparisons to be made between households of different sizes and compositions. If income is equally distributed regardless of age and gender, then we would expect to find 20 per cent of each group in the bottom income quintile.

Figure 12.3 highlights some interesting differences between the countries. Australia has much higher proportions of its single elderly population in the lowest quintile band of the overall distribution of equivalent income. Elderly single Australians appear considerably worse off than younger Australians with the proportions generally

---

4 Caution should be used in considering the concept of 'pre-transfer' income as the basis for assessing the extent to which particular transfer systems reduce inequality between men and women in retirement. As argued by Saunders, Hobbes and Stott (1989), there is a fundamental interdependence between the generation of market income and redistributive policies. In particular, in planning for retirement some individuals might be expected to take account of the interaction between private and transfer incomes.

5 The equivalence scales used approximate closely to those used in the estimation of households below average income statistics calculated for the Department of Social Security in the UK (DSS, 1992c). A couple counts as 1, an additional adult as 0.46 and a child under 18 as 0.23, and a single person household as 0.61.

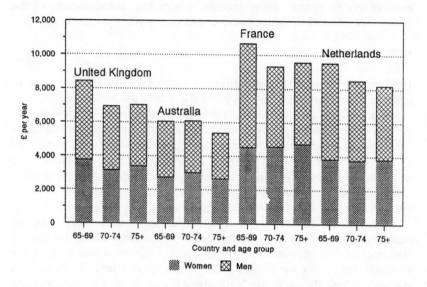

Figure 12.2 Net Household Income of Single Women and Single Men, Adjusted by Purchasing Power Parities, £, 1985

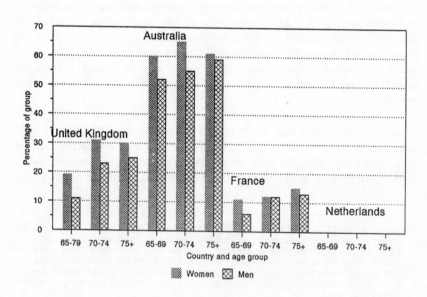

Figure 12.3 Percentage of Single Men and Women in Lowest Quintile of Equivalent Net Income Distribution

increasing with age. Women are more likely to be in the lowest quintile of the income distribution than men. The same trend with age and between men and women is also true of the UK, but the proportions of elderly women in the lowest quintile band of the UK income distribution only reach a maximum of around 30 per cent. The result for the Netherlands is striking, with virtually no single elderly households experiencing low levels of equivalent income.

It should be noted that the relative low income figures given in Figure 12.3 may be sensitive to the choice of equivalence scales, as shown by Buhmann *et al.* (1988) and Bradbury and Saunders (1990). In particular, in Australia many pensioners are clustered around the basic pension levels, so that choice of an equivalence scale that differs from the implicit statutory scale may partly explain the much higher proportion of single person households with low incomes in Australia.

Figure 12.4 shows the average level of household social transfer income. It is lowest in Australia followed by the UK, and then by the Netherlands. France has by far the highest household social transfer income for men and women in any age group. Social transfer income is similar for men and women of all age groups in the UK and the Netherlands, but in Australia, women receive substantially higher levels than men whilst in France, men receive higher transfer incomes than women.

Table 12.1 shows the contribution that income from social transfers makes to total gross household income for men and women in different age groups and breaks this down between social insurance and

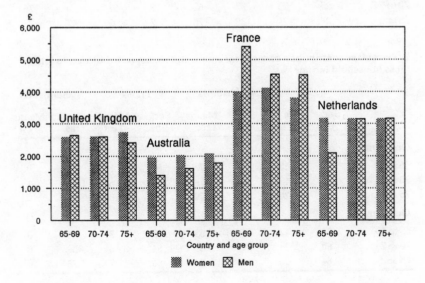

Figure 12.4 Household Social Transfer Income, Single Women and Single Men

means-tested benefits. Transfers are most significant in France, somewhat lower in the Netherlands and the UK, and least significant in Australia. In all countries, social transfers generally make a higher contribution to the gross household income of women living on their own compared with men in the same circumstances. For example, in the UK social transfers as a percentage of income are between 6 and 11 percentage points higher for women than for men of the same age. In Australia the difference is between 9 and 20 percentage points, while in the Netherlands the difference is between 5 and 26 percentage points. This is true of all age groups except in France where transfers are more important for men.

Table 12.1 Sources of Income of Single Elderly Households

A. Percentage contribution of pre-transfer (PT) and social transfer (ST) income to total gross household income

	UK		Australia		France		Netherlands	
	PT	ST	PT	ST	PT	ST	PT	ST
One woman								
65 to 69	25	74	24	75	13	84	18	32
70 to 74	16	84	23	76	12	87	17	82
75 and over	16	84	21	79	12	87	18	82
One man								
65 to 69	32	68	39	55	12	88	44	56
70 to 74	25	73	37	62	9	91	24	76
75 and over	26	74	30	70	7	93	27	73

B. Percentage contribution of social insurance and means-tested income to total gross household income

	UK		Australia		France		Netherlands	
	Soc. Ins.	Means Test	Soc. Ins.	Means Test	Soc. Ins.	Means Test	Soc. Ins.	Means Test
One woman								
65 to 69	59	15	0	75	81	3	82	0
70 to 74	66	19	0	76	81	6	81	1
75 and over	64	20	0	79	77	10	82	0
One man								
65 to 69	56	12	0	55	85	7	56	0
70 to 74	60	14	0	62	84	6	56	0
75 and over	64	10	0	70	86	7	73	0

Source: Estimated from LIS data sets.

The second part of the table shows the contribution of social insurance and means-tested benefits to total gross household income. After Australia (where all transfers are classified as means-tested), income-related benefits are most important in the UK, being between 10 and 20 percent of income, compared to 3 to 10 percent in France and virtually non-existent in the Netherlands. For those over 65 years, the means-tested benefits are more important for women than for men in UK; this is also true for France, but to a much smaller extent.

Figure 12.5 illustrates the extent to which the transfer system equalises the incomes of single women and single men. The figure shows the ratios of men's to women's incomes before and after transfers. A ratio greater than one means that men are more favoured in terms of average incomes received, while a ratio of less than one implies that women benefit more. For example, the first bar in Figure 12.5 shows that in the UK, men's average 'pre-transfer' income between the ages of 65 and 69 was about 1.4 times that of women. Between the ages of 70 and 74, average male income before transfers was nearly twice that of women. The extent to which the transfer system equalises the incomes of men and women will depend on the equality of transfers going to women and men, and the level of transfers as a proportion of total income. The second bar in the figure shows the ratio of male to female incomes after taxes and transfers. In the UK, this ratio is consistently lower than the ratio of before-transfer incomes, implying that the social security and tax systems have reduced inequality between men and women in these groups.

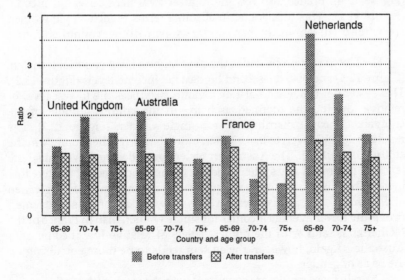

Figure 12.5 Effect of Transfers on Relative Incomes of Single Men to Women

Looking first at incomes before transfers, the pattern is very mixed. Among 65 to 69 year olds, men have the least advantage in the UK and the greatest in the Netherlands. Among 70 to 74 year olds, Dutch men have the highest private incomes relative to women of the same age. The average private incomes of single French men are apparently lower than those of single women over 70 years of age.

The ratios of net incomes after transfers can be taken as a final measure of the extent to which the transfer and tax systems are pro-women in outcomes. For the UK, Australia and the Netherlands, the transfer systems increase the level of women's incomes compared to men, but in France they operate in the opposite direction for those aged 70 years and over. That is, French women over 70 years of age have higher average private incomes than men, but they receive lower transfers and therefore their net incomes are similar. In all countries, the average net income of single men over 65 years is greater than that of single women of the same age although the male advantage tends to decline with increasing age. The differences are generally lowest in Australia, followed by the UK.

12.4   Conclusions

A number of interesting if mixed conclusions flow from this analysis. The French earnings-related system provides the highest levels of transfer income for single women, but provides even higher levels for single men (Figure 12.4). France also has the highest total net household income (Figure 12.2). This means that in absolute terms French single women are better-off in retirement than similar women in other countries (Figure 12.5).

The Dutch system provides the next highest level of social transfers (Figure 12.4) and also the second highest net income levels (Figure 12.2). This system of universal flat-rate benefits produces the lowest level of relative low income (defined as being in the bottom quintile of the equivalent income distribution) for single women (Figure 12.3). The results tend, however, to favour men more than any other country in the study (Figure 12.5). The Australian system provides the lowest absolute levels of income of any system, and the highest incidence of relative low income, but does rather more to equalise the circumstances of single men and women. The British system falls between all of these extremes, providing lower average incomes for single women than in France or the Netherlands, and with the highest levels of relative low income after Australia. Again, however, the system tends to be more equalising on the basis of gender.

Overall, these results are consistent with the working hypotheses put forward in Figure 12.1. Our first hypothesis was that systems that encourage private provision will tend to favour men over women in retirement. In all countries, the net household income of single elderly men was higher than those of women of the same age (Figure 12.2). With the exception of France, private income was a larger source of income for men than for women in all age groups (Table 12.1). Our second hypothesis was that earnings-related public pensions would tend to favour men. This was shown to be the effect of the French system. French men received consistently higher social transfer incomes than did French women (Figure 12.4), and for those aged 70 or over, the French transfer system advantages men. The third hypothesis – that flat-rate benefits will tend to equalise incomes between women and men – is consistent with the results in Figure 12.5 for the UK and the Netherlands. Finally, the finding that the incomes of single men and women are more equal in Australia than in any of the other countries is consistent with the hypothesis that means-tested systems will tend to have the strongest equalising effect.

In considering these conclusions, further issues arise. While Australia had the greatest degree of equality overall between men and women in retirement, it also had the lowest income levels overall, and the highest concentration of both men and women in the lowest quintile of the equivalent income distribution. The French transfer system was most unequal, but gave the highest transfers to both men and women. This suggests that the level of social transfers may not be independent of the form in which those transfers may be provided. As noted previously, the equalising power of transfers depends not only on the structure of benefits, but also on the relative size of those transfers.

Chapter 13

Heading for Hardship: How the British pension system has failed women

Jay Ginn and Sara Arber

Beveridge's social security policy embodies assumptions and constraints which are not gender neutral: for men they are organised around their labour force participation and for women around dependence on men in marriage. In the 50 years since the Beveridge proposals, the assumption that married women had no need of social security in their own right has become increasingly at odds with reality.

In this chapter, we analyse the pension system to show that the gendered assumptions institutionalised in the welfare state have been detrimental to women. Reliance on a husband's pension, both state and private, has proved to be an inadequate means of financial support for women in later life.

We first examine the income of single, married and previously married elderly women, focusing particularly on occupational pensions, whether their own or derived from their husbands' employment. In the second part, we consider the future pensions of working-age women, to assess whether they also are heading for hardship if they marry and have children. We examine membership of occupational pension schemes by women and men, and compare their likelihood of losing entitlement through gendered employment patterns.

13.1 Assumptions underlying the Beveridge Reforms

Gender conflict and equality for women were not addressed by Beveridge's reforms. In spite of the increase in women's labour force participation during the war, the normality of married women's dependence on their husbands was not questioned. Beveridge recognised that married women's 'vital work' in the home benefited

216

society as a whole, but handicapped them in acquiring insurance entitlements in the labour market. However, like most men of his time, he took the domestic division of labour to be natural and inevitable and deemed wives' financial support to be the responsibility of husbands, not the state, both during working life and in retirement.

Beveridge's assumption of married women's financial dependence and his commitment to the contribution principle created two categories of beneficiaries; those, mainly men, who earned rights to benefits through employment, and married and widowed women who earned rights derived from their husband's contribution record. In the state National Insurance retirement pension, three specific provisions were made for women as dependants. First, married women became entitled to a Wife's Allowance, amounting to two-thirds of the pension based on their husband's contributions. Because 39 years of contributions were required for a woman to earn a full pension (and 26 years for two-thirds pension) few married women were able to exceed the Wife's Allowance through their own contributions, which were thus 'wasted'. Second, employed married women were allowed to opt out of the pension portion of the NI contributions, forfeiting entitlement to any pension in their own right. Third, Widow's Benefit was introduced to support married women who lost their husband, reflecting the assumed financial dependence of wives. In these ways, incentives were provided for married women not to seek independent pension entitlements through their own employment. The Beveridge structure of pension insurance encouraged women to rely on marriage rather than employment or the state as their means of financial security in old age. Social security legislation bolstered traditional pressures on both men and women, clarifying the different roles expected of each: men, assumed to be sole breadwinners, were pressured into the labour market and women, assumed to be solely housewives, into the marriage market. As Land (1989) and Lister (Chapter Two in this volume) show, social security policy has contributed in many ways to the construction of women's dependency on men.

The way in which social security systems influence behaviour in the labour market, marriage and fertility varies according to the type of welfare regime. For example, it has been argued that in welfare regimes of the 'Institutional–Redistributive' type such as the Scandinavian countries, workers in the productive (paid) economy have to a larger extent than elsewhere been freed from dependence on the labour market by citizenship rights to a basic income: they have been largely 'de-commodified' (Esping-Andersen, 1990). But this is a male-centred view (Langan and Ostner, 1991; Hutton and Whiteford, Chapter Twelve in this volume). Women may escape commodity status in the labour market through their family role, but usually become dependent on men. Are they merely exchanging one form of commodification for another, compelled to sell their labour for food and shelter in the domestic economy instead of for wages in the paid economy? We suggest that, for women, escape from commodity status in marriage is only achieved if social policy enables them to survive financially, whether or not they have children, without depending on men. How far have women with domestic responsibilities in Britain been decommodified in this sense since 1946? In the next section, we outline changes in demographic structure, in family composition and in women's employment over the last 50 years which have rendered Beveridge's assumption that married women had no need of independent pension income untenable.

13.2   Social Changes Relevant to Women and Social Security

Women have experienced a greater increase in life expectancy than men, resulting in a feminisation of later life. Among those over 65, women outnumber men by 3 to 2 (Arber and Ginn, 1991) and half of these are widows. Although less than 5 per cent of elderly people are currently divorced or separated, this proportion is likely to increase in the future as one-third of current marriages are predicted to end in divorce (Haskey, 1989b). The increase of lone parenthood, cohabitation and divorce is unlikely to be reversed. The decline of marriage as a lifelong contract makes reliance on husbands for income in later life an ever more risky strategy for women. Women now have more need for their own independent pensions than at the time of the Beveridge reforms.

For women who remain married all their lives, there is still a need for an independent income. The marital relationship is characterised by economic inequality, and as feminists such as Delphy (1984) have argued, is one of exploitation and potential conflict. There is an accumulation of research evidence among working-age couples that equitable sharing of family income is not automatic, the wife often having a standard of living below that of her husband (Barrett and McIntosh, 1982; Pahl, 1983; 1989; 1990; Millar and Glendinning, 1989; Brannen and Wilson, 1987). Where income is equitably shared in a marriage, personal dependence on the discretion of another to provide support is often experienced as demeaning (Mason, 1987; Popay, 1989). For these and other reasons, married women responded in large numbers to the post-war opportunities for female employment, boosting the percentage of all women aged 15 to 64 in the labour force from 41 per cent in 1950 to 66 per cent in 1989 (OECD, 1979; 1991d). However, married women's employment has remained overwhelmingly part-time and intermittent (Martin and Roberts, 1984).

Married women's increased employment could be expected to shift the balance of financial support in later life towards a pension income earned through their own paid work. But, as we show later, for the majority of married women in Britain the prospects of obtaining an adequate pension in their own right have remained bleak. This is mainly because private occupational pensions have become the major factor in determining the financial well-being of an elderly person in Britain (Green et al., 1984; Groves, 1987b; 1991; Ginn and Arber, 1991). In order to understand how state policy contributed to the predominant role of occupational pensions and their effect on women's pension income, it is necessary to outline their development in Britain.

13.3   The Growth of Occupational Pensions

Occupational pension scheme membership, including employees in both the public and private sectors, grew from 13 per cent of the workforce (2.6 million) in 1936 to a peak at 49 per cent in 1967 (over 11 million). Subsequently, coverage ceased to rise, settling at around 46 per cent (Hannah, 1986). Coverage by occupational pensions was unevenly distributed by class and gender. In the private sector the gender differential increased during the boom years; between 1956 and 1963, among private sector employees whose employer operated a scheme, the proportion of men covered rose from 49 per cent to 63 per cent, while that of women declined from 27 per cent to 21 per cent (calculated from Shragge, 1984, p. 73, Table 3.3). By 1967, the main scope for further growth in membership lay in extending the coverage of women and manual workers, an option which employers resisted (Brown and Small, 1985).

The importance of occupational pensions as transmitters of structured inequality in the labour market has significantly increased since the 1960s as Green et al. (1984) show: employers' welfare payments (mainly occupational pension contributions) as a proportion of the total remuneration package to all employees doubled between the 1960s and 1980s. But this doubling in total employer contributions was not due to doubling the coverage of the working population. The massive post-war expansion in membership did not continue, and membership only grew by 0.7 million between 1963 and 1979. Thus the growth in occupational welfare expenditure after the mid-1960s was mainly due to improved provision for those fortunate enough to belong to a pension scheme (Green et al., 1984, p. 8).

Post-war growth in coverage was due in part to economic developments; a tight labour market from 1940 to 1960 made occupational pensions attractive to employers as a recruitment and loyalty incentive, while a spate of mergers produced large bureaucratic organisations which favoured formal pension schemes (Hannah, 1986). But these conditions were shared by other European countries where occupational pensions have not seen such rapid growth (Ginn and Arber, 1992).

Generous tax concessions undoubtedly contributed to British employers' enthusiasm for setting up occupational pension schemes. From the employer's point of view, tax reliefs made pensions an efficient alternative to higher wages for core staff, and they were also a less visible advantage, avoiding wage claims from other staff based on restoration of differentials. The low level of state provision was also crucial to the expansion of the occupational pensions industry. For most of the post-war period, the basic National Insurance pension for a single person has remained just below the level of means-tested benefits, at less than one-fifth of average male earnings (Lister, 1975; Evandrou and Falkingham, 1993). Unlike most European countries, Britain made no serious attempt to ensure universal coverage of the workforce by a pension above poverty level until the State Earnings-Related Pension Scheme (SERPS) in 1975.

Provision of public and private pensions are reciprocally related: in spite of differences among countries in the balance of state and private pension provision, the share of GNP which is devoted to old age transfers is broadly comparable (Tamburi and Mouton, 1986), although the distribution of income among the elderly population is not. In countries where the state social security pension provides for a high proportion of earnings to be replaced in retirement, or where a flat rate pension is well above the poverty level, there is less demand from workers and less incentive for employers to operate a private supplementary scheme. The reciprocal relationship between state and private provision was recognised by Titmuss (1958) when he proposed a new state system of earnings-related benefits with a progressive element to redistribute towards the low paid. But this was the 'last practical moment when a state earnings-related scheme could have wiped out the bulk of demand for private provision' (Hannah, 1986, p. 56). By building on a tradition of low state provision, the Beveridge recommendations 'furthered the conditions within social security for the growth of a multi-billion-pound enterprise of private pensions' (Shragge, 1984, p. 33).

The Beveridge Plan and subsequent policy left ample scope for expansion of the private sector. Beveridge preferred a state-based subsistence income for pensioners that would not compete with private occupational pensions. The latter were an optional extra, an incentive to self-reliance, and represented:

> an individual's opportunity to achieve for *himself* in ... old age ... a standard of comfort and amenity which it is no part of a compulsory scheme of social insurance to provide. (Ministry of Reconstruction, 1944, our emphasis)

Whether women would also have this opportunity is obscured by 'man-made language'. However, when Beveridge referred to the merits of additional private provision, he thought of men as breadwinners providing for women as dependants:

The state ... should leave room and encouragement for voluntary action by each individual to provide more than that minimum for *himself and his family* . (Beveridge, 1942, 9, pp. 6–7, our emphasis)

The assumption of married women's lifelong financial support by a husband meant their reduced opportunity to obtain an occupational pension was not seen as a problem.

In spite of this, the cost to the Exchequer of tax reliefs on occupational pension contributions and invested income, was considered an acceptable use of public resources. The small occupational pensions industry in the 1940s, together with other private provision for old age, was seen by Beveridge as avoiding costs to the public purse. However, as writers have pointed out, the loss of public revenue due to tax reliefs on occupational pension schemes reduce the funds available for state pensions. The revenue loss, or 'tax expenditure' was estimated as £3.35 billion in 1983/4 (Wilkinson, 1986), a quarter of the amount paid out in state retirement pensions and greater than the Exchequer's subsidy to the national insurance fund (Lister, 1975; Green *et al.*, 1984; Twine, 1992; Reddin, 1985). The difference between state welfare on the one hand and fiscal and occupational welfare on the other lies not in their policy function (to provide financial assistance) or in their public cost but in who the recipients are, whether working class or middle class – the social division of welfare (Titmuss, 1958).

Unlike state pensions, which are social rights potentially guaranteeing social inclusion and integration, occupational pensions offer only a 'civil opportunity' (Twine, 1992) which depends on position in the labour market. They are more available to men and to non-manual staff than to women and manual employees (George, 1968; Wedderburn, 1970; Green *et al.*, 1984; Ginn and Arber, 1993). Where an employer excludes sections of staff from a pension scheme, these people are subsidising scheme members, since the employer's contribution comes from resources produced by all the employees (Reddin, 1985; Ward, 1985).

There is inequity even among those who join an occupational pension scheme, because those who leave the scheme before retirement lose much of the value of their contributions compared to those who stay. Since the employers' contributions to early leavers' occupational pensions are forfeited and ploughed back into the scheme, the pensions of employees who stay are thereby boosted, and employers have been able to take 'contribution holidays' (Pond, 1990). Thus those who stay with the same employer for many years before retirement (mainly middle class men) are subsidised at the expense of early leavers (mainly married women).

Women, because of their typically interrupted employment histories and periods of part-time working (Bone *et al.*, 1992), are more likely than men to suffer from the restrictions on eligibility for membership of occupational schemes. Women aged 55 to 69 had fewer years of pension scheme membership than men; over half of men had at least 20 years of contributions, compared with less than a third of women, and women were also more likely to have lost pension rights (Bone *et al.*, 1992). Where elderly women have occupational pensions, the amounts are smaller, for all these reasons and also because of their lower wages (Ginn and Arber, 1991). Personal pensions, although portable from job to job, cannot be continued across a career break of over a year, and are in many ways, like occupational pensions, ill-designed for women's needs (Davies and Ward, 1992).

Occupational pensions in combination with low state benefits play a major part in perpetuating married women's labour market disadvantages into poverty and dependence in later life. The effects of the pension system as a whole on women's income in later life can be seen by considering women who are now aged over 65, but who were of working age in the post-war period; their productive and reproductive lives were lived under the social security system shaped by the Beveridge Plan, and during the period of rapid expansion of the occupational pension sector.

13.4 Pensions and Women's Income in Later Life

13.4.1 Research aims and method

We first assess the extent to which elderly women who have been married have acquired their own occupational or personal pension income, rather than having to depend on shared income (as wives) or on pension income derived from their past husband (as widows, divorced or separated). Second, we assess whether later cohorts of women are likely to differ significantly from those who are now elderly in their prospects of obtaining an independent pension income in later life. We therefore examine current membership of occupational pension schemes for working-age men and women of different marital status. Finally we need to know how far the problems of early leavers in transferring or preserving their occupational pensions are likely to obstruct women's acquisition of their own pension entitlements. For this purpose, we analyse gender differences in the outcome of past membership of employers' pension schemes, whether pension rights have been transferred, preserved or lost entirely.

Secondary analysis of data from the 1988 and 1989 General Household Survey (GHS), (Office of Population Censuses and Surveys, 1990a, b) is used to examine the first two issues, but to analyse the fate of previously earned pension rights we use data from the 1987 GHS (Office of Population Censuses and Surveys, 1989), as this is the most recent year in which this question was addressed. With a response rate of over 80 per cent, the GHS provides high quality information about a nationally representative sample of adults living in private households. In each year nearly 2,400 elderly women and over 13,500 people between the ages of 20 and 59 are interviewed.

13.4.2 Derived versus independent income of elderly women

According to Beveridge's assumptions, women who marry would have a lower independent income than that of never-married women, but their total income would be comparable due to the addition of income derived from their relationship to their husband or past husband. The analysis will investigate whether this is so, focussing on the 85 per cent of elderly women who live alone or with their husband only. The amounts and sources of income of widowed, divorced and separated elderly women were similar, so all previously-married women were grouped together. Cohabiting women were grouped with married.

Widowed, divorced and separated women were far more likely than single (i.e. never married) women to be poor enough to receive Income Support, 22 per cent compared with 13 per cent in 1988/89 (authors' analysis of GHS). Thus one-fifth of women who had been married in the past, but who now lacked a husband, needed means-tested benefits. Neither their own pensions, nor any derived from their past husbands, had prevented poverty. Among lone elderly men, 10 per cent of those who had been married and 7 per cent of single men received Income Support. Only 4 per cent of married men received Income Support.

Marital status had a marked effect on elderly women's independent income: single women had a much higher likelihood of receiving an occupational or private pension than married and previously married women (see Figure 13.1). The difference was greatest among women aged 65 to 69, where nearly three-quarters of single women but about one-fifth of married or previously married women (mainly widows) received any pension from their own employment. An inherited pension from a past husband's occupational pension scheme was more common for widows than their own pension. Yet less than two-fifths of the youngest widows, aged 65–69, had an inherited private pension, and in all age groups married and previously married women were much less likely than single women to have any non-state pension.

The percentage of elderly women receiving an occupational or private pension was higher for those in the younger age groups. The difference between age groups was especially noticeable for single women, reflecting the better opportunities to join an occupational pension scheme for those who were still aged under 50 in the 1960s. However, for married and previously married women, age made only a moderate difference to their rather poor chance of having their own

pension, suggesting that they had not benefited from the improved
economic opportunities available to single women.

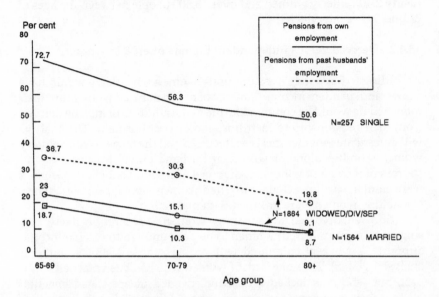

Source: General Household Survey, 1988/1989, authors' analysis.

Figure 13.1 Percentage of Women aged over 65 who Receive an
Occupational/Private Pension, by Marital Status and Age Group, Britain,
1988/1989

The mean amounts of income received from different sources are
shown in Figure 13.2. Mean income from the state to all lone women was
similar, providing a minimal subsistence income (about £46 per week in
1988/89). The majority of married women received little more from the
state than the amount of the Married Women's Allowance (£24.75 in
1988). For elderly married women, it would be unrealistic to assume that
there is no sharing of resources within the household, and married
couples usually benefit from economies of scale relative to elderly people
living alone. However, it would be equally unwise to assume equal
sharing of income between couples (Pahl, 1989; Wilson, 1987) so we have
presented the income of married men and women separately. The
husbands of the younger group of married women had a mean usual
gross income of £123 per week, and those of the older group £96 per week.
Income from other sources such as interest, earnings, and rent was
greater for single than for other women.

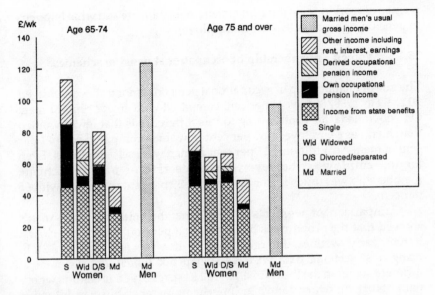

£/wk
Age 65-74   Age 75 and over

Married men's usual gross income
Other income including rent, interest, earnings
Derived occupational pension income
Own occupational pension income
Income from state benefits

S   Single
Wid Widowed
D/S Divorced/separated
Md   Married

S Wid D/S Md   Md   S Wid D/S Md   Md
    Women   Men   Women   Men

Source: See Figure 13.1

Figure 13.2 Mean Weekly Income from Different Sources, Women aged over 65, by Marital Status and Age Group

The mean non-state pension received by married women or widows from their own employment as trivial, about £3 per week for married women, under £3 for older widows and £6 for younger. These amounts were certainly insufficient to provide the extra 'comforts' envisaged by policy makers in the 1940s. The addition to widows' mean income provided by their deceased husbands' occupational pension (£10 for widows under 75 and £5 for those over 75) left them with a much lower pension income than single elderly women. While their own pension income is paltry, widows' pensions from their husbands' employment have provided, on average, barely a quarter of the occupational pension earned by single women in the same age group. The total mean income of widows aged 65 to 74 was nearly £40 per week less than that of single women in this age group. Thus, reliance on a husband's employment to provide an adequate income in later life has, on average, not 'paid off' for the current generation of widows. Only single women have been able to obtain a non-state pension income in significant amounts to add to the subsistence pension provided by the state.

We now turn to women who are currently of working age, with higher rates of employment than earlier cohorts. What are their prospects of earning occupational pensions comparable to men's? There are two aspects of occupational pensions which we consider next for men and women of working age: their current membership rate and what happens to pension rights after leaving an employer.

13.4.3 Women's membership of occupational pension schemes

The rate of membership of occupational pensions among all women aged 20 to 59 in 1988/89 was 24 per cent compared with 46 per cent for men. One obvious factor contributing to this difference is that fewer women than men were employees, 61 per cent of women compared with 71 per cent of men. An additional 16 per cent of men were self-employed. Even among employees, however, women's rate of pension scheme membership was much lower than men's, 39 per cent compared with 66 per cent.

Comparison of women's 1988/89 membership rate with men's showed that the proportions belonging to a pension scheme are closest in their early twenties, diverging sharply after this (see Figure 13.3). In using cross-sectional data, we have a 'snapshot' which shows women at different stages in the life course, as well as successive age cohorts whose patterns of employment and pension scheme membership may differ due to social change. It is not possible to distinguish with certainty the effects of these two sources of variation on the pension scheme membership rate. However, a trough in the age profile of women's membership rate, from

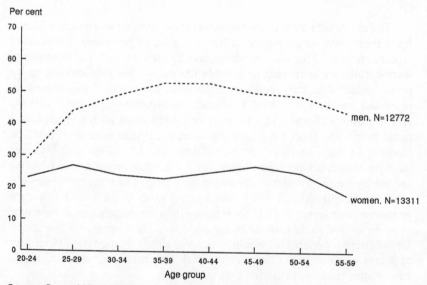

Source: General Household Survey 1988/1989 (authors' analysis).

Figure 13.3 Percentage of Women and Men aged 20-59 who Belonged to an Occupational Pension Scheme, by 5-year Age Groups

the late twenties until the mid-forties, suggests that in spite of women increasingly combining paid employment with childrearing, the latter is still a major constraint on women's pension scheme membership.

Both marital and parental status affected pension scheme membership rates, but in different ways for men and women (see Figure 13.4). Young single women and men had similar membership rates, at about one third, and among older single women their rate was higher than equivalent men's. For women, marriage and having a child in the family had an adverse effect on their likelihood of belonging to a pension scheme. Among ever-married women, only one-fifth belonged to a scheme compared with half of married men, and of women with a child of any age living in the family only 14 per cent belonged to a pension scheme. In the 'career' age group (30 to 44), all men and single women show an increase in their rate of pension scheme membership compared with the youngest age group, while married women's rate remains under a quarter.

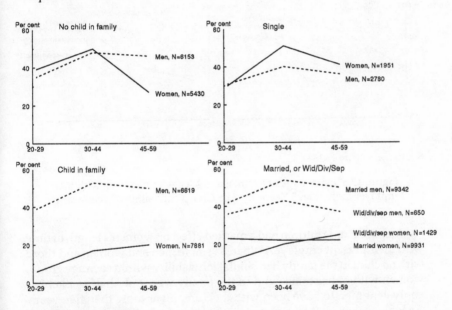

Source: See Figure 13.1

Figure 13.4 Percentage of Women and Men aged 20–59 who Belonged to an Occupational Pension Scheme by Age Group and Family Circumstances

We show elsewhere (Ginn and Arber, 1993) that marital and parental roles affect women's pension scheme membership through the constraints they place on employment. For example, 28 per cent of women work part-time, often due to childcare responsibilities, and only 13 per cent of part-timers belong to a pension scheme. Likelihood of

membership is also reduced by low occupational class, employment in
the private sector, low earnings and shorter length of time in the current
job, all of which are more common among women than men, especially
for married women with children. In Figure 13.5, we show how length
of time with their present employer was reduced for women by their
domestic roles.

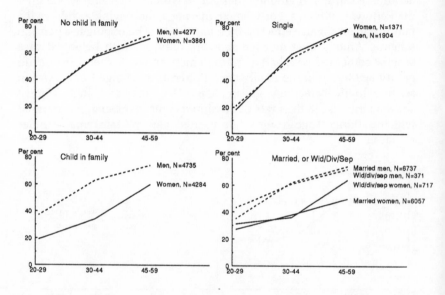

Source: See Figure 13.1

Figure 13.5 Percentage of Women and Men who had been with their
Employer more than 5 Years, by Age Group and Family Circumstances

Marriage and children had a marked effect on women's length of time
with their present employer. Whereas single men and women and those
with no child in the family had similar job stability within each age group,
women with at least one child in the family were only half as likely as
equivalent men to have been with their employer more than five years.
As long as women are expected to shoulder the bulk of domestic work
and childcare, and as long as employment practices and pension
arrangements are designed according to male patterns of employment,
the prospect for a substantial increase in women's occupational pension
scheme membership seems unpromising.

The likelihood of women eventually obtaining adequate
independent pension income depends on pension entitlements over the
major part of a 40-year working life. Occupational pension levels depend,
in all types of scheme, on years of membership, as well as on
earnings-linked contributions. If pension scheme membership is less

than 20 years, the pension is likely to be insignificant in amount. In addition to current scheme membership rates, therefore, it is necessary to analyse the extent to which women lose pension entitlements for which they have already made contributions.

13.4.4 Loss of pension entitlements during working life

The majority of British women who have children have interrupted employment due to the inadequacy of good quality affordable child care (Joshi and Davies, 1992). The exit of women from the labour market because of childbearing, care of elderly dependants and other domestic roles is likely to jeopardise pension rights for those who were able to join an occupational pension scheme.

There are two ways in which an employee's pension rights can be retained on leaving an employer: the fund generated by their own and the employer's contributions may be transferred to a new scheme, or the pension entitlement earned by the combined contributions may be preserved in the old scheme until retirement. Early leavers are penalised because the right to transfer or preserve a pension fund depends on whether the pension is 'vested', that is, the employee has a legal entitlement to the accumulated fund. At present, vesting is not required by law until the employee has been a member of the scheme for two years. Prior to 1987, vesting was not required until membership exceeded five years, and prior to 1980 there was no legal requirement for vesting. Those whose pension is not vested are entitled only to a refund of their own contributions. Employees who withdraw their own contributions lose their pension rights and thus lose also the value of the employer's contributions.

Preservation of pension rights within the previous employer's pension scheme is more common than transfer, but has two major disadvantages. The first is that numerous small pensions are likely to be generated, especially when there are many job changes during the working life. Second, inflation can erode much of the value of preserved pensions before the individual reaches retirement age. It was not until 1990 that some measure of revaluation was required by law. This limited indexation is insufficient to prevent a gradual decline in the value of preserved pensions compared with those which continue to accumulate value until retirement.

Transfer is a more advantageous option. Since the 1985 Social Security Act, employers have been obliged to release early leavers' funds, but there is still no obligation on the new employer's scheme to accept the transfer of funds and associated obligations. The calculation of transfer values is complex, and losses to the employee due to administrative and other costs vary depending on the two pension schemes involved. For those whose new employer does not operate an occupational pension scheme, and for women taking a career break, transfer has generally not been possible.

Transfer and preservation of pension rights and the restriction of vesting to those with a minimum length of pension scheme membership have all discriminated against those with interrupted employment histories. It is quite possible for those with frequent job changes to accumulate no occupational pension at all, in spite of contributing to pension schemes all their working life.

In the 1987 GHS, information was obtained from both employed and economically inactive people as to whether they had ever belonged to an occupational pension scheme with a previous employer. Among all those aged 20 to 59, the proportion of women in this position was lower than for men, 28 per cent compared with 39 per cent (see Table 13.1, second column). The following analysis of loss of pension rights relates to these individuals (1866 women and 2571 men). These people were all asked whether they had kept the right to a pension with any previous employer. Those who were currently members of an occupational pension scheme were also asked whether they had transferred pension rights from the previous to the current scheme.

Table 13.1 Percentage of Women and Men who had Transferred, Preserved or Lost Pension Rights, among those who had Belonged to a Previous Employer's Pension Scheme, by Family Circumstances

	Gender	Sample N=	% previous in scheme	Transferred*	Preserved only	Lost	Row %	N=
All	Women	6701	28	6	28	66	100	1866
	Men	6543	39	9	40	52	100	2571
Single	Women	958	20	16	28	56	100	190
	Men	1365	22	5	29	66	100	303
Wid/d/s	Women	679	27	9	25	66	100	182
	Men	315	41	7	45	48	100	129
Married	Women	5064	30	5	28	67	100	1494
	Men	4863	44	10	41	50	100	2139
No child in family	Women	2623	26	11	31	58	100	693
	Men	2963	33	8	39	54	100	978
Child in family	Women	4078	29	3	26	71	100	1173
	Men	3580	45	10	40	50	100	1593

Note: * A small percentage of those who had transferred rights also had preserved rights.
Source: General Household Survey, 1987, authors' analysis.

Transfer, the option most advantageous to the employee, had only occurred for a small minority, 9 per cent of men and 6 per cent of women (see Table 13.1, third column). Women who had belonged to a pension scheme with a previous employer were less likely than men to have preserved their pension rights, just over a quarter compared with two fifths of the men (see Table 13.1, fourth column). By inference, those who had neither preserved nor transferred their pension rights obtained with a previous employer had lost them, and this was the case for half of the men and two-thirds of the women (see Table 13.1, fifth column).

For single women, the percentage with transferred rights was three times that of married women. Women with a child in the family were much less likely than women without a child to have transferred rights. Thus the more favourable means of keeping pension rights was least available for women with the greatest domestic responsibility.

Fewer women than men had preserved pension rights, irrespective of marital or parental status. Women's greater likelihood of losing previous pension rights only applied among those who were ever married; single women were less likely than single men to lose their pension rights, 56 per cent compared with 66 per cent, but were more likely than married men to have lost rights. The effect of having a child on women's loss of rights was even greater than the effect of marriage, whereas for men a child in the family had no adverse effect.

Thus fewer women than men had belonged to a previous employer's pension scheme, but for those who had done so, the chance of losing their pension rights was greater than for comparable men. The loss of pension rights was associated with family roles for women but not for men.

13.5   Discussion and Conclusions

In the first part of our analysis, we examined the income of elderly women beneficiaries of the pension system shaped by the Beveridge Plan, who had spent a large portion of their adult lives under the post-war welfare state. Elderly previously married women who live alone have an average income below what is generally considered necessary for full participation in society; neither their own nor their past husbands' occupational pension contributions have secured an adequate additional income to the basic subsistence pension provided by the state. Elderly presently married women have a lower personal income, and depend to a large extent on their husbands for money to meet their personal needs. Only single lone elderly women, a rather small group, generally have occupational or private pension income which raises them above the margins of poverty.

In the second part, we showed that women of working age are also heading for hardship in later life if they marry and have children. They are triply disadvantaged compared with men, less likely to belong to an occupational pension scheme, less likely to have belonged to a scheme with a previous employer and also more likely to have lost any entitlements they had. Women who have followed the prescribed pattern of marriage and childbearing, and are 'early-leavers' from occupational pension schemes, are subsidising the pensions of those with long-term membership; mainly men. In spite of increased employment of married women, the nature of their employment is such that their occupational pension rewards are far less than men's.

Married women's low membership rates and high losses of occupational pension stem from schemes' original role as incentives for organisational loyalty and long service. Improvements in terms of access, transfer, preservation and provision of survivors' benefits have been slow, partial, and generally forced on employers by legislation. Legislation since the 1970s to ensure minimum standards in occupational pension schemes are an improvement, but it remains to be seen whether such schemes can remain both financially viable and attractive in their contribution and benefit structure within these new constraints. As long as occupational pension provision is voluntary for employers, the increased costs of required reforms may deter many employers from operating a scheme, so that coverage of the workforce, far from becoming more inclusive, may even decrease. Nor are the rules for uprating preserved pensions adequate to protect them from inflationary erosion. For these reasons, legislative tinkering with occupational pensions seems unlikely to provide protection from poverty for married women in the future, especially if their employment patterns continue as they are.

Personal pensions operated by employers, although avoiding the problem of transfer, have little to offer women, as Davies and Ward (1992) show. Most importantly, as defined-contribution rather than defined-benefit schemes, there is no guarantee as to the level of pension which will be payable at retirement. This is because the pension payable depends on both the performance of the economy as well as on the investment decisions of the pension fund operators. Personal pensions arranged on an individual basis are even less attractive; they are administratively costly and lack the benefit of contributions from an employer. For either type of personal pension, contributions cannot be made during periods when there is no income, even if these could be afforded. Thus women cannot maintain their premiums during a career break. Personal pensions are unlikely to provide a better deal for women than the State Earnings-Related Pension Scheme.

Beveridge's plan bears a share of responsibility for gender inequality of income in later life, for two reasons. First, the assumption of married women's dependence on a breadwinning husband in the social security provisions helped to perpetuate the belief that women's place was in the home; that if they chose to work outside the home, it was for 'pin money' and not the level of pay or occupational welfare required by male breadwinners. The Married Women's Option not only discouraged women from earning their own NI pension record, but may also have conveyed the message that contributions to occupational pension schemes by married women were unnecessary, relieving their employers of the cost of making contributions and leaving women without an independent pension.

Secondly, while other European countries have accorded the state a major role in pension provision, recognising that social objectives cannot be met by reliance on the market, in Britain the low level of state pension set up following the Beveridge proposals helped to boost the growth of occupational pensions, which are inherently ill-adapted to British women's needs. Although any earnings-linked pension scheme will perpetuate inequalities in the labour market into later life, a state scheme (as in Sweden, France or West Germany, for example) provides universal coverage of employees, is fully portable, guarantees indexing of pensions and usually has a more progressive contributions and benefits structure than occupational or private schemes. A state scheme can also ensure adequate survivors' benefits, a feature which occupational pension schemes were slow to introduce in Britain, to the detriment of widows who are now elderly.

Even more beneficial to women with domestic ties and to other groups disadvantaged in the labour market would be the abandonment of contribution tests (Ward, 1985; Parker, 1992). A better and universal basic pension (or citizen's pension), would (as Joshi and Davies show in the next chapter), radically improve the income of elderly women who have been handicapped by their caring role. Such a pension could be funded from general taxation (as in Denmark) and from other forms of taxation, such as a wealth tax. An opportunity was missed in Britain, in the immediate aftermath of the war, to consider ways of enabling women with domestic responsibilities to obtain an independent pension income and to introduce a far more progressive pension system than the market-dominated one which has created two nations.

Recent attacks on state pensions in Britain, especially the ending in 1980 of the link of the basic NI pension with average earnings, the basing of SERPS on lifetime average earnings instead of on the best 20 years and reduction of the SERPS widow's pension from all to half of their deceased husband's pension from the year 2000, will exacerbate the concentration of poverty among elderly women. Pressure to reduce state pensions further is likely to be increased by the moral panic over 'affluent pensioners' (Johnson et al., 1989) which has been based on a rise in pensioners' average income but has ignored structured inequalities. Societies face the question 'Who will bear the financial cost of reproduction – husbands, the state, or women, who have already paid with their labour?' In Scandinavia the state has paid, both by taking over many of the tasks of parenthood and by providing relatively woman-friendly and egalitarian pension systems (Hernes, 1984;

Overbye, 1992). In more traditional family-oriented societies such as Germany, support by husbands is still assumed, and employees' pensions from the state scheme are much higher than in Britain, providing an adequate income for most couples and generous widows' benefits at 60 per cent of the deceased husband's pension (Ginn and Arber, 1992). But in Britain women are left without a clear route to financial security in later life, lacking a guaranteed adequate income either as dependants or as individuals.

We conclude that the pension system shaped by the Beveridge Plan has failed to ensure that elderly women are not penalised for their earlier reproductive role. Occupational pensions are an ineffective means of providing an independent income for women in later life, if their employment is constrained and disrupted by domestic responsibilities. Increasingly women expect and need their own income, but their pension income is unlikely to improve substantially unless state pensions are introduced which are better adapted to women's employment patterns. Occupational and personal pensions cannot protect women from poverty in later life.

Chapter 14

The Paid and Unpaid Roles of Women: How should social security adapt?

Heather Joshi and Hugh Davies[1]

14.1   Introduction

William Beveridge's report expressed the values of his day (Beveridge, 1942). He viewed marriage as a lifelong partnership, with the wife not normally gainfully employed, though very much occupied. The husband–wife team divided its labour into paid work on his part and vital unpaid work on hers, not least in 'ensuring the adequate continuance of the British race and of British ideals in the world' (para. 117). In the scheme proposed (and implemented) a man's contributions covered both partners in the team. There was little point in a married woman making contributions in her own right, at least once she had taken advantage of maternity benefit: she would only be entitled to a reduced rate of other short-term benefits, and in the long run she gained only four–tenths of a pension, since the married team anyway qualified for 1.6 times as much pension as a single person.[2]

For all the rhetoric of teamwork and partnership, the Beveridge Report does refer in its opening paragraphs to 'the individual providing for himself and his family', reflecting the view of wives as dependents of male breadwinners which became apparent in the legislation finally resulting (see chapters by Land and Lister in this volume). The married woman's option, which was suggested by Beveridge, was reinforced by

---

1   We are grateful to Tony Lynes and Jane Falkingham for comments. Errors are our own.
2   This ratio is justified in the context of short-term benefits by the fact that to pay double for a married couple would be covering the same rent twice (para. 112), though (para. 222) a couple is shown as requiring more than a single man for rent.

the half test – not in his Plan – to reduce most married women to the status of appendages in the social security scheme.[3]

By the time Barbara Castle's pension legislation was drawn up, some thirty years later, Beveridge's view of the family was considered dated. It was no longer normal for wives to cease employment on marriage (Hunt, 1968; Martin and Roberts, 1984; Land, Chapter Six in this volume). With the 1975 Social Security Act, women marrying after 1977 lost their option, if employed, to depend on their husband's contributions. Home responsibility (HR) credits were introduced so that certain (administratively identifiable) episodes of unpaid work qualified towards the basic pension.[4] The new arrangements embodied a new presumption that women were normally economically independent individuals, though there might be phases of the life-cycle when they were engaged on 'other duties'.

This all-or-nothing view of women's economic status missed the point that, for much of their lives, women combine paid and unpaid roles, rendering them partially dependent on pooling resources with their husbands (Davies and Joshi, 1992a). The fact of labour force participation tended to be mistaken for independence. Much of the increase in women's employment was by married women working part-time, most of it at markedly lower rates of pay than men's (Joshi, 1989a; Dale and Joshi, 1992). Past, current and presumed future domestic duties have a lot to do with women's low pay (Joshi 1991). As social insurance moved towards earnings-related benefits, the protection of unpaid workers, or of those who combined paid and unpaid work, became more inadequate. Thus women became increasingly reliant on the family, itself becoming increasingly unreliable, given trends in divorce and cohabitation without formal marriage (Kiernan, 1989). The unsatisfactory nature of marriage as a source of security for women in old age would not be entirely redressed even by apportioning pensions on divorce (Joshi and Davies, 1991a,b).

Barbara Castle's reform, like Beveridge's, depended for its success on other measures. As far as equitable treatment of women was concerned, better pensions presumed the success of equal pay (The Equal Pay Act, 1970; Sex Discrimination Act, 1975). The pay differential between men

---

3   The Half Test, in the 1948 National Insurance Act, required a married women to have made full contributions over more than half her married life to be eligible for any pension in her own right.

4   Home Responsibility Protection is awarded automatically to those who receive Child Benefit. It may be claimed by those caring regularly for at least 35 hours per week for recipients of certain disability benefits, and people receiving Income Support because a caring responsibility prevents earning (for more details, see Benefits Agency, 1992). No more than 19 years in a contribution history can be covered by these provisions for Basic Pension. For the state earnings-related scheme (since the 1986 legislation) the averaging of revalued surpluses must take place over at least 20 years.

and women is narrowing only slowly, and may never be eliminated, as much of it reflects a domestic division of labour which is unlikely to disappear completely.

Although Norman Fowler's 1986 legislation extended HR credits to State Earnings-Related Pensions (SERPS), this still tends to leave mothers with smaller pensions in their own right than married women with no children, let alone their husbands (see Joshi and Davies, 1991a,b, and Section 14.4 below). This is because the HR Protection formula, and even its predecessor, the best 20 years rule, does not recognise that past domestic responsibilities reduce earnings even after the circumstances which keep mothers or carers right out of employment. The years which may qualify for HR credit are not the only ones in which earnings are affected. Hence HR credits cannot resolve the paradox of compensating unpaid work with pension related to earnings. The 1980s also saw increased emphasis on private pension provision for old age, via personal or occupational pensions, which would usually be much bigger than the pensions provided solely through the State system. Although the calculation of SERPS implies an element of home responsibility protection even for those who are contracted out, the more valuable of these private pensions would, proportionately, penalize unpaid work even more than Fowler's SERPS. Ginn and Arber (Chapter Thirteen in this volume) show that women currently of working age (especially mothers) are not as likely as men to belong to the better occupational pension schemes. Nothing has changed an earlier conclusion that British women take better care of their families than their pension rights (Owen and Joshi, 1990).

One aim of the 1987 Draft EC Directive completing implementation of the equal treatment of men and women in social security schemes is to promote individual entitlement as an alternative to derived rights, such as widow's pensions. This proposal has caused concern that it dismantles protection many women need, while offering others a positive gain in independence (House of Lords, 1989; chapters by Lister and Cantillon in this volume). Individualisation of benefits is unlikely to be introduced other than gradually, but is unlikely to disappear from the policy agenda.

This chapter explores a range of alternative policies by which the state pension scheme might recognise the 'vital unpaid services' to which Beveridge drew attention. Fifty years on, as Roll (1991, p. 74) has argued, this important work still needs to be made more visible, and rewarded rather than penalised in the social security system.

We use a simulation model to calculate state pensions: under the status quo; under an extended definition of home responsibility; under a system of comprehensive childcare services; and with a better basic pension. The last of these would be 'Back to Beveridge' in that the basic pension would be raised (partially financed by the abolition of SERPS),

Heather Joshi and Hugh Davies

but we also suggest abandoning the contributory principle, enshrined by Beveridge. An extension of state childcare services appears also to stand Beveridge on his head, though one of his unimplemented recommendations for an allied service was to provide housewives with cover for their unpaid responsibilities when hospitalized (para. 344 – family and neighbours were expected to cope with anything less serious!). None of the pension options we consider actually puts a premium on child-rearing, they merely move towards redressing existing penalties.

We confine ourselves to pensions, rather than short-term benefits or cash for children. Beveridge had pro-natalist concerns to perpetuate a race of empire builders. Even now that Europe has become more inward looking, the question of whether there will be big enough generations of future pension contributors remains. We stay out of this area, but note that those who are concerned about the birth rate should also be concerned that the pension system is not unduly unrewarding to those who bring up the next generation. Although we concentrate on the unpaid work involved in caring for children, similar considerations apply to unpaid work caring for sick and disabled adults.

Section 14.2 briefly describes our model; Section 14.3 lays out the policy options considered; Section 14.4 describes the results of the simulations and Section 14.5 discusses our conclusions.

14.2   The Model

14.2.1   Method and assumptions

The simulation model used here extends the one in our work on pensions and divorce, details of which are explained in Davies and Joshi (1992b). In brief, we devise illustrative people and generate their lifetime earnings via econometric equations. The pension rules are then applied to these simulated earnings. We assume that the current National Insurance pension ages for men and women remain at 65 and 60.[5] In our previous work on pensions, the simulations took place in a time warp, neither prices nor earnings changing. Here, real earnings are assumed to rise at a constant annual rate, which shifts the earnings profile upwards over time. Following the Government Actuary (1990b) we chose a real earnings growth rate of 1.5 per cent per annum. We considered two indexation variants for the state pension system: the current policy of indexing the basic pension and the lower and upper earnings limits (LEL and UEL) to prices, and the alternative of indexing these to earnings.

---

5   The Government is committed to equalising State Pension ages for men and women, but has not yet decided how or when to do this.

Under both variants, we assumed that the SERPS entitlements would continue to be calculated on earnings revalued in line with the earnings index, and that all State pensions would continue to be price-indexed post-award.

14.2.2 The individuals

We concentrate on people in middle level occupations, having GCSE-type educational qualifications, and entering the labour force after one year of post-compulsory education. Here, however, the men are given 12.5 per cent more earnings than the mid-level men described in Davies and Joshi (1992b), which brings them closer to average earnings and gives the married couple a hitherto typical educational lead for the husband. We assume that there are no interruptions to earnings histories, apart from those due to childcare responsibilities. Older married women switch into part-time employment, but there is no allowance for sickness or unemployment. Our illustrative people are not average people: some of them are chosen as 'typical' individuals, while others are deliberately extreme cases, chosen to examine the range of effects of policy. There are five types of women in the simulations: an unmarried woman and married women with no, two or four children, as well as a 'career housewife'. The 'career housewife' gives up work permanently on marriage. It is irrelevant whether or not she has children, for she would not have enough contact with the labour market over her life-time to benefit from home responsibility protection. We include her partly in deference to Beveridge, and partly because she, though a *rara avis*, is almost entirely dependent on her husband for her retirement income. A woman who marries does so at age 22.[6] The illustrative people are replicated in successive cohorts covered for their entire careers by current pension rules, assumed to retire in approximately 2040, 2050 and 2060. In each cohort the men are assumed to be five years older than all the simulated women. We adopt this slightly anachronistic assumption so that both sexes retire at the same time: in this respect, as in their non-participation in private pension arrangements, our illustrative people belong more to the age of Beveridge than to that of Fowler. The marriages studied here are lifelong partnerships: even today, 63 per cent of marriages are expected not to end in divorce.

14.2.3 Indexation

The Government Actuary (1990b) estimated that, with 1.5 per cent per annum real earnings growth, the aggregate cost of SERPS is not much

---

6   The woman with two children gives birth when she is 25 and 28. The four-child woman has children when she is 24, 26, 28 and 30.

affected by whether the UEL and LEL are earnings- or price-linked (£14.6 billion or £15.4 billion, 1990 prices, in 2030, respectively). Price-linking would result in savings relative to earnings-linking as more people's earnings outstripped the UEL, but these savings would be approximately offset by the extra amounts paid to those with earnings brought over the LEL. The distributional implications of the two indexation policies are therefore different. In contrast to the roughly equal aggregate costs of SERPS with earnings or price indexation, the total costs of earnings-indexed basic are about double those of price-linked basic by the year 2030 (£63 billion, 1990 prices compared to £34.7 billion). These figures imply that a 45 per cent increase in basic pension (under current indexation policy) could be financed by abolishing SERPS. This would bring basic only half-way up to the level it would have reached in 2030 if linked to 1.5 per cent earnings growth. This reflects both the modest value of SERPS, and the large number of pensioners (many of whom would have been contracted out) who would not give up any SERPS but would presumably be eligible for basic. Disney and Whitehouse (1991) consider a wider range of indexation options, but focusing on their implications for men.

14.2.4 Simplifications

The simulations assume that the earnings profiles of the illustrative people remain unchanged relative to the general level of earnings. This means, firstly, that we have not attempted to model the process whereby part-timers' earnings tend to bunch below the lower earnings limit. Secondly it means that we have not allowed for any adaptation of employment (or indeed fertility) behaviour to hypothetical changes in pension benefits.

14.3 Policy Options

14.3.1 Better home responsibility protection

We attempted to devise a simple rule to extend home responsibility protection to years of low earnings ascribable to a caring responsibility. The idea was to find an analogue of Swedish provisions which treat part-timers with caring responsibilities as if they were full members of the ATP State Earnings-Related Pension. We experimented by allowing any year when the contributor is earning over the LEL but also receiving Child Benefit to be discarded in the calculation of SERPS, as if it were a year below the LEL, if doing so raised the ensuing pension. This experiment has the short-coming of not extending to years of low earnings after the caring is actually being performed.

14.3.2 Better childcare

Another strategy for reducing the pension penalties of motherhood is to imagine that a comprehensive system of childcare were available, from cradle to GCSE. This would help preserve a mother's earnings, and hence her pension rights, even without any changes to the HR rules. We looked at two of the more complete childcare packages that we considered elsewhere (Joshi and Davies, 1992), one based on a Swedish model, and one based on what we call employment-track mothers in France. In both cases we assume that the mother takes a full year's break for each birth, but that thereafter employment is full-time ('French' variant) or well-paid long part-time hours ('Swedish' version). In the 'Swedish' variant we are also (heroically!) assuming that the labour market adapts to provide this opportunity to combine employment and childrearing on reasonable terms. The childcare required would involve daycare and out-of-school care. We do not know what proportion of families would choose this option, if it were available.

14.3.3 Better basic pension

Earnings-related pensions have their limitations when it comes to those who do not earn, so it seems logical to make an extreme assumption about changing the balance between flat-rate basic and SERPS. A cost-neutral increase in basic (45 per cent) financed by the abolition of SERPS has the weakness of redistributing pension away from the contracted-in to the contracted-out, who are generally much better pensioned. Assuming that some way could be found to make the contracted-out help pay for the restructuring of state pension benefits, we experimented with a scenario where basic was doubled and SERPS was abolished.

14.3.4 Scrapping contribution conditions

A further step would be to abolish the notional link between flat rate pension and the 'contribution conditions' which are satisfied now by most paid work and some unpaid caring work. Many of those who fail the test in practice become eligible for means-tested assistance, and so receive the same money from the state. It seems simpler to abandon the pretence of contribution conditions for basic pension, thus offering a form of basic income for the elderly. If the contribution conditions were abolished forthwith, there would be an appreciable effect on the pensions of women retiring before the end of the century, but in our simulations this reform would affect only the (increasingly rare) 'Category B' housewife, giving her a full state pension. State pensions would reward neither paid nor unpaid work, though those in continuous paid work would continue to have the advantage of occupational benefits.

14.3.5 Earnings-linked basic

Another way of providing better basic would be to index it to earnings. This could operate alongside price-linked earnings limits for SERPS. In this option, basic would gradually increase in importance relative to SERPS. Assuming 1.5 per cent earnings growth, it would result in a doubling of basic after about 46 years.

14.3.6 Costs

Better pensions for mothers could be paid for by redistributing income either among pensioners or from the working population to pensioners.[7] The options discussed above will differ both in their total costs and in how these are distributed. Better HR is likely to raise the pension bill least, followed by improved childcare, as both these options are more specifically targeted than the others. Earnings-linking of basic is the most expensive option: it would require (in 2030, the peak year) an increase in NI contribution rates of about seven percentage points (Dilnot and Johnson, 1992), though even this is not obviously infeasible when compared to the reduction in the basic rate of income tax under Mrs Thatcher. These options will require financing entirely by the next century's workers. The resource costs of the provision of services for the childcare option are likely to be more than covered by the gains in earnings they permit (Cohen and Fraser, 1991; Holtermann, 1992). Better basic pension would cost about as much as earnings-linking if it was introduced when our first cohort retired, but would be cheaper thereafter. In this case, however, we also propose abolishing SERPS. In this way, about half the cost would be met by inter-generational redistribution, and about half by intra-generational redistribution among pensioners, from men (and childless women) to mothers.

14.4   Results

14.4.1 Dynamisation of earnings limits

The effects of the indexation method on the amount of SERPS are illustrated in Figures 14.1 and 14.2. Each figure shows earnings for two of our specimen cases: the man and the married mother of two. For each person type, three cohorts (10 years apart) are depicted. Figure 14.1 shows the upper and lower earnings limits assuming price indexation,

---

7   For a more detailed discussion of financing burdens and inter-generational equity, see Johnson and Falkingham (Chapter Fifteen in this volume) who, however, have a sceptical view of the credibility of government pension promises.

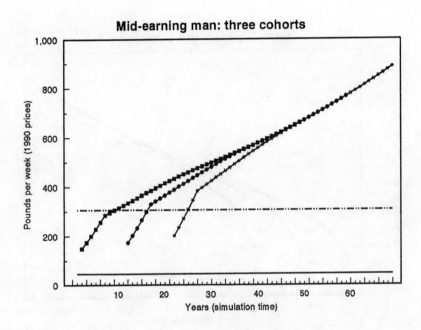

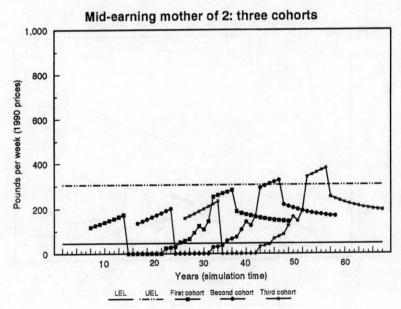

Figure 14.1 Earnings Profiles (LEL, UEL price-indexed)

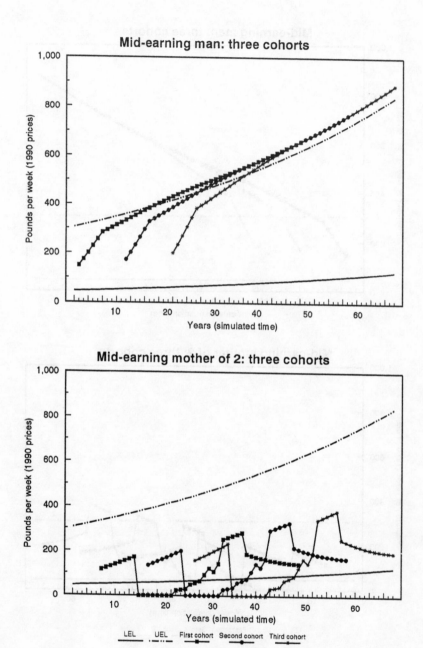

Figure 14.2 Earnings Profiles (LEL, UEL earnings-indexed)

while Figure 14.2 shows earnings indexation. Under price indexation of the earnings limits, the man spends a large fraction of his working life (increasing in successive cohorts) above the UEL, but is never below the LEL. For the mother of two, however, the LEL always excludes some years of part-time earnings (under the current HR rules). This woman always earns less than the UEL in the first cohort, but by the third cohort her second spell of full-time work is entirely above the UEL. With earnings indexation, depicted in Figure 14.2, successive cohorts will make the same proportionate contributions, and reap the same rewards (relative to average earnings on retirement). The married mother of two never earns above the UEL.

14.4.2 Lifetime earnings

For the middle-earning couple, the man's simulated lifetime earnings are more than double his wife's, even if they have no children. This is because we have built in an earning advantage for the man from a number of sources: a pure gender premium on wage rates, an educational lead over the woman worth 12.5 per cent on earnings, his longer hours and his longer working life. Even if the woman did not marry, her earnings would only come to 54 per cent of his. The wife we have modelled would have earned 46 per cent of her husband's earnings even if she had no children (but some part-time employment). If she became a mother, staying out of the labour market while the children were under 5, her earnings would fall to around one-quarter or one-fifth (24 per cent, two children, 18 per cent, four). In the extreme case of the woman living up to Beveridge's expectations of a permanent domestic career, her earnings, entirely gained before marriage, come to 3 per cent of his lifetime total.

14.4.3 State pensions for model middle-wage couple

The ranking of these individuals' earnings is reflected in their state pension entitlements, but the proportional spread is more muted. The relative sizes of pensions depend on what assumptions are made about real growth and indexation, and, under any assumption where pensions grow less than earnings, on the point in time at which the pensions are awarded. We express pensions relative to benchmark weekly earnings in the year they are paid, equivalent in 1990 to £300 per week, close to the average weekly earnings of all male workers and of our illustrative husband. The combined state basic and SERPS never exceed 33 per cent for mid-level earners, though a full final salary occupational pension could be as high as 66 per cent.

In all variants, we assumed that, after award, pensions would be indexed to prices. This implies a decline in the value of the pensions relative to earnings over time. The relative sizes of the pensions under

the two indexation options, and their post-award decline relative to the
benchmark are illustrated in Figure 14.3, for the case of the mid-earning
man.[8] With earnings indexation, successive cohorts enter retirement with
the same pension (relative to the benchmark), but with price indexation,
successive cohorts enter retirement with lower pensions. Price indexation
therefore results in more inequality across cohorts of pensioners than
does earnings indexation.

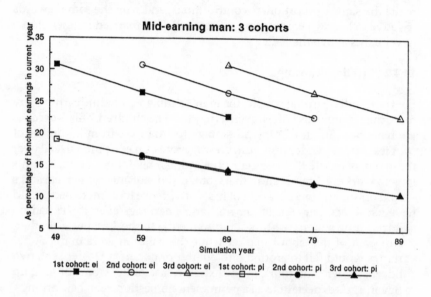

Figure 14.3 Pension over Time (price v. earnings indexation)

The value of the total state pension on award is shown in Figure 14.4
for each of our model middle-earning people under both indexation
assumptions. Under earnings indexation the curve is, by definition,
identical for all cohorts. The mother of two receives a pension just under
two-thirds that of the man, though her lifetime earnings were not quite
one-quarter of his. It is on the current indexation policy, linking pension
and earnings limits to prices but not earnings growth that the picture
changes. The policy of allowing state pension to 'wither on the branch'
is seen in the gradual decline of the values of pensions awarded (as well
as the relative erosion once awarded, shown in Figure 14.3), and in the
fact that even the first cohort considered, men who had spent 48 years
contributing under the new rules, retiring around 2038, would receive
only 19 per cent of benchmark earnings, falling to 14 per cent for those

---

8   The picture would be similar for any of the other model people.

retiring 20 years later (cohort 3). Relativities between men and women are similar for the first cohort to those under earnings indexation, but dwindle in successive cohorts: pensions (except that of the housewife, who receives only category B basic and a tiny amount of SERPS) will converge gradually to basic plus SERPS on lifetime earnings at the UEL.

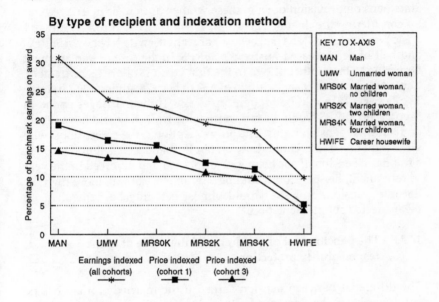

By type of recipient and indexation method

Figure 14.4 State Pension on Award (mid-earners)

Although dynamisation produces a picture of falling relative pensions, the absolute amounts of SERPS are much higher than under the 'time warp' assumption of our previous papers (Davies and Joshi, 1992b). For women, but not men, they would be more than double our previous estimates in the middle of the next century. The increase is precisely because we are assuming that the earnings on which SERPS is based will grow at 1.5% per year. Men's SERPS do not grow so fast, given price indexation of the UEL because less of their earnings fall beneath the limit as time goes by. The relative values of the 'time warp' pensions across couples are virtually the same as those shown for the earnings-linked version.

14.4.4 Widowhood and divorce

If marriages survive until death, the lower pensions of the married women must be considered alongside the higher pension of their husband, who may be presumed (certainly would have been by Beveridge) to pool at least some of it. With no children, the pooled pension of a married person is higher than that of the unmarried woman, and with two children it is about equal to that of the unmarried woman. We have not calculated exactly what pensions the women would receive if their marriages ended in widowhood or divorce, because that depends on a range of assumptions about when the marriages end which are not relevant to present purposes. One can however get a broad idea of the State pension provision open to these women after their marriages end by considering the data in Table 14.1. A widow would receive the full Basic Pension (even if she had been a 'career housewife'), her own SERPS, and half of her deceased husband's SERPS. In the case of bereavement occurring to the mother of two in the first year of cohort 1's retirement, this would amount to an addition of £37 to her £78, giving £115 in total. The housewife would be brought up to £88. If the marriages ended in divorce, no SERPS would be transferred: the women would have to rely on their own pension rights. The only exception is the career housewife who, if divorced late, could draw on her husband's contributions to get a full Basic Pension. If she belonged to cohort 1 and divorced in the year of retirement, her pension would be £51, almost nothing more than the flat-rate pension, and she would almost certainly be dependent on means-tested supplementation.[9]

14.4.5 The pension cost of children and the value of home responsibility protection

The difference between pension earned if the married woman has no children and if she does can be thought of as the pension penalty of motherhood. Because the majority of her pension consists of flat-rate Basic, the mother's forgone pension is proportionately much smaller than forgone earnings, but it is still considerable. Table 14.1 shows these magnitudes in its last two columns for the mother of two and four children respectively – £19 per week forgone pension with two children and around £28 with four children. Expressed in terms of benchmark earnings these pension costs are around 3 per cent and 4 per cent, dropping across the three cohorts. The impact is not proportional to the number of children because lifetime earnings are not proportional to the number of children,[10] and pensions are not proportional to lifetime earnings. Existing home responsibility protection already modifies these costs considerably, as can be seen by comparing the pension evaluated as if there were no HR protection with that we have 'awarded' on current

---

9 For further details of the pension prospects for women after divorce, see Joshi and Davies (1991a), but note that we assumed no real earnings growth there.

10 Especially when the larger family is more closely spaced. The effect for a mother of only one child would be more than half that for two, but the effect for three is likely to be about mid-way between that for two and four (see Joshi, 1990b).

rules. For the mother of two, HR protection allows 11 years to be set aside in calculating SERPS – eight years of non-employment, and three of low earnings under the LEL. This adds around 2.5 points to her 'relative pension'. For the mother of four, 13 years are set aside, protecting her relative pension by around 3 points. The crediting of 11 years for two children and 13 for four can be expressed as 5.5 or 4.3 years per child, which appears relatively generous already in comparison with French and German schemes where pension credits of two or three years per child have been discussed.

Table 14.1 Pensions on Alternative Policies Assuming Price Indexation

	Man	Women					Pension costs of children	
	Not married	Married			House- wife	Mother of:	
		Number of children					
		None	Two	Four		Two	Four
Pounds per week (1990 prices; Basic Pension £46.90; Current HR rules)								
Cohort 1	120	103	98	78	71	33	19	27
Cohort 2	122	108	104	85	76	33	19	28
Cohort 3	123	112	110	90	82	34	19	27
As per cent of benchmark earnings								
Cohort 1								
Current HR rules	19.0	16.4	15.5	12.4	11.2	5.2	3.1	4.3
No HR	19.0	16.4	15.5	9.8	8.2	5.2	5.7	7.3
Better HR	19.0	16.4	15.5	13.1	11.7	5.2	2.4	3.8
Double basic (no SERPS)	14.9	14.9	14.9	14.9	14.9	8.9	0.0	0.0
'Swedish' child care	19.0	16.4	15.5	13.4	13.1	5.2	2.1	2.4
'French' child care	19.0	16.4	15.5	15.2	15.0	5.2	0.3	0.5
Cohort 2								
Current HR rules	16.6	14.8	14.2	11.5	10.4	4.6	2.7	3.8
No HR	16.6	14.8	14.2	9.1	7.6	4.6	5.1	6.6
Better HR	16.6	14.8	14.2	12.2	10.9	4.6	2.0	3.3
Double basic (no SERPS)	12.8	12.8	12.8	12.8	12.8	7.7	0.0	0.0
'Swedish' child care	16.6	14.8	14.2	12.4	12.1	4.6	1.8	2.0
'French' child care	16.6	14.8	14.2	14.0	13.8	4.6	0.2	0.4
Cohort 3								
Current HR rules	14.4	13.2	12.9	10.6	9.7	4.1	2.3	3.2
No HR	14.4	13.2	12.9	8.3	7.0	4.1	4.5	5.9
Better HR	14.4	13.2	12.9	11.2	10.2	4.1	1.7	2.7
Double basic (no SERPS)	11.0	11.0	11.0	11.0	11.0	6.6	0.0	0.0
'Swedish' child care	14.4	13.2	12.9	11.5	11.2	4.1	1.4	1.6
'French' child care	14.4	13.2	12.9	12.7	12.6	4.1	0.2	0.3

Note: HR – home responsibility

14.4.6 Policy experiments: better home responsibility protection

The results of extending home responsibility credits to more years of low earnings are shown in Table 14.1 and in Figure 14.5. The extra credits awarded are for seven years of low earnings while responsible for two children, and eight for the mother of four. They do not add much to the existing effect of HR credits – less than a percentage point on benchmark earnings – and so do not cut the pension costs of children much. One reason for this somewhat disappointing result is that the earnings profiles contain a spell of part-time working after the children are grown up which remains in the calculation of the average. There would have been a greater impact if the mothers had pursued full-time earnings until retirement, but even then the pension cost of motherhood would not be eliminated unless there were no long-term effects of motherhood on rates of pay.

14.4.7 Policy experiments: better child care

Another line of attack on the pension consequences of motherhood is to reduce the earnings losses in the 'standard' scenario by providing alternative care for the children, before and during the years of schooling. Two fairly comprehensive options are reported in Table 14.1, and the more extreme 'French type' option providing full-time cover outside years of maternity is also plotted in Figure 14.5. The latter option almost eliminates earnings and pension costs of childbearing. The remaining margin reflects the impact on subsequent earnings of taking maternity breaks. The 'Swedish' style scenario, permitting long part-time hours, still shows some loss of earnings and pension, though the pension cost of children is a little less than under the better HR scenario.

14.4.8 Policy experiments: better basic

The last variant on current indexation shown in Table 14.1 and Figure 14.5 is 'better basic'. The basic pension is doubled and SERPS scrapped. This brings everybody, including the housewife if contribution conditions go too, to the same state pension (£94). Relative to the benchmark this drops in successive cohorts from 15 per cent to 11 per cent. Uniform state pension implies no (state) pension cost of childbearing, and no pension premium. This would be achieved, in part, by redistribution amongst state pensioners. Among these middle-level earners, men, unmarried women and the employed childless wife would lose more SERPS than they would gain from increased Basic; the mothers and the career housewife would gain. Amongst low earners (based on the unqualified couple we simulated in our divorce analysis – see Davies and Joshi, 1992b) the distribution would still be away from men, and to a small degree the unmarried woman, but all married women would gain. For the mothers, using the French type of childcare cover, the Double Basic option yields slightly less pension than SERPS. Thus, especially as time goes by, the extensive child care appears to be the most 'effective' option in Table 14.1.

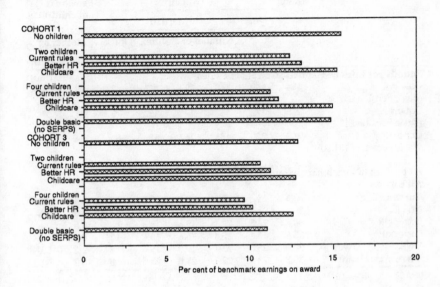

Figure 14.5 State Pension for Mid-earning Women Assuming Price Indexation

14.4.9 Policy experiments: earnings-indexation

Linking pensions to an earnings index would, in this long term, be even more generous. This approach has been presented in Figures 14.3 and 14.4 and is set out in Table 14.2. By the year cohort 1 retires, basic pension would have more than doubled (£97), and it would continue to rise in real terms for successive cohorts. The relative pension costs of motherhood are slightly less under this assumption, as is the impact of the 'Swedish' child care variant. The value of HR itself is greater as the rising LEL allows more years to be dropped. Inevitably, as long as there is a SERPS component in the state pension there are pension costs of motherhood. If there were only earnings-linked basic and no SERPS, the pension costs of children would also disappear, all types of pensioner would lose some (or a lot of) SERPS, but they would all be better off than in the double basic regime considered in the price-linked world of Table 14.1, especially as time went by. By cohort 3 even the man would be better off without SERPS in the earnings-linked world of Table 14.2 compared to the price-linked world of Table 14.1 with SERPS. The married woman would gain from cohort 1.

Table 14.2 Pensions on Alternative Policies Assuming Earnings Indexation

	Man	Women					Pension costs of children	
		Not married	Married				Mother of:	
			Number of children			House-wife		
			None	Two	Four		Two	Four
Pounds per week (1990 prices; Current HR rules)								
Cohort 1 (Basic Pension £97.30)	194	149	140	122	113	62	18	26
Cohort 2 (Basic Pension £112.90)	225	172	162	141	132	72	21	30
Cohort 3 (Basic Pension £131.00)	262	200	188	164	153	83	24	35
As per cent of benchmark earnings **All cohorts**								
Current HR rules	30.8	23.5	22.1	19.3	18.0	9.8	2.8	4.1
No HR	30.8	23.5	22.1	14.1	12.4	9.8	8.0	9.8
Better HR	30.8	23.5	22.1	19.6	18.3	9.8	2.5	3.8
Basic only	15.4	15.4	15.4	15.4	15.4	9.2	0.0	0.0
'Swedish' child care	30.8	23.5	22.1	19.9	19.6	9.8	2.2	2.6
'French' child care	30.8	23.5	22.1	21.8	21.5	9.8	0.3	0.6

Note: HR – home responsibility

14.5 Summary and Conclusions

The Beveridge model of husbands as the main source of insurance for married women is clearly out of date. We have pointed out that reproductive and caring responsibilities still form economic handicaps for many women. We have questioned how far subsequent and projected changes in social security rules allow for this. Women's advances into the labour market have not given them equality with men, and perhaps never will. Contrary to popular perception, they have reduced, rather than eliminated many women's dependency on their partners. We have considered how pensions policy could be adapted to recognise the importance of both the paid and unpaid aspects of women's work. We used simulations of model lifetimes to investigate the implications of alternative indexation policies, and also to examine a number of policy reforms: improving home responsibility protection, providing better basic pension, and the pension consequences of childcare policies.

Our simulations illustrate contrasts between men's and women's lifetime earnings which are mirrored, though muted, in differential state pensions. Wives are still partially dependent on their husbands' pension rights and need access to them on widowhood, particularly if they have raised children. In the pattern of earnings differentials which, we suggest, is still common, women would not be well served by the individualisation of benefits and the abolition of derived rights, particularly to occupational benefits.

We have shown that home responsibility credits mitigate, but do not eliminate, the pensions forgone by mothers. We considered enhancing the individual pension rights of women by extending HR protection to years of low earnings while responsible for children. This only yielded modest advances in entitlement beyond that already afforded by existing HR provision, but might be politically attractive and would have modest costs. Improvements in home responsibility protection, at least along the lines of our simulations, do not entirely redress the pension penalties of motherhood, for, unlike childcare, they do not correct the erosion of mothers' earning power.

Among the other options we considered on current indexation policy, the extensive child-care option was more effective than the specified increases in basic pension at safeguarding for mothers a modest level of income in old age, but only for those who chose to spend time in paid work away from their children. Those doing the childcare job wholly or partly themselves will still end up with relatively little pension in their own right. Of the options we have considered, the child-care policies would be the most difficult to implement, since they entail a wholesale relocation of nurturing work and a near reconstitution of mothers' earning patterns.

It is questionable whether current indexation policy on State pensions, destined to make these 'wither on the branch', is sustainable. Its success depends on privatising pensions, but those with low earnings will be unable to earn themselves a decent pension. The consequences will be continued dependence on means-tested benefits, which pleases no-one, and increasing relative impoverishment of those reliant on the state system. The flip side of the worsening dependency ratio is greater voting power for pensioners, and it is realistic to expect them to exploit it. Without structural changes in the pension system, pressure for better benefits could be achieved either by changing the indexation rules or (perhaps more likely) by periodic hikes in the level of benefit.

Doubling basic pension or linking it to earnings growth yielded approximately the same flat rate pension for those retiring around 2040. The latter option would be increasingly generous over time, especially if SERPS was also retained. In case the working population cannot be persuaded to be so generous, we considered partially financing better basic pension by abolishing SERPS. Provided couples stay together and pool resources married men should not in theory(!) object to the latter transfer. Men who were willing to undertake caring duties could themselves benefit from these arrangements.

Individualised benefit in the form of an adequate (but expensive) basic pension could indeed offer women security and independence in old age, but only to a degree. Independence and equality are not the same. Sex equality in pensions remains elusive as long as access to good private pensions and the burden of unpaid work remain unequal.

We have not, in these experiments, found any scheme for social insurance that is better adapted to partial dependency than a better basic pension. Unless these proposals for what amounts to a basic income in retirement are implemented, it would be premature to abolish the notion of derived rights to pension entitlement – on widowhood or divorce. Spouses' interests in each other's pension rights should not just involve female survivors, and ideally they should not just cover legally married partnerships. The case for this is strengthened by the uneven distribution of private pension entitlements between men and women.

As long as retirement income is earnings related, something is required in the policy package to help restore the earning power and pension-earning power, where possible, of those whose pension rights have taken second place to caring responsibility. Another of Beveridge's proposals still seems relevant, the training allowance for those whose unpaid occupation came to an end (for example, through early widowhood, para. 349). For those whose caring responsibilities continue up to (and into) 'retirement', or those to whom the training opportunity came relatively late, this option would not be much use. For younger women with children it would be more effective if combined with child care provision, yet to discard the idea would be tantamount to accepting the labour market penalties of motherhood as irreversible. After much deliberation, Owen and Joshi (1990) concluded that equitable treatment of women in pensions required both an enhancement of the labour market opportunities for carers and an enhancement of the recognition given to unpaid contributions. These simulations rediscover another of Beveridge's principles, that groups of complementary policies are better than single measures. How social security should adapt to the roles of women is – not in isolation.

Chapter 15

Is there a Future for the Beveridge Pension Scheme?

Paul Johnson and Jane Falkingham

In his 1942 *Report*, William Beveridge identified the problem of adequate income support in old age as 'the most important, and in some ways the most difficult, of all the problems of social security' (Beveridge, 1942, p. 90). In response, he endeavoured to devise a pension system which would be financially sound, provide an adequate income in old age for those with no other resources, and give the maximum encouragement to voluntary saving. The Beveridge pension scheme has failed in each of these three respects, and this failure has been apparent since the inception of the National Insurance (NI) system in 1948.

The basic pension has never been paid at an adequate subsistence level, and a substantial minority of pensioners have consistently had to rely on means-tested income supplements. Voluntary additional saving for old age has never been sufficient, a fact explicitly acknowledged in 1975 with the imposition of compulsory additional savings in the form of state earnings-related pension scheme (SERPS) contributions. The financial basis of the National Insurance scheme has never been sound in the sense used by Beveridge – that is, organised around actuarially-determined contribution and benefit rates. Although Beveridge recommended that pensions should be phased-in over a 20-year period in order to equalise pension contributions and benefits, for reasons of political expediency pensions were paid at the full rate from the very beginning of the NI scheme, and were subsequently uprated independently of any increase in contribution levels. Largely because of this cavalier approach to pension financing, the principle of actuarially-determined NI contributions paid into an NI Fund was prejudiced from the very beginning and was finally abandoned in the late 1950s as graduation and pay-as-you-go practice took over from the principle of flat-rate contributions and partial funding (Dilnot *et al.*, 1984, p. 18).

This multiple failure of the Beveridge pension scheme in terms of structure and performance makes the continued support for the scheme by many welfare state apologists somewhat surprising. Despite half a century of palpable inadequacy, there is still widespread faith in the potential of the flat-rate NI pension scheme. We believe that this faith is misplaced, that few worthwhile elements can be salvaged from the public pension system currently in place in the UK, that future social and economic change will further undermine any lingering functional coherence, and therefore that a fundamental restructuring of the British public pension system is required. The first section of this chapter discusses the present and anticipated problems of the Beveridge pension scheme under the five criteria of adequacy, comprehensiveness, portability, distributional transparency and stability. The second section proposes a new model for a public pension system which satisfies these five criteria. The third section then presents some preliminary estimates of the costs and benefits of this new pension system.

15.1 Problems with the Current Pension System

Some of the problems of the Beveridge pension scheme – such as its inability to prevent pensioner poverty – are well known, whereas others such as its confusion of distributional intent are less immediately apparent. In this brief review of these problems we will devote more space to the less commonly discussed issues.

15.1.1 Adequacy

In the period 1948–82 between 20 per cent and 30 per cent of all NI retirement pensioners were in receipt of means-tested income supplements, with many more on low incomes qualifying for but not claiming this additional benefit (Dilnot *et al.*, 1984, p. 22). Little has changed in the last decade; according to the government's own data in 1988 5.6 million pensioners had incomes so low that they were entitled to means-tested support (DSS, 1988). The reason for this enduring inadequacy of pensioner income is the low replacement rate of the NI retirement pension. Table 15.1 shows that the initial replacement rate of the pension, just under 20 per cent of average male manual earnings, barely changed in the first 25 years, rose marginally in the later 1970s, but has declined in the 1980s. This decline is projected to continue because since 1980 the pension has been uprated in line with prices rather than average earnings. The purchasing power of the pension is now fixed at its 1980 level, and if real incomes rise at 1.5 per cent per annum, the NI

pension will wither to a mere 7 per cent of average male earnings by 2050
– a transformation from the inadequate to the trivial.

Table 15.1 Retirement Pension as Percentage of Average Male Earnings, UK, 1948-2050

	as percentage male manual earnings	as percentage male earnings
1948	19.1	-
1955	18.4	-
1961	19.1	-
1965	21.4	-
1971	19.5	17.5
1975	21.5	19.6
1981	22.9	19.8
1985	22.5	19.2
1990	-	16.0
2000	-	14.0
2010	-	12.0
2020	-	10.0
2030	-	9.0
2040	-	8.0
2050	-	7.0

Note: Projections from 1990 assume the pension is uprated in line with prices and that real earnings grow at 1.5% per annum.
Source: DHSS, 1986, pp. 262–3; Government Actuary, 1990b, p. 18.

The state earnings-related pension scheme (SERPS), introduced in
1975 partly to counter this inadequate replacement rate, now provides a
justification for the further diminution of the NI pension, since all older
workers in the future will receive an earnings-related pension either
through SERPS or from a 'contracted-out' occupational or personal
pension. However the adequacy of the SERPS pension is far from
assured. Atkinson (1991b, p. 125) has calculated that, on current rules
and assuming the NI pension replacement rate remains fixed at 16 per
cent, a person with lifetime average earnings equal to the national
average for males and retiring after 2009 would receive at the date of
retirement a combined NI and SERPS pension equal to 33 per cent of final
gross earnings or 43 per cent of net earnings. This compares
unfavourably with gross replacement rates of around 56 per cent in
Germany (65 per cent net) and between 59 per cent and 71 per cent in
France. If, however, the NI pension follows the declining course
projected in Table 15.1, the gross replacement rate for a British worker
with average income would fall from 33% to 27%.

These calculations apply only to workers with average earnings and
in the SERPS scheme – around half of the labour force is 'contracted-out'

of SERPS and enrolled in occupational or personal pension schemes which meet certain minimum requirements. In general the net replacement rate of final salary occupational pension schemes is much higher than in SERPS – typically over 70 per cent – but this is received only by workers with uninterrupted service records. Despite recent improvements in vesting procedures (since 1988 rights have been vested after two years qualifying service), frequent job movers can find their occupational pension entitlements are disappointingly small. Moreover, the pay-out from any earnings-related pension scheme, whether public or private, will largely be a function of income, and casual, low-paid and temporary workers in the secondary labour market are seldom likely to have the opportunity to accumulate adequate earnings-related pension entitlements. Some people will continue to rely on the basic NI pension, and if this pension dwindles in size, the problem of old age poverty will be exacerbated.

Of course, if the NI pension replacement rate were to be raised substantially, the problem of old age poverty could be averted, but at enormous cost. A doubling of the replacement rate from the present 16 per cent to 32 per cent of average male income could be achieved at a cost of £18 billion, equivalent to an increase in the basic and higher rates of income tax of seven percentage points, to 32 per cent and 47 per cent respectively, or to the abolition of the NI upper threshold and an increase in employee NI contributions to 17 per cent.[1] Quite apart from questions about the practicality of such a move, we believe it would be the least best way of providing an adequate and assured income for all older people. This is because the Beveridge pension system incorporates a number of structural attributes which make it a necessarily imperfect mechanism for providing guaranteed pensions.

15.1.2 Comprehensiveness

The first, and possibly the most obvious (though not the most important) of these structural attributes is the contribution principle upon which the NI system is based. This principle is discussed in greater detail elsewhere in this volume (see the chapters by Ginn and Arber, and Lister) and we will only briefly touch upon the problems that arise from it here.

Beveridge believed that automatic entitlement should be based upon an adequate contribution record. Since contribution in the NI scheme is a function of employment, only people with a long-term employment record, or with protected periods out of the labour force through registered unemployment, disability or home responsibilities, gain the right to a full NI pension. According to estimates made by the

---

1   These estimates were derived from the TAXMOD tax-benefit model, using October 1991 parameters. For further details of the model, see Atkinson and Sutherland, 1988.

Government Actuary, about 6 per cent of male pensioners retiring in 1990 did not qualify for a full-rate basic pension, while fewer than 70 per cent of women currently reaching pension age have a pension entitlement in their own right, and few of these are full-rate entitlements (Government Actuary, 1990b, pp. 51–2). In a society in which women undertake the majority of non-waged domestic and caring work, the contributory principle is inevitably sexist and exclusive. We believe than an adequate income in old age for everyone can be assured only if the minimum pension is unrelated to previous labour market experience, and if all individuals are treated equally regardless of their past, present or future marital status.

15.1.3 Portability

In the unified labour market of the EC pension entitlements need to be portable across national boundaries, and this is as true of public as of private pensions. At present preserved state pension entitlements remain paid-up in the country of origin, with partial pensions eventually paid according to the rules (retirement age, replacement rate, indexing procedure) of that country and in the currency of that country. A highly mobile European worker could, therefore, secure state pension benefits from all 12 member states of the EC. For any worker with even a modest degree of inter-country mobility during her working life, it becomes practically impossible to develop any clear idea about the expected value on retirement of her several public pension entitlements.

Much the same is true of occupational pensions. The enormous variation across EC countries (and even across firms in the same country) in the way occupational pension schemes treat vesting and transfers means that, despite the apparent simplicity of moving individual entitlements between funded pension schemes, there are in many countries considerable practical constraints, while occupational pensions in Germany, France and Denmark are in effect non-transferable across national boundaries. Jolliffe (1991, p. 200) notes the need to harmonise the tax and actuarial treatment of pension entitlements across EC borders. In Section 15.2 we will present an outline of a pension scheme that can circumvent these portability problems.

15.1.4 Distributional transparency

The distributional consequences of the Beveridge pension scheme are highly complex and largely hidden from view, barely identifiable even for skilled pension analysts. We believe that the working principles and distributional outcomes of any pension scheme should be completely transparent so that pension scheme contributors, beneficiaries and administrators can all make fully-informed decisions.

Public pension schemes in practice normally involve three distinct types of redistribution:

i) The redistribution of an individual's resources over her life-cycle, so that some of the income received during peak earning years is saved for later consumption during a period of retirement – we call this *intrapersonal* redistribution.

ii) The redistribution of resources between rich and poor people alive at any particular point in time – we call this *interpersonal* redistribution.

iii) The redistribution of resources between people born at different dates, i.e. between different birth cohorts – we call this *intergenerational* redistribution.

The Beveridge pension scheme has evolved since 1948 from being aimed largely at *intrapersonal* redistribution to being much more complex in performance and confused in intent. The objective of Beveridge was to ensure that the flat-rate contributions paid by workers into the NI scheme during their working life were set so as to provide an adequate actuarially-assessed income sufficient to cover five-sixths of pension payments (one-sixth was to come from general tax revenue). This was supposed to provide a mechanism for intrapersonal redistribution across the life-course; the flat-rate nature of both contributions and benefits meant that interpersonal redistribution was limited to that brought about by differential mortality. Since 1948 the distributional outcomes of public pension schemes in Britain have fundamentally diverged from Beveridge's design for two quite different reasons.

First, the flat-rate principle has been gradually eroded. In April 1961 graduated contributions replaced the flat-rate impost, and from 1975 contributions have been related to earnings for all income between the lower and upper NI contribution thresholds. A very meagre element of graduation in benefits was introduced in 1961 to compensate for the change in the contributory principle, but the pensioning effect of this has been trivial. Much more important has been the distributional consequence of the change to earnings-related contributions which, when tied to a primarily flat-rate benefit, has automatically brought about an interpersonal redistribution from higher to lower earners.

Secondly, the Beveridge pension scheme has, since its inception, worked to transfer resources between people born at different dates, i.e. it has brought about an intergenerational transfer of resources, the scale of which was further increased by the introduction of SERPS in 1975. This intergenerational transfer is the outcome both of the way in which the Beveridge pension scheme was inaugurated and of the subsequent evolution of public pension entitlement and contribution rules. By paying a full-rate pension immediately after the Second World War to people over the pension qualifying age (65 for men, 60 for women), a substantial and direct transfer was made from central government funds to pensioners who had, in many cases, made no earlier contributions to the preceding contributory public pension scheme. This first generation of pensioners received, in effect, a windfall gift from the government, paid largely from the contributions of the working population.

These pension windfalls were paid for by dipping into the NI fund, with the result that the fund was always in actuarial deficit, a problem neatly resolved when the funding principle was dropped in 1958 to be replaced by pay-as-you-go financing, with each year's contribution being used to pay that year's pensions. This might not have mattered had the system been in a 'steady state' – that is with a fixed population size and age structure and fixed contribution and pension levels. In these circumstances payments into and out of a mature, fully-funded pension scheme are identical to the annual flow of funds through a pay-as-you-go scheme, and so the two systems are functionally equivalent. But the pension system since the Second World War has not been in a steady state because the ageing of the population has increased the ratio of pensioners to contributors.

This changing age structure was entirely foreseen by Beveridge who noted that 'the cost of pensions relatively to the rest of social security will increase inevitably through increase in the proportion of people of pensionable age in the population' (Beveridge, 1942, p. 90). The introduction of pay-as-you-go financing into this ageing pension system has had the inevitable effect of increasing the cost of the pension for successive generations. The financing conditions for a flat-rate contributory pension scheme can be written as:

$$L(w.c) = P(w.r) \tag{1}$$

where L is the number of contributors in the labour force, P the number of pension recipients, c the contribution or tax rate, r the pension replacement rate, and w the real wage. Since the real wage appears on both sides of the equation, economic growth can have no impact on this financing identity. Rearrangement of [1] shows that:

$$c = P/L.r \tag{2}$$

so if the replacement rate remains fixed at some constant level, an increase in the size of the pensioner population relative to the contributor population must increase the contribution rate c.

This is just what happened in Britain to the Beveridge pension scheme. In 1951 there were 23.96 million NI contributors and 4.22 million pensioners, figures which had risen by 1974 to 25.18 million and 8.74 million respectively. The increase in pension costs brought about by this ageing of the population is reflected in two different sets of figures. First, pensions as a proportion of all NI expenditure rose from 57 per cent in 1950/51 to 69 per cent in 1974/5. Second, the income from contributions received by the NI Fund as a proportion of total income from employment[2] (a proxy measure for the contribution rate, c) which stood at 5.0 per cent in 1951 and declined marginally to 4.7 per cent by 1957 then rose to 7.4 per cent in 1968 and reached 9.5 per cent in 1974. Preservation of the replacement rate at around 20 per cent and a near doubling in the pensioner support ratio inevitably led to a near doubling in the contribution rate. Although real pension levels remained virtually constant over this period, different cohorts of pensioners have paid contributions which have varied widely depending solely upon when they were born. Extensive intergenerational transfers have been made from later-born generations of workers to earlier-born generations of pensioners. The effect of this has been to give highly divergent real rates of return to pension contributions.

The introduction of SERPS in 1975 increased the scale of intergenerational transfers. Pay-as-you-go financing was adopted to permit the early payment of pensions (at a reduced rate from 1978, full rate from 1998) even though SERPS would not become fully mature, with pensions based upon contributions paid over a full working life, until 2020. In the 1970s the immediate cost of SERPS was low because there were many contributors supporting very few pensioners. Official projections made in 1975 indicated that the necessary contribution rate for SERPS would rise to no more than 3–4 per cent by 2009, but these projections failed to take account of either the maturing of SERPS after 2020 or the projected increase in the ratio of pensioners to contributors between 2011 and 2031 as the share of people in the population over the current pension age (60 for women, 65 for men) rises from 19 per cent to 24 per cent. An independent estimate by Hemming and Kay of the long-run costs of SERPS suggested that the ultimate contribution rate would be around 13 per cent. They concluded that 'we have, in effect, secured the finance to impose lower rates of taxation on the working population now by selling promises that our children will pay more generous pensions than we are willing to pay to our parents' (Hemming and Kay, 1982, pp. 314). Partly in response to this concern about the apparently unfair financial burden placed by yesterday's electors and legislators on tomorrow's workers (many of whom are as yet unborn), and partly to contribute to a general reduction of social security provision and expenditure, the SERPS scheme was substantially modified by the 1986 Social Security Act. From 2000 benefits will be reduced from 25 per cent to 20 per cent of maximum pensionable earnings, the entitlement basis will be changed to average lifetime earnings from best 20 years, and

---

2   The definition of total income from employment published in the *Annual Abstract of Statistics* changes over the post-war period. For these calculations a standard definition has been used, which consists of: wages, salaries, pay in cash and kind to the armed forces and employers' National Insurance and other contributions.

the long-run costs of the scheme will be approximately halved (Fry *et al.*, 1990).

We believe that pension systems should be structured in order to prevent the transfer of the cost of current pension promises onto future generations who are not party to the promises, to encourage awareness of the true financial implications of securing a pension with an adequate replacement rate, and to make explicit the welfare function of a minimum pension provision. This can best be done by ensuring that the intergenerational, intrapersonal and interpersonal transfers are all separately identifiable and independently resourced. The pension scheme proposed below is designed to meet these objectives.

15.1.5 Stability

Perhaps the most important attribute of any pension scheme is the long-run guarantee given to current contributors/savers that at some defined point in the future they will become eligible for a pension of some value fixed relative to their current living standards. Unfortunately no pension scheme can realistically give such a commitment. Although promises are continually made, the history of pension scheme provision over the past century is one of exaggerated claims and disappointed expectations. There are two reasons for this.

First, few pension schemes guarantee to maintain the real value of the pension. Although most pension schemes now uprate pension payments to take some account of inflation, this is often an *ad hoc* procedure, and the indexation is usually linked to prices rather than incomes, as is now the practice in the basic NI pension scheme.

Second, the value of the initial pension is contingent on a number of variables that change over an individual's life course, and which necessarily make pension expectations probabilistic rather than certain. This is true of all pension schemes, whether public or private, funded or pay-as-you-go, although this is not always fully recognised. For instance Schmähl (1991, p. 52) in his excellent survey of European supplementary pension schemes, makes the common but incorrect assertion that defined-benefit pensions permit explicit target-income saving for retirement which is not possible in defined-contribution schemes. In the same vein Atkinson (1991b, p. 130), in a discussion of the decision of several million British workers to enrol in defined-contribution personal pension schemes rather than defined-benefit occupational schemes, remarks that 'a guarantee is replaced by a lottery' because of the uncertainty in defined-contribution schemes over both the capital sum available at retirement and the value of the annuity it will buy. In truth, however, both systems are lotteries, with capital market gambles in the defined-contribution pension set against labour market gambles in the defined-benefit system where workers who fail to achieve their expected career progression, or who are demoted towards the end of their career, will find their actual pension is below their long-run expectation. For female workers who, on average, have flatter age–earnings profiles than men and more discontinuous employment histories, gambling on capital market performance may well be a better bet than gambling on the chance of a high income in the years immediately preceding retirement.

The element of chance is equally apparent in public pension schemes. The uprating of the NI pension with average earnings between 1948 and the mid-1970s depended upon repeated *ad hoc* political decisions to maintain the financing conditions of equation [1], but in 1980 the government decided to change the financing conditions to:

$$L(w_t .c) = P(w_{1980} .r) \tag{3}$$

thereby fixing the value of the basic pension at its 1980 level. Few older people could have reasonably expected any such fundamental change in financing principles and incorporated this in their long-term saving plans. Public pensions are in some ways the least stable of pension schemes – almost every industrialised economy has introduced major changes to public pension entitlements, qualifying ages, benefit levels or indexing principles over the last decade (OECD, 1988b). This generic absence of stability in public and private pension systems militates against rational individual retirement planning and encourages people to adopt short-term attitudes towards long-run saving.

The Beveridge pension scheme fails to satisfy all five criteria of adequacy, comprehensiveness, portability, distributional transparency and stability. Rather than attempt to remove the manifest inconsistencies and inefficiencies which are deeply embedded in the structure of the Beveridge pension scheme, we think it is preferable to develop a new pension system designed explicitly to meet the five criteria discussed here.

15.2   Alternative Systems of Pension Provisioning

What alternatives are there to the existing combination of NI and SERPS pensions? Occupational pensions provided by employers do not offer a plausible alternative to public pension provision because their coverage is limited. Occupational schemes attained their maximum coverage of the labour force in 1967 at 53 per cent, and since then coverage has declined to 49 per cent, so they fail to satisfy the criterion of comprehensiveness. Personal pensions, although increasingly popular, are also an inadequate substitute for a public pension system because they provide only minimal pensions to people who have low lifetime incomes. They therefore fail to meet the adequacy criterion. If adequate pensions in retirement are to be provided for all people, regardless of their past labour market history, then they must involve a substantial transfer of resources from the life-time rich to the life-time poor, and this can only be achieved through some degree of public intervention.

The Institute for Fiscal Studies has recently proposed a reform to the existing NI pension system that would involve the gradual addition of a means-tested supplement to the basic state pension (Dilnot and Johnson, 1992). They argue that this is the only way of containing the cost of the NI pension while also ensuring that an adequate income is provided to the poorest of the elderly. Any move in this direction would involve all the well-known problems and costs of operating a means test, and would do nothing to unravel the distributional complexity of the existing NI system. A rather different way of providing better incomes for the poor elderly is by means of a Citizen's Income (or basic income) which would be provided tax free to all people every month, with this financed by the abolition of existing income tax relief and by the payment of tax on earned income (Citizens Income, 1993). This proposal also does nothing to clarify the extent to which the system involves intrapersonal, interpersonal and intergenerational transfers, and also introduces potentially important labour supply disincentives.

We propose a quite different pension system which explicitly unifies basic and supplementary pension provision. We call this system a Unified Funded Pension Scheme (UFPS) because it is designed to replace the existing NI basic pension and the majority of state, occupational and personal earnings-related pension schemes with a single pension that combines minimum pension guarantees with earnings-related provision. This UFPS would meet all five criteria established above and in addition would increase labour mobility, the stock of investible funds in the economy and personal choice over the timing of retirement. The scheme is based on the principle of every individual building-up a personal retirement fund (PRF) over his or her adult life which is used, at some age, to purchase a pension annuity. Combined with this is a system of annual tax-financed capital transfers to people with low incomes or not in the labour market, together with investment insurance designed to spread portfolio risk across people of different generations.

In the UFPS all adults aged over 21 are required to contribute a set percentage of their pre-tax income into a personal retirement fund (PRF) which is a tax-privileged personal long-term savings account designed to facilitate intrapersonal income transfers over the life-cycle. These PRFs will normally be collectively managed by a number of competing retirement trust funds, and to encourage management competition everyone will have the right to a free transfer of their PRF between trust funds once every five years. The percentage contribution rate will be fixed so that an individual in receipt of average age-specific income across the earning life-span will have accumulated by some age (say 65) a PRF sufficient to purchase an index-linked annuity equal to some fixed amount (say 50 per cent) of average earnings. Anyone with lifetime earnings above the average would necessarily accumulate a larger PRF and so would have a pension with a gross replacement rate greater than 50 per cent of average income, and anyone would be entitled (and encouraged) to raise their percentage contribution rate if they wished to raise their ultimate pension replacement rate. We believe that the long-term retirement saving plans of each individual are too important to be placed in the hands of employers and made subject to their labour market management objectives. It would be open to employers to devise other remuneration packages designed to reward worker loyalty, but PRFs would be entirely paid for and vested in the individual.

What happens to people who receive less than average lifetime earnings, or who receive no earnings at all because of illness, disability, unemployment or non-waged caring responsibilities? To ensure that people in these categories have access to a minimum acceptable pension at age 65, they will require direct capital transfers into their PRF for each and every year in which their contribution into the PRF is inadequate to maintain the required path of PRF capital growth. This capital transfer will be financed from taxes on current income, and so will be a direct interpersonal tax transfer. This will provide a guaranteed income for all elderly people irrespective of their past labour market history or marital status, but to preserve savings incentives and a sense of equity this guaranteed pension should be set at a level below the 50 per cent replacement rate accumulated by a worker with an average lifetime earnings trajectory. A replacement rate of 33 per cent of average male earnings might be an acceptable minimum level. This means that for any individual whose income consistently falls significantly below the average age-specific income, then her PRF will consistently receive a capital top-up sufficient to maintain a fund that will buy an index-linked annuity at age 65 equal to 33 per cent of average income. If, however, an individual is sometimes in the labour force in a well-paid job but sometimes in a low-paid job or out of the labour force, her PRF capital top-up would be paid only at the point when the PRF falls below the required minimum age-specific amount.

There are two obvious sources of uncertainty about ultimate pension income within this model of a UFPS. First, the long-run real rate of return on PRF assets and the rate of real income growth may not correspond with expectations, and secondly short-term fluctuations in asset values may impose windfall PRF gains or losses at the point of retirement, thereby unexpectedly enhancing or undermining long-term saving plans. The first problem is, to some extent, automatically corrected by the minimum pension rule. If the growth rate of real earnings significantly exceeds its expected value but the real rate of return maintains its expected growth rate, then the replacement rate of the annuity purchasable with any PRF will fall over time. To the extent to which this invokes additional PRF top-ups it brings about an interpersonal transfer from prime-age workers (who benefit most from the high real income growth) to lower-paid workers close to retirement. Even so, long-run inadequacy of financing cannot be resolved in this manner, so we would propose that the required pension contribution rate be subject to change by not more than one percentage point each year, and that such a change should be automatically imposed if age-specific PRFs fall below the level required for a 50 per cent replacement rate for a person on average income.

The second problem is more tricky. One of the weaknesses of funded, personal pensions is that with each cohort reliant on its own savings it is difficult to insure against risks such as abrupt movements in asset values that affect any particular generation. Within a UFPS several methods can be adopted to spread this risk across cohorts without introducing opportunities for intergenerational buck-passing of the sort provided by SERPS. First, trust funds responsible for managing PRFs could be required to value PRFs on, say, a three-year moving-average basis. The cost of this, either in terms of insurance premia or charges in the options/futures market would be part of the overall management cost and so spread across all birth cohorts. Secondly, more overt insurance protection can be provided by levying an extraordinary capital gains tax on PRF asset growth in times of very high and unanticipated capital appreciation which can be used to build up an asset protection reserve fund to provide, in a period of declining asset values, capital top-ups to the PRFs of people within, say, five years of retirement. Some combination of these strategies is probably optimal; although such a system could not give an absolute guarantee of ultimate pension value to someone in mid-career, it would provide greater security than existing pension schemes.

How well would this Unified Funded Pension Scheme meet the five criteria established in Section 15.1? Adequacy and comprehensiveness would both be achieved through the minimum PRF provision and the system of tax-funded capital top-ups. Minimum pension entitlements would be provided regardless of gender, marital status or labour market history. The system is gender blind in so far as the contribution rate is common to men and women, though the replacement rate and average age-earnings profiles used in the calculation of the necessary age specific PRF value relate to males. This will impose some degree of redistribution within the system from high-income (male) taxpayers to low/zero income (female) recipients of a PRF capital top-up.

Portability is ensured by the fully-vested nature of the individual's PRF. By removing all control of the PRF from the employer the long-term savings plans of individuals are removed from the shackles of work-place loyalty, and decisions over when to retire are freed from any manipulation of pension values which can be effected by employers in final-salary pension schemes. The absolute ownership by individuals of their PRF means that no complex calculations of transfer values are needed if a person moves to another country. It also means that if an individual dies before the conversion of her PRF into an annuity at age 65 the PRF would be included in her estate (though the government might wish to reserve the right to claw back any capital top-ups from the PRF of people who die before pension age).

Distributional transparency is ensured by separating the financing of intrapersonal, interpersonal and intergenerational transfers. Contributions into a PRF are each person's means of redistributing resources across her own life-cycle, the tax-financed capital top-up is the cost of intrapersonal transfers from rich to poor in any particular year, and an exceptional capital gains levy on PRFs is the cost of intergenerational solidarity. This financing structure has two important outcomes. First it makes it impossible to make pension promises today while deferring the cost for several decades, as happened in 1975 with SERPS. In the UFPS a decision to raise replacement rates for everyone requires an immediate and sustained increase in the PRF contribution rate and in the tax-transfer costs of topping-up the inadequate PRFs of people near retirement. Second, it makes explicit the real cost of long-term retirement saving, thereby increasing public awareness of the enormous scale of pension funds, the value of each individual's pension savings, and the importance of pension rules and regulations. Finally, stability is provided by distancing the pension system from interference from governments and employers, and by building-in some intergenerational solidarity and index-linking of pension benefits.

15.3 Costing the UFPS

The viability of any new pension system must ultimately depend on its affordability. We have presented detailed estimates of the cost of a UFPS elsewhere (Falkingham and Johnson, 1993), and here we will simply indicate some likely outcomes. Using individual work history data for a cohort of persons generated by the microsimulation model, LIFEMOD (Falkingham and Lessof, 1991; 1992), we can estimate the numbers of men and women in any one cohort who, over their contribution life-cycle (ages 21–64) will have an income too low to allow the accumulation of a PRF which, at any age, is on a growth path sufficient to buy an annuity equal to at least one third of average male income at the point of retirement – i.e. the population that will need PRF capital top-ups.

With a contribution rate of 15 per cent of earnings, and a minimum UFPS pension of 33 per cent of average male earnings, 82 per cent of men but only 15 per cent of women had accumulated a PRF of sufficient size to purchase an annuity equal to the minimum pension. The average amount of capital top up required by men was £2,400 compared to £26,700 for women in 1991 prices. This demonstrates the low lifetime income position of the majority of women *vis-à-vis* men. If contributions are modified to be levied on joint earnings during marriage and are equally split between the spouses' PRFs then the proportion of men reaching retirement age with a shortfall in their PRF increases to 37 per cent (with a mean capital top-up requirement of £5,000) whilst the proportion of women falls to 45 per cent (£10,600).

By grossing up these figures we can estimate the cost of capital top-ups for the 564,000 UK citizens who reached age 65 in 1991, assuming they had the same average lifetime earning profiles as the LIFEMOD population. For a funded pension system based on individual contributions of 15 per cent of earnings and a minimum pension target of 33 per cent of average male full-time earnings, the cost is £8.4 billion, and for joint contributions the cost is £4.4 billion. This tax cost would be compensated for by the abolition of the current NI pension and associated means-tested benefits to the elderly which currently cost about £26.5 billion. In addition, if tax thresholds are kept at their present level, the higher income of pensioners would, according to TAXMOD estimates, generate an additional £3.7 billion in income tax revenue, so the combined saving would be £30.2 billion, and the net saving, after paying for the UFPS capital top-ups, would be between £21.8 and £25.8 billion.

Currently employee NI contributions produce a revenue of £17.4 billion, so the cost of a mature UFPS could be covered by the abolition of employee NI contributions, and this would leave between £4 and £8 billion for additional income tax cuts or for some reduction in employer NI contributions. Employer NI contributions would continue to be levied and would pay for unemployment, sickness and disability benefits, but would not be part of UFPS income.

For the government, therefore, there need be no net expenditure implication in replacing a mature NI pension system with a mature UFPS. For workers there would be the additional cost of PRF contributions of 15 per cent of gross earnings, against which would be set the saving on employee NI contributions plus income tax cuts of up to 5 per cent. Clearly all workers would be paying more into the UFPS than they do into the NI system, but they would receive much better pensions in return. For employers there would no longer be any need to operate an occupational pension scheme or become involved with the long-term savings plans of individual workers. There may be some beneficial effects to capital markets from an increase in the savings rate; total annual contributions within a mature system would be £44.5bn.

However, estimates of the cost of a mature pension system in a steady state take no account of any additional costs that may be incurred in making a transition between different types of system. These costs may be considerable, particularly if the change is from a pay-as-you-go to a funded system. Elsewhere (Falkingham and Johnson, 1993) we demonstrate that although substantial, the costs of transition are not insurmountable and therefore that fundamental reform of the public pension structure in Britain, with movement from today's PAYG system to tomorrow's UFPS, is a viable option.

15.4   Summary and Conclusion

In this chapter we have argued that the current mix of pension systems in Britain is inadequate, and that the NI and SERPS systems are based upon structural conditions which preclude effective reform.

We have presented outline plans for an entirely new type of funded pension system that incorporates annual capital top-ups for the life-time poor so that they can purchase an adequate pension annuity at normal retirement age. Our proposed UFPS embodies a number of attributes that we think would be desirable in any reform of the British pension system, whether or not it follows the model proposed in this chapter. The most important of these are:

- individual pensions regardless of labour market or marital history;
- joint contributions for married or co-habiting couples;
- provision of annual statements to all contributors of the value of past contributions and the expected value of pensions at retirement;
- removal of employer interference in pension arrangements;
- full vesting of pension savings in the individual;
- separation of inter- and intra-personal redistribution functions of pension schemes;
- higher basic replacement rates, which necessarily require higher contribution rates than at present;
- annualisation of the cost of tax-financed subventions to prevent transfer by government of current pension costs onto future generations.

List of Contributors

Emily K. Abel is an Associate Professor in the UCLA School of Public Health. Recent publications include: *Who Cares for the Elderly? Public policy and the experience of adult daughters* (Temple University Press, 1991), and *Circles of Care: Work and identity in women's lives* (State University of New York Press, 1990, co-editor).

Sara Arber is a Senior Lecturer in Sociology at the University of Surrey. Recent publications include: *Gender and Later Life* (Sage, 1991, co-authored with J. Ginn), *Women and Working Lives* (Macmillan, 1991, co-authored with N. Gilbert), and *Ageing, Independence and the Life Course* (Jessica Kingsley, 1993, co-edited with M. Evandrou).

Sally Baldwin is Director of the Social Policy Research Unit and Professor of Social Policy at the University of York. Recent publications include: *The Cost of Caring: Families with disabled children* (Routledge, 1985), *Social Security and Community Care* (Avebury, 1988, co-edited with G. Parker and R. Walker), and *Quality of Life: Perspectives and Policies* (Routledge, 1989, co-edited with C. Godfrey and C. Propper).

John Blackwell was Lecturer in Environmental Studies at University College Dublin and formerly Principal Administrator, Social Affairs Division, OECD. Recent publications include: 'The relationship between cost of community care and dependency in old people' (*Social Science and Medicine*, 37, 1993, co-authored with E. O'Shea), and *Low Pay – The Irish Experience* (The Combat Poverty Agency/Irish Congress of Trade Unions, 1990, co-authored with B. Nolan).

Bea Cantillon is a Professor at the Universities of Antwerp and Brussels and Director of the Centre for Social Policy (UFSIA, University of Antwerp). She has written on the distribution of welfare outcomes, pensioners and resources of the elderly, social security and social and demographic change, international comparisons, and social security reform.

Anne Corden is a Research Fellow in the Social Policy Research Unit, University of York. Recent publications include: *Perceptions of Family Credit* (HMSO, 1991, co-authored with P. Craig), and *Measuring Low Incomes: Self-employment and Family Credit* (HMSO, 1993, co-authored with R. Boden).

Hugh Davies is a Lecturer in Economics at Birkbeck College, University of London. Recent publications include: 'Pension splitting and divorce' (*Fiscal Studies*, November 1991) and 'Daycare in Europe and mothers' forgone earnings' (*International Labour Review*, 1992), both co-authored with H. Joshi.

Tony Eardley is a Research Fellow in the Social Policy Research Unit, University of York. Recent publications include: *Housing Benefit Reviews* (HMSO, 1991), and 'Managing appeals: The control of housing benefit internal reviews by local authority officers' (*Journal of Social Policy*, 4, 1993), both co-authored with R. Sainsbury.

Jane Falkingham is a Lecturer in Population Studies at the London School of Economics. During the preparation of the manuscript, she was a Research Fellow on the Welfare State Programme at the LSE. Recent publications include: *Ageing and Economic Welfare* (Sage, 1992, co-authored with P. Johnson), and *The Dynamic of Welfare* (Harvester Wheatsheaf, forthcoming, co-edited with J. Hills).

Jay Ginn is a Research Fellow in the Sociology Department, University of Surrey. Recent publications include: *Gender and Later Life: A sociological analysis of resources and contraints* (Sage, 1991), and 'Pension penalties: The gendered division of occupational welfare' (*Work, Employment and Society*, 1993), both co-authored with S. Arber.

Sandra Hutton is a Research Fellow at the Social Policy Research Unit, University of York. Recent publications include: 'Men and women's incomes: The evidence from survey data' (*Journal of Social Policy*, forthcoming), 'Incomes and assets of older people' (*Ageing and Society*, forthcoming), and 'The costs of ageing and retirement' (in *Money Matters*, Sage, 1987, R. Walker and G. Parker (eds.), co-authored with R. Walker).

Heather Joshi is a Reader in Social Statistics and Deputy Director of the Social Statistics Research Unit, City University. Recent publications include: *The Changing Population of Britain* (Blackwell, 1989, editor), 'The cash opportunity cost of childbearing' (*Population Studies*, 1990), and 'Pensions, divorce and wives' double burden' (*International Journal of Law and the Family*, 1992, co-authored with H. Davies).

Paul Johnson is a Lecturer in Social History at the London School of Economics. Recent publications include: *Ageing and Economic Welfare* (Sage, 1992, co-authored with J. Falkingham), and *Labour Markets in an Ageing Europe* (Cambridge University Press, 1993, co-edited with K. Zimmermann).

Hilary Land is Professor of Social Policy at Royal Holloway College, University of London. Recent publications include: 'Time to care' (in *Women's Issues in Social Policy*, M. Maclean and D. Groves (eds.), Routledge, 1992), and 'Whatever happened to the social wage?' (in *Women and Poverty*, C. Glendinning and J. Millar (eds.), Routledge, 1992), and 'Families and the law' (in *Politics, Policy and the Law*, A. Cochrane and J. Muncie (eds.), Open University Press, 1993).

Ruth Lister is Professor of Social Policy and Administration at Loughborough University of Technology and a member of the Commission on Social Justice. Recent publications include: *The Exclusive Society: Citizenship and the poor* (CPAG, 1990), and *Women's Economic Dependency and Social Security* (EOC, 1992).

Susan Lonsdale is a Senior Lecturer in Social Policy at South Bank University. Recent publications include: *Work and Inequality* (Longman, 1985), *Women and Disability* (Macmillan, 1990), and *In the Best of Health?* (Chapman and Hall, 1992, co-edited with E. Beck, S. P. Newman and D. Patterson).

Jane Millar is a Reader in Social Policy at the University of Bath. Recent publications include: *Lone-parent Families in the UK* (HMSO, 1991, co-authored with J. Bradshaw), and *Women and Poverty in Britain: The 1990s* (Harvester Wheatsheaf, 1992, co-edited with C. Glendinning).

Chris Phillipson is Professor of Applied Social Studies and Social Gerontology at the University of Keele. Recent publications include: *Capitalism and the Construction of Old Age* (Macmillan, 1982), *Ageing and Social Policy* (Gower, 1986, co-edited with A. Walker), and *Changing Work and Retirement* (Open University Press, 1991, co-authored with F. Laszcko).

Jennifer Seddon has recently graduated from the University of Bath, having studied Economics and Politics.

Steven Webb co-ordinates personal sector research at the Institute for Fiscal Studies, and is an adviser to the all-party Social Security Select Committee and member of the Commission on Social Justice. Recent publications include: *Time for Mortgage Benefits* (Joseph Rowntree Foundation, 1991, co-authored with Steve Wilcox), and *Poverty Statistics: A guide for the perplexed* (Institute for Fiscal Studies Commentary, 1993, co-authored with C. Giles).

Peter Whiteford is a Senior Research Fellow at the Social Policy Research Unit, University of York, and previously worked at the Social Policy Research Centre, University of New South Wales. Recent publications include: *A Family's Needs: Equivalence scales, poverty and social security* (Social Policy Research Centre, Australia, 1985), *Measuring Poverty: A review of the issues* (Office of Economic Planning Advisory Council, Australia, 1989, co-authored with P. Saunders), and *Immigrants and the Social Security System* (Bureau of Immigration Research, Australia, 1991).

References

Abbott, E. and Bompas, K. (1943), *The Woman Citizen and Social Security*, London: Mrs. Bompas.

Abel, E. K. (1991), *Who Cares for the Elderly? Public Policy and the Experiences of Adult Daughters*, Philadelphia, PA: Temple University Press.

Acker, J. (1988), 'Class, gender and the relations of distribution', *Signs*, **13**, 3.

Alba-Ramírez, A. (1991), 'Fixed-term employment contracts in Spain: labour market flexibility or segmentation?', Madrid, Universidad Carlos III de Madrid, mimeo.

Allen, D. and Hunn, A. (1985), 'An evaluation of the Enterprise Allowance Scheme', Employment Gazette, **93**, 8, pp. 313–317.

Allen, S. and Truman, C. (1992), 'Women, business and self-employment: a conceptual minefield', in *Women and Working Lives: division and change*, Arber, S. and Gilbert, N. (eds.), London: Macmillan.

Amann, A. (1981), *The Status and Prospects of the Aging in Western Europe*, Vienna: Eurosocial Occasional Papers No. 8.

Arber, S. and Gilbert, N. (1992),*Women and Working Lives: division and change*, London: Macmillan.

Arber, S. and Ginn, J. (1991), *Gender and Later Life: a sociological analysis of resources and constraints*, London: Sage.

Archbold, P. G. (1983), 'Impact of parent-caring on women,' *Family Relations*, **32**, pp. 39–45.

Atkinson, A. B. (1991a), 'Poverty, statistics and progress in Europe', STICERD Welfare State Programme Discussion Paper WSP/60, London: London School of Economics.

Atkinson, A. B. (1991b), 'The development of state pensions in the United Kingdom', in *The Future of Basic and Supplementary Pension Schemes in the European Community – 1992 and Beyond*, Schmähl, W. (ed.), Baden-Baden: Nomos Verlagsgesellschaft.

Atkinson, A. B. (1993), 'Beveridge, the national minimum and its future in a European context', STICERD Welfare State Programme Discussion Paper WSP/85, London: London School of Economics.

Atkinson, A. B. and Micklewright, J. (1988), 'Unemployment compensation, employment policy and labour market transitions', paper for meeting of experts at the OECD, mimeo.

Atkinson, A. B. and Micklewright, J. (1989), 'Turning the screw: benefits for the unemployed 1979–88', in *The Economics of Social Security*, Dilnot, A.W. and Walker, I. (eds.), Oxford: Oxford University Press.

Atkinson, A. B. and Sutherland, H. (1988), 'TAXMOD', in *Tax-Benefit Models*, Atkinson, A. B. and Sutherland, H. (eds.), STICERD Occasional Paper 10, London: London School of Economics.

Atkinson, J. (1985), 'Flexibility: planning for an uncertain future', *Manpower Policy and Practice*, **1**, Summer, pp. 26–29.

Bacchi, C. (1990), *Same Difference*, Sydney: Allen and Unwin.

Bacchi, C. (1991), 'Pregnancy, the law and the meaning of equality', in *Equality, Politics and Gender*, Meehan, E. and Sevenhuijsen, S. (eds.), London: Sage.

Baldwin, S. and Parker, G. (1989), 'The Griffiths report on community care', in *Social Policy Review 1988–9*, Brenton, M. and Ungerson, C. (eds.), Harlow: Longman.

Baldwin, S., Parker, G. and Walker, R. (1988), *Social Security and Community Care*, Aldershot: Avebury/Gower.

Barr, N. and Coulter, F. (1990), 'Social security: solution or problem?', in *The State of Welfare: the welfare state in Britain since 1974*, Hills, J. (ed.), Oxford: Oxford University Press.

Barrett, M. and McIntosh, M. (1982), *The Anti-social Family*, London: Verso.

Bartholomew R., Hibbett A. and Sidaway J. (1992), 'Lone parents and the labour market: evidence from the Labour Force Survey', *Employment Gazette*, pp. 559–577.

Bayer, R. (1986–87), 'Ethical Challenges', *Generations*, II, pp. 44–47.

Belous, R. S. (1989) 'How human resource systems adjust to the shift toward contingent workers', *Monthly Labor Review*, 112, 3, pp. 7–12.

Benefits Agency (1992), *Caring for Someone*, Leaflet FB31, London: HMSO.

Berkowitz, E. D. (1987), *Disabled Policy*, Cambridge: Cambridge University Press.

Berkowitz, M. and Hill, M. A. (1986), *Disability and the Labour Market*, Ithaca, NY: ILR Press.

Bernard, M. and Meade, K. (eds.) (1993), *Women Come of Age: Perspectives on the lives of older women*, London: Edward Arnold.

Bertghold, L. (1987), 'The impact of public policy on home health services for the elderly', *Pride Institute Journal of Long-Term Home Health Care*, 6, pp. 12–21.

Best, F. (1990), 'Does flexible life scheduling have a future' in *Re-Thinking Worklife Options for Older Persons*, Habib, J. and Nusberg, C. (eds.), Washington, DC: International Federation on Ageing / JDC Brookdale Institute on Ageing.

Beveridge, W. (1942), *Social Insurance and Allied Services*, Cmnd 6404, London: HMSO.

Beveridge, W. (1943), *Pillars of Security*, London: Allen and Unwin.

Beveridge, W. (1944a), *Voluntary Action*, London: Allen and Unwin.

Beveridge, W. (1944b), *Full Employment in a Free Society*, London: Allen and Unwin.

Beveridge, W. (1949) Epilogue to the 1949 edition of *The Disinherited Family*, Rathbone, E., London: Arnold.

Bjorklund, A., Haveman, R., Hollister, R. and Holmlund, B. (1991), *Labour Market Policy and Unemployment Insurance*, Oxford: Clarendon Press.

Blackwell, J. and Nolan, B. (1990), 'Low pay – the Irish experience', in *Low Pay - The Irish Experience*, Harvey, B. and Daly, M. (eds.), Dublin: Combat Poverty Agency and Irish Congress of Trade Unions.

Blank, R. M. (1990), 'Are part-time jobs bad jobs?', in *A Future of Lousy Jobs? The changing structure of U.S. wages*, Burtless, G. (ed.), Washington, DC: The Brookings Institution.

Blum, S. R. (1987), *New and Continuing Impediments to Improving the Quality of Life and Quality of Care in California's Nursing Homes*, A Report of the Commission on California's State Government Organization and Economy.

Board of Inland Revenue (1991), *Inland Revenue Statistics 1991*, London: HMSO.

Bogenhold, D. and Staber, U. (1991), 'The decline and rise of self-employment', *Work, Employment and Society*, 5, 2, pp. 223–239.

Bone, M., Gregory, J., Gill, B. and Lader, D. (1992), *Retirement and Retirement Plans*, Office of Population Censuses and Surveys, London: HMSO.

Borchorst, A. and Siim, B. (1987), 'Women and the advanced welfare state: a new kind of patriarchal power?' in *Women and the State*, Showstack Sassoon, A. (ed.), London: Hutchinson.

Bornat, J., Phillipson, C. and Ward, S. (1985), *A Manifesto for Old Age*, London: Pluto Press.

Bosworth, D. (1991), 'Employment contracts, job tenure and work histories: precarious employment in the UK', Institute for Employment Research, Discussion Paper No. 46, Coventry: University of Warwick.

Bradbury, B. and Saunders, P. (1990), 'How reliable are estimates of poverty in Australia? Some sensitivity tests for the period 1981–82 to 1985–86', Social Policy Research Centre, Discussion Paper No. 18, Sydney: University of New South Wales.

Bradshaw, J. and Deacon, A. (1983), *Reserved for the Poor: The means test in British social policy*, Oxford: Basil Blackwell and Martin Robertson.

Bradshaw, J. and Gibbs, I. (1988), *Public Support for Private Residential Care*, Aldershot: Avebury.

Bradshaw, J. and Huby, M. (1989), 'Trends in dependence on supplementary benefit', in *The Economics of Social Security*, Dilnot, A.W. and Walker, I. (eds.), Oxford: Oxford University Press.

Bradshaw, J. and Millar, J. (1991), *Lone-parent families in the UK*, Department of Social Security Report No. 6, London: HMSO.

Branch, L. G., Callahan, J. J. and Jette, A. M. (1981), 'Targeting home care services to vulnerable elders: Massachusetts' Home Care Corporations', *Home Health Care Services Quarterly*, 2, pp. 41–58.

Brannen, J. and Wilson G. (1987), *Give and Take in Families*, London: Allen and Unwin.

Brindle, D. (1993), 'Sperm donors face maintenance bills', *The Guardian*, 16.1.93.

Brocas, A., Cailloux, A. and Oget, V. (1990), *Women and Social Security: Progress towards equality of treatment*, Geneva: International Labour Office.

Brody, E. M. (1981), '"Women in the middle" and family help to older people', *The Gerontologist*, 21, pp. 471–480.

Brody, E. M. and Schoonover, C. B. (1986), 'Patterns of parent care when adult daughters work and when they do not', *The Gerontologist*, 26, pp. 372–381.

Brown, C. (1988), *Taxation and the Incentive to Work*, Oxford: Oxford University Press.

Brown, J. (1988), *In Search of a Policy*, London: National Council for One-parent Families.

Brown, J. (1989), *'Why Don't they go to Work?' Mothers on benefit*, London: Social Security Advisory Committee/HMSO.

Brown, J. (1990a), *Victims or Villains? Social security benefits in unemployment*, London: Joseph Rowntree Memorial Trust/Policy Studies Institute.

Brown, J. (1990b), *Social Security for Retirement*, York: Joseph Rowntree Foundation.

Brown, J. (1992a), 'Which way for the family; choices for the 1990s' in *Social Policy Review 4*, Manning, N. and Page, R. (eds.), Canterbury: Social Policy Association.

Brown, J. (1992b), *A Policy Vacuum: Social Security for the Self-employed*, York: Joseph Rowntree Foundation.

Brown, J. and Small, S. (1985), *Occupational Benefits as Social Security*, London: Policy Studies Institute.

Brown, R. (1990) 'A flexible future in Europe?: Changing patterns of employment in Europe', *British Journal of Sociology*, 41, 3, pp. 301–327.

Büchtemann, C. and Quack, S. (1989), '"Bridges" or "traps"? Non-standard employment in the Federal Republic of Germany', in *Precarious Jobs in Labour Market Regulation: The growth of atypical employment in Western Europe*, Rodgers, G. and J. (eds.), Geneva: International Institute for Labour Studies.

Büchtemann, C. and Schupp, J. (1988), 'Socio-economic aspects of part-time employment in the Federal Republic of Germany', Labour Market and Employment Research Unit, FSI 88–6, Berlin: Social Science Centre (WZB).

Buhmann, B. Rainwater, L., Schmaus, G. and Smeeding, T. (1988), 'Equivalence scales, well-being, inequality and poverty: sensitivity estimates across ten countries using the Luxembourg Income Study (LIS) database', *The Review of Income and Wealth*, June, pp. 115–141.

Burwell, B. O. (1986), 'Shared obligations: public policy influences on family care for the elderly', Medicaid Program Evaluation Working Paper 2.1, Health Care Financing Administration, Department of Health and Human Services.

Bussemaker, J. (1991), 'Equality, autonomy and feminist politics' in *Equality Politics and Gender*, Meehan, E. and Sevenhuijsen, S. (eds.), London: Sage.

Bytheway, B. (1986), 'Making way: The disengagement of older workers' in *Dependency and Interdependency in Later Life.*, Phillipson, C., Strang, P. and Bernard, M. (eds.), London: Croom Helm.

Calcoen, F., Eeckhoudt, L. and Greiner, D. (1988), 'Unemployment insurance, social protection and employment policy: An international comparison', *International Social Security Review,* XLI, 2, pp. 119–134.

Callender, C. (1992), 'Redundancy, unemployment and poverty' in *Women and Poverty in Britain: the 1990s,* Glendinning, C. and Millar, J. (eds.), Hemel Hempstead: Harvester Wheatsheaf.

Campbell, M. and Daly, M. (1992), 'Self-employment into the 1990s', *Employment Gazette,* June, pp. 269–292.

Carby, H. (1982), 'White women listen: black feminism and the boundaries of sisterhood' in *The Empire Strikes Back,* Centre for Contemporary Cultural Studies, London: Hutchinson.

Caro, F. G. and Blank, A. B. (1987), *Caring for the Elderly at Home: A Policy Perspective on Consumer Experiences with Publicly-Funded Home Care Programs in New York City,* New York, NY: Community Service Society of New York.

Casey, B. (1988), 'The extent and nature of temporary employment in Britain', *Cambridge Journal of Economics,* 12, pp. 487–509.

Casey, B. and Creigh, S. (1988), 'Self-employment in Britain: its definition in the Labour Force Survey, in tax and in social security law', *Work, Employment and Society,* 2, 3, pp. 381–391.

Casey, B. and Creigh, S. (1989), 'Marginal groups in the Labour Force Survey', *Scottish Journal of Political Economy,* 36, 3, pp. 282–300.

Casey, B. and Laczko, F. (1991), 'Older worker unemployment in the 1990s: some evidence from the Labour Force Survey' in *Fordism and Flexibility: Divisions and Change,* Gilbert, G. and Burrows, R. (eds.), London: Macmillan.

Casey, B., Dragendorf, R., Heering, W. and John, G. (1989), 'Temporary employment in Great Britain and the Federal Republic of Germany', *International Labour Review,* 128, 4, pp. 449–466.

Cass, B. (1990), 'Gender and social citizenship', paper presented to the Social Policy Association conference, University of Bath.

Cass, B., Gibson, F., and Tito, F. (1988), *Towards enabling policies: income support for people with disabilities,* Issues Paper No. 5, Canberra: Australian Government Publishing Services.

Castles, F. and Mitchell, D. (1991), 'Three worlds of welfare capitalism or four?', Public Policy Discussion Paper No. 21, Canberra: Australian National University.

Central Statistical Office (1990a), *Social Trends,* No. 20, London: HMSO.

Central Statistical Office (1990b), *Family Expenditure Survey: Report for 1989,* London: HMSO.

Central Statistical Office (1992), *Family Spending: A report on the 1991 Expenditure Survey,* London: HMSO.

Chew, A. N. (1912), 'Mother interest and child training', *Freewoman,* 2, 40, quoted in Pederson, S. (1989), 'The failure of feminism in the making of the British welfare state', *Radical History Review,* 43, pp. 86–110.

Citizens Income (1993), 'Citizens income and elderly people', Aspects of Citizens Income No. 9. London: Citizens Income.

Cohen, B. and Fraser, N. (1991), *Childcare in a Modern Welfare System: Towards a new national policy,* London: Institute for Public Policy Research.

Committee for Racial Equality (CRE) (1983), *Ethnic Minority Hospital Staff,* London: HMSO.

Committee on Nursing Home Regulation, Institute of Medicine (1986), *Improving the Quality of Care in Nursing Homes,* Washington, D.C.: National Academy Press.

Community Council of Greater New York (1978), *Dependency in the Elderly of New York*, New York, NY: Community Council of Greater New York.

Comptroller General of the United States (1977),*The Well Being of Older People in Cleveland, Ohio*, Washington, D.C.: General Accounting Office.

Cooke, K. (1987), 'The withdrawal from paid work of the wives of unemployed men: a review of research', *Journal of Social Policy*, 16, 3, pp. 371–382.

Corden, A. (1987), *Disappointed Applicants: A study of unsuccessful claims for Family Income Supplement*, Aldershot: Avebury.

Corden, A. and Craig, P. (1991), *Perceptions of Family Credit*, London: Social Policy Research Unit/HMSO.

Corden, A., Eardley, T. and Smellie, R. (1993), 'Assessment of self-employed earnings for family credit', *Public Money and Management*, January.

Cotterill, P. G. (1983), 'Provider incentives under alternative reimbursement systems,' in *Long-Term Care: Perspectives from research and demonstrations*, Vogel, R. J. and Palmer, H. C. (ed.), Washington, DC: Health Care Financing Administration.

Council of Europe (1989), *Equality between Women and Men: The Council of Europe's standard-setting activities relating to equality of the sexes*, Strasbourg.

Coutière, A. (1983), 'Arguments sur l'impôt sur le revenu: des mesures de portée inégale', *Economie et Statistique*, pp. 21–35.

Coward, R. T. and Rathbone-McCuan, E. (1985), 'Illuminating the relative role of adult sons and daughters in the long-term care of their parents', paper presented at the professional symposium of the National Association of Social Workers, Chicago, November.

Cragg, A. and Dawson, T. (1984), *Unemployed Women: A case study of attitudes and experiences*, Research Paper No. 47, London: Department of Employment.

Craig, G. (1992), *Cash or Care: A question of choice?*, York: Joseph Rowntree Foundation/Social Policy Research Unit.

Creigh, S., Roberts, C., Gorman, A. and Sawyer, P. (1986), 'Self-employment in Britain: results from the Labour Force Surveys 1981–1984', *Employment Gazette*, June, pp. 183–194.

Crystal, S. (1982), *America's Old Age Crisis: Public policy and the two worlds of aging*, New York, NY: Basic Books.

Crystal, S. (1986), 'Measuring income and inequality among the elderly', *The Gerontologist*, 26, pp. 56–59.

Curran, J. (1990), 'Rethinking economic structure: exploring the role of the small firm and self-employment in the British economy', *Work, Employment and Society*, special issue, pp. 125–146, May.

Dahl, T. S. (1987), *Women's Law: An introduction to feminist jurisprudence*, Oslo: Norwegian University Press.

Dale, A. (1986), 'Social class and the self-employed', *Sociology*, 20, 3, pp. 430–434.

Dale, A. and Joshi, H. (1992), 'The Economic and social status of British women', *Acta Demographica* , pp. 27–46.

Daly, M. (1991), 'The 1980s – a decade of growth in enterprise: self-employment data from the Labour Force Survey', *Employment Gazette*, March, pp. 109–134.

Davies, B. (1988), 'Financing long-term social care: challenges for the nineties', *Social Policy and Administration*, 22, 2.

Davies, B. and Ward, S. (1992), *Women and Personal Pensions*, London: HMSO/Equal Opportunities Commission.

Davies, H. and Joshi, H. (1992a) 'Sex, sharing and the distribution of income', Birkbeck College Discussion Paper in Economics, 9/92, London.

Davies, H. and Joshi, H. (1992b), 'Constructing pensions for model couples', in *Microsimulation Models for Public Policy Analysis: New frontiers*, Hancock, R. and Sutherland, H. (eds.), STICERD Occasional Paper 17. London: London School of Economics.

Davis, G. and Murch M. (1988), *Grounds for Divorce*, Oxford: Clarendon Press.

Dean, H. and Taylor-Gooby, P. (1990), 'Inequality and occupational sick pay', *Policy and Politics*, 18, 2, pp. 145–150.

de Jong, P., Herweijer, M. and de Wildt, J. (1990), *Form and Reform of the Dutch Social Security System*, Amsterdam: Commissie Onderzoek Sociale Zekerheid.

Deleeck, H. and Van den Bosch, K. (1990), 'The measurement of poverty in a comparative context: empirical evidence and methodological evaluation of four poverty lines in seven EC countries' in *Analysing Poverty in the European Community*, Teekens, R. and Van Praag, B.M.S. (eds.), Luxembourg: Eurostat News Special Edition (1).

Delphy, C. (1984), *Close to Home: A materialist analysis of women's oppression*, London: Hutchinson.

Department of Employment (DE) (1991a), 'Revised employment estimates for September 1987 to September 1990', *Employment Gazette*, April, pp. 197–204.

DE (1991b), Information supplied to the authors by the Training, Enterprise and Education Directorate.

DE (1992a), *Gazette*, November, London: HMSO.

DE (1992b), *Labour Force Survey Quarterly Bulletin*, No.1, Spring, London: HMSO.

Department of Health (DoH) (1989), *Caring for People: Community care in the next decade and beyond*, Cm 844, London: HMSO.

DoH (1991), *Social Services Inspectorate*, London: HMSO..

Department of Health and Social Security (DHSS) (1974), *Social Security Provision for Chronically Sick and Disabled People*, House of Commons 276, London: HMSO.

DHSS (1978), *A Happier Old Age: A discussion document on elderly people in our society*, London: HMSO.

DHSS (1980), *The Self-employed and National Insurance: a discussion document*, London: DHSS.

DHSS (1981), *Growing Older*, Cmnd. 8173, London: HMSO.

DHSS (1986), *Social Security Statistics 1986*, London: HMSO.

DHSS (1989), *Family Credit Take-up Estimate 1988: Technical Note*, Statistical and Research Division, 3/89, London: HMSO.

Department of Social Security (DSS) (1988), *Social Security Statistics 1988*, London: HMSO.

DSS (1990a), *Children Come First*, London: HMSO.

DSS (1990b), *Social Security Statistics 1990*, London: HMSO.

DSS (1991) *Stocktaking*, Report of the Working Group on Households Below Average Income, November, London: HMSO.

DSS (1992a), *Social Security: Government Expenditure Plans 1992–1993 to 1994–1995*, Cmnd. 1914, London: HMSO.

DSS (1992b), *Social Security Statistics 1991*, London: HMSO

DSS (1992c) *Households Below Average Income: a statistical analysis 1979 – 1988/89*, London: HMSO.

DSS (1992d), *Social Security Statistics 1992*, London: HMSO.

DSS (1992e), Press release 15 July 1992.

DSS (Australia) (1989), *The Circumstances of Long-term Sickness Beneficiaries: Past, present and future*, Social Policy Division, Policy Research Paper No. 54, Canberra: DSS.

DSS (Australia) (1990), *The Disability Reform Package*, Canberra: DSS.

DSS (Australia) (1992), *DSS Statistics*, Canberra: DSS.

Deven, F. and Cliquet, R. (eds.) (1985), *One-Parent Families in Europe*, Brussels: NIDI.

De Vroom, B. and Blomsma, M. (1991), 'The Netherlands: an extreme case', in *Time for Retirement: Comparative studies of early exit from the labour force*, Kohli, M., Rein, M., Guillemard, A.M. and Gunsteren, H. (eds.), Cambridge: Cambridge University Press.

Dex, S. (1987), *Women's Occupational Mobility: A Lifetime Perspective*. London: Macmillan.

Dex, S. and Phillipson, C. (1986), 'Older women in the labour market', *Critical Social Policy*, Issue No. 15, pp. 79–83.

Diamond, T. (1992), *Making Gray Gold: Narratives of nursing home care*, Chicago, IL and London: University of Chicago Press.

Dilnot, A. W. and Johnson, P. (1992), 'What pension should the state provide?' *Fiscal Studies*, 13, 4, pp. 1–20.

Dilnot, A. W. and Morris, C.N. (1981), 'What do we know about the black economy?', *Fiscal Studies*, 2, 1, pp. 58–73.

Dilnot, A. W. and Walker, I. (eds.) (1989), *The Economics of Social Security*, Oxford Oxford University Press.

Dilnot, A. W. and Webb, S. J. (1988), 'Reforming National Insurance Contributions', *Fiscal Studies*, 9, 4, pp. 1–24, London: Institute for Fiscal Studies.

Dilnot, A. W. and Webb, S. J. (1989), 'Reforming National Insurance Contributions: A progress report', *Fiscal Studies*, 10, 2, pp. 38–47, London: Institute for Fiscal Studies.

Dilnot, A. W., Kay, J. A. and Morris, C. N. (1984), *The Reform of Social Security*, Oxford: Oxford University Press.

Disney, R. F. and Webb, S. J. (1989), 'Is there a market failure in occupational sick pay?', in *The Economics of Social Security*, Dilnot, A.W. and Walker, I. (eds.), Oxford: Oxford University Press.

Disney, R. F. and Webb, S. J. (1990), 'Why social security expenditure in the 1980s has risen faster than expected: the role of unemployment', *Fiscal Studies*, 11, 1, pp. 1–20.

Disney, R. F. and Webb, S. J. (1991), 'Why are there so many long-term sick in Britain?', *Economic Journal Conference Volume*, 101, 405, pp. 252–262.

Disney, R. F. and Whitehouse, E. (1991), 'How should pensions in the UK be indexed?', *Fiscal Studies*, 12, 3, pp. 47–61.

Ditch, J. (1992), *Social Policy Implications and Information Requirements of the Single European Act*, Occasional Paper No. 24, Policy Planning and Research Unit, Belfast: Department of Finance and Personnel.

Dombois, R., and Osterland, M. (1987), 'New forms of flexible utilization of labour: Part-time and contract work', in *Flexibility in Labour Markets*, Tarling, R. (ed.), London: Academic Press.

Donovan, R. (1989), '"We care for the most important people in your life": Home care workers in New York City', *Women's Studies Quarterly*,

Eardley, T. (1991), *Self-employment and Social Security: A review of research and other literature*, Social Policy Research Unit Working Paper DSS 868, York: University of York.

Eardley, T. and Hutton, S. (1992), 'Family credit and self-employment: an analysis of administrative statistics', Social Policy Research Unit Working Paper DSS 890, York: University of York.

Economic Council of Canada (1990), *Good Jobs, Bad Jobs: Employment in the service economy*, Ottawa: Supply and Services Canada.

Eekelaar, J. (1991), 'Child Support – an evaluation', *Family Law*, December, 511–517.

Ekert, D. (1985), 'Les effets redistributifs du système des prestations familiales sur le cycle de vie' in *Cycles de vie et générations*, Kessler, D. and Masson, A. (eds.), Paris: Economica.

Equal Opportunities Commission (EOC) (1986), *Childcare and Equal Opportunities: Some policy perspectives*, London: HMSO.

Ermisch, J. (1990), 'Demographic aspects of the growing number of lone-parent families' in *Lone-parent families: The economic challenge*, Paris: OECD.

Ermisch, J. (1992), 'Policy implications of demographic changes', in *Income Security in Britain: A Research and Policy Agenda for the Next Ten Years*, Swindon: Economic and Social Research Council.

Esam, P. and Berthoud, R. (1991), *Independent Benefits for Men and Women*, London: Policy Studies Institute.

Esping-Andersen, G. (1990), *The Three Worlds of Welfare Capitalism*, Cambridge: Polity Press.

Estes, C. L. (1979), *The Aging Enterprise*, San Francisco: Josey Bass.

Estes, C. L (1991), 'The new political economy of aging: Introduction and critique', in *Critical Perspectives on Aging: The Political and Moral Economy of Growing Old*, Minkler, M. and Estes, C. L. (eds.), New York: Baywood Publishing Company.

Estes, C. L. and Wood, J. B. (1985), 'The non-profit sector and community-based care for the elderly in the U.S.: A disappearing resource?', unpublished paper.

European Industrial Relations Review (1987), 'Netherlands: Flexible Working Survey', 160, May, pp. 16–19.

European Industrial Relations Review (1988), 'Survey of Fixed-term Contracts', December, pp. 20–25.

European Industrial Relations Review (1989), 'Survey of Temporary Work Contracts', 182, March, pp. 11–16.

Eurostat (1988), *EC Labour Force Survey*, Luxembourg: Eurostat.

Eustis, N., Greenberg, J. and Patten, S. (1984), *Long-Term Care for Older Persons: A Policy Perspective*, Monterey, CA: Brooks/Cole.

Euzéby, A. (1988), 'Social security and part-time employment', *International Labour Review*, 127, 5, pp. 545–557.

Evandrou, M. and Falkingham, J. (1993), 'Social security and the life course: Developing sensitive policy alternatives' in *Ageing, Independence and the Life Course*, Arber, S. and Evandrou, M. (eds.), London: Jessica Kingsley.

Evans, M. and Glennerster, H. (1993), 'Squaring the circle? The inconsistencies and constraints of Beveridge's plan', STICERD Welfare State Programme Discussion Paper WSP/86, London: London School of Economics.

Falkingham, J. and Johnson, P. (1993), 'A unified funded pension scheme (UFPS) for Britain', STICERD Welfare State Programme Discussion Paper WSP/90, London: London School of Economics

Falkingham, J. and Lessof, C. (1991), 'LIFEMOD: The formative years', STICERD Welfare State Programme Research Note 24, London: London School of Economics.

Falkingham, J. and Lessof, C. (1992), 'Playing God or LIFEMOD – The construction of a dynamic microsimulation model' in *Microsimulation Models for Public Policy Analysis; New Frontiers*, Hancock, R. and Sutherland, H. (eds.), STICERD Occasional Paper 17, London: London School of Economics.

Family Policy Studies Centre (1991), *Supporting our children: The family impact of child maintenance*, London: Family Policy Studies Centre.

Featherstone, M. and Hepworth, M. (1989), 'Ageing and old age: Reflections on the postmodern lifecourse' in *Being and Becoming and Old Age*, Bytheway, B., Keil, T., Allatt, P. and Bryman, A. (eds.), London: Sage.

Feder, J. and Scanlon, W. (1980), 'Regulating the bed supply in nursing homes', *Milbank Memorial Fund Quarterly/Health and Society*, 58, pp. 54–88.

Feldblum, C. R. (1985), 'Home health care for the elderly: Programs, problems, and potentials', *Harvard Journal on Legislation*, 22, pp. 193–254.

Ferguson, S. and Fitzgerald, H. (1954), *Studies in the Social Services*, London: Longman and HMSO.

Ferreira, J. et al. (1989), *Caracterizoao de Factores e Tipos de Pobreza em Portugal*, Lisbon: ISCTE.

Fevre, R. (1987), 'Subcontracting in steel', *Work, Employment and Society*, 1, 4, pp. 509–527.

Fevre, R. (1991), 'Emerging "alternatives" to full employment', in *Poor Work: Disadvantage and the Division of Labour*, Brown, P. and Scase, R. (eds.), Milton Keynes: Open University Press.

Finch, J. (1989), *Family Obligations and Social Change*, London: Polity Press.

Finch, J. (1992), 'State responsibility and family responsibility for financial support in the 1990s' in *Income Security in Britain: A Research and policy agenda for the next ten years*, Swindon: Economic and Social Research Council.

Finch, J. and Groves, D. (1980), 'Community care and the family: A case for equal opportunities', *Journal of Social Policy*, **9**, 4, pp. 487–511.

Finch, J. and Mason, J. (1992), *Negotiating Family Responsibilities*, London: Routledge.

Finer, M. (1974), *Report of the Committee on One-Parent Families*, Cmnd 5629, London: HMSO.

Forde, M. (1979), 'The self-employed and the EEC social security rules', *Industrial Law Journal*, **8**, 1, pp. 1–18.

Fox Piven, F. (1990), 'Ideology and the state: women, power and the welfare state' in *Women, the State and Welfare*, Gordon, L. (ed.), Madison, WI: University of Wisconsin.

Fraser, N. (1987), 'Women, welfare and the politics of need interpretation', *Hypatia*, **2**, 1.

Fraser, N. (1990), 'Struggle over needs: outline of a socialist–feminist critical theory of late-capitalist political culture' in *Women, the State and Welfare*, Madison, WI: University of Wiconsin.

Freudenheim, M. (1988), 'Nursing homes face pressures that imperil care for elderly', *The New York Times*, May 28, p. 19.

Fry, V. and Stark, G. (1993), *The Take-up of Means-tested Benefits 1984 - 1990*, London: Institute for Fiscal Studies.

Fry, V., Smith, S. and White, S. (1990), *Pensioners and the Public Purse*, London: Institute for Fiscal Studies.

Fuchs, V. C. (1988), *Women's Quest for Economic Equality*, Cambridge, MA: Harvard University Press.

Galbraith, J. K. (1992), 'Culture of Contentment', *New Statesman*, **5**, 201, pp. 14–16.

Garfinkel, I. and Wong, P. (1990), 'Child support and public policy' in *Lone-parent Families: The Economic Challenge*, Paris: OECD.

George, L. K. and Gwyther, L. P. (1986), 'Caregiver well-being: A multidimensional examination of family caregivers of demented adults', *The Gerontologist*, **26**, pp. 253–259.

George, V. (1968), *Social Security: Beveridge and after*, London: Routledge and Kegan Paul.

Giddens, A. (1991), *Modernity and Self-Identity*, Oxford: Polity Press.

Ginn, J. and Arber, S. (1991), 'Gender, class and income inequalities in later life', *British Journal of Sociology*, **42**, 3, pp. 369–396.

Ginn, J. and Arber, S. (1992), 'Towards women's independence: Pension systems in three contrasting European welfare states', *European Journal of Social Policy*, **2**, 4, pp. 255–277.

Ginn, J. and Arber, S. (1993), 'Pension penalties: the gendered division of occupational welfare', *Work Employment and Society*, **7**, 1, pp. 47–70.

Glendinning, C. (1992a), 'Employment and "community care": Policies for the 1990s', *Work, Employment and Society*, **6**, 1, pp.103–112.

Glendinning, C. (1992b), *The Costs of Informal Care*, London: Social Policy Research Unit/HMSO.

Glendinning, C. and Millar, J. (eds.) (1987), *Women and Poverty in Britain*, Brighton: Wheatsheaf Books.

Glendinning, C. and Millar, J. (eds.) (1992), *Women and Poverty in Britain: The 1990s*, Hemel Hempstead: Harvester Wheatsheaf.

Glennerster, H. and Midgley, J. (eds.) (1991), *The Radical Right and the Welfare State*, Hemel Hampstead: Harvester Wheatsheaf.

Goffman, E. (1961), *Asylums*, Harmondsworth: Penguin.

Gordon, L. (1990), *Women, the State and Welfare*, Madison, WI: University of Wisconsin.

Government Actuary's Department (1990a) 'Occupational pension schemes 1987', *Eighth Survey by the Government Actuary*, London: HMSO.

Government Actuary's Department (1990b), *National Insurance Fund Long-Term Financial Estimate. Report by the Government Actuary on the Second Quinquennial Review under Section 137 of the Social Security Act 1975*. London: HMSO.

Green, F., Hadjimatheou, G. and Smail, R. (1984), *Unequal Fringes: Fringe benefits in the United Kingdom*, London: Bedford Square Press/National Council for Voluntary Organisations.

Griffiths, Sir Roy (1988), *Community Care: Agenda for Action*, London: HMSO.

Groves, D. (1987a), 'Women and occupational pension provision: Past and future', in *Social Gerontology: New Directions*, di Gregorio, S. (ed.), London: Croom Helm.

Groves, D. (1987b), 'Occupational pension provision and women's poverty in old age' in *Women and Poverty in Britain*, Glendinning, C. and Millar, J. (eds.), Brighton: Wheatsheaf Books.

Groves, D. (1991), 'Women and financial provision for old age', in *Women's Issues in Social Policy*, Maclean, M. and Groves, D. (eds.), London: Routledge.

Groves, D. (1993), 'The incomes of older people', in *The Future of Family Care*, Allen, I. (ed.), London: Policy Studies Institute.

Guillemard, A. (1989), 'The trends towards early labour force withdrawal and the reorganisation of the life course: A cross-national analysis' in *Intergenerational Justice in an Ageing World*, Johnson, P. Conrad and Thomson, D. (eds.), Manchester: Manchester University Press.

Guillen, E. (1989), 'La Pauvreté en Espagne: Rapport contextuel', report for the EC anti-poverty programme, mimeo.

Hakim, C. (1985), 'Employers' use of outwork', Research Paper No. 44, London: Department of Employment.

Hakim, C. (1987), 'Trends in the flexible workforce', *Employment Gazette*, November, pp. 549–560.

Hakim, C. (1989a), 'Workforce restructuring, social insurance coverage and the black economy', *Journal of Social Policy*, 18, 4, pp. 471–503.

Hakim, C. (1989b), 'New recruits to self-employment in the 1980s', *Employment Gazette*, 97, 6, pp. 286–297.

Hancock, R. (1988), 'Income variation and Family Credit: Evidence from the Family Finances and Family Resources Surveys', STICERD Discussion Paper no. TIDI/109, London: London School of Economics.

Hannah, L. (1986), *Inventing Retirement: The development of occupational pensions in Britain*, Cambridge: Cambridge University Press.

Harding P. and Jenkins, R. (1989), *The Myth of the Hidden Economy*, Milton Keynes: Open University Press.

Harel, Z., McKinney, E. A. and Williams, M. (eds.) (1990), *Black Aged: Understanding diversity and service needs*. Newbury Park, CA: Sage.

Harper, S. and Thane, P. (1989), 'The consolidation of old age as a phase in life, 1945–1965' in *Growing Old in the Twentieth Century*, Jefferys, M. (ed.), London: Routledge.

Harrington, C. and Swan, J. H. (1985), 'Institutional long-term care services', in *Long-Term Care of the Elderly: Public policy issues*, Harrington, C. (ed.), Newcomer, R. J., Estes, C. L. and Associates. Beverly Hills, CA: Sage.

Haskey, J. C. (1989a), 'One parent families in Great Britain', *Population Trends*, 45, pp. 5–11.

Haskey, J. C. (1989b), 'Recent trends in marriage and divorce and cohort analysis of the proportions of marriages ending in divorce', *Population Trends*, 54, pp. 34–39.

Haskey, J. C. (1991), 'Estimated numbers and demographic characteristics of one-parent families in Great Britain', *Population Trends*, 65, pp. 35–47.

Hatchuel, G. (1985), *Transfert Sociaux et Redistribution*, Paris: CREDOC.

Haveman, R. H., Halberstadt, V., and Burkhauser, R. V. (1984), *Public Policy Towards Disabled Workers*, Ithaca, NY: Cornell University Press.

Hayes, M. (1991), 'Making and enforcing child maintenance obligations: will the proposed scheme cause more harm than good', *Family Law*, March, pp. 105–109.

Hemming, R. and Kay, J. (1982), 'The costs of the State Earnings Related Pension Scheme', *Economic Journal*, 92, pp. 300–19.

Hepple, B. (1986), 'Restructuring employment rights', Industrial Law Journal, 15, 2, pp. 69–83.

Hernandez, B. B. (1991), 'Not so benign neglect: Researchers ignore ethnicity in defining caregiver burden and recommending services', The Gerontologist, 31, pp. 271–272.

Hernes, H. (1984), 'Women and the welfare state. The transition from private to public dependence', in Patriarchy in a Welfare Society, Holter, H. (ed.), Oslo: Norwegian University Press.

Hernes, H. (1988), 'Scandinavian citizensnip', Acta Sociologica , 31, 3, pp. 199–215.

Hewitt, P. (1993), About Time: The revolution in work and family life, London: Institute for Public Policy Research.

Hinrichs, K. (1991), 'Irregular employment patterns and the loose net of social security: Some findings on the West German development', in The Sociology of Social Security, Adler, M., Bell, C., Clasen, J. and Sinfield, A. (eds.), Edinburgh: Edinburgh University Press.

Hinrichsen, G. A. and Ramirez, M. (1992), 'Black and white dementia caregivers: A comparison of their adaptation, adjustment, and service utilization', The Gerontologist, 32, 3, pp. 375–381.

HM Treasury (1986), 'The Government's Expenditure Plans 1986–87 to 1988–89', Volume II, Cmnd 9702–II, London: HMSO.

Hobson, B. (1991), 'No exit, no voice: a comparative analysis of women's economic dependency and the welfare state', European Feminist Research Conference, Aalborg, Denmark.

Holtermann, S. (1992), Investing in Young Children, London: National Children's Bureau.

hooks, B. (1982), Ain't I a woman? London: Pluto.

Horowitz, A. (1985), 'Sons and daughters to older parents: Differences in role performance and consequences', The Gerontologist, 25, pp. 612–617.

Horton, C. and Berthoud, R. (1990), The Attendance Allowance and the Costs of Caring, London: Policy Studies Institute.

House of Commons (1991a) Hansard, Written Answers, col. 147, 30 April.

House of Commons (1991b) Hansard, Written Answers, col. 527, 12 December.

House of Commons Employment Committee (1990), Part-time Work, Vol. 2, HC 1 22 II, London: HMSO.

House of Commons Social Services Committee (1982), Age of Retirement: Evidence, London: HMSO.

House of Commons Social Services Committee (1990), Community Care: Carers, Report No. 5, London: HMSO.

House of Lords (1982), Select Committee on the European Communities, Voluntary Part-time Work, HL 216, London: HMSO.

House of Lords (1989), Equal Treatment for Men and Women in Pensions and Other Benefits, London: HMSO.

Hunt, A. (1968), A Survey of Women's Employment, London: HMSO.

Industrial Injuries Advisory Council (1991), The Industrial Injuries Scheme and the Self-employed in Construction and Agriculture: A consultation paper, London: HMSO.

Inland Revenue (1992), Information supplied to the authors by the Inland Revenue, Statistics and Economics Office.

Institute for Employment Research (1987), Review of the Economy and Employment, Coventry: University of Warwick.

International Labour Office (1989), Conditions of Work Digest, 8, 1, Geneva: International Labour Office.

Itzin, C. and Phillipson, C. (1993), Age Barriers at Work: Maximising the potential of mature and older people, Solihull: METRA.

Jacobs, J. (1992), 'December 1942; Beveridge observed: Mass-Observation and the Beveridge Report', Benefits, 5, September/October.

Jefferys, M. (ed.) (1989), Growing Old in the Twentieth Century, London: Routledge.

Jenkins, S. (1991), 'Poverty measurement and the within-household distribution: Agenda for action', *Journal of Social Policy*, **20**, 4, pp. 457–483.

Jenkins, S. and Millar, J. (1989), 'Income risk and income maintenance: Implications for incentives to work', in *The Economics of Social Security*, Dilnot, A. W. and Walker, I. (eds.), Oxford: Oxford University Press.

Johnson, N. (1991), *Reconstructing the Welfare State*, Brighton: Harvester Wheatsheaf.

Johnson, P. (1989), 'The structured dependency of the elderly: A critical note', in *Growing Old in the Twentieth Century*, Jefferys, M. (ed.), London: Routledge.

Johnson, P., Conrad, C. and Thomson, D. (1989) (eds.), *Workers versus Pensioners: Intergenerational conflict in an ageing world*, Manchester: Manchester University Press.

Johnson, P. and Falkingham, J. (1992), *Ageing and Economic Welfare*, London: Sage.

Joint Statement of the Department of Community Services and Health, Department of Social Security and the Department of Employment, Education and Training (August, 1990), *New opportunities for people with disabilities*, Canberra: DSS.

Jolliffe, J. A. (1991), 'The portability of occupational pensions within Europe' in *The Future of Basic and Supplementary Pension Schemes in the European Community – 1992 and Beyond*, Schmähl, W. (ed.), Baden-Baden: Nomos Verlagsgesellschaft.

Jonczyk, M. and Smith, T. (1991), 'Barriers to employment facing people with disabilities: Summary of the results of a survey of DSS clients', *Social Security Journal*, **PR 011**, pp. 35–43.

Jordan, A. (1987), *Sickness Beneficiaries – Background Discussion Paper No. 16*, Social Security Review Research Paper No. 35.

Jordan, B. (1987), *Rethinking Welfare*, Oxford: Basil Blackwell.

Jordan, B., James, S., Kay, H. and Redley, M. (1992), *Trapped in Poverty: Labour market decisions in low income households*, London: Routledge.

Joshi, H. (1989a) 'The changing form of women's dependency', in Joshi, H. (ed.), *The Changing Population of Britain*, Oxford: Blackwell.

Joshi, H. (ed.) (1989b), *The Changing Population of Britain*, Oxford: Blackwell.

Joshi, H. (1990a), 'Obstacles and opportunites for lone parents as breadwinners in Great Britain', in *Lone-Parent Families: The Economic Challenge*, Paris: OECD.

Joshi, H. (1990b) 'The cash opportunity cost of childbearing: An approach to estimation using British evidence', *Population Studies*, **44**, March, pp. 41–60.

Joshi, H. (1991), 'Sex and motherhood as sources of women's economic disadvantage', in *Women's Issues in Social Policy*, Maclean, M. and Groves, D. (eds.), London: Routledge.

Joshi, H. and Davies, H. (1991a), 'The pension consequences of divorce', CEPR Discussion Paper 550, London: Centre for Economic Policy Research.

Joshi, H. and Davies, H. (1991b), 'Pension Splitting and Divorce', in *Fiscal Studies*, **12**, 4, pp. 69–91.

Joshi, H. and Davies, H. (1992), 'Childcare and mothers' lifetime earnings: Some European contrasts', CEPR Discussion Paper 600, London: Centre for Economic Policy Research.

Kamerman, S. B. and Kahn, A. J. (1988), *Mothers Alone*, MA: Auburn House Publishing.

Kane, R. A. and Kane, R. L. (1987), *Long-Term Care: Principles, programs, and policies*, New York: Springer.

Kell, M, and Wright, J. (1990), 'Benefits and the labour supply of women married to unemployed men', in *Economic Journal*, Conference Papers Supplement, pp. 119–126.

Kelly, K. and Nichol, W. (1987), 'Sickness beneficiaries – trends and characteristics', Research Paper No. 48, Research and Data Analysis Section, Social Policy Division, Department of Social Security.

Kestenbaum, A. (1992), *Cash for Care: The experience of Independent Living Fund clients*, London: Independent Living Fund.

Kiernan, K. (1989), 'The family: Formation and fission', in *The Changing Population of Britain*, Joshi H. (ed.), Oxford: Blackwell.

Kiernan, K. (1992), 'Men and women at work and at home' in *British Social Attitude: the 9th Report*, Jowell, R. (ed.), London: Social and Community Planning Research.

Klein, V. (1960), *Working Wives*, Occasional Paper No. 5, London: Institute of Personnel Management.

Kohli, M. (1988), 'Ageing as a challenge to sociological theory', *Ageing and Society*, 8, 4, pp. 367–395.

Kohli, M. and Rein, M. (1991), 'The changing balance of work and retirement', in *Time for Retirement: Comparative studies of early exit from the labour force*, Kohli, M. et al. (eds.), Cambridge: Cambridge University Press.

Kohli, M., Rein, M., Guillemard, A. M. and Gunsteren, H. (1991), *Time for Retirement: Comparative studies of early exit from the labour force*, Cambridge: Cambridge University Presss

Korpi, W. (1989), 'Can we afford to work?', in *The Goals of Social Policy*, Bulmer, M., Lewis, J. and Piachaud, D. (eds.), London: Unwin and Hyman.

Laczko, F. (1990), 'New poverty and the old poor: Pensioners' incomes in the European Community', *Ageing and Society*, 10, 3, pp. 261–278.

Laczko, F. and Phillipson, C. (1991a), *Changing Work and Retirement*, Buckingham: Open University Press.

Laczko, F. and Phillipson, C. (1991b), 'Great Britain: The contradictions of early exit' in Kohli, M. et al. (eds.) *Time for Retirement: Comparative studies of early exit from the labour force*, Cambridge: Cambridge University Press.

Land, H. (1988), 'Women, money and independence', *Poverty*, 70, Child Poverty Action Group.

Land, H. (1989), 'The construction of dependency', in *The Goals of Social Policy*, Bulmer, M., Lewis, J. and Piachaud, D. (eds.), London: Unwin Hyman.

Land, H. (1992), 'Whatever happened to the "social wage"?', in *Women and Poverty in Britain: The 1990s*, Glendinning, C. and Millar, J. (eds.), Hemel Hempstead: Wheatsheaf.

Langan, M. and Ostner, I. (1991), 'Gender and welfare', in *Towards a European Welfare State?*, Room, G. (ed.), Bristol: School for Advanced Urban Studies.

Lave, J. R. (1985), 'Cost containment policies in long-term care', *Inquiry*, 23, pp. 7–23.

Lee, R. (1985), 'The entry to self-employment of redundant steelworkers', *Industrial Relations Journal*, 16, 2, pp. 42–49.

Leece. D. (1990), 'Redundancy, unemployment and self-employment', *International Journal of Manpower*, 4, 4, pp. 35–40.

Legal and General (1984), *The Self-employed Report*, London: Legal and General Insurance Company.

Le Grand, J. and Bartlett, W. (eds.) (1993), *Quasi-markets and Social Policy*, London: Macmillan.

Le Grand, J. (1991), 'Quasi-markets and social policy', *Economic Journal*, 101, 408, pp. 1256-1267.

Leighton, P. (1983), 'Employment and self-employment: some problems of law and practice', *Employment Gazette*, May, pp. 197–203.

Leighton, P. (1986), 'Marginal workers', in *Labour Law in Britain*, Lewis, R., (ed.), Oxford: Blackwell.

Leira, M. (1989), *Models of Motherhood*, Oslo: Instittut for Samfunns Forskning.

Leutz, W. (1986), 'Long-term care for the elderly: public dreams and private realities', *Inquiry*, 23, pp. 134–140.

Lewin and Associates, Inc. (1987), *An Evaluation of the Medi Cal Program's System for Establishing Reimbursement Rates for Nursing Homes*, submitted to the Office of the Auditor General, State of California.

Lewis, J. (1984), *Women in England, 1870- 1950*, Brighton: Wheatsheaf.

Lewis, J. (1990), 'Equality, difference and state welfare: the case of labour market and family policies in Sweden', London, mimeo.

Lewis, J. (1992), 'Gender and the development of welfare regimes', *Journal of European Social Policy*, 2, 3, pp. 159–173.

Lindeman, D. and Wood, J. (1985), *Home Health Care: Adaptations to the Federal and State cost containment environment*, San Francisco, CA: Institute for Health and Aging, University of California.

Lingsom, S. (1992), 'Paying for informal care in Norway', report to the international research project 'Payment for Care', Vienna, 1992, mimeo.

Lister, R. (1975), *Social Security: The case for reform*, London: Child Poverty Action Group.

Lister, R. (1990), 'Women, economic dependency and citizenship', *Journal of Social Policy*, 19, 4, pp. 445–467.

Lister, R. (1992), *Women's Economic Dependency and Social Security*, Manchester: Equal Opportunities Commission.

Liu, K., Manton, K. G. and Marzetta Liu, B. (1985), 'Home care expenses for the disabled elderly', *Health Care Financing Review*, 7, pp. 51–58.

Lowe, R. (1992), 'Santa Claus versus the five giants', *Times Higher Education Supplement*, March, p.16.

Lubben, J. E. and Becerra, R. M. (1987), 'Social support among Black, Mexican, and Chinese elderly', in *Ethnicity and Aging: New Perspectives*, Gelfland, D. E. and Barresi, C. (eds.), New York: Springer.

Luckhaus, L. (1991), 'New technology, social security and the self-employed', paper given to the European Institute of Social Security International Colloquium on Social Security and Technological Innovation, Florence, October 1991.

Luckhaus, L. and Dickens, L. (1991), *Social protection of atypical workers in the United Kingdom*, a report produced for the European Commission, Brussels.

Lynes, T. (1988), 'The take-up of family credit among self-employed people is low - because the regulations are so absurd', *New Statesman and Society*, 16, p. 25.

Lynes, T. (1989), 'The self-employed deserve a better deal', *New Statesman and Society*, 6, 2.

MacAffee, K. (1980), 'A glimpse of the hidden economy in the national accounts', *Economic Trends*, 316, pp. 81–87.

McCoy, J. L. and Weems, K. (1989), 'Disabled-worker beneficiaries and disabled SSI recipients: A profile of demographic and program characteristics', *Social Security Bulletin*, May, 52, 5.

MacDonald, R. and Coffield, F. (1990), 'Youth, enterprise and business start up in a depressed area of Britain'. Paper given to the ESRC 16–19 Initiative Education, Training and Employment Conference, Sheffield, 28 March 1990.

McGregor, A. and Sproull, A. (1992), 'Employers and the flexible workforce', *Employment Gazette*, May, pp. 225–234.

McIntosh, M. (1981), 'Feminism and social policy', *Critical Social Policy*, 1, 1.

McLaughlin, E. (1991a), 'Work and Welfare Benefits: social security, employment and unemployment in the 1990s', *Journal of Social Policy*, 20, 4, pp. 485–508.

McLaughlin, E. (1991b), *Social Security and Community Care: The Case of the Invalid Care Allowance*, London: Department of Social Security/ HMSO .

McLaughlin, E. (1992a), *Understanding unemployment*, London: Routledge.

McLaughlin, E. (1992b), 'Paying carers: conceptualising systems of financial support for carers', unpublished paper: presentation to Annual General Meeting of Social and Health Research Society, 20 May 1992, Belfast.

Macrae, S. (1991), *Mothers in Employment*, London: Policy Studies Institute.

Maier, F. (1991), 'Part-time work, social security protections and labour law: An international comparison', *Policy and Politics*, 19, 1, pp. 1–11.

Markson, E. W. (1980), 'Institutionalization: Sin, cure, or sinecure for the impaired elderly', in *Public Policies for an Aging Population*, Markson, E. W. and Batra, G. R. (eds), Lexington, MA: D.C. Heath.

Marsden, D. (1974), 'What action after Finer?' *New Society*, December, pp. 817–818.

Marsh, C. (1991), *Hours of Work of Women and Men in Britain*, London: Equal Opportunities Commission/HMSO.

Marshall, T. H. (1963), 'Citizenship and social class', in *Sociology at the Crossroads,,* London: Heinemann.

Martin, J. and Roberts, C. (1984), *Women and Employment: A Lifetime Perspective*, London: HMSO.

Martin, J. and White, A. (1988), *Financial Circumstances of Disabled Adults Living in Private Households*, London: HMSO.

Mason, J. (1987), 'A Bed of roses? Women, marriage and inequality in later life' in *Women and the Life Cycle: Transitions and turning points*, Allatt, P., Keil, T., Bryman, A. and Bytheway, B. (eds.), London: Macmillan.

Mead, L. (1986), *Beyond Entitlement: The social obligations of citizenship*, New York: The Free Press.

Meager, N. (1992), 'Does unemployment lead to self-employment?', *Small Business Economics*, 4, pp. 87–103.

Means, R. and Smith, R. (1983), 'From public assistance institutions to "sunshine hotels": Changing state perceptions about residential care for elderly people', *Ageing and Society*, 3, 2, pp. 157–181.

Means, R. and Smith, R. (1985), *The Development of Welfare Services for Elderly People*, London: Croom Helm.

Micklewright, J. (1990), 'Why do less than a quarter of the unemployed in Britain receive Unemployment Insurance?', Taxation, Incentives and the Distribution of Income Programme, Discussion Paper No. TIDI/147, London: London School of Economics.

Micklewright, J. and Giannelli, G. (1991), 'Why do women married to unemployed men have low participation rates?', European University Institute working paper, ECO No. 91/56, Florence: European University Institute.

Millar, J. (1989), 'Social security, equality and women in the UK', *Policy and Politics*, 17, 4, pp. 311–319.

Millar, J. (1992), 'Lone mothers and poverty' in *Women and Poverty: The 1990s*, Glendinning, C. and Millar, J. (eds.), Hemel Hempstead: Harvester Wheatsheaf.

Millar, J. (1993), 'State, family and personal responsibility: the changing balance for lone mothers in the UK', in *Gender and Family Change in Industrialised Societies*, Oppenheim Mason, K. and Jensen, A. (eds.), Oxford: Oxford University Press.

Millar, J. and Glendinning, C. (1989), 'Gender and poverty', *Journal of Social Policy*, 18, 3, pp. 363–381.

Millar, J. and Whiteford, P. (1993), 'Child support in Australia and the UK', *Policy and Politics*, 21, 1, pp. 59–72.

Millar, J., Leeper, S. and Davies, C. (1992), *Lone Parents: Poverty and public policy in Ireland*, Dublin: Combat Poverty Agency.

Miller, B. (1990), 'Gender differences in spouse management of the caregiver roles', in *Circles of Care: Work and Identity in Women's Lives*, Abel, E. K. and Nelson, M. K. (eds.), Albany, NY: State University of New York Press.

Ministerie van Sociale Zaken en Werkgelegenheid (1990), *Social Security in the Netherlands*, Den Haag: Kluwer Law and Taxation Publishers.

Ministry of Labour (1947a), *Report for the Years 1939–46*, Cmd. 7225, London: HMSO.

Ministry of Labour (1947b), *Gazette*, June, London: HMSO.

Ministry of Labour (1951), *Gazette*, April, London: HMSO.

Ministry of Reconstruction (1944), *Social Insurance Part I*, Cmnd. 6550, London: HMSO.

Ministry of Social Affairs and Employment (1990), *Statistic Van de Algemene Bijstand 1985–1987*, Den Haag: Central Bureau of Statistics.

Mink, G. (1990), 'The lady and the tramp: gender, race and the origins of the American welfare state', in *Women, the State and Welfare*, Gordon, L. (ed.), Madison, WI: University of Wisconsin.

Mitchell, D. (1991a), 'Comparing income transfer systems: Is Australia the poor relation?', Luxembourg Income Study Working Paper No. 56, Walferdange, Luxembourg: Luxembourg Income Study.

Mitchell, D. (1991b), *Income Transfers in Ten Welfare States*, Aldershot: Avebury.

Mitchell, D. and Bradshaw, J. (1992), 'Lone parents and their incomes: a comparative study of ten countries', Social Policy Research Unit Discussion Paper, York: University of York.

Moller Okin, S. (1989), *Justice, Gender and the Family*, New York, NY: Basic Books.

Morginstin, B. (1989), 'Impact of demographic and socio-economic factors on the changing needs for services for the very old', *International Social Security Review*, **42**, pp. 123–163.

Morginstin, B., Baich-Moray, S. and Zipkin, A. (1992), 'Assessment of long-term care needs and the provision of services to the elderly in Israel: the impact of long-term care insurance', *Australian Journal on Ageing*, **11**, 2, pp. 16–24.

Moss, P. (1988/89), 'The indirect costs of parenthood: a neglected issue in social policy', *Critical Social Policy*, **24**, pp. 20–37.

Muckenberger, U. (1991), 'The trend to non-standard forms of work and the role of changes in labour and social security regulations', paper given at Anglo-German conference, Nottingham.

Murray, C. (1984), *Losing Ground: American social policy*, New York, NY: Basic Books.

Myrdal, A. and Klein, V. (1956), *Women's Two Roles: Home and work*, London: Routledge and Kegan Paul.

Nasman, E. (1990), 'Models of population policy – the Swedish case', paper presented at Population, Social and Demographic Policies for Europe conference, Turin.

National Audit Office (1990), *Department of Social Security: Support for lone parent families*, London: HMSO.

National Audit Office (1991), *Support for Low Income Families*, London: HMSO.

National Prices and Incomes Board (NPIB) (1968), *Report No 60. Pay of Nurses and Midwives in the NHS*, Cmnd. 3585, London: HMSO.

National Social Insurance Board (1990), *Social Insurance Statistics Facts 1985*, Stockholm: National Social Insurance Board.

NCOPF (1990), *Barriers to Work: A study of lone parents' training and employment needs*, London: National Council for One Parent Families.

NCOPF (1991), *A Response to the Government's Proposals on Child Maintenance*, London: National Council for One Parent Families.

Nelson, B. (1984), 'Women's poverty and women's citizenship: Some political consequences of economic marginality', *Signs*, **10**, pp. 209–231.

Nelson, B. (1990), 'The origins of the two-channel welfare state: workmen's compensation and mother's aid', in *Women, the State and Welfare*, Gordon, L. (ed.), Madison, WI: University of Wisconsin.

Nichol, W. (1988), 'Invalid Pension, 1970–1987: Numbers and characteristics', Research Paper 47, Research and Data Analysis Section, Social Policy Division, Department of Social Security.

Noble, M., Smith, G. and Munby, T. (1992), *The Take-up of Family Credit*, Oxford: Department of Applied Social Studies and Social Research.

Noelker, L. S. and A. L. Townsend (1987), 'Perceived caregiving effectiveness: The impact of parental impairment, community resources, and caregiver characteristics', in *Aging, Health and Family: Long-Term Care*, Brubaker, T. H. (ed.), Newbury Park, CA.: Sage.

NOP (1990), *A Report of a Survey Conducted by NOP Market Research Limited on behalf of the National Audit Office: A Survey Among Family Credit Recipients*, London: National Opinion Polls.

OECD (1979), *Demographic Trends*, Paris: OECD.

OECD (1983), *Employment Outlook*, Paris: OECD.

OECD (1986), *Employment Outlook*, Paris: OECD.

OECD (1987), *Employment Outlook*, Paris: OECD.

OECD (1988a), *Employment Outlook*, Paris: OECD.

OECD (1988b), *Reforming Public Pensions*, OECD Social Policy Studies No. 5, Paris: OECD.

OECD (1989), *Employment Outlook*, Paris: OECD.

OECD (1990a), *Employment Outlook*, Paris: OECD.

OECD (1990b), *Lone Parents: The economic challenge*, Paris: OECD.

OECD (1991a), *Employment Outlook*, Paris: OECD.

OECD (1991b), *The Tax/Benefit Position of Production Workers 1987–1990*, Paris: OECD.

OECD (1991c), *Labour Force Statistics 1969–1989*, Paris: OECD.

OECD (1991d), *Labour Force Survey*, Paris: OECD.

OECD (1992), *Employment Outlook*, Paris: OECD.

Offe, C. (1985), *Disorganised Capitalism*, Oxford: Polity Press.

Offe, C. and Heinze, R. (1991), *Beyond Employment*, Oxford: Polity Press.

Office of Population Censuses and Surveys (OPCS) (1989), *General Household Survey 1987*, London: HMSO.

Office of Population Censuses and Surveys (OPCS) (1990a), *The General Household Survey 1988*, London: HMSO.

Office of Population Censuses and Surveys (OPCS) (1990b), *General Household Survey 1989*, London: HMSO.

O'Higgins, M. (1984), 'Inequality, redistribution and recession: The British experience', Rockefeller Foundation's Bellagio Conference Centre, mimeo.

O'Higgins, M and Jenkins, S. (1990), 'Poverty in the EC: 1975, 1980, 1985', in *Analysing Poverty in the European Community*, Teekens, R. and Van Praag, B. (eds.), Luxembourg: Eurostat News Special Edition.

Oldman, C. (1991), *Paying for Care: Personal sources of funding care*, York: Joseph Rowntree Foundation.

O'Reilly, J. (1992), 'Banking on flexibility: A comparison of the use of flexible employment strategies in the retail banking sector in Britain and France', *International Journal of Human Resource Management*, 3, 1, pp. 35–58.

Overbye, E. (1992), *Public or Private Pensions? Pensions and pension politics in the Nordic countries*, Oslo: Institutt for Sosialforskning.

Owen, S. and Joshi, H. (1990), 'Sex, equality, and the state pension' *Fiscal Studies*, 11, 1, pp. 53–74.

Pahl, J. (1983), 'The allocation of money and the structuring of inequality within marriage', *Sociological Review*, 13, 2, pp. 237–262.

Pahl, J. (1989), *Money and Marriage*, London: Macmillan.

Pahl, J. (1990), 'Household spending, personal spending and the control of money in marriage', *Sociology*, 24, 1, pp. 119–138.

Pahl, R. E. (1988), 'Conclusions: Whose problem?', in *Underground Economy and Irregular Forms of Employment*, Final Synthesis Report, Brussels: Commission of the European Communites, CDG V/A(1).

Pahl, R. E. and Wallace, C. (1985), 'Household work strategies in economic recession', in *Beyond Employment: Household, Gender and Subsistence*, Redclift, N. and Mingione, E., (eds.), Oxford: Blackwell.

Parker, G. (1990), *With Due Care and Attention: A Review of Research on Informal Care, 2nd Edition*, Occasional Paper No. 2, London: Family Policy Studies Centre.

Parker, H. (1989), *Instead of the Dole*, London: Routledge.

Parker, H. (1991) (ed.), *Basic Income and the Labour Market*, London: Basic Income Research Group.

Parker, H. (1992), 'Onwards from Beveridge: Labour market effects of work-tested benefits and their replacement by Citizens' Incomes', paper presented to the International Conference on Social Security 50 Years After Beveridge, University of York, September.

Parker, R. A. (1987), *The Elderly and Residential Care*, Aldershot: Gower.

Pascall, G. (1986), *Social Policy: A feminist analysis*, London: Tavistock.

Patel, N. (1990), *A 'Race' Against Time*, London: Runnymede Trust.

Pateman, C. (1989), *The Disorder of Women*, Cambridge: Polity.

Pederson, S. (1989), 'The failure of feminism in the making of the British welfare state', *Radical History Review*, **43**, pp. 86–110.

Pederson, S. (1990), 'Gender, welfare and citizenship in Britain during the Great War', *The American Historical Review*, **95**, 4. pp. 983–1006.

Pepper Commission, U.S. Bipartisan Commission on Comprehensive Health Care (1990), *A Call for Action*, Washington, DC: U.S. Government Printing Office.

Phillipson, C. (1978), 'The emergence of retirement', Working Paper No.14, Durham: University of Durham.

Phillipson, C. (1993), 'The sociology of retirement' in *Ageing in Society* (2nd edn.), Bond, J., Coleman, P. and Peace, P. (eds.), London: Sage.

Piachaud, D. (1986), 'Disability, retirement and unemployment of older men', *Journal of Social Policy*, **15**, 2, pp. 145–162.

Pissarides, C. and Weber, G. (1989), 'An expenditure-based estimate of Britain's black economy', *Journal of Public Economics*, **39**, pp. 17–32.

Pollert, A. (1988), 'The flexible firm: fixation or fact?', *Work, Employment, and Society*, **2**, pp. 281–316.

Pollert, A. (1991) (ed.), *Farewell to Flexibility?*, Oxford: Blackwell.

Pond, R. (1990), *Pension Fund Surpluses Survey*, London: Labour Research Department.

Popay, J. (1989), 'Poverty and plenty: Women's attitudes towards and experience of money across social classes', in *Women and Poverty: Exploring the Research and Policy Agenda*, Popay, J. and Rimmer, L. (eds.), Thomas Coram Research Unit/University of Warwick, London: Institute of Education.

Qureshi, H. and Walker, A. (1989), *The Caring Relationship: Elderly People and Their Families*, London: Macmillan.

Rabin, D. L. and Stockton, P. (1987), *Long-Term Care for the Elderly: A factbook*, New York: Oxford University Press.

Rainbird, H. (1991), 'The self-employed: Small entrepreneurs or disguised wage labourers?', in *Farewell to Flexibility?*, Pollert, A (ed.), Oxford: Blackwell.

Ray, J. (1990), 'Lone mothers, social assistance and work incentives: The evidence in France', in *Lone-Parent Families: The Economic Challenge*, OECD, Paris: OECD.

Reddin, M. (1985), 'A view by Mike Reddin', in *Can We Afford our Future?*, Reddin, M. and Pilch, M. (eds.), Mitcham: Age Concern England.

Reno, V. and Price, D. N. (1985), 'Relationship between the retirement, disability and unemployment insurance programmes: the US experience', *Social Security Bulletin*, May, **48**, 5.

Report of the Committee on the Economic and Financial Problems of the Provisions for Old Age (1954), *The Phillips Report*, Cmnd 9333, London: HMSO.

Ricardo-Campbell, R. (1988), 'Aging and the private sector', *Generations*, Spring, pp. 19–22.

Riksforsakringsverket (RFv) (1991), *Social Insurance Statistics Facts 1991*, Statistical Division.

Ringen, S. (1991), 'Do welfare states come in types?' in *Social Policy in Australia: Options for the 1990s*, Saunders, P. and Encel, D. (eds.), Reports and Proceedings No. 96, Social Policy Research Centre, Sydney: University of New South Wales.

Rivlin, A. M. and Wiener, J. M. (1988), *Caring for the Disabled Elderly: Who will pay?*, Washington, DC: The Brookings Institute.

R.L. Associates (1987), *The American Public Views Long-Term Care*, Princeton, NJ: R.L. Associates.

Roche, C. (1992), *Rethinking Citizenship*, Cambridge: Polity Press.

Roll, J. (1988), *Family Fortunes: Parents' incomes in the 1980s*, London: Family Policy Studies Centre.

Roll, J. (1991), *What is a Family? Benefit models and social realities*, London: Family Policy Studies Centre.

Roll, J. (1992), *Lone-parent Families in the European Community*, London: European Family and Social Policy Unit.

Room, G. (1990), *New Poverty in the European Community*, London: Macmillan.

Room, G. (ed.) (1991), *National Policies to Combat Social Exclusion*, Bath: Commission of the European Communities / Centre for Research in European Social and Employment Policy.

Rosenbaum, S. (1971), 'Social services manpower' in *Social Trends 1971*, CSO, London: HMSO.

Rosenthal, C. J. (1986), 'Family supports in later life: Does ethnicity make a difference?', *The Gerontologist*, **26**, pp. 19–24.

Rosenwaike, I. (1985), 'A demographic portrait of the oldest old,' *Milbank Memorial Fund Quarterly/Health and Society*, **63**, pp. 187–205.

Rowntree, B. S. (1941), *Poverty and Progress: A second social survey*, London: Longman Green.

Royal Commission on Population (1949), London: HMSO.

Sager, A. (1983), 'A proposal for promoting more adequate long-term care for the elderly', *The Gerontologist*, **23**, pp. 13–17.

Saunders, P., Hobbes, G. and Stott, H. (1989), 'Income inequality and redistribution in Australia and New Zealand: An international comparative analysis', in *Social Policy and Inequality in Australia and New Zealand*, Saunders, P. and Jamrozik, A. (eds.), Reports and Proceedings No. 78, Social Policy Research Centre, Sydney: University of New South Wales.

Scanlon, W. J. (1980), 'Nursing home utilization patterns: Implications for policy', *Journal of Health Policy, Politics and Law*, **4**, pp. 619–641.

Schmähl, W. (1991), 'On the future development of retirement in Europe especially of supplementary pension schemes – An introductory overview', in *The Future of Basic and Supplementary Pension Schemes in the European Community - 1992 and Beyond*, Schmähl, W. (ed.), Baden-Baden: Nomos Verlagsgesellschaft.

Schuller, T. (1989), 'Work-ending: Employment and ambiguity in later life' in *Becoming and Being Old*, Bytheway, B., Keil, T., Allat, P. and Bryman, A. (eds.), London: Sage Books.

Schulte, B. (1989), *The Role of Social Security in Providing Social Protection to the Very Old*, Working Paper ISSA/RDS/EG/89/2, Geneva: International Social Security Association.

Schultz, J. (1991), 'Epilogue: The "buffer years": Market incentives and evolving retirement policies', in Myles, J. and Quadagno, J. (eds.), *States, Labour Markets, and the Future of Old Age Policy*, Philadelphia, PA: Temple University Press.

Schultz, J., Borowski, A. and Crown, C. (1991), *The Economics of Population Ageing*, New York: Auburn House.

Seebohm Report (1968), *Report of the Committee on Local Authority and Allied Personal Social Services*, Cmnd. 3703, London: HMSO.

Short, P. and Leon, J. (1990), *Use of Home and Community Services by Persons Ages 65 and Older with Functional Difficulties*, DHHS Publication No. 90–3466. National Medical Expenditure Survey Research Findings 5, Agency for Health Care Policy and Research, Rockville, MD.: Public Health Service.

Showler, B. and Sinfield, R. (eds.) (1981), *The Workless State*, Oxford: Martin Robertson.

Shragge, E. (1984), *Pensions Policy in Britain: A socialist analysis*, London: Routledge and Kegan Paul.

Simonen, L. (1991), 'The Finnish caring state in transition – Reversing the emancipatory mothering?', Aalborg: European Feminist Research conference, Denmark.

Sinclair, I. A. C., Parker, R., Leat, D. and Williams, J. (1990), *The Kaleidoscope of Care: A review of research on welfare provision for elderly people*, National Institute for Social Work, London: HMSO.

Sinfield, A. (1981), *What Unemployment Means* ,Oxford: Martin Robertson.

Sjerps, C. M. (1988), 'Dames en heren, en dan nu: Gelijke Behandeling', *Sociaal Maandblad Arbeid*, 4, pp. 306–324.

Smeeding, T., Saunders, P., Coder, J., Jenkins, S., Fritzell, J., Hagenaars, A., Hauser, R., and Wolfson, M. (1992), *Non-cash Income, Living Standards, and Inequality: Evidence from the Luxembourg Income Study*, Luxembourg Income Study Working Paper, Walferdange: Luxembourg Income Study.

Smith, A. (1981), 'The informal economy', *Lloyds Bank Review*, 141, pp. 45–60.

Smith, S. (1986), *Britain's Shadow Economy*, Oxford: Oxford University Press.

Social Security Committee (1991), *Changes in Maintenance Arrangements: The White Paper 'Children Come First' and the Child Support Bill*, London: House of Commons.

Sociale Verzekeringsraad (SVr) (1992), *Statistics 1980-1990*, Den Haag. SVr

Soldo, B. J. (1985), 'In-home services for the dependent elderly', *Research on Aging*, 7, pp. 281–304.

Soldo, B. J. and Manton, K. G. (1985), 'Health status and service needs of the oldest old: Current patterns and future trends', *Milbank Memorial Fund Quarterly/Health and Society*, 63, pp. 286–319.

Special Committee on Aging, United States Senate (1987), *Developments in Aging: 1987, Volume 3: The Long-Term Care Challenge*. Washington, DC: Government Printing Office.

Special Committee on Aging, United States Senate (1988), *Home Health Care at the Crossroads: An Information Paper*, Washington, DC: Government Printing Office.

Special Committee on Aging, United States Senate (1991), *Developments in Aging: 1991*, Volume 1. Washington, DC: Government Printing Office.

Standing, G. (1992), 'The need for a new social consensus', in *Arguing for Basic Income*, van Parijs, P. (ed.), London: Verso.

Steinmetz, G. and Wright, E.O. (1989), 'The fall and rise of the petty bourgeoisie: Changing patterns of self-employment in the post-war United States', *American Journal of Sociology*, 94, 5, pp. 973–1018.

Stephens, S. A. and Christianson, J. B. (1986), *Informal Care of the Elderly*, Lexington, MA: Lexington Books.

Stone, R., Cafferata, L. and Sangl, J. (1987), 'Caregivers of the frail elderly: A national profile', *The Gerontologist*, 27, pp. 616–625.

Subcommittee on Human Services of the Select Committee on Aging, House of Representatives (1987), *Exploding the Myths: Caregiving in America*, 100th Congress, 1st Session, Comm. Pub. No. 99–611.

Sullerot, E. (1984), *Pour le meilleur et sans le pire*, Paris: Fayard.

Tamburi, G. and Mouton, P. (1986), 'The uncertain frontier between private and public pension schemes', *International Labour Review*, 125, 2, pp. 127–40.

Task Force on Long-Term Health Care Policies (1987), *Report to Congress and the Secretary*,Washington, DC: Government Printing Office.

Taylor-Gooby, P. (1991), *Social Change, Social Welfare and Social Science*, Hemel Hempstead: Harvester Wheatsheaf.

Therborn, G. and Roebroek, J. (1986), 'The irreversible welfare state. Its recent maturation. Its encounter with the economic crisis. Its future prospects' in *The Future of the Welfare State*, Albeda, W. (ed.), Maastricht: Presses Universitaires Européennes.

Thomas, J. J. (1988), 'The politics of the black economy', *Work, Employment and Society*, 3, 2, pp. 169–190.

Thomson, D. (1983), 'Workhouse to nursing home: residential care of elderly people in England since 1840', *Ageing and Society*, 3, 1, pp. 43–69.

Titmuss, R. (1958), *Essays on the Welfare State*, London: Allen and Unwin.

Titmuss, R. (1970), 'Equity, adequacy and innovation in social security' in *International Social Security Review*, Geneva: International Social Security Association, 2, pp. 259–268.

Townsend, P. (1962), *The Last Refuge*, London: Routledge and Kegan Paul.

Townsend, P. (1981), 'The structured dependency of the elderly: a creation of social policy', *Ageing and Society*, 1, 1, pp. 5–28.

Trinder, C., Hulme, G. and McCarthy, C. (1992), *Employment: The role of work in the third age*, London: Public Finance Foundation.

Twigg, J. (ed.) (1992), *Informal Care in Europe*, papers presented at a European conference held at the University of York, September 1991, York: Social Policy Research Unit.

Twine, F. (1992), 'Citizenship: Opportunities, rights and routes to welfare in old age', *Journal of Social Policy*, 21, 2, pp. 165–75.

Université des Femmes (1987), *Sécurité sociale: Individualisation des droits dérivés*, Actes du colloque du 26 Septembre 1987.

U.S. Department of Health and Human Services (1992), *Social Security Bulletin: Annual statistical supplement 1970-91*, Summer.

U.S. House Committee on Ways and Means (1986), *Background Material and Data on Programs within the Jurisdiction of the Committee on Ways and Means*, Washington, DC: Government Printing Office.

Varesi, P. A. and Villa, P. (1988), 'Home-working in Italy, France and the United Kingdom', *Social Europe* (Commission of the EC), January.

Vittas, D. and Iglesias, A. (1992), 'The rationale and performance of personal pension plans in Chile', World Bank Policy Research Working Paper WPS 867, Washington, DC: World Bank.

Vladeck, B. C. (1980), *Unloving Care: The nursing home tragedy*, New York, NY: Basic Books.

Wadensjo, E. (1984), 'Disability policy in Sweden', in *Public Policy towards Disabled Workers*, Haveman, R. *et al.* (eds.), Ithaca, NY: Cornell University Press.

Wadensjo, E. (1990a), 'Early exit from the labor force in Sweden', Institutet for Social Forskning, mimeo.

Wadensjo, E. (1990b), 'Recent labor market experiences of older workers in Sweden', mimeo.

Wadensjo, E. (1991), 'Sweden: partial exit' in *Time for Retirement: Comparative studies of early exit from the labour force*, Kohli, M. Rein, M. Guillemard, A.M. and Gunsteren, H. (eds.), Cambridge: Cambridge University Press.

Waerness, K. (1989), 'Dependency in the welfare state', in *The Goals of Social Policy*, Bulmer, M., Lewis, J. and Piachaud (eds.), London: Unwin Hyman.

Walker, A. (1980), 'The social creation of poverty and dependency in old age', *Journal of Social Policy*, 9, 1, pp.49–75.

Walker, A. (1982), *Community Care: The family, the state and social policy*, Oxford: Basil Blackwell/Martin Robertson.

Walker, A. (1987), 'The poor relation: Poverty among older women', in *Women and Poverty in Britain*, Glendinning, C. and Millar, J. (eds.), Brighton: Wheatsheaf Books.

Walker, A. (1989), 'Poverty and inequality in old age', in *Ageing in Society*, Bond, J. and Coleman, P. (eds.), London: Sage Books.

Walker, R. (1988), 'The financial resources of the elderly, or paying your own way in old age', in *Social Security and Community Care*, Baldwin, S., Parker, G. and Walker, R. (eds), Aldershot: Avebury.

Walker, R. and Hutton, S. (1988): 'The costs of ageing and retirement' in *Money Matters: Income, Wealth and Financial Welfare*, Walker, R. and Parker, G. (eds.), London: Sage Publications.

Walker, R., Hedges, A. and Massey, S. (1987), *Housing Benefit: Discussion about reform*, London: Housing Centre Trust.

Wallace, S. P. (1991), 'The political economy of health care for elderly blacks', in *Critical Perspectives on Aging: The Political and Moral Economy of Growing Old*, Minkler, M. and Estes, C. L. (ed.), Amityville, NY: Baywood.

Ward, S. (1985), 'The financial crisis facing pensioners', *Critical Social Policy*, **14**, pp. 43–56.

Wedderburn, D. (1970), 'Workplace inequality', *New Society*, April 9th, p. 393.

Weissert, W. G. (1985), 'Seven reasons why it is so difficult to make community-based long-term care cost-effective', *HSR: Health Services Research*, **20**, pp. 423–33.

Weissert, W. G. (1988), 'The national channeling demonstration: What we knew, know now, and still need to know' *HSR: Health Services Research*, **23**, pp. 175–187.

West, P. (1984), 'The family, the welfare state and community care', *Journal of Social Policy*, **13**, iv, pp. 417–446.

Whiteford, P. (1985), 'A family's needs: Equivalence scales, poverty and social security', Research Paper No. 27, Canberra: DSS.

Whiteford, P. (1991), 'The tax-benefit position of average production workers: A research note', Working Paper No. 903, Social Policy Research Unit, York: University of York.

Whiteford, P. and Hicks, L. (1992), 'The extra costs of lone parents: evidence from Family Budget Standards', Family Budget Unit, York: University of York.

Wilkinson, M. (1986), 'Tax expenditure and public expenditure in the UK', *Journal of Social Policy*, **15**, 1, pp. 23–49.

Williams, F. (1989), *Social Policy: A critical introduction*, Cambridge: Polity/Basil Blackwell.

Wilson, E. (1977), *Women and the Welfare State*, London: Tavistock.

Wilson, E. (1983), 'Feminism and social policy', in *Social Policy and Social Welfare*, Loney, M., Boswell, D. and Clarke, J. (eds.), Milton Keynes: Open University Press.

Wilson, G. (1987), *Money in the Family*, Aldershot: Avebury.

Wolf, D. A. and Soldo, B. J. (1986), 'The households of older unmarried women: Micro-decision models of shared living arrangements', paper presented at the Annual Meeting of the Population Association of America, San Francisco, CA.

Wollstonecraft, M. (1792/1985), *Vindication of the Rights of Women*, London: Penguin.

Wood, D. and Smith, P. (1989), 'Employers' labour use strategies: First report on the 1987 survey', Department of Employment Research Paper 63, London: Department of Employment.

Wood, J. B., Fox, P. J., Estes, C. L., Lee, P. R. and Mahoney, C. W. (1986), *Public Policy, the Private Nonprofit Sector, and the Delivery of Community Based Long-Term Care Services for the Elderly*, Final Report: Executive Summary. San Francisco CA, Institute for Health and Aging, University of California.

Worobey, J. L. and Angel, R. J. (1990), 'Poverty and health: Older minority women and the rise of the female-headed household', *Journal of Health and Social Behavior*, **31**, pp. 370–383.

Yudkin, S. and Holme, A. (1963), *Working Mothers and their Children*, London: Sphere Books.

Index